THE SECRET SHIRE OF COTSWOLD

THE
SECRET SHIRE
OF
COTSWOLD

VOLUME I: HOBBITON-RIVENDELL

Steve Ponty

Matador
9 Priory Business Park,
Wistow Road, Kibworth Beauchamp,
Leicestershire. LE8 0RX
Tel: 0116 279 2299
Email: books@troubador.co.uk
Web: www.troubador.co.uk/matador
Twitter: @matadorbooks

Paperback ISBN 978 1838595 531
Hardback ISBN 978 1800460 034

British Library Cataloguing in Publication Data.
A catalogue record for this book is available from the British Library.

Printed and bound in Great Britain by 4edge Limited
Typeset in 11pt Adobe Garamond Pro by Troubador Publishing Ltd, Leicester, UK

Matador is an imprint of Troubador Publishing Ltd

To: Dylan

'It was fifty years ago today
Sergeant Pepper taught the band to play'

Preface

'I fear you may be right that the search for the sources of The Lord of the Rings is going to occupy academics for a generation or two. I wish this not to be so. To my mind it is the particular use in a particular situation of any motive whether invented, deliberately borrowed, or unconsciously remembered that is the most interesting thing to consider.'

Contents

APPENDICES (415)

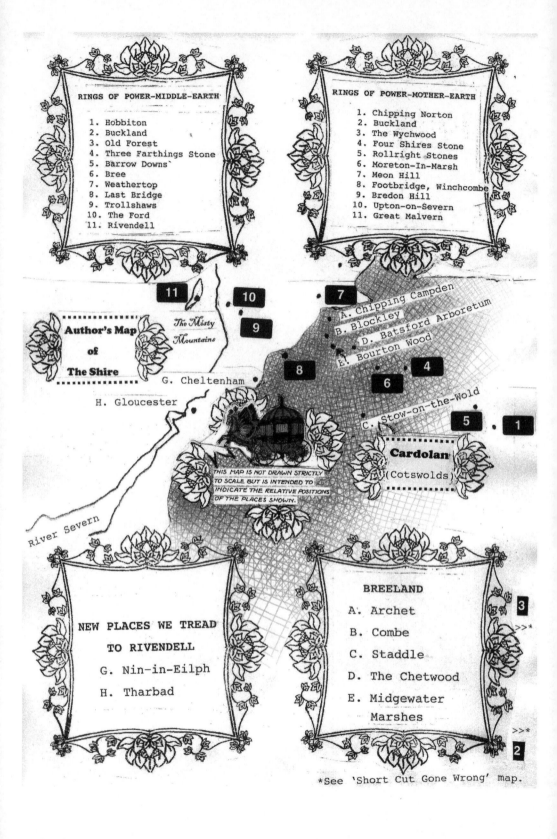

RINGS OF POWER—MIDDLE-EARTH

1. Hobbiton
2. Buckland
3. Old Forest
4. Three Farthings Stone
5. Barrow Downs`
6. Bree
7. Weathertop
8. Last Bridge
9. Trollshaws
10. The Ford
11. Rivendell

RINGS OF POWER—MOTHER-EARTH

1. Chipping Norton
2. Buckland
3. The Wychwood
4. Four Shires Stone
5. Rollright Stones
6. Moreton-In-Marsh
7. Meon Hill
8. Footbridge, Winchcombe
9. Bredon Hill
10. Upton-on-Severn
11. Great Malvern

Author's Map of The Shire

The Misty Mountains

A. Chipping Campden
B. Blockley
D. Batsford Arboretum
E. Bourton Wood

G. Cheltenham

H. Gloucester

C. Stow-on-the-Wold

THIS MAP IS NOT DRAWN STRICTLY TO SCALE BUT IS INTENDED TO INDICATE THE RELATIVE POSITIONS OF THE PLACES SHOWN.

River Severn

Cardolan (Cotswolds)

NEW PLACES WE TREAD TO RIVENDELL

G. Nin-in-Eilph

H. Tharbad

BREELAND

A. Archet
B. Combe
C. Staddle
D. The Chetwood
E. Midgewater Marshes

>>*

>>*

*See 'Short Cut Gone Wrong' map.

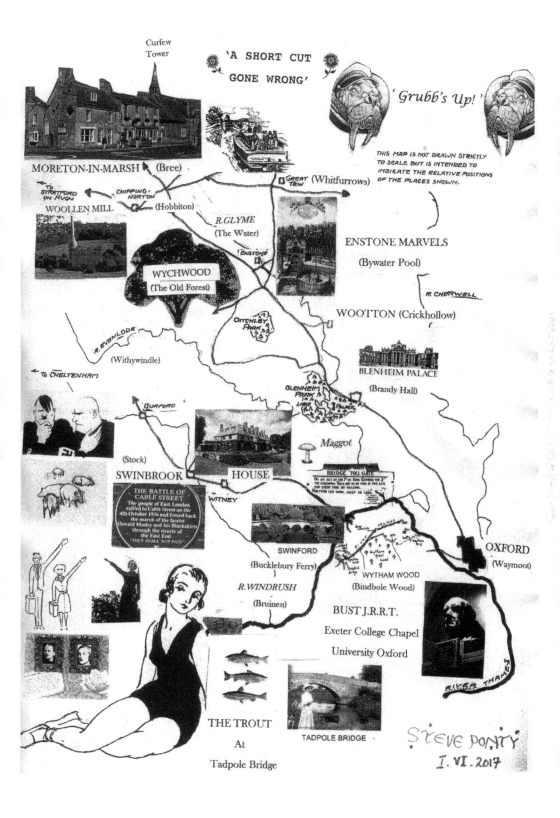

Curfew
Tower

'A SHORT CUT
GONE WRONG'

'Grubb's Up!'

THIS MAP IS NOT DRAWN STRICTLY
TO SCALE BUT IS INTENDED TO
INDICATE THE RELATIVE POSITIONS
OF THE PLACES SHOWN.

MORETON-IN-MARSH   (Bree)

GREAT TEW (Whitfurrows)

TO STRATFORD ON AVON

CHIPPING NORTON   (Hobbiton)

WOOLLEN MILL

R. GLYME
(The Water)

ENSTONE

ENSTONE MARVELS
(Bywater Pool)

WYCHWOOD
(The Old Forest)

R. CHERWELL

WOOTTON (Crickhollow)

OTTCHLEY PARK

R. EVENLODE
(Withywindle)

TO CHELTENHAM

BLENHEIM PALACE
(Brandy Hall)

BURFORD

BLENHEIM PARK LAKE   PALACE

Maggot

BRIDGE TOLL GATE

(Stock)

SWINBROOK   HOUSE

THE BATTLE OF
CABLE STREET
The people of East London
rallied to Cable Street on the
4th October 1936 and forced back
the march of the fascist
Oswald Mosley and his Blackshirts
through the streets of
the East End.
'THEY SHALL NOT PASS'

WITNEY

SWINFORD
(Bucklebury Ferry)

R. WINDRUSH
(Bruinen)

OXFORD
(Waymoot)

WYTHAM WOOD
(Bindbole Wood)

BUST J.R.R.T.
Exeter College Chapel
University Oxford

RIVER THAMES

THE TROUT
At
Tadpole Bridge

TADPOLE BRIDGE

STEVE PONTY
I. VI. 2017

Preamble

'I wonder what sort of a tale we've fallen into?'
(Samwise Gamgee, The Two Towers)

The Quest is mined on two levels; the first was a quest for the topography of the Shire of Middle-earth in and around England's Cotswold Hills; but, tracking ever onwards beyond the Shire, there, at Rivendell, the Author falls into the deepest tunnels below the pitheads of the Shire, which you, our Audience, will come to know as the *Rings of Power*; and trucks on from our account of *The Council of Elrond,* ever onwards to Mordor: for at the Council there begin shifts, night and day, to Mordor, to shed new shafts of light on some of the doctrines underpinning the story in The Lord of the Rings: the Wheel of Fire, the essence of Frodo, Gandalf and Saruman and Sauron in opposition; Free Will and the One Ring; Good and Evil; and, for an initial revelation until it resurfaces from time to time up the road ahead, the following from Letter Number 142 ...

"The Lord of the Rings' is of course a fundamentally religious and Catholic work; ... the religious element is absorbed into the story and symbolism."

The mining industry may be asleep, rather like Smaug within The Lonely Mountain, but the words of the lyricists awaken it for unearthing the pure gold of poetry, just below the road ahead ...

Gollum: ... Ach s-ss ... Gerron wivvit, Awffer Mas-sster ...

Smeagol: ... yes, indeed, My Luvvs, make haste! Time is short ... a bit like wot hobbitses is like! ...

' abstract threats too noble to neglect ...'

It is copyright Steve Ponty in the present form effective December 10, 2016; that date matters ... before that date, the voice was called

First Voice; yet now *The Nobel Voice*: and in that of Leonard Cohen, gone on just the month before …

'[the award of the Nobel Prize]
is like pinning a medal on Mount Everest
for being the highest mountain.'

Dylan's lyrics are so well resourced in the public domain that we analyse them on the same level (for purposes of criticism or review within context) as any of the other great poets in the domain; even though The Nobel Voice will not play the game …

'Not once have I ever had the time to ask myself, 'Are my songs literature?'
So, I do thank the Swedish Academy, both for taking the time to consider that
very question,…'

(Speech: Award Nobel Prize)

'It Ain't Me Babe'

Even so …

'Everybody knows by now that there's a gazillion books on me either out or coming out in the near future. So I'm encouraging anybody who's ever met me, heard me or even seen me, to get in on the action and scribble their own book. You never know, somebody might have a great book in them. (bobdylan.com)

Those of the Audience in doubt about the respect due the lyrics of Bob Dylan, *prized* by the Author on our Quest, might like to consider the following …

'Only a fool in here would think
he's got anything to prove'

Dylan earned yet another distinction in a 2007 study of US legal opinions and briefs that found his lyrics were quoted by judges and lawyers more than those of any other songwriter, 186 times versus 74 by the Beatles, who were second. Among those quoting Dylan were US Supreme Court Chief Justice John

Roberts and Justice Antonin Scalia, both conservatives. The most widely cited lines included 'you don't need a weatherman to know which way the wind blows' from 'Subterranean Homesick Blues' and 'when you ain't got nothing, you got nothing to lose' from 'Like a Rolling Stone'.

'The highest purpose of art is to inspire ... What else can you do for anyone but inspire them?'
(Dylan)

If the American Justices admire the inspiration of sung lyrics, then so might we. We bring to mind, when confronted with critics of the quality of the writing in the Lord of the Rings, Professor Tolkien's retort that the reaction did not trouble him, because he may not like his critics' work either, and so we offer the following to those (and there are many, the Author has heard from some, and, of, others, and is expecting more if they react to this) who choose to undermine, criticise, ultimately to ignore the ethos, sincerity and hidden, yet ever humble, boldness (born of Bilbo Baggins, no doubt) of the Quest ...

'Boldness has genius, power and magic in it ...'
(Goethe)

Poetry is Emotion

Re-echoing the prayer of Dylan Thomas ...

Read the poems you like reading. Don't bother whether they're 'important', or if they'll live. What does it matter what poetry *is*, after all? If you want a definition of poetry, say:

'Poetry is what makes me laugh or cry or yawn, what makes my toenails twinkle, what makes me want to do this or that or nothing', and let it go at that. All that matters about poetry is the enjoyment of it, however tragic it may be.'

(The Colour of Saying; Dent 1963)

xvii

… that one should read those poems one enjoys reading without reference to the status accredited by others, that may yet not be enough; the Author was, indeed, *inspired* by the intent of the following, which, as an aside, one might not imagine being politically correct nowadays (but, for fawkes sake, we are to burn that bonfire of vanity, somewhere up the road ahead), it being far too didactic for the modernists in literature …

'It may be useful … to suggest how they may find and absorb all the manifold beauties of a poem. Such a consummation can only be achieved after many readings, for the joy of great poetry, as of all literature, is that every time we read it we find new interest and new beauties that have escaped us before. To find these beauties and the true significance of literature we must search for them, for, as Ruskin has said, they are hidden away like gold in the earth, and to find them we must work as a gold-miner would.

'The metal you are in search of being the author's mind or meaning, his words are as the rock which you have to crush and smelt in order to get at it. And your pickaxes are your care, wit and learning; your smelting furnace is your own thoughtful soul. Do not hope to get at **any good author's meaning** without those tools and that fire; often you will need sharpest, finest chiselling, and patientest fusing, before you can gather one grain of the metal.'

(Sopwith, The Companion Poets: Tennyson)

The final lines (throw aways because he's too smart for any of us) come from Dylan, in belated recognition of the Nobel Prize (Daily Telegraph, October 29, 2016) …

'He has never, of course, been one to explain his lyrics. 'I'll let other people decide what they are,' he tells me. 'The academics, they ought to know. I'm not really qualified. I don't have any opinion …'
When it comes to meaning, Dylan is, it becomes clear, no more keen to explain his paintings than he is his lyrics.

'Different people read different things into what they see,' he says. 'It's all subjective.' '

It follows that we shall never, ever mine the full metal jacket of Mithril: and that we are merely picking at the seams for the moment.

The Ruskin is a perfect mirror image of the words of Professor J.R.R. Tolkien that you, our Audience, first read above, before our Index, indeed a *Mantra of Middle-earth* throughout our Quest,(... *'the most interesting thing to consider'* ...) and the perfect justification for it, because the mining discipline is to be no less demanding in discovering *the truth of the prose legend that is The Lord of the Rings.*

'He panned poetry gold,
whether on purpose or by accident is irrelevant ...
He gave back to poetry its elevated style,
lost since the romantics.'
(Nobel Prize Award Speech)

And so to a comparative evaluation by Professor J.R.R. Tolkien:

'No dwarf could be unmoved by such loveliness. None of Durin's race would mine those caves for stones or ore, not if diamonds and gold could be got there ... We would tend these glades of flowering stone, not quarry them. With cautious skill, tap by tap – a small chip of rock and no more, perhaps, in a whole anxious day – so we could work, and as the years went by, we should open up new ways, and display far chambers that are still dark, glimpsed only as a void beyond fissures in the rock ... '

Hi Ho! ... Hi Ho! ... and it's off to work we go ...

The Bridge at Khazad Dum

'The Twenty-first Hall ...
on the Seventh level,
that is six above the level of the Gates'

We open our minds in the Mines of Moria, tunnelling down into tight terrain, in search of the voided architraves and vaulted staves of frames in windows so long gone and good bye in time; Gimli surveying the same place we depart this Volume I: down below in Moria … yet at the highest point reached by the Fellowship within those Mines before eventual descent and *'out'* … at the unbroken rock-solid wall downward tread of steps … and no other exit available to the mind of even the wizard Gandalf …

*… from **The Twenty-first Hall** … **on the Seventh level, that is six above the level of the Gates** … **down** to **the First Deep, the level immediately below the Gates …***
The shock of this avalanche of invention dumbs the cerebrum down, into a neverending numbness …

> **'There rolls the deep where grew the tree.**
> **O earth, what changes hast thou seen! …'**
> (In Memoriam: Tennyson)

Did the Professor borrow the *deep* (rather than *depth*) from the Poet Laureate of Victorian times? How many Halls and Levels and Gates *are* there? … and, if there is the *First* Deep, is there and where is there a *Second* … or further … Deep? … adding that even the staggermental vision of Karen Wynn Fonstad's Atlas does not truly see through the confusticating maelstrom blowing over the snowbound Caradrhas …)…

Professor Tolkien may well have been unaware of the atrophy wrought by these points of reference; at least in the Author's ever moribund mind. In our little three-second retention brain (within the recall only of those who wish goldfish for psycoanalyshish), this fantasy scenery of fleetingly transient walls of half-windowed rock, tunnels and stairways broken in half, and steps up and down by several levels and depths, the whole show leading somehow to gates *out,* blows my mind beyond comprehension … lasting not even a millisecond … let alone any second within the three-fold capacity of the goldfish (but not a lot of people know that, or want to remember it …)… and leading to nothing, but nothing, to see or hear …

> **'Ears in the turrets hear**
> **Hands grumble on the door,**

Eyes in the gables see
The fingers at the locks ...'
(Ears in the Turrets Hear; Dylan Thomas)

... for there is nothing reaching our eyes or ears, nor any clue ...
of what we hoped transparent through the translucent snow-dome
that is the Professor's Caradrhas: recalling the quarrelsome squall
of weathers slicing through, snow and icy cold, there up high, the
forewarning of war sent by Sauron, signal of a cruel and wicked
curse; yet there we are left, gawping gormless through the globe, to
the banter of Little Britain, slapped wet fish-face, chav-town gutter-
chatter ...

OMG!'*Scuse* me? Awesome!!!

As we observe further up the road ahead, and moreover in Volume II,
as the scene stands, one imagines one has wandered into some one off
dream, a bad one at that, or some virtual reality game set, with turrets,
passages, tunnels, levels and walls and halls and steps and depths down
to the gate **'out'** that one shall never find in reality, not just yet, or at all,
if ever ...

Is there anybody out there truly follows the pathways leaving Moria
... ?

Déjà vu

'At dawn my lover comes to me
And tells me of her dreams
With no attempts to shovel the glimpse
Into the ditch of what each one means'

... in a cacophony of resurrection in celluloid,
memories young and old are rising
from the coffins in the void
beyond the backyard of your cemetery brain cerebrum,
each dream of coming back characters
one new out the cutting room,

each host of spirits a new one out without repeat,
not coming again to your cinema seat;
no more to video, with most, but by no means all,
forgotten as soon as the lights go up in the hall,
but the odd one out to return, flesh and blood,
sometime later, as you somehow knew it would …

… We shall see, O yes, we shall see …

More Mystery

'With blinded lantern, that all night
Had never shot a spark
Of comfort through the dark,
So ghostly in the cold sunlight
It seemed, that we were struck the while
With wonder all too dread for words …

(… with the *Flannan Isle* disappearance by W.W. Gibson one equally deep as the secret egress of Moria is high …)

Smeagol: … we hopes to find answers insides of hills wiv seven levels inbetweens heavens and hells of earthsly paradises, My Luvvs, an' each level a Sin of them po' Dead Sinner Souls …

Gollum: … yes-ss, yes-ss indeed … ins-sside Danty's Nas-ssty Infernose … los-sst like nas-ssty noser Bagginses-ss atter Back Door in Goblinstowns-ss …

Smeagol: … Dante's *Inferno*, My Luv …

Voices over Shire (whooping, gloating applause)-

'All my loyal and my much-loved companions
They approve of me and share my code
I practice a faith that's been long abandoned …'

Gollum: … enemies-ss inner Shire, Audiences-ss-ss … enemies-ss ss, yes-ss … (screams) … ***enemies-ss-ss-ss*** …

'But this is terrible!' … 'Far worse than the worst that I imagined from your hints and warnings … What am I to do? For now I am really afraid. 'I am sorry,' … 'But *I am frightened* …'

Smeagol: … Keep the faiff, hobbitses, My Luvvs …

The Chamber of Mazarbul: Lost

'You say you've lost your faith,
but that's not where it's at
You have no faith to lose,
and you know it …'

Gollum: … Is it los-sst pre-e-ecious-ss-ss …?

Smeagol(gap in rock wall): … Smeagol helps find it … Good Smeagol always helps! …

We hear echoes of Bilbo Baggins, sometime lost, all so many years ago, some 12,000 feet below in the Misty Mountains, at the back-door of Goblin-town in The Hobbit …

Smeagol: … It doesn't know, and it can't go far. It's lost itself, … It doesn't know the way out. It said so …

The floor plan in the halls of Moria may become a little less confused given the virtual reality tour we have in mind for Volume II of our Quest; for we may indeed have got at a *good author's meaning* there, all by virtue of the plan of Mother-earth.

Gollum: … Awffer Mas-sster finks we knows-ss whereaboutses-ss is-ss, My Precious-ss … on Muvver-erff … is-sser mos' trickssey bisnes-ss-ss uppertop Caradrhas-ss, precious-ss-ss … is-ss a most deepes-sst of bisnesses-ss up there … deepest down many, many steps-ss like Saints Paul Caffedrals-ss-ss,… so say Awffer Mas-sster quests-ss, far off inner Vollum Twos-ss … and … (mischievous) … dussn't Smeagol say so his-sselfs-ss-ss … *los-sst* like Bagginses…?

Smeagol: … Tricksy, yes, … high and deep, yes, indeed … Lost, No, … we doesn't say so, O No, My Luv, Author Master by no means *lost … remembers, My Luv … Not all those who wander are* **lost** *…* so many, many months and months and yearses of wandring searches for troof of Herefords Beaconses, My Luv …

Gollum: … Ooops-sy days-sseees-ss-ss …! Smeagol says-ss Awffer Mas-sster secrets-ss out lu-o-o-wd …!!!

Smeagol: … silly … Audiences knows British Camps from ol' Magic Mirror Mapses, silly, silly, … mus' trust us, My Luvvs … mus' trust good Smeagol helps find lost Audiences way down from Mazarbul … Good Smeagol always helps …

Gollum; … Ach s-ss … Gerron wivvit, Awffer Mas-sster … when dus-ss we knows, precious-ss-ss … when exacly dus-ss we knows ss…?

Smeagol: … yes, indeed, My Luv, make haste! Time is short … (grinning) … a bit like wot hobbitses is like! … We shall see, O yes, we shall see, abowt seven sinful levels of Caradrhas, … somewhere's over the rainbows of Rivendells, My Luvvs!!!

The Author's own faith was rewarded when we found the St. Paul's Cathedral comparable already made, in poem, and by a true local; Ivor Gurney, 'The Comparison': see if your own is. For the Author, there is a distinct possibility, even probability, that Professor J.R.R. Tolkien drew some of the imagery of Cruel Caradrhas from that of the contemporary Ivor Gurney's poem. There is absolutely no doubt that the Professor would know it, from all the connections we discover further up the road ahead in Volume II.

'But God wondered, when Wren heaved up Dome above Thames,
Worcestershire to Herefordshire Beacon
learnt shapes and different names.'

Inspiration of Lyrics

Finally, for those at odds with our lyrical inspirations ...

'... Read the poem ... so that you may appreciate the music of it. For poetry is music; it has the rhythm of music, and the rhythm is sad or gay, light or grave, quick or slow, according to the matter of the verse.'

(Sopwith; ibid.)

> **'Bright is the ring of words**
> **When the right man rings them**
> **Fair the fall of songs**
> **When the singer sings them**
> **Since they are carolled and said**
> **On wings they are carried**
> **After the singer is dead**
> **And the maker buried.'**
>
> ('Bright is the Ring of Words': Robert Louis
> Stephenson)

Thus poetry is music and music is poetry; they have a synergy for those prepared to listen to the words: and here now are some of one Samwise Gamgee, desolate at the Tower of Cirith Ungol, and unable to find Frodo Baggins ensconced with the Tower Guard.

Sam (recites or sings):

> **'Though here at journey's end I lie**
> **in darkness buried deep,**
> **beyond all towers strong and high,**
> **beyond all mountains steep, ...'**

Gollum (elbows Samwise, still in recitation, praps singing, off stage): ... Journeys-s? ... Darknes-ss?... the Fat One be *climbin' evry mountains-ss* wivvat Mary Poppins-s girls-ss upper road ahead nexs-sst if Awffer Mas-ster dursnt makes-ss silly hobbitses-ss shurrup his fat face ...!!! No mo' po'try! No mo' songs-ss! No more such nonsenses-ss-ss !!!

Smeagol: … Good Smeagol does all po'try lyrrix an' songses and dances on this quest, Author Master… any more chances fix summore my po'try lyrix … fascinating lyrical miracles indeed, My Luv, or my songses and dances so awsums, … upper road ahead … Author Master …?

Gollum: … Awffer Mas-sster …?

Voice Off: … only The Nobel Voice, the occasional other and you two …

Gollum (scowling): … ach-s-ss … isser deal …

Smeagol (nodding, smiling) … We shall see O yes, we shall see … !

Bob Dylan's works are so well known (and if you don't, you might not yet know enough to argue or to judge) that the Author merely echoes the words, without designation of title, or other resource for them, because you members of the Audience might need to be inspired, by finding them, like the Author, over some fifty years: at least one plays out in my head *every single day of my life:* and so, as far as the Author is concerned, that's how good he is.

> **'For three years, out of key with his time,**
> **He strove to resuscitate the dead art**
> **Of poetry; to maintain 'the sublime'**
> **In the old sense. Wrong from the start—'**
> (Hugh Selwyn Mauberley, Ezra Pound)

Wrong, indeed, The Nobel Voice has striven over 50 and is still striving … the Author knows very little of the works of Ezra Pound (except for his *'fighting in the Captain's Tower'* with T.S. Eliot), yet we have adapted Pound's self-appraisal for the context. The Dylan lyrics are in good company: other poets take the stage where their words might be considered applicable, especially in terms of place, where we hear local vocals (Shaw, Auden, Houseman) in such as Rivendell. Samwise Gamgee is the only yokel and he gets his chance (but not for long); indeed, at Rivendell.

'Certainly I have not been nourished by English Literature, in which I do not suppose I am better read than you; for the simple reason that I have never found much there in which to rest my heart (or heart and head together). I was brought up in the Classics, and first discovered the sensation of literary pleasure in Homer.'

(Letter number 142)

A belated reference to the works of Victorian Poet, Alfred, Lord Tennyson, not *so* well known to the Author preparatory to the Quest, becomes obligatory; indeed Alfred is emblazoned upon our escutcheon as we march on to war, for Professor J.R.R. Tolkien clearly knew the poetical works intimately, and allusions are more prevalent than some might imagine. Hardly surprising given the Professor would have been schooled in these, they prove the testament of the three commentators below (Faulkner, Woolf, Einstein) with regard to a writer's sources. The Audience may be quite Tennystoned by any number of parallels of life and death: indeed there is a synergy within Fangorn Forest which is, to the Author's mind, staggermental, yet by no means synchronicity.

William Wordsworth also came late to the fold, especially at Lothlorien up the road ahead. Here are many fields beyond the Daffodils; luckily for the Author, to assist us through the golden pastures of Lothlorien about Tintern Abbey.

In the result, the road ahead is galleried in classical style with the word-pictures of any number of the Romantic poets: Tennyson, Wordsworth, Shelley, Keats and Coleridge, such that in Rivendell up the road ahead, and recalling the Mantra of Middle-earth, we proffer it sometimes seems to the Author that any number of scenes in The Rings have their source in these works. There are also some later ones; for instance the Professor's focus on the natural world (frog, badger, worms and crows) is complimented by the languid, relaxing and lovely ... leisurely treasure in the pleasure of nature ... and also otherwise sensuous language of Ted Hughes, such that this later Poet Laureate may be the poet most tactile that you will ever come to touch upon.

'… [Dylan] gave back to poetry its elevated style, lost since the romantics …'

'To her death is quite romantic …'

Romantic in this context does not (as some seem to think) mean the love interest of a Valentino, Gable or Errol Flynn, but has to do with emotion produced by appropriate, sometimes conflicting, imagery or thought: romantic in the sense of the beautiful unreal … the Professor's pictures in the mind (like a 'green sun' or 'dead life'); Coleridge goes large on this up the road ahead: it may involve a suspension of belief from reality (a 'secondary world'), indeed such as in The Lord of the Rings, and *fantasy,* meaning spaced out from reality, may be an aspect of the genre.

Alice, Huck and Tom

Real *Alice in Wonderland* stuff; but the Author's assertion turns into a perfect reality down along the banks of the River Thames up the road ahead, given the following in the context of the reversal of maps from Mother-earth into Middle-earth …

> *'She puzzled over this for some time, but at last a bright thought struck her. 'Why, it's a Looking-glass book, of course! And if I hold it up to a glass, the words will all go the right way again."*
> (Alice Through the Looking-Glass)

… and 'The Jabberwocky' poem (read back to front) illustration is merely to make an early marker for the Professor's map reversals, and, moreover, to queery (Doh!) the claim that …

'Certainly I have not been nourished by English Literature'

… because Mark Twain's Huckleberry Finn and Tom Sawyer are in the swim, too, at about the Brandywine Bridge and Bucklebury Ferry; a little ahead of Alice, lost in The Marish in the approaches of

The Old Forest on the exact same stretch of the River Thames … as a glimpse at our 'Short Cut Gone Wrong' should show.

It was on a 'golden afternoon' in 1862 that Charles Dodgson (who is better known as Lewis Carroll), a Mathematics don at Christ Church, took Alice Liddell and her sisters on a boat trip along the River Thames. As usual, they pestered him for a story – which became Alice in Wonderland and was followed by Through the Looking-Glass.

You can retrace that magical journey aboard an Edwardian-style electric river launch, along the sleepy backwaters, past Binsey the real 'treacle' ('healing') well and as far as The Trout – made famous as one of Inspector Morse's preferred watering holes.

In our book, because of the proximity of Buckland of Mother-earth, 'The Trout' manifests in The Rings as 'The Golden Perch'.

'It's either one or the other or neither of two'

And so it shall remain, even though Binsey has its own claimant, having its own 'Perch' …

The Perch *is a historic public house in the village of Binsey, northwest of Oxford and close to the River Thames.*

The Perch was frequented by author Lewis Carroll and is noted as one of the first places that he gave public readings of Alice in Wonderland. It was also a favorite of C. S. Lewis …

There is more of this 'queer' (a word, we are to suggest, derived, to some extent, of the Alice stories), stuff down along the river embankment ahead, especially in the midst of The Old Forest where the Professor makes explicit reference to the *queerness* of things.

'Ring out the false, ring in the true'
(Elegy; Tennyson)

'Do not let the writer's
authority or learning influence you,
be it little or great,

but let the love of pure truth
attract you to read.'
('Sed Quaere' … *Latin*, My Loincloff …?)

Here is the ethos of our Quest in The Rings: by way of tribute
to Professor J.R.R. Tolkien, all within the theatre of majesty,
magnificence, and above all munificence in Professor J.R.R.
Tolkien's generosity of gift to all future generations, and remarkably
consistent in ideology with Dylan's philosophy of art …

'But once upon a time (my crest has long since fallen) I had a
mind to make a body of more or less connected legend, ranging
from the large and cosmogonic to the level of romantic fairy-
story … The cycles should be linked to a majestic whole, and
*yet leave scope for other minds and hands, wielding paint and music and
drama* … Absurd …'
('J.R.R. Tolkien A Biography'; Humphrey Carpenter).

**'I have spread my dreams under your feet;
Tread softly because you tread on my dreams.'**
(The Cloths of Heaven; W.B. Yeats)

Professor J.R.R. Tolkien's dreams are legend, and we tread softly,
forever in the certainty that we are merely fulfilling the Professor's
final dream; clearly hinted at in Letter number 183 …

'The theatre of my tale is this earth, the one in which we now live,
but the historical period is imaginary. The essentials of that abiding
place are all there (at any rate for inhabitants of N.W. Europe), so
naturally it feels familiar, even if a little glorified by the enchantment
of distance in time.'

Smeagol: … come, come … come see what Smeagol finds …

Elf Warning

With all applause for the trappings of our clapping lauds of poetry
but a whisper now, time to focus on the geography of Middle-

earth; yet, as in 'Magic Mirror Maps' preceding this Quest, we offer similar warning about the build-up to departure from Hobbiton (some dozens of pages further up the road ahead) …

'Patience is a virtue, but in these days of instantaneous communication, many of the Audience will fidget through PARTS ONE TO THREE. Those of impatient disposition might proceed straight away to RING M:I, where our Quest for the Shire of Middle-earth really begins.

The Rolling English Road

'Before the Roman came to Rye or out to Severn strode,
The rolling English drunkard made the rolling English road.
A reeling road, a rolling road, that rambles round the shire,
And after him the parson ran, the sexton and the squire;
A merry road, a mazy road, and such as we did tread
The night we went to Birmingham by way of Beachy Head.'
(The Rolling English Road)

Those of the Audience following on from our quest in The Hobbit by Magic Mirror Maps will be aware that Professor J.R.R. Tolkien clearly knew the works of G.K. Chesterton very well, denoting attention to the 'queerness of things' when once sighted from another direction. The Rolling Road poem is one of such works, and we think possibly among the impulses for, dare we say it, the direction that the Lord of the Rings was ultimately to take.

'Everything I've ever known to be right has been proven wrong'

Whether or not the Audience is familiar with Magic Mirror Maps, the Author is here to tell you that the same trick of the eye has been pulled by Professor Tolkien in The Lord of The Rings: all is in Reverse. The *Reverse* is so perversely ironic in terms of Chesterton: the Author is bound to tell that the vision of the Audience will turn from Birmingham and towards Beachy Head on this our quest to

Mordor: for we are to find Birmingham (Fornost on the Maps), then to cross the English Channel, via Beachy Head or any other point of coastal departure,(Dover being the most usual), in order to reach … eventually in Volume III … Rohan, Gondor and indeed Mordor: respectively France, Spain and Germany.

'Whom now I conjure to stand as thief
In the memory worked by mirrors, …'
(To Others Than You; Dylan Thomas)

The Audience may care to recall the following from the Magic Mirror Maps …

In humble defence of our aims open to challenge, we must rise to that challenge; for some of you, a frolic of fantasy foreclosed: and all my fault. The Hobbit is so close to the heart of so many of you, this quest of ours may destroy your dearest dreams. Yet the Professor gloves us up game for the giant challenge ahead …

'I was most pleased by your reference to the description of 'glittering caves'. No other critic, I think, has picked it out for special mention. It may interest you to know that the passage was based on the caves in Cheddar Gorge and was written just after I had revisited these in 1940 but was still coloured by the memory of them much earlier …'
(Letter number 321)

The exact same things may be said of The Lord of the Rings: if the Author destroys dreams, then that may be in favour of building new ones. Professor Tolkien turned the fact of places into fantasy fiction, and we suppose, ultimately, legend. Legend will give rise to further fact as the places become known to everyone who cares to take interest in these places, or even go there. Those journeys will, in time, themselves become the legend of the connectivity of Mother-earth and Middle-earth … or it may be the other way about. Middle-earth may be allowed to operate on two levels, or in two dimensions, as it were. So grand the purpose of inspiration, on the other hand, the Quest may be dismissed for the load of eyewash some have suggested: yet we can assure the Audience of the presence of the Eye … found there in a corner, in a wood, in a box, in a house, the waters of the River Severn swashing by … and first sighted in Volume II close by Amon Hen, as one might expect …

The Audience may even visit online. If you go personally, you will have the joy that you will have read and now tread in the footsteps of Professor J.R.R. Tolkien; and that on the matter of the Professor's influences, there is this to be said …

> 'There is no special reference to England in the 'Shire' – except of course that as an Englishman brought up in an 'almost rural' village of Warwickshire … I take my models like anyone else – from such 'life' as I know …'
>
> (Letter number 181)

'And my whole heart under your hammer …'
(ibid.)

Personally, the Author finds nothing more satisfying than 'following in father's footsteps' to quote a Musical Hall favourite; it is not every day one gets to psychoanalyse (if we are) the author of the bestselling story of all time.

**'A writer needs three things,
experience, observation, and imagination,
any two of which, at times any one of which,
can supply the lack of the others.'**
(William Faulkner)

Some seem to think that Middle-earth spirited itself into Professor Tolkien's consciousness, somehow out of the ether, and then into print by some kind of magic; but every writer has only personal experience to draw upon in his work and that, coupled with imagination, is more or less how Middle-earth took off; but without question with the maps of Mother–earth to shove start the Professor off on his way … the Professor would be on bicycle, a favoured mode of transport about The Shire, … and Professor J.R.R. Tolkien himself will be telling us that was exactly how it all did, as a matter of actual fact, get started …

'Every secret of a writer's soul,
every experience of his life,
every quality of his mind,
is written large in his works.'
(Virginia Woolf)

We shall be hearing that within 'The Shire' the Professor lives with experience of Winston Churchill, the notorious six Mitford sisters and Vita Sackville-West; whilst in rampaging Roy Campbell, we have more than the rumour of Aragorn in armour.

'Learning is experience.
Everything else is just information.'
(Albert Einstein)

Runes plus Tunes

' Now I've heard there was a secret chord
That David played, and it pleased the Lord
But you don't really care for music, do you?'
(Hallelujah; Leonard Cohen)

'I wanted to understand things and then be free of them. I needed to learn how to telescope things, ideas. Things were too big to see all at once, like all the books in the library – everything laying around on all the tables. You might be able to put it all into one paragraph or into one verse of a song if you could get it right.'
(Dylan; Chronicles, Vol. I)

For those who doubt the relevance of sung lyrics in 'serious' literature or poetry (and recall the words of Dylan Thomas who says all that matters about poetry is the personal *enjoyment* of it), we have this …

'Dylan had been working on what was supposed to be a book of prose poems. He said that when he wrote 'Like a Rolling Stone' he realised that he did not need to divide his talents – a song could contain as many ideas or subjects as a novel or poem could.'

(Liner Notes; The Cutting Edge)

Perhaps it is only those who have limitations themselves who place limits on what is entitled to be called literature ...

'All good art cannot help but confront denial on its way to truth.'
(Pete Townshend)

'It's either one or the other or neither of two'

Whether or not we give Gollum express credit for po'try lyrrix or songs and dances-ss, wherever the Audience hears one (unless we tell you otherwise) the voice is most definitely that filffy stinker creature with (like an old-time 45 or 33 rpm) two sides, all because Gollum so wants It ... but you shan't know what it is until ...

Smeagol: ... we tells you at the end ...

Gollum: ... Smeagol doesn't know, my precious and we doesn't want to know ... until the ends-s of ends-ss-ss-ss...

The final notation would be that in The Lord of the Rings, Professor J.R.R. Tolkien himself encapsulates so many thoughts and ideas in poem ('One for the Dark Lord ...) and song ('The Road goes ever on and on ...'): it is sometimes forgotten that The Rings has its own separate index of Songs and Verses, running to dozens ... and the Audience may come to accept that all are homogenous.

Gollum: ... Ach-ss, big words-ss-ss, Gerron wivvit, Awffer Mas-sster ...

Smeagol: ... yes, indeed, My Luv, make haste! Time is short ... (grinning) a bit like wot hobbitses is like! ...

FOREWORD, FORWARD & BACKWARDS

**'She knows there's no success like failure
And that failure's no success at all'**

Once upon a time, this initiation in Professor J.R.R. Tolkien's creation by code of cartography bore the mark 'Foreward', a weird concoction in a worrisome word, damned by every reader put to proof of the quest herein; and so, for peace of mind, we turn to the Professor, who forewords and forwards our Quest onwards with the truth of what underpins the purpose of our Quest …

'I fear you may be right that the search for the sources of The Lord of the Rings is going to occupy academics for a generation or two. I wish this not to be so. To my mind it is the particular use in a particular situation of any motive whether **invented, deliberately borrowed, or unconsciously remembered** *that is the most interesting thing to consider.'*

This is our *Mantra of Middle-earth;* and you will be hearing it again, it so represents the rationale, purpose and justification (for anyone who thinks we might need one) for this our Quest.

Not to suffer the charge of 'academic', we remain, even so, interested in considering the motives of Professor Tolkien in his code of cartography, and, moreover, in the nomenclature of places of the Professor's maps; but we fear we may yet stand condemned for a heresy such as follows.

… and say do you want to make a d-e-e-e-a-al?

Smeagol: … we doesn't know and we doesn't want to know any recrimminayshuns … we's only inner Author Master's three Vollums to tell Audiences what Smeagol finds …

**'You my friend there with a winning air
Who palmed the lie on me when you looked
Brassily at my shyest secret, …'**
(To Others Than You; Dylan Thomas)

This Quest most cruelly underpinned in witches, their craft so pervades it that 'forward' from time to time manifests itself 'backwards' by corruption of ritual in the dark arts.

Some of you out there have already put two and two and two together ... Frodo and Sam, Saruman and Sauron, and their Two Towers, 3 times 2 making 6, as indeed we make 3 times 6, the number 666, in Our Cauldron in Appendix C, but it is yet very early days ...

'... one who tries to hide what he don't know to begin with ...'

So many consciously pretentious to knowledge that they play blind man's bluff (with the keychain), letting you catch a glimpse of the treasure, but not really knowing what and where the real stuff is.

A Web contribution ...

On Tolkien's maps, the Shire is located at about the same position as England is on modern European maps and has been cited as an example of Merry England ideology. Throughout the narrative, Tolkien also implies numerous points of similarity between the two, such as weather, agriculture and dialect.

In particular, the central part of the Shire corresponds to the West Midlands region of England, extending to Worcestershire (where Tolkien located his 'home' in particular, his mother's family being from Evesham), Gloucestershire, Shropshire, Warwickshire, Herefordshire and Staffordshire ...

'Though a Tolkien by name, I am a Suffield by tastes, talents, and upbringing, and any corner of that county [Worcestershire] (however fair or squalid) is in an indefinable way 'home' to me, as no other part of the world is.'

(Letter number 44)

Tolkien is a boy local to Worcestershire and as good a reason as any to be where I am, writing this right now, in Evesham Library of Worcestershire, where All Saints' Church carries a plaque listing several (Eighteenth Century) generations of the Suffield family, being Professor J.R.R. Tolkien's mother's family name, and whose connections with the counties of Worcestershire and Gloucestershire, Warwickshire and Oxfordshire, become manifest throughout our Quest in The Rings, none more so than for the Professor's marriage(eventually) in Nin-in–Eilph of the Shire.

A glimpse at the two maps (Author's 'of the Shire' and 'Short Cut Gone Wrong') makes plain the essence of these words: these are the areas Professor Tolkien knows best.

PART ONE Genesis of the Quest

'How many roads must a man walk down
Before you call him a man?'

Greetings from the Shire!

This collection of written works concerns the places of Middle-earth encountered by Frodo Baggins and Samwise Gamgee on their journey from Hobbiton to Mordor in J.R.R. Tolkien's 'The Lord of the Rings'.

The purpose of this work, the Quest, is to find those places on our own Mother-earth.

The Quest is our interpretation of many places of Middle-earth, based upon our learning to read the Maps in The Lord of the Rings, but on Mother-earth: for there is indeed a learning process involved; and this learning extends to the method adopted by Professor Tolkien in drawing the Maps, and in the construction of several of the location names; and many examples follow.

Rhudaur

A good example of word building might be 'Rhudaur', an area easy enough to find in the Shire of Middle-earth, mapped with the Trollshaws in its midst; and translating (in the Welsh language, but fear not, at least not yet) easily enough into the 'Golden Valley': and so the Audience must appreciate our assumption that one will be familiar with our quest in The Hobbit; this Quest is far more difficult if not ... 'Rhudaur' a bullseye in one, there are countless others, of more or less difficulty, as we play Professor Tolkien's game of plucking allusion from the air in an infinite sky of words. Aquiver with arrows, we hit the target of such as 'Tuckborough' of the Green Hill Country, a feature of the 'Map of Part of the

Shire': this Map proves so difficult to interpret that we are to call our rationale of it the 'Enigma of the Shire Map', or 'Shire Map Enigma'.

We steadfastly refuse to reduce the title of The Lord of the Rings to 'LOTR', considering that style should be confined to directions to the Film scenery in NZ. On the other hand, we do remain hopeful that our revelations of the actuality of such as the Old Forest, Weathertop, Rivendell, Lothlorien and Fangorn Forest, not forgetting The Lonely Mountain of our prior quest in The Hobbit, may do something for the British Tourist Industry, as has the scenery in NZ for that of the land of the Long White Cloud ... and so we place ourselves ever *at your service* ...

Gollum: ... why the pruffes-s-ssur Tolkkun say *'absurd'* abowt *'scope for uvver minds and hands, wielding paint and music and drama'* ... precious-ss ...?

Smeagol: ... 'cos of what follows by the Author Master, My Luv ... O, yes, My Luv ... becos of wot that Ponty wally valley boy have done *this* time ... *absurd* ...

Gollum: ... abs-ssur-r-rd stuff, yes-ss-ss, that silly, silly ... s-s-silly pons-ssey pretenshuss Ponty ... ort to have ffrottled him back in Wales ... O yes-ss ... back there we ort of ffrottled him ... O yes-ss, indeed ... an' that wino Nogood Boyo an' whine of The Nobel Voice he won' shurrup about on his silly little questses allurtime ... ort have rung their filffy little neckses-ss allur same time-s-ss-ss ...

Structure of the Quest: Rings of Power in Three Volumes

'The Rings'

Throughout the 'Letters' (of which there is much more to come), Professor Tolkien most often refers to the development of 'The Rings' or 'Rings' and even occasionally 'Ring'. Thus our abbreviation could not be bettered.

'... a structural invention of the highest order'

(C.S. Lewis of *The Lord of the Rings*, from 'The Dethronement of Power'; cited in Humphrey Carpenter's Biography of Professor J.R.R. Tolkien)

The shape of the Quest will to some be quite inordinate; following our Genesis, we undertake the Quest in Three Volumes; and magically enough,(as are the Rings magic), the works in Volumes I and II bind together all of ***nineteen*** Rings of Power.

> **'Three Rings for the Elven-kings under the sky,**
> **Seven for the Dwarf-lords in their halls of stone,**
> **Nine for mortal men doomed to die ...'**

Yet –

> **'One for the dark Lord on his dark throne ...**
> **One Ring to rule them all, one Ring to find them,**
> **One Ring to bring them all**
> **and in the darkness bind them ...'**

The certainty and power in such declaration *forces* one to believe in the unbelievable; and no doubt its purpose: in the dark speech of the street-cred, are you *hard enough* to try arguing?

The focus upon the One Ring is so intense that the remaining Nineteen are sometimes overlooked, forgotten, even lost from our thoughts completely. These two initial Volumes (taking us from Hobbiton to Fangorn Forest) comprise nineteen works which we have chosen (don't even ask me why) to call 'Rings of Power'. This otherwise strange number is made up of Nine Rings of power of the Men, Seven of the Dwarves and Three of the Elves, in order to match Professor Tolkien in The Rings.

Our content implies that there are nineteen places of Middle-earth which we claim to have identified upon Mother-earth. Actually there are any number more than that, counting in the 'new places' within each Ring; and we have clustered two groups of four within Ring D II (in which we offer the Mother-earth location of features

3

in and about the Misty Mountains, namely the peaks of Caradrhas, Silvertine and Cloudyhead, the Lake Mirrormere alongside);and three within Ring M:IX (for the localities of Amon Hen, overlooking the River Anduin, with Tol Brandir in its midst, and Amon Lhaw in the distance) in order to adhere to a 9,7,3 configuration.

Rings DII and MIX must await Volume II of the Quest: we come on to explain further the Volumes I to III which comprise the Quest. None of the Audience will have anticipated a Trilogy; any more than did Professor Tolkien, who wrote Six Books comprising The Rings, but whose publishers, eventually with the Professor's approval, called for a division into three.

There is some method in all of this structural madness; witness the words of Gandalf the Grey:

' … many Elven-Rings were made, magic Rings as you call them, and they were, of course, of various kinds: some more potent and some less. The lesser Rings were only essays in the craft before it was full-grown, and to the Elven-smiths they were but trifles – yet still to my mind dangerous for mortals. But the Great Rings, the Rings of Power, they were perilous.'

Thus, quite apposite that we call our introductory *essay* 'Genesis of the Quest', being, we trust, beyond a trifle, yet created merely to introduce the subject-matter of the Quest; but hardly dangerous (albeit our publisher winced at the sheer volume(sic)of the length and breadth of our original introductory essay, running to 3 times the words of the present); our Genesis is followed by the nineteen Rings of Power: which if again not perilous, then at the very least representative of our craft full-grown.

Why the Professor wrote of *Nineteen* Rings in all, all bound or governed by the One Ring, is for contemplation by the Audience: we know of no commentator who has posed the question; yet question whether the choice of a number may have significance. The Author gives a form of answer at some point during the Quest, having ventured out to find them not *all*, but the Rings as far as Rivendell in this Volume I.

4

Appendices

The Author had no intention of mirroring the form of The Rings (and the Audience will, by now, assuming the quest in The Hobbit is familiar, fully appreciate the sublime irony in our description of form) until the content of the Quest became so unmanageable as to make its reading tortuous without; it is perhaps torture even with: but there is much material derived of other sources which we have included; and so we have relegated it to six Appendices, A to F, of which more in Part Two of this Volume I.

Maps of The Rings and The Hobbit

Both The Rings and The Hobbit have their own sets of Maps, so for ease of reference, we call them respectively the 'Ring-Maps' and the 'Hobbit-Maps'. Many ideas are based upon the fine detail of the Ring-Maps and the Author is obliged to recommend that ready sight of the Ring-Maps is essential for comprehension of the Author's own position of understanding. So much so that the Quest is meaningless without the Ring-Maps immediately accessible. But 'easy sight' may (literally) mislead, because we mean that the Audience will not get very far without a copy of the Ring-Maps right to hand alongside the Quest; and whilst we are planning the *modus operandi* of embarking upon the Quest, the same comment applies regarding the maps of Mother-earth. We need to be in a position to compare the Maps of Middle-earth with those of Mother-earth; and to go straight there: which is enough said for the moment of the plan of our route; for such knowledge is, indeed, precious.

'Roll up, roll up, for the Magical Mystery Tour, Step right this way ...'

Many will have read The Rings but never studied its Maps with the attention equivalent to that paid by the Professor in their creation; hence our recommended *modus operandi*. This is not to forget that there is an impressive array of Web on-line maps of Mother-earth to scroll up and down on; and most if not all the locations we visit will have a write-up, some with photoshoots, on the right website.

The Quest would never have been written without the resource of the Web. How the Professor expected anyone to crack the Secret of the Shire without such resource is beyond this author; but he evidently did: one conjures with the early film image of Gandalf fleeting off to Minas Tirith on horseback to dig out some old tome about the history of the One Ring.

The Professor

We are accustomed to refer to Professor J.R.R. Tolkien as 'the Professor' and acknowledge having considered the Gaffer (like Gaffer Gamgee), and The One (already taken, by the Professor himself), so 'the Professor' it shall be; sometimes 'Professor Tolkien' but never, ever 'Tolkien' which for the Author is derogatory, dated and even class-ridden; just as the Public Schoolboy might use one of another; or, indeed as the Academic hierarchy was accustomed in the Professor's teaching days: see the Letters of the Professor addressed 'Dear Auden'.

Tolkienistwyr; Tolkien Boys

There are worldwide vast numbers of scholars in the works of Professor J.R.R. Tolkien, whose depths of knowledge of The Rings and all of the Professor's other works will make light of the Author's imprint. The Professor's approach to the construction of place-names in particular was no doubt born of logical progression from a basic principle expressed in the Letters-

'We do not know the 'original' meaning of any word, still less the meaning of its basic element (sc. the part it shares or seems to share with other related words: once called its 'root') ... there is always a lost past ...'

We find a label for the Tolkien experts by means of the Welsh language, which (if not yet) is to become of supreme relevance upon the Quest: and from simple basis in root; but with no other past. Ultimately we settled on 'Tolkienistwyr' because we believe the Professor would have approved of the invention. The 'wyr' ending simply adds "men' or 'men of' in the Welsh language, so the 'men of Tolkien', Tolkien followers, experts or even 'aficionados' or something similar: colloquially 'The Tolkien Boys', perhaps. For fear of parochiality, and as part of the last throes of this volume, we decided to use 'Tolkienistwyr' where Welsh may be relevant, but 'Tolkien Boys' where it is not.

The simple ending in Welsh ('gwr/wyr')may be coloured up into whatever counterpart suits in English, the ancient nature of the language often providing no direct specific translation, but one to be derived from the sense of the Welsh 'root', or roots.

A powerful example: 'rhyfelwyr'(a word sung proudly in the National Anthem of Wales)is compounded of the word for 'war'(rhyfel),which together with the 'wyr' ending signifies fighting men, soldiers, or warriors; in the Anthem the word is coupled with 'gwrol' in 'gwrol rhyfelwyr'; 'gwrol' is (most appropriately in this present context), derived of the singular 'gwr' of the plural 'wyr' and so gives us warriors described as 'manly', thus brave or courageous fighting men, soldiers, or warriors: typifying how the Welsh language often builds words from simpler compounds. Excuse the Author while a 'cleddyfwr'(from 'cleddyf' meaning 'sword' and 'gwr' mutated by 'lenitation' to the 'wr' ending, and thus 'swordsman') unsheaths his for a charge.

(The Professor spends an Appendix(E) on pronunciation; we do not, yet for phonetic guidance and strictly for those interested in such details: in 'rhyf-el-wyr', beginning with a 'rrr' sound, the first element rhymes with 'shove'; 'el' sounds like the letter 'l' and 'wyr' sounds as in 'win' with the rolled 'rrr' sound once more at the end. 'Gwrol' begins to sound like (sticky) 'goo' and we end up in the Tyrol of Austria).

Those not one bit interested in such details may struggle with our methodology in sounding the place names of The Rings, the foregoing phonetic charade being our stance; but why not pick up your 'cleddyf', become a brave warrior and do battle for the first time with the sounds of a new language? If the Professor liked them well enough to include in his Masterpiece, so might we in our servitude.

We come to know that Professor Tolkien often thought in similar phonetic terms. A charming example is afforded in the 'Father Christmas Letters' written for his young sons in the 1930's and through the War years: the Polar Bear writes in his 'Arktik Langwidge', an example of the word games that the Professor delighted in. The Letters may return in Volume III of our Quest, giving some insight into the Professor's train of thought through those War years.

> **'But pluck an ivy branch for me**
> **Grown old before my time.'**
> (Song; Christina Rossetti)

Our final warcry: the double 'dd' of such as 'cleddyf' is as in *the* cat sat on *the* mat, and so nothing could be easier. Even so, the 'dd' sound is hidden (from the Welsh language), in the ivy bushes within the name of the river 'Mitheithel', as is the 'Ivy Castle' in the town which is home to the river: as is 'The Last Bridge' of the Ring-Maps in the township the subject of Ring M:VIII. The more resourceful of our Audience will check the Welsh Dictionary for 'Ivy'; and, trading 'th' for 'dd', may even make some sense of this preceding sentence: but the 'Ivy Castle' is hard to find, entwined in the tendrils of a lost history as it is; but by golly (a word chosen simply for its rhyme with 'holly', to carol with Ivy at Christmas), Gollum is already peering from behind the Ivy up the road ahead, buried in fun and games.

Not to tantalyse, *Mitheithel* has its root in the Welsh word for *Ivy,* which is *Eiddew.*

Saruman

The White Wizard's name may of itself suggest a further example of Professor Tolkien's trickery with words, and specifically with elision: two sided, two-faced and duplicitous, not unlike the character of Saruman, the Wizard white before Gandalf returns as The White, … and so says Mithrandir in Fangorn Forest, as what Saruman *should have been,* had the original white wizard remained *true:* and so Gandalf metamorphasises into the role that should have been that of Saruman.

We believe the name reveals two compounds. Professor Tolkien's is yet a double trickery, for he mixes a first Welsh root with a second, English component, derived of the equivalent of the Welsh word for man, being 'gwr', the singular of 'wyr' of previous mention.

The Author is to suggest little difficulty with the first root, being derived of the Welsh word 'Sarhau', meaning to injure, hurt or insult the objective of the one who does so: perhaps, in the language of the Christian Church Evensong service, the 'miserable offender'. Thus after Sauron, Saruman is a prime offender of Middle-earth.

To recall our mention, eons ago on our quest in The Hobbit, the suffix 'wyr' to denote the *men* who perform a function, then the singular 'gwr' added to 'sarhau' produces sarhau(g)wr, and by converting the second root *back into the English language*, the result produced is 'Sar(ha)u-man'. Again we recall from our quest in The Hobbit, the Professor's comment that most names of Middle-earth are derived from Welsh, and this is indeed our only rationale, adding the note that the name must derive from *some* root or other; yet the Tolkien Boys may have that other, but if so the Author has not read of any.

Mind Games

> **'We all been playing those *mind games … fore-ever***
> **Some kinda druid dudes lifting the veil**
> **Doing the mind guerrilla**
> **Some call it magic … the search for the grail'**

As that Lennon tune recalls itself to one's aural sensitivities (as it hopefully will be for many), we might here recall our quest in The Hobbit: where there were Druids, Magic, a search for the Grail; and, furthermore, our first ever exposure to Professor J.R.R. Tolkien's games with words in mind.

The Professor's place names in The Rings appear often to be built in the same fashion as in The Hobbit, from compound roots, with games in mind. One will never at this early stage comprehend the extent to which the Professor contrived to make up the place names in The Rings: most are obviously made up; but also quite literally 'made up' from simpler components when broken down: we are to mention Tharbad, a Docklands; by such simple process, a haven for boats, built down in Welsh. Thus it will come as no surprise when we aim to show that many place names are built in the same way: Bindbole Wood, Frogmorton and Whitfurrows (each of the Shire Map), but in these cases the build is not from the Welsh language, but by application of the same process in English.

Some will recall the meaning and use of 'elision' from our quest in The Hobbit.

We fear to put the Audience through the impact of the Welsh language upon our Quest in The Rings, but it is there in substantial degree, as we have proffered on our quest in The Hobbit and as we come on to share further. Much of the Shire is indeed sheep country, within the Cotswold Hills, *Cardolan* on the Ring-Maps, and the Welsh roots and elisions will be equally lost on some …

> **'… and though the rules of the road**
> **have been lodged,**
> **Its only peoples' games**
> **that you got to dodge …'**

Wails and Whales (to a triplicity in Wales …)

We hear the Audience wails: is the Author mesmerised in all this cacophony of terminology … presumably by the One Ring; just so Bilbo at Rivendell?

The wails are about to morph into Whales and thence to Wales. The Author regards the Quest as a shred of plankton fodder in the oceanful of Whales of the Professor's creation; the Professor ever ahead of school. In all candor, the complex structuring and labeling of everything is devised so as not to get lost like 'The Precious': simply because it made the Quest far easier to write and hopefully to follow by the Audience. We are bound to define our terms for the arduous journey that we face, in order that we know what we are talking about when we get there.

At some stages that may remain open to doubt.

Rangers

Occasional reference to *Rangers* upon the Quest is meant to mean those of the Audience tracking the Quest so closely that they may wish to do their own researches of places and names, whether of the association where they are mentioned, or up the road ahead; not forgetting that the Author was a 'ranger' once, starting from the same place of zero knowledge; and our claim to have tracked so much from Middle- to Mother-earth is a challenge open to the Rangers in following the same progress.

The 'Ranger' name is commonplace in the USA; indeed we have mentioned in The Hobbit 'Magic Mirror Maps' the debt the Tolkien Boys and all other readers of The Rings owe to America, which was the fount of the book's success; we come the nearest we may to Texas, by reference to the Mississippi, at the Brandywine Bridge and Bucklebury Ferry; only to meet a lone one in the Old Forest: which is indeed, quite possibly, where Professor Tolkien derived the concept of a band of rangers in the first place.

'All the world's a stage,
And all the men and women merely players …'

Not to forget that the appeal of The Lord of the Rings is indeed worldwide, some 150,000,000 copies later and translated into most

11

languages of Mother-earth: so we had better get on and open the curtain …

Exploration, Exploitation and Elaboration from Premise

The Professor fully expected the Rings to be *researched,* beyond just the reading of it as a story. The Rings is beyond mere story; its entire nature is uncertain because it is one of its only kind. It may seem a virtual documentary-history-textbook, whose Appendices and Indices confirm as much. Is there any other work of 'Fiction' that affords an extensive index-list of (inter alia) 'Places' and 'Things', giving rise to the implication that one may wish to check back on these for context, relevance and meaning? And so, the Author has been checking back on any number of the 'Places', to discover that The Rings may not be so much fiction after all.

We are to learn that the Professor drew the Maps first and constructed the edifice of his story around them. Upon reflection, one wonders whether there was realistically any other method of creation. We contemplate the Professor's methodology at great length; and make the point that the story of a journey is impossible to tell unless one knows where to go next.

We might preliminarise some thoughts more fully expanded later on in terms of the Professor's sense of mischief. Appendix E to The Rings (Useful Hints on Writing and Spelling and especially Pronunciation) is introduced by the following:

'The following points may be observed by those who are interested in such details.'

That is exactly the sentiment we wish to underpin the ethos of the Quest. It underpins everything; so much so, that we parrot the words over and over and over again until it sinks in, as it will. We are not expert on Professor Tolkien, his life or his works, no more than the average reader qualifies as expert. We share with our Audience what we think we know, or at least what we know we think, and leave the rest to its members if it happens the Audience is interested.

Even so, 'cunning devilry' (by Bilbo of Smaug in The Hobbit) on the part of the Professor is gross understatement.

Proof of want of expertise strikes first at Bree; just so the Black Riders or Nazgûl. When Frodo puts on the Ring, he becomes invisible to mortal man. At Bree it is the force field of the Nazgûl that wills Frodo to put on the Ring, so that he becomes visible to them. This simple duality from one dimension to another, which will be commonplace for the Tolkien Boys, escaped the Author until the latter stages of the Quest. We may have appreciated either facet, but not the subtlety of the mutuality: saved in one dimension, so to speak, Frodo immediately becomes imminently vulnerable in the other.

Professor Tolkien thought in dualistic terms in matters beyond putting on the Ring. Elements of The Rings operate on a level of invisibility beyond that in plain sight. The primary duality is inherent in the purpose of the Quest, for we contend that the maps of Middle-earth are capable of being read on Mother-earth; but the Professor's illusion, or trick, may be seen to extend beyond even this first 'hey presto'.

Difficult to convey at this early stage, but beyond the duality of Middle-and Mother-earth, places on the Ring-Maps sometimes allude to two places on Mother-earth; and this incomprehensible generalisation is best illustrated by the example of 'Stock', by which the Professor takes us one step beyond: where 'stock' implies swine or pigs, in Rings M:II and M:V we aim to reveal *two* places of that same root by name. The Quest becomes rather complicated in these areas, meaning those in and around Stock; but we do believe Professor Tolkien designed it so.

Research for the simple truth started out as a basic exercise: observation of points for those who may be interested; but developed into research on disparate levels: so many more than once upon a time, and so multifarious, one is required to believe in them; fairies that is, lots of them.

But we told you about them on our quest in The Hobbit.

Now we must get started; and in doing so, we may permit ourselves a number of premises, in the sense of a statement from which others may be inferred. It is of the essence to understand that each premise, and most of the views we take on the Quest, were catalysed by words written or spoken by Professor J.R.R. Tolkien himself; and so heaven forbid that we should be taken to undermine a masterpiece.

The following is a synthesis of what the Professor has written or said on the subject of physical setting of The Rings:

(1) The action of the story takes place in North-west of Mother-earth, equivalent in latitude to the coastline of Europe and the north shore of the Mediterranean;
(2) If Hobbiton and Rivendell are taken (as intended)to be about the latitude of Oxford then Minas Tirith, 600 miles south, is at about the latitude of Florence … ' (and we intend the subject of Volume III of the Quest);
(3) The theatre of the tale is our earth and Professor Tolkien assured us that he had *'kept his feet on Mother-earth'* for his field of action.

One can read the full words, spoken in a journalist's interview, in The Tolkien Encyclopaedia of David Day (1991); which was the Author's original source of the Professor's words; and which it will be readily acknowledged started us off on the Quest in the first place. We feel obliged to credit our first conception of the Mother-earth analogy, which set us off on track, but the Professor indicates the same general comparable in many of his Letters, notably number 183, the text of which concludes this Part One. For our purposes, the Audience is asked to mark very carefully the words of the Professor; *we are told that the setting of the Rings is Mother-earth;* with hints as to whereabouts we need to look for our locations.

Some have attempted their explanation; indeed, some of the places are already located and in the public domain, so why not, literally, go further? The Third of the Wise and the Great (explained in Appendix A) spends a Chapter drawing parallels between Mother-earth and Professor Tolkien's 'contrived' Middle-earth; and yet he concludes it is not so much contrived:

'… a secondary world must be 'credible, commanding Secondary belief'. And he manifestly expected that secondary worlds would combine the ordinary with the extraordinary, *the fictitious with the actual…*' (Author's italics)

This is a lovely chapter with wondrous insight into Professor Tolkien's method of writing. Here Paul Kocher means the trees, birds and weather of the real world; all of which we see are features of Middle-earth; yet, on the Quest, we claim also the actual locations of Mother-earth.

The best example of Mother Nature on the Quest might be the Silver Birch; which the Professor clearly adored: the Letters (number 50) show as much-

'At no time do birches look so beautiful: their skin snow-white in the pale yellow sun, and their remaining leaves shining fallow-gold …'

The Silver Birch of Mother-earth are precisely where they should be according to the Professor's secret of the Shire: Lothlorien; but now we look too far ahead; so the Audience must simply look forward to Lothlorien, where we shall not be disappointed with what we find; rapturous, more like, or in the terminology of the Professor, in 'eucatastrophe'.

And yet our actuality extends beyond trees, birds and weather: to the real places of their environment. We have mentioned the resource of the Web in determining the outcome of the Quest, which would never have been born at all without it. The same is true of 'The Letters of J.R.R. Tolkien'(edited by Humphrey Carpenter), whose insight into the Professor Tolkien's 'motives' is beyond words. Even so, there follow those of another-

'Just as in history, a lot of Tolkien scholarship can be dated 'B.C.'; but in this case it would mean 'Before Carpenter', referring to Humphrey Carpenter, author of *Tolkien: a Biography* and editor of *The Letters of J.R.R. Tolkien* (1981). Prior to the publication of those books, some brave souls did their best – often producing very good work – with limited success to Tolkien's own thoughts about Middle-earth. Since then, nearly every worthwhile book about Tolkien, whether for a general audience or for academics, has relied on Carpenter's books as essential sources. This volume is no exception.'

(The Magical Worlds of the Lord of the Rings, David Colbert (2002)).

Neither is this Volume; the only remaining questions being three: is there an audience, who is in it (general reader or academic) and whether it is worthwhile: only time will tell, and some hundreds of pages of patient reading, and once more we stress the requirement of patience.

And so to a number of premises: three.

A Reality Check

"Every writer making a secondary world, he declared, 'wishes in some measure to be a real maker, or hopes that he is drawing on reality: hopes that the peculiar quality of this world (if not all the details) are derived from Reality, or are flowing into it."

('J.R.R. Tolkien A Biography'; Humphrey Carpenter).

The First of the Wise (sometimes questionable) and the Great (likewise) comprise newspaper reviews; but all are replete with appreciations in the same vein: all is Glory, but, … *let me take you down* …

> ' …'cos I'm going to …
> **Strawberry Fields,**
> **nothing is real …**'

Other authorities have gone along with this perception of the story's creation. Some, like the Second of the Wise and the Great think it *entire* fantasy. Any question of fact is dismissed in favour of *'sheer invention'*. We maintain that most of this is barely half-truth. The Rings is **not** *pure* invention, and indeed has a basis in reality, a reality of places. It is perhaps something akin to what in popular terms is called 'faction', that is, fiction based on fact, where the facts are in this instance the reality of the places.

Does anyone out there imagine that even the brow of the superbrained Professor Tolkien might make up the epic of The Lord of The Rings from *sheer invention* ... any writer who has ever written *anything* knows full well that there are sources, resources and forces (mine's the Welsh triplicity) being drawn upon in putting pen to paper ... and we are about to begin a search for those of Professor J.R.R. Tolkien ... with the abiding question ever ... Why? ...

'I fear you may be right that the search for the sources of The Lord of the Rings is going to occupy academics for a generation or two. I wish this not to be so. To my mind it is the particular use in a particular situation of any motive whether invented, deliberately borrowed, or unconsciously remembered that is the most interesting thing to consider.'

Some, like the Author, have attributed more weight to Professor Tolkien's *actual words*, especially those of the Prologue to The Rings; witness the perceptive analysis of the Third of the Wise and the Great. The intuition of Paul Kocher is wise and great enough to bring forward his material from Appendix A –

'... the maps of Europe in the Third Age drawn by Tolkien to illustrate his epic show a continent very different from that of today in its coastline, mountains, rivers and other major geographical features. In explanation he points to the forces of erosion, which wear down mountains, and to advances and recessions of the sea that have inundated some lands and uncovered others.'
                    (Paul Kocher: 'Master Of Middle-earth'(1972))

This commentator is saying in effect: it may all be here on earth, we simply have to find it if we wish.

Together we shall.

The conclusions we draw much depend upon the map of the World, and specifically that of Europe, being very different from what we see and know today. Our theories necessarily involve Continental Europe(not least because Professor Tolkien declared that such was the case, as in (2)of the foregoing synthesis), yet we have so much for sharing within this Volume I of the Quest, Continental Europe will have to wait another day.

Yet our findings there up the road ahead do, indeed, bear out Fonstad's Atlas, which proffers the reference (from Niekas fan magazine) that …

'Tolkien once commented that Mordor corresponded more or less with the Mediterranean volcanic basin; and Mt. Doom, Stromboli. At every turn volcanism was suggested …'

Whilst 'more or less' is a big window on maps newly drawn of the old world, we look forward to the concept of the changing shape of the world over time, with specific reference to the absence on the Ring-Maps of the English Channel separating England from France, and on smaller scale the Bristol Channel separating England from Wales. For the moment we simply make reference to that future analysis.

''Middle-earth', by the way, is not a name of never-never land without relation to the world we live in … imaginatively this 'history' is supposed to take place in the period of the actual Old World of this planet."

(Letter number 165)

Just before we pretend about history: a thought which had occurred to the Author, whose theoretical was to be confirmed by much discussion on the Web: that the flood of the Holy Bible is man's subliminal memory of the end of an ice age, when vast areas of the planet would be under water; for instance, the Shire was under sea: see The Cotswold Edge below.

Pretend History

A second premise follows from the Professor's comment-

'I much prefer history, true or feigned, with its varied applicability to the thought and experience of readers …'

The history of the Lord of the Rings is obviously not fact, but feigned or pretend, thus clearly involving invention: *the history may be invented around places ostensibly fictional but in reality actual.*

It is common ground that such as Dickens set stories in actual places and allowed the locations to invent and develop the story around them. Our first dart a bullseye: Jacob's Island, the scene of Bill Sykes's literal fall from grace in 'Oliver Twist' represents the London Bridge and Bermondsey areas. The island is still there, as a matter of fact of geographical association. Thomas Hardy, too, of several places in England: Dorchester (Casterbridge), Salisbury (Melchester)and Winchester (Wintoncester) in his works of the shire of Wessex. The Christminster of 'Jude the Obscure' is a well recognised location; as is Waymoot of the Ring-Maps, best studied (remembering where we are beneath the Dreaming Spires) from the Shire Map and our RING M:I, new light shining on Waymoot from Hobbiton.

Waymoot represents Oxford; and Hobbiton is more or less unquestionably ... to be found in RING M:I.

Association from real places is by no means a new phenomenon in fictional history. Upon reflection, perhaps Hardy is after all amongst the best illustrations of the methodology we contend for the Professor's mapping of The Rings. There is perhaps an even better; for the Audience's own reflection: think on, Pilgrim.

The Maps are Key; the Key is the Maps

Gandalf to Merry ...

'There are many maps in Elrond's house, but I suppose you never thought to look at them?'

Background material concerning the Professor's motives in the writing of the Rings is replete with commentary in the following vein ...

'If you're going to have a complicated story you must work to a map; otherwise you'll never make a map of it afterwards.'

('J.R.R. Tolkien A Biography'; Humphrey Carpenter).

All demonstrate that the Maps are in fact the key to all comprehension of The Rings.

The Fourth of the Wise and the Great is formidable authority: Tom Shippey is unequivocal that Professor Tolkien started with the Maps and moved the story on by use of the locations. Our resource is navsatisfyingly second sightful in the comment that Aragorn is often made to speak *as if he were reading and following a Map-*

'But even the characters of *The Lord of the Rings* have a strong tendency to talk like maps, and historical ones at that.'

We have included this author's neat examples within the Fourth of the Annals of the Wise and the Great. We foresee our own within RING M: VIII(for a second time, since we first challenged the Audience to a sword fight in the midst of the 'Tolkienistwyr'), in relation to The Last Bridge of the Ring-Maps, where the words of Aragorn of the river 'Mitheithel' cause us to look (in local, perhaps Barliman Butterbur, accent) *loively* ... for *Ivy*; and a Welsh translation.

The Fifth of the Wise and the Great expresses himself convinced that the Professor's favourite tool is the *inside joke*; and *what* a joke: Professor Tolkien's mischievous nature underscores one of the central tenets of the Quest. Namely that the Maps are not all they might first appear. In fact they may just be one great riddle, feint or act of trickery.

'... in such story one cannot make a map for the narrative, but must first make a map and make the narrative agree ...'

(Letter number 137)

Many, if we thought about it at all, will have assumed the process was the reverse ... pun intended; story then Maps, but we may all agree; Professor Tolkien ought to know: the maps came first, and the Professor has said so time and again. In fact, for some the Maps

20

are mere afterthought, whose detail is all but ignored by many. For the third time of asking, the Professor explains:

'I wisely started with a map, and made the story fit…'
(Letter Number 144)

It must go without saying that Professor Tolkien could not have started with a finished concept or product. Indeed, we know that The Rings took many years of his life in the writing:

'It had taken twelve years to write *The Lord of the Rings*. By the time that he had finished it, Tolkien was not far from his sixtieth birthday.'
('J.R.R. Tolkien A Biography'; Humphrey Carpenter).

We have Professor Tolkien's own words on the subject of the story development. Of its writing, in the Letters-

'… in the same period (1938-39) when The Lord of the Rings was beginning to unroll itself and to unfold prospects of labour and exploration *in yet unknown country* as daunting to me as to the hobbits. At about that time we had reached Bree, and I had no more notion than they had what had become of Gandalf or who Strider was; and I had begun to despair of surviving to find out.'

So for those who imagine that The Professor first sketched out an outline of the whole story, then filled in the gaps with detail, we are wrong: we come to understand that he sketched *the Maps* and then filled in the story detail, no doubt filling in the gaps (sometimes ahead and sometimes working backwards) from station to station.

This piece of esoteric information may have been missed by some of our Audience but it is the one single, vital piece of information which gives credence to the Quest.

The exact truth has one staggering, presumably ever backwards-

' … from time to time I made rough sketches or synopses of what was to follow, immediately or far ahead; but these were seldom of much use: the story unfolded itself as it were. The typing-up was achieved, so far as it is achieved, *by constant re-writing backwards ...'*

(Letter Number 199; Author's italics)

'Bewitched, bothered and bewildered ...'

For a tantalysing first instance of rewriting backwards, the Author is of the belief that the events at Weathertop were written on the Professor's journey backwards through the writing of The Rings: all because of the events occurring in the Shire in 1945; and we may even know the date: February 14, 1945: indeed St. Valentine's Day ...

If the places of the Shire are written backwards, then, not unlike the Ringwraiths and their unwelcome visitation upon Weathertop, the secret is soon enough to shock us ... not unlike a Morgul blade: in RING M (V: VII), where there is to be blood shed in unlikely ritual of Witchcraft.

And so, backwards to the future and our Exploration of the Professor's Cartography.

From Premise to Exploration, Exploitation and Elaboration

Analysis by the Fourth of the Wise and the Great suggests to us threefold banners for the genesis of The Rings: *exploration; exploitation;* and *elaboration.*

(I)
Exploring Cartography

The Fourth of the Wise and the Great ...

> ' ... ***maps,*** names and languages came *before* plot...'

We have valued commentary upon the Professor's methodology; as ever, the Fourth of the Wise and the Great is well ahead of us, having read, seen and heard it all before-

'[Professor Tolkien] created Middle-earth before he had a plot to put in it, and at every delay or failure of 'inspiration' he went back to the map and to the landscape...'

Even the superbrow of Professor J.R.R. Tolkien could not conceptualise and encapsulate the breadth of vision of The Rings at a stroke. The scale of Tolkien's achievement is no better described than in the writing of the Seventh of the Wise and the Great, W.H. Auden, a commentator of the highest calibre upon the achievement of The Rings, and one not shy to share his long and winding road of opinion ...

It is indirectly through Auden that we may perceive a secret identity for Lobelia Sackville-Baggins; keeping company with the Mitford sisters (Nancy, Pamela, Diana, Unity, Jessica and Deborah, each of whom merit portrayal on the Quest) in the shires of Mother-earth: these in our Portrait Gallegory at the Crossroads up the road ahead.

> **'All these people that you mention**
> **Yes, I know them, they're quite lame, ...**
> **I had to rearrange their faces**
> **And give them aaall another name ...'**

In a locality-orientated history such as this, essentially the tale of a journey or quest, Professor Tolkien, in our submission, needed 'somewhere to go' for the purposes of his developing storyline. We have already postulated the first instance of the feigned nature of his historical account: the story is imagined but the places have a bearing in reality. Given that the places may be real then we supposed a further feint in giving them another name, and possibly imprecision of location one to another, meaning there may be some leeway in the relativity of the actual locations on Mother-earth by comparison with their relativity on the Maps of Middle-earth. As we are enlightened by the Third of the Wise and the Great, the territory may look quite different from what we see today.

We do not claim a carbon copy of the maps of Middle-earth on Mother-earth; but at the very least we demonstrate how the Professor used places of Mother-earth for his trail to Mordor (or in this Volume I, to Rivendell),and sequentially from one to the next. Professor Tolkien says in the Letters(number 169) that his is a 'dramatic' representation of Mother-earth; which is the best description; those looking, perhaps naively, for a 'facsimile' (if that is any different from a carbon copy) will be disappointed, but even so we hold that by the Professor's Secret of the Shire the congruence between Middle-earth and Mother-earth is demonstrably remarkable.

If we trace no 'facsimile', we shall nevertheless be riding with 'Shadowfax'.

Whilst we were lead to a number of the associations of the Quest by need to think laterally, and loosely or 'outside the box' in modern parlance, our starting place had been very much a conclusion drawn from the other end of the spectrum; in terms of the rigidity of the detail and minutiae of the Professor's map-making. They show the concentrated focus of a Cyclops. The Professor is meticulous in thought, word and deed, and he, above all, knows it …

'Among my characteristics that you have not mentioned is the fact that I am a pedant devoted to accuracy, even in what may appear to others unimportant matters.'

(Letter number 294)

The Maps are drawn in such detail and with such abundant depth of thought process that they must surely indicate the fixated focus of a logical progression. One cannot credit the suggestion that the Professor simply made them up. One cannot credit the idea that the Professor created the Maps arbitrarily. If so, they do amount to pure fiction or fantasy, a doodle, and there is no riddle, feint, trick, game or 'Code' and nothing more to add: except that the Audience might like to work out for yourselves how the Maps were first envisioned and then executed.

Perhaps the most likely conclusion is that Professor J.R.R. Tolkien copied, modeled and recreated the maps by some trick, illusion or (upping the level of the game), some 'Secret' within the maps: and unless the Professor knew the geography of some other planet(not

24

beyond the Professor), one assumes the places relevant are on a Mother-earth well known to him.

Smeagol: ... We guesses, yes, we knows ...

Gollum: ... Ach,-ss!... Yes-ss, My precious-ss, we knows ... We guesses, yes,... like allur riggle games wiv bagginses ... an' wot hobbitses had got in his nas-ssty little pocketses ... *and* wot hobbitses have got round his filffy little neckses-ss ...

William Ready: The Tolkien Relation

We come to the writings of William Ready, our Ninth of the Wise and the Great, held in great store on the Quest. Bill Ready seems to the Author to have known so much more over fifty years ago, as his work reveals; but then he did have an advantage, which we also come on to explain, somewhere up the road ahead. When we hear him on the subject of the Maps, in the Ninth of the Annals of the Wise and the Great, one is obliged first to question the suggestion (from within such of the Annals) that the Hobbits did ever '*seek for*' the pass over the Misty Mountains through which the Hobbits '*made it*' to the Shire ...'?

It should not take one of our Tolkien Boys to twig that the Hobbits did not cross the Misty Mountains to 'make it' *to* the Shire, but the reverse. They crossed the mountains alright, but *leaving* the Shire. As it is explained further, this might conceivably be Bill Ready's rather clumsy way of telling us something he wished not to make manifestly clear: he was leaving a clue, as the Professor does throughout The Rings.

A single ray of light shone upon the troubled waters: the Author ultimately discovered that William Ready will have had privileged knowledge in the making of such statements. He may have been playing his own Riddle-Game; his Gollum to our Bilbo. Especially startling for the Author are Bill Ready's comments about Wales and the Welsh. Bill Ready openly declares that Middle-earth *is* Wales, albeit with some of England in its midst, in the following words:

'The place of the great Hobbit action is Middle-earth, something like a Europe of these days … and Britain is Wales, with the heart of England in the middle of the principality.'

The Author now previews our revelation in regard to Bill Ready with the statement of the Author's discovery that the Hobbit-Maps were indeed made by the Professor on the basis of the geography of Wales, and equally to the point: the geography of the Hobbit-Maps are drawn from the Maps of Wales on Mother-earth *by means of the same process as the Ring-Maps.*

We repeat that, at time of writing, the Author envisages a Trilogy (not an entirely original concept) for the Quest: a second Volume comprising Frodo's journey in The Rings beyond Rivendell to Fangorn Forest; and a third Volume in relation to the journey beyond, involving Continental Europe. That count makes four Volumes in all; naturally, all will depend on whether there is anyone interested in such details. Over some part of Frodo's journey in The Rings, Bilbo had gone before, in The Hobbit. The implications of this are profound for the Quest; for if we aim to show how Professor Tolkien created the Ring-Maps from Mother-earth, so too (one assumes) the maps in The Hobbit.

But you may know about that already.

There is a duality here, but the journeys are not co-extensive: their trails diverge at or about Rivendell. But we determine that both crossed into Wales; and so Dylan Thomas (whom we rechristen the 'Nogood Boyo' after the character of that name in 'Under Milk Wood') is bound to come wending his wanton way, there and back again –

> 'I, in my intricate image, stride on two levels,
> Forged in man's minerals, the brassy orator
> Laying my ghost in metal,
> The scales of this twin world tread on the double,
> My half ghost in armour hold hard in death's corridor,
> To my man-iron sidle.'

There are at least seven allusions to duality here; but we may have imagined a number. The Nogood Boyo has looked in the mirror, only to see an imperfect double image. And so, in our next section, to the Professor's creation of Middle-earth in his image of Mother-earth; by the Secret of the Shire. Upon reflection (for a third time of looking), having rewound with Bill Ready to 1968, who might be recording a further creation that same year?

**'Go to the Mirror, Boy!
Go to the Mirror ... Boy!'**

Professor J.R.R. Tolkien's Secret of the Shire

The Author struggled long and hard for a description of the Professor's technique of map-making. Perhaps the best ever was already written; 'A Cartographic Plot' in 'The Road to Middle-earth' of the Fourth of the Wise and the Great. That writer indicates the truth we have already addressed; that the Professor's plot in The Rings followed the Maps of The Lord of the Rings in conception and time.

The Author aims to demonstrate that there is a further, deeper 'plot' or 'Secret' concealed or hidden within the Ring-Maps themselves.

Assumptions

As Shakespeare has it-

**'In their poor praise he humbled. Such a man
Might be a copy to these younger times;
Which, follow'd well, would demonstrate them now
But goers backward ...'**
('All's Well That Ends Well' of Shakespeare)

And so, with the best Will in the world, backward to the future. Is Frodo making a journey backwards? In a sense, he is. If the Audience will for the time being bear with the Author in making some assumptions with reference to the story detail in The Rings, it is hoped, given time and patience, the Audience will achieve full reward.

At least two associations of place are recognised by the Tolkien Boys and already in the public domain. The Audience may confirm that this is so on the Web. The Professor's basis for the location popularly claimed as Bree is Moreton In Marsh. The Professor's basis for the location popularly claimed as The Barrow Downs is The Rollright Stones. The degree of association of both these locations is discussed in some detail in RINGS M:V and M:VI following. Let us assume firstly that both of these 'associations' are valid. The location of The Rollright Stones in relation to Moreton In Marsh became a problem and thence a complex, at least for the Author.

On Mother-earth, the Stones are to the East of Moreton. On the other hand, in the Ring-Maps, The Barrow Downs are to the West of Bree. The Hobbits' journey is Eastward, as the Professor consistently reminds us. They arrive at Bree (meeting Strider who is Aragorn) *following* the trauma of the Downs.

The Professor's mapping appears to present difficulty in progressing with any proposition that there may be further associations. The problem is that the subjects of both associations occupy *opposing compass points* in relation to one another for the Professor's mapping to be credible in terms of position on Mother-earth: what is West on the Ring-Maps (The Barrow Downs) is East on Mother-earth (The Rollright Stones) and vice-versa.

So on the basis of the Ring-Maps, further inquiry of the next location(s) of a journey on Mother-earth breaks down and appears fruitless and pointless. One's thoughts eventually turned to consider whether this may be an indication of the Professor's feint, trickery, plot, game or Secret of the Shire.

Gandalf upon departing Rivendell-

'There are many maps in Elrond's house, but I suppose you never thought to look at them?'

Which of us can say that we have studied the Maps in the Lord of the Rings *closely*?

The Author arrived at this single all-important, earth-shattering (!) further Assumption: that the journey in The Rings is made by reference to geographical features, as they appear on a map of Mother-earth today, which are by design *reversed* on the Map of Middle-earth.

A feature shown on the Professor's Map of Middle-earth as East of that other, exists on our map of Mother-earth to the West of that other.

The Ring-Maps are drawn in reverse or *backwards*.

They represent a mirror image.

The result of course is that whilst Frodo is in The Rings journeying Eastward on the Ring-Maps, were he making the same journey on Mother-earth, he would be traveling Westward. This is a truth, according to the Author, in relation to the first two of the Ring-Maps, showing Middle-earth from the Gulf of Lhun in the West (albeit, we naturally start the Quest at Hobbiton), through to Mirkwood in the East, and we end the Quest in this Volume I at Rivendell; but go ever onwards in Volume II beyond the Great River Anduin, to Lothlorien and Fangorn Forest on the hinterland of Mirkwood.

In these instances the compass points fall to be reversed.

We might add that the remainder of the Maps, representing Continental Europe, are *not* reversed in the same way.

The Nogood Boyo returns amongst his many mentions within the Quest. For the moment, (Dylan returns in his rightful place, when we get to Wales or, according to his own legend, wherever he so chooses), one recalls Dylan's own famed reversal, of the name of the town in Under Milk Wood: Llareggub. There is yet a further, still much earlier, reversal. We imagine Professor Tolkien may have had somewhere at the back of his mind the work of Samuel Butler's 'Erewhon' (1872) which, whilst not literally spelt backwards, is a close anagram of 'Nowhere', the ideal commonwealth in the philosophical novel of that name. Further back still: Leonardo

Da Vinci writes letters and notes intended for secrecy by 'mirror writing', that is to say *in reverse*.

Edging us on as we cower towards the witchcraft of Weathertop, we offer a portent of things to come: there is much to say about Witchcraft and its tendency to orientation backwards. Appendix C convokes the three primary features of Witchcraft, one of which is the mutation of accepted ritual, notably by the reversal of symbol or procedure: the subversion of the Cross, the saying of Prayer backwards, or the desecration of that which is sacred. A mirror shows everything in reverse, and imports the significance of the Witch's glass or mirror: under wraps pending Weathertop, the mystery of the bloodshed there includes the disappearance of the victim's witch glass or mirror…

'It was not until the summer of 1960 … that the old man's pocket watch was discovered. But … his witch's looking glass, the crystal used for weaving spells or seeing into the future was never found …'

And so, beyond the Professor's mere trickery, there may be implied a dark art of an illicit nature, covert in the very process.

It may be the height of fun to turn the Map backwards, but there may be other implications.

'Fair is foul, and foul is fair:
Hover through the fog and filthy air.'

Just how the Professor came to think regressively or 'backwards' in these terms (and we acknowledge that we have yet to demonstrate it) is anyone's guess, but the following provides a clue to his thought processes. The Professor had acquired a copy of –

' …Joseph Wright's Primer of the Gothic Language. Tolkien opened it and immediately experienced 'a sensation at least as full of delight as first looking into Chapman's Homer'… He was not content simply to learn the language, but began to invent 'extra' Gothic words to fill gaps in the limited vocabulary that survived, and to move on from this to the construction of a supposedly unrecorded but historical Germanic language… Tolkien also began to develop his invented languages **backwards**; that is, to posit the hypothetical 'earlier' words which he was finding necessary for invention by means of an organised 'historical' system.'

('J.R.R. Tolkien A Biography'; Humphrey Carpenter).

The Author supposes it is far easier to draw a map back-to-front than it is to invent a language backwards. Further in defence of our sanity in all this madness, we offer from the Biography, an account of just how far the Professor thought to take the trickery with the Hobbit-Maps:

'The Hobbit maps had to be redrawn by him because his originals had incorporated too many colours, and even then his scheme of having the general map as an endpaper and Thror's maps placed within the text of Chapter One was not followed. The publishers had decided that both maps should be used as endpapers, and in consequence his plan for 'invisible lettering', which would appear when Thror's map was held up to the light, had to be abandoned.'

The Professor loved a Game.

What of Bilbo's Riddle-Game with Gollum?

Does not Bilbo see Thror's map only by holding it up to the light of a special Moon?

To read the Ring-Maps one needs to hold them to … a *Mirror*.

The Professor's Secret of the Shire is pure Witchcraft.

Crafty if one cannot have invisible ink.

A Witch for company on the Quest is one's own choice.

**'Crimson flames tied through my ears
Rollin' high and mighty traps
Pounced with fire on flaming roads
Using ideas as my maps'**

Our heads are at last into gear; going backwards: from maps to ideas.

(II)
Exploiting Etymology

The Fourth of the Wise and the Great …

' … maps, **names and languages** came before plot …'

'Exploit' is one of those rare words having two possible meanings, each the opposite of the other; to use with good or bad intent; here we mean the former.

Wails, Whales; to Wales and the Welsh Language

'I love Wales (what is left of it, when mines [etc.] have done their worst), and especially the Welsh language …'

(Letter number 213)

There follows a segment to complete a trilogy with Wails and Whales.

There is a deal of Wales and the language to come, because once again the Professor learned, and came to love, the language. Those of the Audience not attuned to 'loving' a language for an inherent quality, such as its musicality, may fail to pick up on such nuances.

What the Dickens, this is nothing new. The names of characters of 'Great Expectations' are apt to fill the Author with delight in poetry, or musicality: Pip Pirrip, Joe Gargery, Mr. Pumblechook, Bentley Drummle and to leave the worst till last, Dolge Orlick; each sings a symphony, for the Author at least; perhaps to leave the best until last: Abel Magwich bewitches like a charm.

Those who fail to *hear* what we are talking about may never understand what we *are* talking about.

At times the Welsh language will mimic poetic device: where two words occur in sequence, which may together produce an unfavourable sound to the ear, the second word will 'mutate' in order to enhance sound production: my father: fy tad: fy nhad.

We do so hope the Audience is not to be deterred in this sub-quest. We are in good company, for the Professor was entirely conscious of potential difficulties in the transfer of Welsh 'lenitations' into Sindarin-

'I have not bothered to explain the S.[Sindarin]lenitations in the Appendices, already overloaded, because I am afraid they would have been passed over, or have been felt unintelligible and tiresome, by practically all readers, since that is the normal attitude of the English to Welsh. The lenitations or 'mutations' of S. were deliberately devised to resemble those of W[elsh]in phonetic origin and grammatical use ...'

(Letter number 347)

The Professor openly acknowledged the influence of the language:

'the names of persons and places in this story were mainly composed on patterns deliberately modeled on those of Welsh (closely similar but not identical). This element in the tale has given perhaps more pleasure to more readers than anything else in it.'

The Fourth of the Wise and the Great-

'The distinction between the Quenya and Sindarin language is important for the purpose of the understanding of the labyrinth of language built by the Professor:

'Quenya' was derived, as any 'real' language would have been, from a more primitive language supposedly spoken in an earlier age; and from this 'primitive Eldarian' Tolkien created a second elvish language, contemporary with Quenya but spoken by different peoples of the Elves. This language was eventually called 'Sindarin', and he modeled its phonology on Welsh, the language that after Finnish was closest to his personal linguistic taste.'

The Fourth of the Wise and the Great picks up on a perceived exaggeration of the statement made by Professor Tolkien –

"Mainly' is a bit of an exaggeration; the Welsh-modeled names are only those of Gondor and of Elvish, or more accurately of Sindarin, and these are precisely the most doubtful cases ...'

Our initial perception concurred with this view, but has changed; to the extent that derivation from the Welsh language extends well beyond Rohan, albeit the names of the peaks of the White Mountains appear to the Author almost exclusively made up of Welsh words; but also any number of the Shire, and of Middle-earth generally: the locations of *Ered Waith, Eryn Vorn*, and *Ered Luin* came to the Author from Welsh translation belatedly upon the Quest, but now at least I believe I have them ... but you do not, until Volume II ... for which their treatment in full is reserved. All three are drawn on the western section of the first of the Ring-Maps, as you will see: but you are yet to hear why they may be respectively associations for the Midlands of England (Ered Waith), Sheffield of Yorkshire (Eryn Vorn),and the Pennines of England into the Highlands of Scotland (Ered Luin) ... and the Rangers will need to be satisfied with that, because we need ample time to change our mind, and (if we are not already) get it right, pending Volume II ...

Smeagol: ... Author Master's getting even tricksier, My Luv ...

Gollum: ... We shall see, O yess, we shall see ...

Victory in our first battle amongst the Tolkienistwyr far from assured (some will have laid down their 'cleddyf', horrified by the prospect of more of the Welsh language), once more unto the breach: the Audience should not recoil in horror at the prospect of a language of which one has absolutely zero knowledge; there is entirely no need whatsoever; for the Author predicates simple steps of cross-translation. Examples may encourage us all to persevere.

Of places in the text, we have Amon Hen, Lhaw and Sul (with circumflexed vowel), each of which we afford a Welsh derivation.

Remarkably, not one of the three Hills appears on the Ring-Maps; of no significance in itself, except that where in Volume II upon the Quest we come to designate the location of Amon Hen, we do proffer our own suggestion of why indeed the Professor purposefully wished not to pinpoint Amon Hen by map.

There is so much material to adduce that we cannot possibly offer our explanation at this early stage; but we look forward to the light dawning in our Volume II. It almost went without saying (but we say it now) that we first share identification of all three hills upon Mother-earth, before sharing the Professor's naming methodology; yet, having a ring binding for Amon Sûl (Weathertop) in RING M:VII of this Volume I, we are also to proffer a derivation of the name from Welsh, and also make an attempt at proper pronunciation, one based on the derivation of its root in Welsh.

And so we see Amon Hen in Volume II, but hear about Amon Sûl in this Volume I.

As for 'Amon Lhaw', the Hill or seat of Hearing, we can guarantee the Audience will never have heard anything like it before; where we hear the 'Lh' of 'Lhaw' sounding like the (in)famous 'll' of Welsh, most prominent in the 'Llan' ('church')root of so many place names in Wales.

As a matter of another curiosity, we are to discover where Professor Tolkien will almost certainly have dug up the badge of the silver hand symbol; having literally excavated it alongside Sir Mortimer Wheeler amongst the ruins of the Temple of Nodens, for those who recall our digging about Lydney Park as a station within The Mines of Moria on our quest in The Hobbit: that, too must await Volume II ...

Smeagol: ... Author Master's not any Professor, not any Gandalf, My Luv ...

Gollum: ... O No ... can't get it all in, all in one go, O No ... but best Awffer Mas-sster get on with it ... We wants it! We wants it! We wants it! We must have It ...!

'Tharbad', just to the south-west of the Misty Mountains, is another place in the process of translation. 'Tharbad' is, in most simplistic terms, a place for boats; but for reasons of geographical congruence on the Ring-Maps, a Docklands; not a boat-yard, mooring, harbour, quay or marina, but definitively, purely and simply, the *Docklands* … at *Gloucester.*

Our simple aim is to let the Audience know when we hear an inkling of Welsh; a concept indeed best captured by this further of the Fourth of the Wise and the Great-

'… it would be wrong to say that readers understand nothing of alien songs as to say they understand everything. As with place-names, landscapes, mythic fragments, 'feel' or 'style' is enough, however much it escapes a cerebral focus.'

This is all we seek to do with our derivations from the Welsh language.

By the end of the Dictionary we believe the Professor's statement no exaggeration at all; but to return to south of Gondor …

' …Minas Tirith, 600 miles south, is at about the latitude of Florence… '

The comparative latitudes of Hobbiton and Minas Tirith are indeed some 600 miles distant.

We appear to be treading where the Professor left off, following closely in his tantalyzing footsteps; the Professor's hints tease us towards those latitudes about the hills of Florence; being at about the Dinas of … and so to the Welsh Dictionary: for there's wisdom in the Welsh lands and Welsh hills, all sounding much the same, named for the Forest River of Mother-earth … or for Sabrina who holds within herself the number of the wonders of the world, and in this case, the pillars of this wisdom …

Smeagol: … 'tiroedd' and 'Tirith' is sounding much the same to me, My Luv …

Gollum: … and to me, my precious … Welsh *hills* …

Smeagol: … Sabrina … Severn … seven … we knows, yes, we guesses … the City of the seven hills of **Rome** … O yes, O yes, it mos' s-s-sertainly is, My Luv …

Gollum: … Ach,-ss!… Yes-ss, My precious-ss, we knows … We guesses, yes, … like allur riggle games wiv bagginses … *an'* wot hobbitses had got in his nas-ssty little pocketses … **and** wot hobbitses have got round his filffy little neckses-ss …

Light Finds The New Places We Tread

Our subheading is a subversion of the title of a poem ('Rain Cuts the Places We Tread') of Dylan Thomas. We anticipate now the introductory paragraphs of each of the nineteen Rings of Power, where we set out in full how we came to many new places, both with regard to geography and with regard to the derivation of place names of the Shire and beyond.

These places are 'new' because they were discovered well after the primary associations (our nineteen 'Rings of Power'), but lend a brand new level of credence to those associations, or at least those as far as Rivendell, where we end this Volume I.

Before we cut the light, it made no sense whatsoever to share the Professor's naming patterns with the Audience before we had proceeded to identify the places upon Mother-earth (corresponding with the names) which is the primary task of the Quest; and so, the Quest is written in the chronology of their genesis; generally speaking the places first, name derivations afterwards.

Again before we cut the light entirely, the Author has made as clear as day two previous derivations from the Welsh language: Tharbad and Minas Tirith; not one to miss a third opportunity, we repeat the challenge to the Audience with *Rhudaur*, the first task being to find it on Middle-earth; the second the source of translation from Welsh; the third its location on Mother-earth.

Smeagol (grinning): … not to worry … yes, My Luv … we goes the Golden Valley, RING D:I …

Gollum (Nodding): … yes, my precious, very close The Last Bridge and Trollshaws shall we find that Golden Valley we seek …

Some of the Audience may yearn for further contribution; others may not; but merely to warn again of a continuing presence along the Quest; for they appear ever eager for *it*.

'We must have it. We wants it, we wants it, we wants It!'

We do so wonder what It is.

And we are to find It in Rivendell.

Cut The Light; at least for the time being …

**'Do not go gentle into that good night,
Rage, rage against the dying of the light …'**

(III)
Elaborating Mythology

The Fourth of the Wise and the Great …

' … maps, names and languages came before plot… Elaborating them was in a sense Tolkien's way of building up enough steam to get rolling, but they had also in a sense provided the motive to want to. They were 'inspiration' and 'invention' at once …'

The Shire of Middle-earth: the Shires of Mother-earth

'But, of course, if we drop the 'fiction' of long ago, 'The Shire' is based on rural England … The toponomy of the Shire … is a 'parody' of that of rural England, in much the same sense as are its inhabitants: they go together and are meant to.'

(Letter number 190)

This letter is written in the context of translation into other languages (where the Professor has fundamental objection – for the purpose of the reading in any other language – to translation into that other language of the *place* names of the tale); yet 'parody' is a most unusual choice of word: one we revisit in The Portrait Gallegory at the Crossroads up the road ahead.

Once through the Door of the Portrait Gallegory at the Crossroads up the road ahead, we may come to realise that the Shire is more a 'parody' of places of Mother-earth than we might ever have imagined; especially, indeed, with regard to 'toponomy', the *naming* of places: 'Stock' being perhaps the most squealing oinkling, teetering up the road ahead.

'Po' boy
'Neath the stars that shine,
washing them dishes,
feeding them swine ...'

Amongst the Tolkien Boys, the four counties (noting each a 'Shire') of Oxfordshire, Worcestershire, Gloucestershire and Warwickshire in England had, so far as in the public domain, become especially receptive to lending up sites. This was so, in part, because of the Professor's personal background connections with these areas, notably Oxford, and Evesham in Worcestershire, where he regularly visited his brother Hilary.

Apparently little has been written about any locality beyond the original Oxford locale referenced by Professor Tolkien. The Barrow Downs, Bree and perhaps some others have been coupled with real places in materials already in the public domain. Not that there should be need, for the Professor himself approves, but we defend our rationale in the attribution of association: the Professor is quite happy to have 'critics' recognise a transfer from Mother- to Middle-earth:

'I was most pleased by your reference to the description of 'glittering caves'. No other critic, I think, has picked it out for special mention. It may interest you to know that the passage was based on the caves in Cheddar Gorge and was written just after I had revisited these in 1940 but was still coloured by the memory of them much earlier .... '

(Letter number 321)

Professor Tolkien is 'most pleased' if we find places upon which his descriptions are based; *which is all the Author and the Audience require for rationale of the Quest.*

Our Mother-earth locations of such as The Last Bridge, the Trollshaws, Tharbad, Nin-In-Eilph and the River Anduin, to say nothing of Amon Hen, Tol Brandir and Amon Lhaw are all within fifty miles of the Cheddar Gorge of Mother-earth, and what is more; there are so many more, we do not count them: other than for nineteen primary associations: with these named and other new places scattered all about.

Equally within such distance is Rivendell and the Misty Mountains, and in Ring E:II we explore once more the Professor's willingness to acknowledge an imagination based on real locality, in that case the Alpine valleys of Switzerland; but in our view transposed in map-location to Middle- via Mother-earth.

A glance backward over the rambling and wandering words of this Genesis will disclose upwards of 30 pre-references to locations of Middle-earth which we claim to have mapped on Mother-earth. It should be tolerably clear that the Author has come a long way; but even more clearly that there is a long way to go: in the hope that the Audience will join us on the Quest.

A Slow Pace to Start

'In the sun that is young once only,
Time let me play and be
Golden in the mercy of his means, ...

**... And the sabbath rang slowly
In the pebbles of the holy streams.'**

We should perhaps mention the slow progress of The Rings at the outset of Frodo's quest. ***Our own is consciously designed to match it.*** Most of the Audience will be aware of this almost somnolent build-up: the encounters with an Elven funeral procession, with Farmer Maggot's mushrooms, and with Tom Bombadil, provide a somewhat easy and comfortable backdrop to the first glimpses of a Black Rider; and the first real indication of trouble ahead.

Indeed the film-makers omit virtually any account of the tale until the story lifts off at Bree; granted the Ringwraiths are lurking, but there is nothing of the Old Forest, the Barrow Downs nor, (thankfully for some), Tom Bombadil and Goldberry.

Once more the Fourth of the Wise and the Great (Tom Shippey) says it better than anyone before or since –

'But for their first hundred-odd pages the hobbits seem to be wandering through a very closely localised landscape ... They force themselves into the story. But while they slow its pace, appear strictly redundant, almost eliminate the plot centred on the Ring, they also do the same job as the maps and names: they suggest very strongly a world which is more than imagined, whose supernatural qualities are close to entirely natural ones ... many people believe that names fit; *and that places have a character of their own ...'*

Very nearly time to end our slowly wandering words; we are very nearly where we want to be: nineteen Rings of entirely natural places, to which we hope to give some character.

The Rings of Power

The focus of The Rings is very much upon the One Ring of Power whose destruction is the objective of Frodo on his journey to Mordor: so much so that we may forget there are numerous other Rings (nineteen in all) to account for, comprising-

**'Three Rings for the Elven-kings under the sky,
Seven for the Dwarf-lords in their halls of stone,
Nine for mortal men doomed to die ...'**

The Quest became one divined by the number of the Rings (3, 7 and 9) and their association, whether to Elves, Dwarves or to Men ... or so it came to pass for the Author ... whose task it became to 'find them' and 'bring them' all, that is to say RINGS M I to IX for Men, RINGS EI to III for the Elves and RINGS DI to VII for the Dwarves, to our Audience.

Conjecture as may be, the Author has sufficient confidence to give the loose assurance that in our Volumes I and II we have indeed found them all; and these are quite apart from those New Places where light shines; and apart again from the sites of Continental Europe whose blocks we are building towards Volume III as we speak.

We began this Genesis of the Quest with the poem of the Rings around which the entire tale of the Rings is forged; and what is more with the Wise and the Great who have helped us to analyse what may lie at the heart of the matter ...

*'One for the dark Lord on his dark throne ...
One Ring to rule them all,
One Ring to find them,
One Ring to bring them all
and in the darkness bind them.'*

We close the circle with the wise words of the Eighth of the Wise and the Great ...

'The ambiguous reference to the 'Dark Lord' and the nature of his power adumbrates the ambiguity of Sauron in the story. No-one ever is sure in just what his corruption lies, whether it is the deadly sin of pride, Machiavellian power-perversion, or alliance with death-forces.'

Some of the Audience may have the special knowledge, supposed by the Eighth within the Annals of the Wise and the Great, to be required for understanding the poem; for those without, Gandalf the Grey comes to our aid for the first time:

'The Enemy still lacks one thing to give him strength and knowledge to beat down all resistance ... He lacks the One Ring.

The Three, fairest of all, the Elf-lords hid from him ... Seven the Dwarf-kings possessed, but three he has recovered, and the others the dragons have consumed. Nine he gave to Mortal Men, proud and great, and so ensnared them. Long ago they fell under the dominion of the One, and they became Ringwraiths, shadows under his great Shadow, his most terrible servants. Long ago ...'

We are not to overlook the question of Nineteen Rings plus One.

As for the challenge thrown down by the Eighth of the Wise and the Great ... of an understanding of Sauron, the Dark Lord of the Rings ... the Enemy, the One, and of the Ringwraiths or Nazgûl, this may pass all understanding; but the Cauldron of One's Own in Appendix C goes some way; for the rest we must go all the way ...

Gollum (shaking head): ... to Mordor, my precious ... and such a very long way for all of us-ss-ss ...

'A Hard Rain ...'

'All that matters about poetry is the enjoyment of it, however tragic it may be ...'
(Dylan Thomas; quoted in The Colour of Saying; Dent 1963)

Each of the Rings carries a caption taken from the song by Bob Dylan, The Nobel Voice, lyrics which the Author happens to believe are inspired by The Rings; and it really does not matter whether the Audience agrees or not, the view being mere personal conjecture. Perhaps someone will ask him. The Nobel Voice is entirely dominant in the quality of lyrical output over the period of the acclaim originally given to The Rings; the mid-nineteen sixties, into the seventies, of which Bill Ready and the other authorities within the Annals of the Wise and the Great are evidence: in many ways these analyses of The Rings remain the foundation of 'academic' thought, perhaps because they were closest in time to the new phenomenon and thus freshest in outlook.

Again, in the Author's view, The Nobel Voice has no rival in terms of quality and ingenuity of lyric, but then again, reverting to our quest in The Hobbit: how would I know, any better than the Audience? The Author simply loves the stuff, and it may show. Then again, the same applies to the Nogood Boyo, and that may show, too. To revert once more, you need not share the opinion; yet the Audience might be interested in such details, one never knows. Some of the Author's other tastes will manifest themselves as our Quest unfolds …

Chosen for its ominous foreboding, possibly akin to that of Professor J.R.R. Tolkien in The Rings, the song simply fits and belongs on the Quest, at least in the Author's ears. Each line has its' own 'applicability', within the terminology of the Professor, and we endeavour our own, but let that not deter the members of the Audience from questioning the applicability, nor, indeed from asking the very same questions in the relevant context …

> **'Oh, where have you been, my blue-eyed son?**
> **And where have you been my darling young one?'**
> **'Oh, what did you see, my blue eyed son?**
> **And what did you see, my darling young one?'**
> **'And what did you hear, my blue-eyed son?**
> **And what did you hear, my darling young one?'**
> **'Oh, what did you meet my blue-eyed son?**
> **And who did you meet, my darling young one?'**
> **'And what'll you do now, my blue-eyed son?**
> **And what'll you do now, my darling young one?'**

… and that the ethos of the chorus is closer to the fatalistic words of poet W. H. Auden (closing this Part One) than one might care to imagine …

So many tens of pages in, we are to hear a Hard Rain fall on the moronic reign of Sauron …

Gollum (nodding head): … yes, my precious … all the ways to the Land of Mordor … where the Shadows lie …

The Final Word

And so to the final word; from the pen of Professor J.R.R. Tolkien in Letter number 183, words which surely underpin the tenet of the Quest, and specifically for those of the Audience (of the Tolkien Boys or otherwise)who doubt an exercise in association, of this kind, can ever produce results-

'The theatre of my tale is this earth, the one in which we now live, but the historical period is imaginary. The essentials of that abiding place are all there (at any rate for inhabitants of N. W. Europe), so naturally it feels familiar, even if a little glorified by the enchantment of distance in time.'

On this (rare) occasion, we take the Professor *literally*: the essentials of that place *'are all **there**';* on Mother-earth; and the Quest is an attempt to show ***where*** those essentials are.

The Audience will need a respite, what with all this terminology and map- and name-game complication to contend with; quite apart from the following Part Two containing details of six Appendices (A to F),each of which is a challenge of itself: the Annals of the Wise and the Great, the Bureau of Shire-history, A Cauldron of One's Own and the Door through the Portrait Gallegory at the Crossroads up the road ahead.; to say nothing of the Enigma of the Shire Map in Appendix E and finally to the Fanfare for the Tolling of The Rings in Appendix F.

And so, for the time being, until we are through the Appendices, yet ever conscious of impending doom …

**'The sky is darkening like a stain,
Something is going to fall like rain
And it won't be flowers.'**
(The Two/The Witnesses; W.H. Auden)

'Farewell from the Shire!'

PART TWO: Appendix A to F

The Appendices

The Author had no intention of mirroring the form of The Rings but the Audience *will by this stage* (by reason of the theory of the Secret of the Shire), be fully aware of the sublime irony in our description of form; and so to six Appendices, A to F.

Appendix A

'Come writers and critics who prophesize with your pen'

The Author becomes accustomed to borrowing in the course of the Quest, but we prefer to call it taking counsel. We are naturally bound to borrow the words of Professor Tolkien from time to time; but we take great counsel from other commentators on the subject of hobbits and The Rings; of itself a prediction of the Professor; indeed as early as page 2 of the Prologue to The Rings, where…

' … in the days of Bilbo, and Frodo his heir, they suddenly became, by no wish of their own, both important and renowned, and troubled the counsels of the Wise and the Great.'

And so it came to pass (the speech of many long years ago, even though we have farewelled the Shire for the time being) that the Author elected to transcribe the counsels of the Wise and the Great in the 'Annals of the Wise and the Great' in Appendix A; and references to 'the First, Second of the Wise and the Great' etc. may be researched in the authorities within Appendix A; for those interested in such details.

Appendix B

' … to memorizing politics of ancient history …'

Throughout the Quest, we make reference to resources of historical input; these are stored within the 'Bureau of Shire-history', the Shire-historians being referred to but once in The Rings, in reference to 'the Battle of Bywater, 1419, the last battle fought in the Shire' … whose dim distant archive prompted inclusion of the historians of the Shires of Mother-earth; the relevant historical archive is set out in Appendix B, referenced by the name of the relevant Binding of the Ring: some historical input may be of general application beyond the Shire, and even some of further social history, to include the United Shires of America.

Many of the archives of the Shire-historians in Appendix B are pre-Second World War. There is nothing, so far as we know, available today to match such as 'Wold Without End' (H.E. Massingham) whose 1932 vintage makes our point. There are several books of similar vintage dedicated to description of local geography, history and above all folklore; but there are so very few today. We suppose much material published formerly in book format is now scattered on the Web in the form of local authority records, the contributions of local history societies, together with those of individuals by means of received folklore. We offer spectacular confirmation as much: our associations for the Bywater Pool (by shepherd Mont Abbot) and of The Last Bridge (by local history), to say nothing of important elements of the geography of the Mines of Moria, (in relation to May Hill), were born of these.

Appendix C

'… treacherous young witches …'

This Appendix comprises a 'Cauldron of One's Own'.

Once we depart our Portrait Gallegory at the Crossroads up the road ahead, and following Bree, we reach Weathertop, where Frodo suffers the cut of the Nazgûl blade of the Witch King of Angmar, primary of the Black Riders, Ringwraiths or Nazgûl; and so we contemplate the craft of the Witches in Appendix C, by our recipe for 'A Cauldron of One's Own': a stab at the origins of the folklore of Fairies and Witches, and especially relevant for its insight into the origins of the 'Little People' on whom, we are to suppose, that hobbits are based.

We may be shocked by the fact that the primary authorities in the craft, one Fairyseeker and one Witchfinder, are writers contemporary with the Professor; and indeed the Fairyseeker's witch-group is convened at the Professor's University of Oxford.

Appendix D

'Yes, I received your letter yesterday, about the time the doorknob broke'

We are to learn of the Professor's many Dental metaphors; jagged teeth and green gums at The Barrow Downs, the blunted sawteeth of the Misty Mountains, and so on. We learn, from Humphrey Carpenter's Biography, that the Professor might leave false teeth (his own) smiling amongst loose money change; and perhaps there is just one more ache lies in the mouth.

The Author has also learned that, certainly amongst the Tolkien experts, if not others, there is something nagging at the back of the mind (not unlike a toothache), whose anguish will simply not go away: not only the uneasy discomfort, wanting relief, that Professor Tolkien modeled areas of Middle-earth upon real places; but a deeper, silent abscess: there must be more, festering innocently beneath the first 100 pages of The Rings, than meets the first cut.

Many non-experts give up on the story for a tissue of slow rot; all but anaesthetised before reaching Bree, never to recover: out of it for good. For some, Tom Bombadil is pure intravenous anaesthetic, to say nothing of Goldberry, Tom's own dental nurse in the Old Forest, perhaps.

Yet now the ache, nagging but uncomfortably dumb, is to be given voice; one may scream a little: no gain without pain yells Marathon Man; and we must run some distance before we are to know *is it safe* (?) to look behind the mask. Open ajar our Portrait Gallegory at the Crossroads up the road ahead(a deliberate Tolkienesque contrivance), accessed by a Door through Appendix D: at 'the Crossroads' is our designation of the portraiture in the Gallegory; where we look up to see many faces, framed in the facade of the Shire.

The characters of our Portrait Gallegory at the Crossroads up the road ahead, belong in the Shire of Professor Tolkien's Middle-earth; but by a transfer from Mother-earth, whose accretion of four Shires (Oxfordshire, Worcestershire, Gloucestershire and Warwickshire)is endemic to the Professor's Shire of Middle-earth.

This gap has never been filled before.

Yet the final analogy; none of us will ever forget this, our very first visit to the Portrait Gallegory at the Crossroads up the road ahead.

Analgesia, at last, through the Door at the Crossroads.

Waiting patiently for it to open, the Door may not be the same as that of the Dentist; and, metaphorically speaking, we have really no idea how we have got them mixed; except for the question posed of the One Ring by Gandalf in the Film screenplay, upon his return from Minas Tirith to investigate the history of the Ring, and upon Frodo's imminently departing the Shire: the question posed whether unconsciously, subconsciously or entirely consciously **three** times by the screen writers,(but not once in the text of The Rings),the third (conscious question) being the only credible answer, one to leave us gasping –

'Is it safe?'

A retrospective: the sheer volume (sic) of the Quest dictates that a few words of introduction at the Crossroads give rise to some truncated words of entry into the Portrait Gallegory in Appendix D. The doors may be thrown fully open, of necessity within the Shire, but on our return from Mordor, close to the Scouring of the Shire materials up the road ahead. That is appropriate enough, because the materials of Fascism are indeed those on canvas within the gallery: many of the literati, glitterati and other scatty members of the dignitary classes are there; from Edward and Mrs. Simpson down to Oswald Mosley: and we may go even lower with such as Unity Mitford, who probably couldn't help her sense for indignity, being brazenly bonkers.

Appendix E

' Yes, I wish that for just one time
you could stand inside my shoes
You'd know what a drag it is to see you ...'

A second retrospective to be going on with: the Author might blame the size of the Quest for the truncated version of the Shire Map Enigma in Appendix E, yet this is the plain truth of the version much shorter than we had first envisaged ...

'... patience will hold the Audience in good stead, because there are so many new difficulties discovered at time of writing (February 2017) that the Author has made the easy decision to withhold the details of the Shire Map Enigma for a possible Volume II; should anyone still be interested in such details; merely to add that the text of the Enigma already runs to some 40 pages of A4 text.'

The 'Enigma of the Shire Map' discusses the anomalies of the 'Map of Part of the Shire', which are noted by Professor Tolkien himself:

'The small map 'Part of the Shire' is most at fault and much needs correction (and some additions), and has caused a number of questions to be asked...'

(Letter number 274)

The 'Enigma' in Appendix E contains many references from the Letters to Professor Tolkien's dissatisfaction with the process of production of maps and especially the Shire Map. In our view, this map discloses many anomalies and flaws, at least so far as concerns consistency with our theory of the Professor's Secret of the Shire:

it is difficult to reconcile the Shire Map with the proven (at least in the Author's view) existence of the Secret of the Shire.

Yet we have no knowledge of the questions asked of the Professor. In the Enigma, the Author poses several questions of the making of the Shire Map; down to the detail of precisely how it was drawn. These issues by no means receive adequate response by two extracts from the Letters, but which do serve, on the other hand, to demonstrate the Professor's fastidiousness, measured (within a millimetre) by the following with regard to the Shire Map-

'The chief fault is that the ferry at Bucklebury and so Brandy Hall and Crickhollow have shifted about 3 miles too far north (about 4mm.) ...'
(Letter number 274)

If that is indeed the chief fault, then our solution of the Enigma is already doomed to failure. Even so, we do our best to explain how the Three Farthing Stone happens to be where it is on the Shire Map in relation to Hobbiton; for we find a perfectly acceptable 'Four Shires Stone' no distance away from our Hobbiton of Mother-earth, but in an entirely different situation from where the Secret of the Shire would dictate that the Three Farthing Stone *should* be.

The plot thickens; and is thicker still by reference to a 'Three *Shires* Stone' of Mother-earth.

Yet we cannot leave the important letter number 274 without voicing the ultimate proof that the Quest is not in vain; for we share the congruity of text and Maps by the following perception of a further deficiency in the Shire Map:

'There is also no trace of the wood described at the top of p.99.'

This second omission clearly mattered to the Professor, but once again other discrepancies seem to the Author to matter a lot more. For instance, the Green Hill Country of the Shire Map is to the Author a perfectly recognisable representation of an area of Mother-earth some 60 miles in expanse: but again the area is shown not where it *ought to be* in relation to the remainder of the (decoded) Shire Map.

Perhaps time to leave the Letters whilst we read of the wood in question.

But the wood leaves no question of us barking up the wrong tree.

Appendix F

'Forever young … may you stay …'

Appendix F ('Fanfare for the Tolling of The Rings') is unabashed nostalgia on behalf of the Author for one's recollections of a first exposure to The Rings. One may regard it as social history; some may regard it as antisocial hysterics. For what it is worth, it is there.

Those who read the nostalgia as a succession of rolling waves, literally spaced out, are swinging in the psychedelic sixties in the common speech of the day.

'Dig Gandalf?' was also of the common speech.

We were ever perplexed by the notion that we 'dig' not only Gandalf and The Rings, but other things that may or may not appeal, albeit the digging of rings is hinted at in the text…

'Busy as ants orcs were digging, digging lines of deep trenches in a huge ring …'

Far out, man.

That period is legend to those who experienced it, and as such a light-hearted chronicle of it is permitted us within Appendix F, being something of a commentary on the popular culture of the period, not confined to the Shire, but countrywide in the United Kingdom and most definitively, in the United States.

Those of no such age will take surprise to hear that this quintessentially English and European tale caught a fire which spread to England, rather than the reverse. To mix more metaphors, it raised a storm sufficient to get Harry Potter out of bed. Many will not begin to understand the pivot of the moment, but the Author felt the moment should not be lost in contemplation of the mythology of The Rings, quite separate from that intrinsic and of its own creation. The Author is to suggest that The Rings gave birth to many of the strands of philosophy born to the generation of its youth.

Nostalgia for this period of social history took us off on another track entirely, for whilst Aragorn is to track us through to Rivendell in this Volume I, there is something of a soundtrack to our Quest. Our account of a place, location or situation might plug us into song in the Author's headphones, and quite apart from the supposed aptitude of the lyrics there, our soundtrack should not only share the nostalgia with those who may have heard them all before, but even tune in some new pairs of ears, possibly the younger of the Audience, to groove the vibe, once more in the common speech of the day; and so to just once more in the common speech ...

'Tune in, turn on, drop out' was, for some, the ethic of the day.

There were dozens until we dropped them (like acid) in favour of a more established po'try: probably an improvement (if there is anything of value on the road ahead); yet I can push the Rock version to any old hippy interested.

We invite the Audience to tune in, but ignore the sum of the rest; knowing at the same time, however, that Professor Tolkien apparently detested the adoption of his works as ingredient in this melting pot of youth culture. Our account of each association of place is what we call a 'Binding of the Ring'; our only criterion for selection being material pre-millennium, with (virtually, except for The Nobel Voice) nothing beyond. Professor Tolkien included songs, and covert reference to contemporary personalities, uncovered in the Portrait Gallegory at the Crossroads up the road ahead, and we have simply joined in the game. Yes, indeed, My Luvvs, this one is for ...

'My generation
My generation
My generation
Baabaaay ...'
... hope I die before I get old ...

Gollum: ... he's better not ... it got this Quest to write for ...

Smeagol: ... you means he got this Quest to write for It, My Luv ...

Gollum: ... yess, tha's exacly wot we means, My Pre-e-e-cious ...

As ever, the soundtrack may be ignored by those not interested in such details.

Just as Gollum is sneeeaking about any and everywhere upon the Quest, so too the Author sneaks in two more: song titles, that is, in sections headed 'Rambling Man' and 'Wandering Star': of appeal simply because, albeit the Audience suffering enough, they each have a 'ring' in them; and so naturally we couldn't resist. In those sections we ramble and wander to places around and about the Rings of Power with history and other tales.

Third and Final Retrospective

We are at this point reminded of Professor Tolkien's observation that he avoided any reference to the Sindarin lenitations (mutations, modeled on those from Welsh) inherent in his invented language, because the Appendices in The Rings were deemed already 'overloaded'; and that is how the Author now feels, for the Portrait Gallegory and Shire Map Enigma probably (if at all) deserve a small volume in themselves. Thus, each may form part of any Volume following this.

Coda Part Two: Modus Scribendi
(writing style ... or lack of it)

'Who among us has not dreamed, in his ambitious days, of the miracle of a poetic prose, musical without rhythm or rhyme, supple enough and jarring enough to be adapted to the soul's lyrical movements, the undulations of reverie, to the twists and turns that consciousness takes?'
(Charles Baudelaire)

Gollum (whispers to Audience): ... *Coda*, wot a plonker ... *Latin,* my loincloff ... got some kinduvva lyric prose such as Awffer Mas-sster say his mates-ss d' call his-ss silly skribblings-ss ... la-dee-da prole parole pusher, if you please ... bit of a show off wivvit, fancys his-ss chances-ss olrite ... so pons-ssey poetic ... paffetick pretenshussnes-ss ... arty farty, artful fartful, poser, todger, prose-bodger ... dreams of miracles-ss musicals-ss-ss ... likes that Charles-ss Baudelaires-ss-ss ... more like that mate of Charlie's ... Edgar Allen Po ...

Smeagol: ... Poe, My Luv,...

Gollum: ... embarrassin' flatulence personified Awffer-Mas-sster is-ss, ... ach-ss, so full of it sumtimes ...

Smeagol: ... full of *it* from that Esgaroff place inner Kumreyses of his ...

Gollum: ... least Awffer Mas-sster nonsenses durstn't start til Rushock Bogses-ss or maybe's Bywater Poolses-ss, some ways-ss in, can't remembers-ss ... an' he so besotted by his Last Bridge, Audiences-ss be wishing he jumps-ss off of it ... an' a neverending drivel in Rivendells-ss-ss ... yes, sumtimes s-ss-ssso-o-o full of ...

Smeagol: ... *the twists and turns that consciousness takes,* My Luv ...

This is an imprint of what Baudelaire might be dreaming of ...

'I know we're not saints or virgins or lunatics; we know all the lust and lavatory jokes, and most of the dirty people; we can catch buses and count our change and cross the roads and talk real sentences. But our innocence goes awfully deep, and our

discreditable secret is that we don't know anything at all, and our horrid inner secret is that we don't care that we don't.'

This is mesmeric lyrical prose, and much in the Author's admiration: exciting; the most crazed romantic output in the process of thought; yet with a truth on offer in an insect-orchestrated individualistic touch: wild whirlings to beeswax lyrical your while away … honeycomb honest within a hive activated and workered by the bizzy bee Nogood Boyo: within his own description of the writing style in Under Milk Wood …

'Prose with blood pressure …'

Welcome

And so, at last, to Frodo and Sam, (but not forgetting the other two), … the plankton author tagging along … who sings now for the first and last time on all our questses, and very, very late at night …

★**'I sit before my only candle,
Like a pilgrim sits beside the way
Now this journey appears before my candle
As a song that's growing fainter
The harder that I play
But I fear before I end, I'll fade away
But I guess I'll get there,
Though I wouldn't say for sure … '**
★ Jackson Browne

'Welcome to the Shire!'

PART THREE: Rings of Power

'Sing and howl through sand and anemone
Valley and sahara in a shell, ...
See what the gold gut drags from under
Mountains and galleries to the crest! ...
Out of the house that holds a town
In the continent of a fossil ...'
(The Ballad of the Long-Legged Bait; Dylan
Thomas)

Visions poured one upon another into the waves, a difficult conceptual poem, we imagine an underwater sea-world brought high to profile.

'Over that undersea isle, where the water is clearer than air
Down we look'd: what a garden!
O bliss, what a Paradise there!'
(Voyage Maeldune; Tennyson)

'To begin at the beginning' ...

... about 200 million years to the Jurassic period when something called oolitic limestone rock was formed by the layers of mud and sand that lay at the bottom of the shallow tropical sea covering the country at that time. Over the course of the millennia oolitic limestone became the stone we know today, golden coloured and full of fossils and without doubt one of the most beautiful stones in the world.

'... There where the long street roars, hath been
The stillness of the central sea.'
(In Memoriam; Tennyson)

'... it was the Romans who discovered the Cotswold stone and began quarrying and building with it. Can you imagine Bath without the inspiring combination of the Romans and the stones?

The most notable builders after the Romans were the rich sheep merchants, who created the quintessential Cotswold tapestry ...

57

But why did this special stone cover the Cotswolds and not the Vale? They were once made of the same layer of limestone, called lias stone, a pretty humdrum stone in comparison.

But then something happened to split hill from vale. It wasn't glacial movement in the Ice Age. No, the hill was created when the bottom layer tilted up to create something called a cuesta. The scar of this tilt can still be seen at Dover's Hill.

The escarpment was then fortunate enough to be covered by oolitic limestone, whilst the valley had nothing but the lias stone.

(Alice Gillman: Vale Magazine; March 2014)

Many will puzzle over the pronunciation of diphthong *lias,* and indeed it is, for at least in Wales, I have heard it to rhyme with *farce.*

We are to climb the *Weather* Hills, central within the Shire, whose higher ground is of much prominence above the lower level of the Vale of Evesham, which the Cotswold Edge, or Escarpment, overlooks. Notable amongst the hills along the Edge is that of Dover's Hill: where Dover's Hill lies out down below you like the distant boundaries of Lords Cricket Ground stretched out before the Long Room …

> **'But below, as we look around,**
> **The deep long plains appear,**
> **Like a lost country drowned**
> **In a tranquil flood of air …'**
> (Dover's Hill; Edward Shanks)

… the Author just wishes the Audience might see the accuracy of the poet's words here: once upon a time deep, lost drowned and flooded in the wind …

The Cotswold Way

… the ridge extending over Cardolan, down through Archet, passing nearby Tharbad and Nin-in-Eilph(via Cleeve Hill and its Belas Knap neolithic long barrow chamber), topping Amon Hen, skirting Rhudaur and to the hills beyond and below … onwards Somerset and *Bath* …

Bath Thermal Waters

The water fell as rain around 10,000 years ago and then sank to a depth of about 2km. Here it is heated by high temperature rocks before rising back up through one of the three hot springs in the centre of the City, the Cross Spring, Hetling or King's Spring, which supplies the Roman Baths.

'O Fons Bandusiae Splendidior Vitro'
(*After* the Ode of Roman Poet, Horace)

**O drip, water, drop, wash crustacean inertia,
O drip, water, drop, wet the floor of a *camera* …
O sing kettled enclaves,
pipe up hot rippled waves, …
Aquae Sulis the raindrops of yesteryear craves.'**

Gollum: … Ach s-ss, conversashuns wivver plummin' inner caves-ss-ss … *Latin* my Loincloff … gone all akwaaatics-ss-ss in Barff …

Smeagol: … whose Royal Crescent is arched … not to be forgett'n Chipping Campden is Archet … as we shall see, O, yes, we shall see, My Luvvs …

At the other end of the Escarpment, west of Dover's Hill, there lies a hill Professor J.R.R. Tolkien calls Weather*top*.

In a climatic outlook uphill, each *is* its weathers; even if one's eye is an ocean.

**'I fled the earth and, naked, climbed the weather,
Reaching a second ground far from the stars; …'**
(I Fellowed Sleep; Dylan Thomas)

One of the '18 Poems' published in 1934, it is not unlikely Professor Tolkien knew these (and perhaps this one), which stood out against the emotional restraint of contemporary poets; the Oxford educated generation of Auden, Spender, Isherwood and the rest: their poetry presumably known to Professor Tolkien; the Professor certainly knew W.H. Auden personally in later days.

Roy Campbell, in some ways the Professor's model for Aragorn, was an exception; so, too, Thomas himself ...

'For literary undergraduates will tend to write in the manner and mood of their time ... In 1937 this meant that they would be surrealists, sound like Dylan Thomas ...'
                              (The Auden Generation; Samuel Hynes: 1976)

'The Hobbit' is published that same year.

The world is at war two years later.

That is more or less the last of the Nogood Boyo (as far as the Author recalls)until Dylan steps up to the bar in the Portrait Gallegory at the Crossroads up the road ahead; but it is well to remember that the new poet wonderkid on the block was a pervasive influence cavorting about the Shire (to the absolute mortal distraction of famed historian A.J.P. Taylor, but to whose wife, Margaret, Dylan was dissolute immortal attraction), concurrent within the period of Professor Tolkien's work, yet in the year before publication of the Lord of the Rings in 1954, poor Dylan is dead. The Author happens to know exactly where I was at the time of death: En Ventre Sa Mere ...

Gollum: ... Ach s-ss ... *French* my Frogslegs ...

Smeagol: ... No, My Luvvs, not on the French rivvyairers, by the France seasideses, No, No My Luvvs ...

Gollum: ... Dursnt make silly lingos jokes-ss about it, it is-ssn't funny ... Gerron wivvit, Awffer Mas-sster ...

Smeagol: ... yes, indeed, My Luv, make haste! Time is short ... (grinning) ... a bit like wot hobbitses is like! ...

'I told you I was trouble,
You know that I'm no good,'
(Amy Winehouse)

One day I have promised myself to write a dialogue between the two men, on a chance meeting (it would be 1945) between Tolkien and Thomas in a pub in Oxford.

Here is a foretaste ...

Professor Tolkien:... do you understand, Thomas, old chap, how much I yearn to be free of the cursed disease of the internal combustion engine of which all the world is dying ...?

Dylan (crafty, ingratiating artifice): ... *before the motor car, before the wheel, ... when we rode the daft and happy hills bareback ...**

(whispers: ... err ... your round, Tollers ...)

I doubt it will ever be made public; or maybe it already has ... The War of the *Worlds* ... or perhaps The War of the *Wolds,* given the confrontation is bound to take us to the very *Edge* of our sanity ... but my favourite would be The War of the *Words,* because each has limitless supply of cannon fodder, countless battalions and boundless reserves and reinforcements, such that the thing will hopefully end in peace; with both still standing: although, admittedly, that would be far less likely in the case of ...

Gollum: ... wheedling wino Dylans Thomas-ss-ss ...

Smeagol: ... yes, indeed, My Luvvs ... is a mystery murder ... 1945 ... hill of Meons in Cotswoldses, but not nobody knows whosdunnit, My Luvvs ...

---

*   *A Child's Christmas in Wales*; Dylan Thomas:
    The recording ... Thomas made on 22 February 1952,... Marianne Mantell later stated that she believed Thomas may have been drunk during the recording ... The recording ... eventually became his most popular prose work in America.

Professor Tolkien: ... quite a mystery, Thomas, old chap, poor fellow slashed to ribbons, pitchfork bestride his neck, blood running into the earth, witchcraft symbolism it would seem, so says Fabian of Scotland Yard at any rate ... story might well be adapted to fiction, I suppose ... what do you say, as a poet of the *avant garde* ...?

Dylan(propping up bar, incapable, paralytic; slurring ...):

'Perhaps it was Trolls' ...*

'Let's go in and see if there's any jelly left,' Jack said. And we did that.

It is on record that the Nogood Boyo read and much admired The Hobbit: Collected Letters; Paul Ferris.

Here we go, with A Wish ...

> **'MINE be a cot beside the hill;**
> **A bee-hive's hum shall soothe my ear;**
> **A willowy brook, that turns a mill,**
> **With many a fall shall linger near.'**
> (A Wish: Samuel Rogers; 1763-1855)

Smeagol: ... we tells Audiences about waterfallses an' hard rainses in Rivendells, My Luv ...

> **'The sky is darkening like a stain,**
> **Something is going to fall like rain**
> **And it won't be flowers.'**

---

* 'Perhaps it was a ghost,' Jim said.
'Perhaps it was trolls,' Dan said, who was always *reading*.

RING: M I
Hobbiton

'Where the home in the valley meets the damp dirty prison'

Hobbiton and the Shire are to suffer 'The Scouring of the Shire': we return to the 'Scouring', appropriately, upon our return journey from Mordor in Volume III.

Middle-earth

We cite a small yet compact … like a hobbit … Web source to condense into abbreviated form … like a hobbit … what Hobbiton is like.

Hobbiton Hill also called The Hill was a hill in the Westfarthing between Hobbiton and Overhill.
It was on this hill that Bag End stood as well as Bagshot Row and its residents, the Party Field, and the Party Tree. The hill had many other large trees as well.
During the Shire's rule by Lotho and Saruman much of the hill's places and trees were dug up and destroyed, and a large sand and gravel quarry stood in the place of Bagshot Row.
During the Scouring of the Shire, the Party Tree was replaced by a Mallorn, and Bagshot Row was replaced by New Row.

This source chooses to evoke Hobbiton in terms of three main features; its two hills (The Hill and Overhill), the Party Field and Tree and finally the events that befall it. By way of preliminary, the Author is first to recognise that we were not as struck by the significance of the *two* hills of Hobbiton as some might be. No doubt the Tolkien Boys assume as much, but the double feature is not one that strikes the Author with immediacy with regard to the layout of Hobbiton; one would need to be thoroughly familiar with the text of the Rings (such as in preparation for Mastermind questions) but the phenomenon is not one that bowls one over from a general reading, (at least not the Author over), and we do not recall the Film versions making a great deal of the twofold hill landscape. It is on the other hand true that very close inspection of the Shire Map indicates a double-header, specifically 'The Hill' and 'Overhill'. It becomes of no small importance in our candidature for association with Hobbiton; as does the Party Tree, which caused us a headache we cured very late in the Quest, indeed after the event(as the worst hangover), the morning following; that is to say, following our head clearing to the Professor's allusion of the Party Tree. The Audience must by now have read the symptoms: we believe the allusion something to do with parties and their ill after effects.

But here we think that the prescription of the Tree is misleading. The Party Tree is not at all 'replaced' by the Mallorn: the Tree is torn out and discarded and it is Sam who, following the events of the Scouring of the Shire, plants Mallorn seeds, we suppose to commemorate those sad events and by way of hope for the future: the seeds being a gift from the Lady Galadriel at Lothlorien, herself a symbol of light, purity and hope.

Binding of the Ring: Preview

Determined not to identify Hobbiton until much of our exploratory material is set down, our first association happens in so many ways to be the most dramatic in the mind of the Author. This is for the very honest reason that it was just about the last that we put together: two and two that is, of Hobbiton and our eventual association, eventually making two: *hills*, that is to say. Extraordinarily enough, these fell into place long *after* the other Rings were sorted and written up. Of interest to nobody but the Author, somehow only *after* the places the subject of the succeeding 'Light Shines' section (on Waymoot, Bindbole Wood, Rushock Bog, Needlehole, Nobottle, and the Bywater Pool) had first been contemplated.

The Author recognises a second failure in vision, (the first was way back in our omission to account for the *two* hills of Hobbiton), that our original conception of Hobbiton was the City of Oxford, or some enclave within its sprawling extent; more than likely by focus on Northmoor Road whose legend we discuss at some point up the road ahead. We came to change our mind not least for the factors of the two hills of Hobbiton, and the Party Tree, but for three other facets emerging from analysis of the Ring-Maps; these three being the relative position of Waymoot, Bindbole Wood and finally (and most vitally) the Bywater Pool.

Light Finds the New Places We Tread: Waymoot and Bindbole Wood; Rushock Bog; the Bywater Pool

Waymoot

'He always remembered the appearance of the afternoon on which he awoke from his dream. Not quite knowing what to do with himself, he went up to an octagonal chamber in the lantern of a singularly built theatre that was set amidst this quaint and singular city. It had windows all round, from which an outlook over the whole town and its edifices could be gained. Jude's eyes swept all the views in succession, meditatively, mournfully, yet sturdily. Those buildings and their associations and privileges were not for him. From the looming roof of the great library, into which he hardly ever had time to enter, his gaze travelled on to the varied spires, halls, gables, streets, chapels, gardens, quadrangles, which composed the ensemble of this unrivalled panorama. He saw that his destiny lay not with these, but among the manual toilers in the shabby purlieu which he himself occupied, unrecognized as part of the city at all by its visitors and panegyrists, yet without whose denizens the hard readers could not read nor the high thinkers live.'

(Jude the Obscure: Thomas Hardy)

The prominence of Waymoot to the far west of the rest of the Shire, and therefore to the East of all according to the Professor's Secret of the Shire, promotes it as mapped for the City of Oxford in our ultimate conclusion. One may detect it a conurbation somewhat greater than Hobbiton for the suggestion by its markings on the Ring-Maps; but apart from such mere hint, we rely upon the relative position of Bindbole Wood.

A small word of self-justification: when we had thought Oxford for Hobbiton, the position of Bindbole Wood was problematic: to the North-West of Hobbiton on the Ring-Maps, thus North East on Mother-earth. According to the Secret of the Shire, the Wood is supposed to be *North-West* on Mother-earth: our Bindbole Wood does indeed nestle to the north-west corner of the City of Oxford; thus the inherent reversal process of the Professor's Secret of the Shire works for Waymoot = Oxford: but not Hobbiton = Oxford; assuming, of course, that we have location for Bindbole Wood.

Very little is said of Waymoot in The Rings, other than for more we share in relation to the Shire Map Enigma in Appendix E; but accept it as a focal point from which all else falls into place.

Eriador

Whilst we are indeed beneath the Dreaming Spires, so evocative of the educational aspirations of Jude the Obscure, we might acquire a little more 'book-learning' as Samwise Gamgee (to whom it was Bilbo Baggins taught Sam his 'letters') would speak of it: through a perceived etymology of the region labelled 'Eriador' by Professor Tolkien.

We look back once more to Bilbo's adventures in The Hobbit, most specifically in 'Barrels out of Bond' and the Wood-elves' partiality for the wine of Dorwinion. We fancy the 'dor' of Eriador precisely the same use by reference to cutting (in geographical terms), or otherwise break, interval, space and possibly any cognate word meaning a place, possibly of quiet respite, depending upon context.

Here we think the context unequivocally the Professor's own: the use of words in philology, indeed at the University of Oxford. If Philology is about words, then so might 'Eriador' be: the Welsh word, indeed for 'words' is 'geiriau'; and the Author (at least) has little difficulty in the elision of Geiriau and 'Dor' to 'Eriador' in the manner that became so familiar on our quest in The Hobbit. Once again try the test of rapid repetition, and one comes out with a result sounding very much like 'Eriador'.

'Geiriau' is Guy – reee – I: 'Dor' is as through the keyhole...

What happened to the 'g' of 'geiriau'? The same thing that happened to the 'g' of 'Dor-gwynion': it got gone by god-given mutation/ lenitation; once again as we spoke of on our former quest. We offer the perfect example from the endearing Welsh entreaty, emotive and much-loved, *'Myfanwy'*, an ode to a lost love ...

'Pa le mae'r wên oedd ar dy wefus
Fu'n cynnau 'nghariad ffyddlon ffôl?
Pa le mae sain dy *eiriau* melys,
Fu'n denu'n nghalon ar dy ôl?

Where is the smile that once most tender
Kindled my love so fond, so true?
Where is the sound of your sweet *words*,
That drew my heart to follow you?'

A fair copy of 'Eriador' might well be 'a Place of Learning': the Professor's University at Oxford: albeit the knowledge emanating from the place is shown to be spreading far wider and farther than reality on Mother-earth might indicate, what with the (sniff) *laddish* culture *so* prevalent today ...

'Time to get drunk!
Don't be martyred slaves of Time,
Get drunk!
Stay drunk!
On wine, virtue, poetry, whatever!'
(Get Drunk; Charles Baudelaire)

In our own youth, mixed with vermouth, some of the more uncouth of us drank to this truth; but I'll always lie for a rhyme and I only ever drank beer and was with Ruth that night at The May Ball.

'When Ruthie says come see her ...'

Upon further reflection, and written long after the preceding paragraphs, it occurs to the Author that 'Eriador' may simply be one of Professor Tolkien's private jokes: loosely speaking, 'Eriador' marks the region where *these* words are written, meaning that the words *of The Lord of the Rings* are written here in the four shires of middle England that we are to demonstrate to be 'the Shire' on Mother-earth.

The Arkenstone Amidst Academia

Troubling the Bureau of Shire History since the days of Smaug in The Hobbit (and the Author's Magic Mirror Maps theory), a Broadway scholar reveals to the Author the word *Eorcanstan*, Anglo-Saxon for jewel, topaz or other precious stone; but also that, buried deep in the vaults of the Ashmolean Museum in Oxford there lies the **Alfred Jewel** ...

Discovered in 1693 at Petherton Park in Somerset, it is the single most important artefact from that era. It is dated to late 9th century in the reign of King Alfred. It is inscribed with AELFRED MEC HEHT GEWYRCAN: Alfred ordered me to be made.

It may well be that the search for the Professor's Arkenstone allusion is over at last: not least because Professor Tolkien would be acutely aware of its radiance from his Place of Learning in Oxford. Of course, you can gaze into the clouds upon the glory of Smaug's golden hoard from your own seat of acquired learning, wherever that may be.

... and Michel Delving ...

Ranking with Buckland and the Yale for easier spotting on our Quest, the similarity here with the small Hampshire village of Micheldever is beyond denial, and the Author for one regards this as one of the less subtle tinkerings with names that Professor Tolkien simply could not resist. On reflection, I believe that Professor Tolkien was simply fascinated by the name, and could not resist temptation.

We have yet to delve deep for the etymology of Dever, but the following of fishing the river was just too good to miss in terms of associations in The Rings ...

The Dever or Bullington Stream joins the River Test at Newton Stacey just upstream of Wherwell. Like the other Upper Test tributaries it is known for the clarity of its water. The fish tend to be highly visible, hanging in front of big beds of starwort and lazily tipping up from time to time to sip down passing insects. In recent years the river Dever has suffered from a shortage of water due to abstraction, perhaps more so than the other chalk streams.

*Of other tributaries of the River Test **The Dun** enjoys some of the characteristics of a true chalkstream, but does not run as clear as the main tributaries, and has, like the Nadder on the Avon system, a tendency to colour after rain. It rises not far from Salisbury at East Grimstead, and joins the Test at Kimbridge.*

The Wallop Brook is a small stream that joins the Test at Bossington.

*The **Blackwater** is a peaty stream coming out of the New Forest and joining the Test on the Broadlands Estate at Romsey.*

We have all heard of *Dun-land* and of the *Greyflood* and *Loudwater;* and the *Redwater* takes us back to the Carnen in our quest in The Hobbit.

I only wish there was a *Nadder* or a *Wallop Brook* on the maps: perhaps The *Ivy Bush*, *Prancing Pony*, or *Golden Perch* might do for the *wallop*, sometime local reference to a pint of beer.

One day the Author will find the Inns of the Shire: certainly the *Prancing Pony*, and less certainly *The Golden Perch* up the road ahead; for the moment, The Ivy Bush is unknown.

Micheldever is in pretty good relative position for Michel Delving, especially when we locate the Downs somewhere on the road up ahead.

Bindbole Wood

'Sittin' on a Barbed Wire Fence'

Professor Tolkien was certainly prone to tease about the secrets of the nomenclature of Middle-earth. Apparently, son Christopher remained certain about the existence of a 'Bindbole Wood' on

Mother-earth, but never discovered it. The Professor(less than helpfully) adds merely this …

'The reason for the name is not, of course, given in the map – but there is one.'
(Ref: The Lord of the Rings A Reader's Companion; 2005: Hammond & Scull, and on the Quest 'H&W').

Bindbole Wood hides within it a witty and endearing truth of the Professor's technique with word name games. No doubt thoroughly familiar with the Wood from his University bolthole in Oxford, it may be no surprise that he seems to have bowled a hole for this bold little wood in the Ring-Maps. Within the ownership and control of his University, we deem it bold indeed in its staunch resistance against outside influence adverse to the preservation of nature.

From the University's own Department for Continuing Education-

Wytham Woods in Oxfordshire, UK, is one of the most highly monitored ecological survey sites in the world. Wytham is a magnificent tract of semi-natural woodland belonging to the University of Oxford. It has been the focus of numerous long-term monitoring projects conducted by the University and other research organisations interested in monitoring environmental change, climate change, and ecological processes...
*The site itself lies a few kilometres **north-west** of Oxford city, and can be reached via Wytham village. Wytham Woods cover approximately 430 ha sited across two low hills that rise up from the surrounding agricultural lands of the Thames valley: the northern Wytham Hill (164 m) and the southern un-named hill rising to 148 m. From the higher points of the site you can gain some wonderful views of the historic city. Access to the site is by permit only.*
The main tree species are oak (Quercus robur), ash (Fraxinus excelsior), beech (Fagus sylvatica), hazel (Coryllus avellana), sycamore (Acer pseudoplatanus), which grow in Wytham's semi-natural woodland habitat (ancient and recent), as well as plantation. The entire site is surrounded by a deer fence, which keeps the deer in the Woods and prevents them causing damage to surrounding agricultural land. As well as three species of deer, the Woods support badgers, foxes, small mammals, bats and numerous bird species. Where there are springs, small water features have arisen including a species-rich valley fen, adding to the diversity of this beautiful site.'

'Underneath the abject willow,
Lover, sulk no more ...'
(Underneath an Abject Willow; W.H. Auden)

Withy (and 'Wytham') implies 'willow' in the vocabulary of the Anglo-Saxon and so the 'bind' of 'Bindbole' offers several connotations. Strips of willow may be said to be binding and bound to others when woven into fences or gates in the traditional agricultural craft of England. The enclosed land is tied, bound or fenced in. The Audience will have noticed that the whole of the Woods is fenced in, to preserve the Woods and its Deer from outsiders.

We shall be reviewing as entirely typical of the Professor's wordplay games that a name may contain any number of allusions. Here we believe we have an instance: where 'bind' relates to fencing in the sporting sense, once we learn that 'bind' connotes –

A way of removing an attacking blade by making a half circular movement with the tip of the sword when the blades are already in contact.'

Now we have no evidence that the Professor was learned in the sport of Fencing; but once more we come to realise upon the Quest that Professor Tolkien knew all manner of unexpected things: and to our conclusion that in the days pre-Computer, Internet and Google days, one simply asked the Professor. With final reference to this style of name game, one comes to learn that, in the vernacular, there is an awful lot of it about upon the Quest; and perhaps one of our tasks is to diagnose the causes: the Professor's motives.

Bole or 'boll' is ancient usage for the trunk of a tree.

Thus, ultimately, 'Witham' being in the reality of Mother-earth a wood fenced or bound, 'Bindbole' is the fenced or gated woodland.

A little pertinent history of the University connection is within(sic) the Bureau of Shire-history in Appendix B.

Step into Bindbole Wood on the Author's 'Short Cut Gone Wrong' map.

71

Needlehole

'And again I say unto you, It is easier for a camel to go through the eye of a needle, than for a rich man to enter into the kingdom of God.' (Matthew 19:24)

Reminiscent of our fun with fables in The Hobbit, and the rich man losing something he really doesn't need, yet covets that thing once more: an accurate representation of Professor Tolkien's comment upon Smaug missing the cup taken by Bilbo in order to prove himself to the Dwarves … *want* and *need* are two entirely different things, as the supposed simple tale in The Hobbit tells. With ancient moral little place on this our quest, (yet there it is in The Hobbit), the message is as old as the hills of the Shire …

'Jesus Christ was a man who travelled through the land
Hard working man and brave
He said to the rich, 'Give your goods to the poor.'
So they laid Jesus Christ in his grave.'
(Jesus Christ: Woody Guthrie)

By the medium of the Secret of the Shire, we are eyeing a site east of Oxford, presumably having some connection with *needles,* having become aware, as we are, of the Professor's liking for allusion of this kind. We sew the seed at Aylesbury, which has a long tradition of lace-making in its history.

In the 17th and 18th centuries there was a lace making industry in Aylesbury. But it was the only significant industry in the town. There were some craftsmen such as carpenters, butchers, bakers and blacksmiths serving the local community but that is all. For centuries Aylesbury continued as a large village rather than a town with many of its inhabitants farming the surrounding land.

(A Brief History of Aylesbury, Tim Lambert)

Found, so look no further, in a haystack about Aylesbury …

Needle lace is made using a needle and thread. This is the most flexible of the lace-making arts. While some types can be made more quickly than the finest of bobbin laces, others are very time-consuming. Some purists regard needle lace as the height of lace-making. The finest antique needle laces were made from a very fine thread that is not manufactured today.

'Needle*hole*' is easily grounded by allusion to 'bury', an entirely typical Tolkienesque contrivance along our way of the Quest. That might be enough, except that the root of 'Ayles' bury intrigued us. With 'Bierton' no distance away, one might readily imagine a brewing connection, but such is periforal in Aylesbury. One supposed derivation is that from 'Aegel', an early citizen of prominence, but unidentifiable apart from the name. The Author was drawn by the eye of the 'awl', a kind of needle for making holes in material such as leather, and hooked on to the French word for 'needle', being 'aiguille', whose pronunciation could be said to have a similar ring about it; frilled as we were with the fancy, we laughed it off, in stitches at yet another loose thread.

Bobbin' to and fro for further allusion, the needle of lace making is perhaps sufficient.

Aylesbury is indeed some 25 miles east of Oxford; and 'Nobottle' is 10 miles to the north-east of Aylesbury.

Nobottle

*While the sand slipped through the opening ...

Professor Tolkien's allusion here, (the Author in delusion until we peer through the glass, not darkly, but through the shifting of time), implies refraction through the glass of the hour ... to sand. Silica sand is fundamental to the glass and bottle-making process, and is or *was* to be found (hence we conjecture *No*-more-bottle) in the vicinity of the township of Leighton Buzzard.

And their hands reached for the golden ring ...

Leighton Buzzard is a town in Bedfordshire, England near the Chiltern Hills and lying between Luton and Milton Keynes. The

---

*   Jackson Browne

'Buzzard' element might have us flying off in all directions, yet it is easy prey …

There are a number of theories concerning the derivation of the town's name, but the most likely is that 'Leighton' came from Old English language Lēah-tēn, meaning a 'farm in a clearing in the woods'. The 'Buzzard' was added by the Dean of Lincoln, in whose diocese the town lay in the 12th century. Having two communities called 'Leighton' and seeking some means of differentiating them, he added the name of his local Prebendary or representative to that of the town. At that time it was a Theobald de Busar and so over the years the town became known as Leighton Buzzard. The other Leighton became Leighton Bromswold.

With their hearts they turned to each other's hearts for refuge …'

Frodo and Sam, perhaps?

The business of the Dean and Theobold being buzzed off in the beeline we had made, straight for its history, we can bottle up the truth no longer: Leighton Buzzard has been famous through the centuries for the production of sand, notably that refined in bottle making; and we don't have to wait to get the message in …

The upper part of the Woburn Sands Formation of the Lower Greensand in the vicinity of Leighton Buzzard, Bedfordshire is a source of sand for foundry and horticultural applications, and water filtration. Coarse-grained, well-rounded quartz sands are particularly suited for water treatment and are produced by the selective screening of sands from a number of quarries. Construction and silica sands are normally derived from the same quarry and their production is interdependent.

(British Geological Survey; Silica Sand)

In the troubled years that came before the deluge.'
(Jackson Browne)

We can perhaps do no better than have the Audience partake of the delights of the 'Woburn Sands Area Bottles' collection on the Web; unless all the bottles have fallen off the wall by now. What a right load of Codswallop; the Author's off to get smashed.

74

Rushock Bog

*'If everything seems under control,
you're just not going fast enough.'*
(Mario Andretti)

Before we wallow in the mire … (come on baby light my fire) … let us not get bogged down with the placement of Rushock Bog to the south of Needlehole on the Shire Map; one to clear up in the Enigma of the Shire Map in Appendix E.

Some distance north of Oxford, the primary feature of the Bog is indeed as clear as mud, with the boggy terrain of virtual swamp much as expected. Perhaps less clear is the reason for the Professor's epithet, Rushock: yet we are indeed to find oak trees rushing about the swampy forest here: at the same time hiding a concern for the preservation of nature against intrusion, a theme unearthed in so many sites chosen by Professor Tolkien for inclusion upon the Ring-Maps. It occurs to the Author that by the end of the Quest, we should create a grid of the sites chosen and the concerns then and now, to measure progress or, we fear, regress. We might make a start here at Whittlebury Forest of the Hazelborough Wood in Northamptonshire; where the grid has been in place for some time.

Our main focus must be on the relative geographic position, which we claim to have now found; then its muddy, boggy terrain, which is profound; thence the rhyme or reason for anyone rushing about the oaks in this neck of the woods; so we discover, to the sound: of roaring motor engines. One will find the relative position of Whittlebury oneself upon the OS maps of Mother-earth, yet the primary focus might well fall upon the Silverstone motor racing track, boasting the 'home of British Racing', here for all to see, just round the bend; which we have little doubt matches the Professor's dismal view of the development.

No doubt a major tragedy for the Professor were the race circuit to have involved major forest clearance in the leisure pursuit of others, such foul tactic may not be levelled at Silverstone, whose origins are those of a disused Wartime airfield; but this turn of events checkers the last lap: at the final bend, just up the road ahead, we flag up the Professor's inner wheels screeching in parallel with those of the racing cars.

Silverstone was opened as a World War Two airfield in 1943, near the leafy village of the same name. Once the war had ended in 1945 Britain was left with a number of redundant airfields but without a major race track … The Royal Automobile Club was interested in Silverstone as a potential site and approached the Air Ministry in 1948 and a lease was arranged. At this time the centre of Silverstone Circuit was a farm producing cereal crops and also a piggery so the RAC employed farmer James Wilson Brown to create the first Grand Prix circuit at the site and gave him just two months to build it.

On October 2nd, 1948, amid straw bales and ropes, Silverstone's first event took place, the RAC Grand Prix. The crowds came in their thousands, thrilled to see the return of Grand Prix racing after so many years of war austerity. The 3.67 mile course sent the 23 competing cars racing round part of the perimeter track, up the two former runways and back to the perimeter. This layout meant cars were racing towards each other head-on until they turned sharp left and returned to the perimeter …

Even so, we suspect the Professor would have failed to see the humorous side of Mutton Racing …

*Silverstone was first used for motorsport by an ad hoc group of friends who set up an impromptu race in September 1947. One of their number, Maurice Geoghegan, lived in nearby Silverstone village and was aware that the airfield was deserted. He and eleven other drivers raced over a two mile circuit, during the course of which Geoghegan himself ran over a sheep that had wandered onto the airfield. The sheep was killed and the car written off, and in the aftermath of this event the informal race became known as the **Mutton Grand Prix** …*

'Hung for a sheep as a lamb' reverberated around and around, and around one's head once more; until we hit the skids:

> **'Mud, mud, glorious mud,**
> **Nothing quite like it for cooling the blood,**
> **So follow me, follow,**
> **Down to the hollow …'**

Children such as the Author thrilled to the sounds of Flanders & Swann, the latter, Donald (referred to in the Professor's Letters), sometime collaborator of Professor Tolkien, whose wordplay evokes the Professor, and whose thrills equally reminisce an innocence in youth, perhaps long gone … for we thought hippos and mud hilarious in those days …

… then there was one about a London Double-Decker Bus …

… as we write,(August 2011), the kids have just set fire to one of London's …

At some point, (in the context of 'Catcher in the Rye'), we muse over how times have changed. Flanders & Swann just brought it back to us: what might the average teenager make of the Double-Decker Bus song …

'Hold very tight please, Ding! Ding!'

Cockney Rebel: …*Yer 'aving a tin barff, aincha, mate?*

Perhaps (entirely from memory) there is some innocent fun still wellying about …

> **'If it wasna' for yur wellies,**
> **Where would ya be?**
> **Yu'd be in the Hospital or Infirmary …**
> **Yu'd have a dose of the Flu,**
> **Or even Pleurisee …**
> **If it wasna' fur yur feet in yur *we-ellies* …'**

Before the Author raced back in time, (and before we bang on about 'the good old days', which the over 50's of every generation seem wont to do, including Professor J.R.R. Tolkien), we were floundering, fast and furious, in a dodgem dogfight down through the mire … all mud and blood on the tracks, and all over the tyres too …

> **'So great a soldier taught us there,**
> **What long-enduring hearts could do**

In that world-earthquake, Waterloo!'
(Ode on Death Wellington, Alfred Lord Tennyson)

The Author has yet to venture more than a first time into the wet woodlands of northern Northamptonshire. We are forewarned to take our Wellies ... named for the Duke of Wellington, victorious over Napoleon at Waterloo, and a lot gone under the bridge since 1815, the scene thereabouts of a battle, very moody for Napoleon because Bonaparte is missing his Josephine; so no boney part, tonight or any night soon, I'm afraid, Mon Petit General ... lying low in the stinking, stenching trenches to explain (to the USA) what Wellies are ... gumboots for a yankee doodle doddle in the doo doo boue boue (the French by now booted out of Belgium by Wellington) on a Sunday morning of all times ... we share (via the Geocached website) the mudbath of Rushock Bog with those who like to get down, deep and dirty themselves on a Sunday morning this time ... when there's nothing like a good few inches ...

'There's nothing like a good few inches of mud first thing on a Sunday morning! ... Did anyone inform you that it was muddy here? Mud Mud glorious mud ... at times hard to even stand up let along to keep moving... were ready for more boggy walking but not quite this bad, it was really hard going in places to find a way through, very boggy, ... Very very muddy – mud nearly came over the top of our walking boots!!!!! But a nice easy find to make up for all the mud! ... Muddy, muddy, muddy. But what fun! Saw a small deer as I clambered through the forest tracks ... Muddy but warm walk, well-hidden and took a bit of hunting ...It was muddy and slippy under foot especially on the route we took to the cache...'

And so on and so forth of our perception of the boggy forests of Hazleborough Wood, of which the site has ample photoshots. The Professor was no doubt right all along-

Hazelborough Wood is an ancient woodland site with both majestic oak and younger conifer plantations. The wood is gradually being restored to native broadleaf woodland under the 'Ancient Woodland Project'.

**' ... without freedom of speech
I might be in the swamp ...'**

Rush-oak …?

' … [Tolkien] was similarly sensitive to the damage that was inflicted on the Oxfordshire countryside by the construction of *wartime aerodromes* and the 'improvement' of roads. Later in life, when his strongest-held opinions began to become obsessions, he would see a new road that had been driven across the corner of a field and cry 'There goes the last of England's arable!' By this time of his life he would maintain that there was not one unspoilt wood or hillside left in the land, and if there was, he would refuse to visit it for fear of finding it contaminated by litter.'

('J.R.R. Tolkien A Biography': Humphrey Carpenter).

In case it missed you, Rushock has the oaks rushing to be missed by motorcars; a lap to warm up for Treebeard in Fangorn Forest. Those of sound memory may recall 'Rushock' cemetery in Worcestershire, where lies the drummer voted by most drummers the best rock drummer ever, John Bonham: we believe the Professor may have linked the Bog of Hazelborough with a place name he would know already, for its vision of oaks rushing through the mud.

The Bywater Pool

' … through all his thoughts there came the memory of water; and every brook or stream or fount that he had ever seen … He felt the cool mud about his toes as he paddled in the pool at Bywater with Jolly Cotton and Tom and Nibs, and their sister Rosie …'

We are to play a game of water-pistols: submerging Thomas Bushell in the firing line, for it was he we must thank for successfully sussing hydrocephalus into our Quest, there being water on our brain … what with the hissing-lawn games of the Bywater Pool our target, all shooting up soon … with a load of balls …

'The Hissing of Summer Lawns'

We learn first that 'Bywater' is an uncommon English surname of Anglo-Saxon origin which can most frequently be found in the

English region of Yorkshire. It is a topographical surname given to those who were situated near a body of water.

The Author tapped the resource of the Bywater Pool in the very latest stages of the Quest, indeed much later than the recitations heard from Master Ancient Mariner Gollum, which are reservoired for Rivendell up the road ahead: such that it may be thought the Author has always had water on his mind, now and in the future, indeed at Rivendell. As much as those future outpourings are to be of water resource harnessed by man to modern utility, (at the British Camp Reservoir of the Malvern Hills), we now dowse a verse or worse in memory of mechanical contrivances in the facile use of nature. These are now long disappeared; a folly in the whimsy of nature: a right Royal game of water pistols.

The Bywater Pool is of no great import on the Ring-Maps, but for the avid reader of The Rings and the 'Scouring of the Shire' chapter in particular, much more so, because it lays a marker through mileage to several other locations. Most of all its position, (for the Author in any event), pins down (for us, definitively), the location of Hobbiton. The Bywater Pool shows itself a feature of the Shire Map: it will be noticed to the south-east of Hobbiton, and most markedly the north-west of the Three Farthing Stone.

In much the same (*yet **not** reverse*) position in relation to our association for Hobbiton upon Mother-earth ... and by now those attentive to maps must surely foresee Hobbiton ... lies the township of Enstone, as a matter of fact a collection of villages, including Neat Enstone. Neat as may be, before we describe the water theatricals of neat little Enstone, we must tidy up our deadly italicised parenthetical ('yet not reverse'): for therein lies one of the most significant anomalies of our Shire Map Enigma. The Author does indeed have *some* rationale for exactly *why* Enstone might not be shown on the opposite side of *Chipping Norton*, to its south-*west,* (... and now at last you *do* see Hobbiton, because this paragraph wouldn't work unless we told you ...) for conformity with the Secret of the Shire, but yet again we must crave patience to await our solving the Shire Map Enigma.

'Why didn't they ask Evans?'

Neat Enstone is itself the ancient site of a mechanical water entertainment of some renown in the Seventeenth Century, but long since jetted off in the sluices of time. All that remains is the Pool and small stream feeding it; which belies its grand history: which is exactly what the Professor would have found out about in his day of mapping (and writing) The Rings. *We* know as much from a contemporary authority (Highways and Byways in Oxford & the Cotswolds, H.A. Evans,1927), which is where the Author first got caught up in our line of thinking towards Thomas Bushell's 'Rock' pool; whose details, (so as not to interrupt our flow), appear in the Bureau of Shire-history in Appendix B.

The Rock pool is not shown on any map we are aware of, and so the Author trusted to our scouting instincts, with no knowledge whether there was anything left to see of the ancient waterworks. Once one finds it up a very long driveway though woods and eddying rivulets all about, it turns out(or rather up) that Enstone is dominated by the presence of Heythrop Park at the top of the rising hill that overlooks the village. The otherwise unremarkable vicinity of Enstone is remarkable for the grandeur of Heythrop House whose best comparable we are able to proffer is something like Buckingham Palace: indeed here in the middle of the quiet Oxfordshire countryside. Perhaps we should not be too surprised, with Blenheim Palace no distance away and the Cliveden pile (of the Astor dynasty) not so far down the road.

We trudged the grounds of the double hotel arrangement which now crowns the rise of the hill overlooking Enstone, and the Golf Course its nether regions. Yet we were lost for the watercourse. We uncovered a splendid possibility to the right on the downward slope ... where a crescent waterpond enclave of 200 foot pine trees shelters the wildest and most wanton waterlillies we had ever seen ... and the Park worthy of a visit for this treasure alone ... becoming our best candidate as we departed Heythrop Park ... but no, nobody was quite sure of the hiding place of the old Grotto.

' ... politicians pumping out the *piss* ...'

And so we found it not on foot, but initially in the clouds. 'Heythrop Park Grotto' gushed forth the most invaluable local knowledge of the Rock Grotto or Bywater 'Pool'. This is the sort of knowledge the locals share in the local Pub over a drink, but the Author's first visit to the Harrow Inn, Enstone, missed that welcome relief. Caught short and holding on to 'pay a visit' a second time, ironically, we heard the magic by-water words, not from within the Inn (closed for business even on our second, later visit), but right out the back side.

From a local history site-

The Harrow Inn on the edge of Enstone is close to the site of a fabulous grotto and fountains, visited by King Charles I and Queen Henrietta in 1636.On the day of the royal visit, two jets of rose-coloured water each raised up a golden ball and held it suspended in the air. The King plucked one from the water and found a portrait of the queen inside it, painted on ivory. The gardens and their ballroom fell into decline after the civil war. The Enstone shepherd Mont Abbott told how, in his young days, 'Queen Henrietta's waterworks' became the privy at the back of the pub.

We go one better than the retelling second-hand of the thoughts of Mont Abbot upon 'Queen Henrietta's Waterworks', with his own words from 'Lifting the Latch', a biographical account of the shepherd's life and times, within the Bureau of Shire-history in Appendix B.

And here now is the report of that return visit.

The objective is not as close behind the Harrow Inn as our shepherd friend might suggest. Across the road ('The Drive') and down the bankside, there runs a rivulet whose source is an arched tunnel-like structure just visible beneath the undergrowth. It was our companion who astonished the Author by 'comparison' with the structure of similar shape running beneath the house in the old engraving of mention by Evans, our Shire-historian: *the Audience now sees how easily we shoot down the squirts who avoid the Appendices …*

… and surely, at long last, we would all like to see what it looked like; and having waited since 1677, wait just a few paragraphs hence.

We believe that we had just come upon the cavern tunnel filling Bushell's Enstone Marvels: so similar, nay identical, we agreed it was the only visible vestige of the waterworks, whose pipework now runs underneath the main road into Neat Enstone. It appears indeed to be the same piece of engineering. The unearthing of the pipework cavern, there since sixteen hundred and some more, was in the terminology of Professor Tolkien, 'eucatastrophe'.

On Mother-earth today, beyond the fairly recently laid tennis court which rises on a plateau above the fast flowing stream, and through some scrub undergrowth, there ponders an accumulation of water in a shallow pool; but such appears now to be housed on private land. Those with never a chance to visit Neat Enstone may take comfort in the engraving of mention … yet still a few paragraphs away … where instead of Bushell's sumptuous banqueting facility, there now runs the road through Neat Enstone: of much disappointment by the absence of water feature, we aim to include photographic evidence (maybe the Author's website) of the cavern pipework … all that remains of the Bywater Pool.

Those of the Audience minded, quite naturally, to check the text of the Rings for reference to Bywater and its Pool will be further disappointed, as was the Author. There are but two, somewhat inconclusive in terms of the Quest, except for the focus of Bywater within the 'Scouring of the Shire' chapter. Yet the path we have beaten thus far was now, in our submission, to be given greater credence than ever before.

With the Bywater Pool, we contend that we have a rock solid illustration of our understanding that Professor Tolkien sketched the Ring-Maps first, then made the story fit around them. Quite apart from the fact that in his Letters the Professor says as much, there is a single feature of the Bywater Pool which makes it clear that the Ring-Maps were drawn in abstraction from the story, but nevertheless drawn to match the Professor's visual recollection: or, at least, recollection of what the Enstone Rock Grotto, pool of water in its midst, will have looked like.

The Bywater Pool has in turn an island in its midst.

Of no relevance whatsoever to the storyline, then why sketch it so in the Shire Map? Because Bushel's Waterworks so too had its own island. Not unnaturally in despair for absence of any vision of how the waterworks might have looked, we first corroborate the island through previous authority. Some may have already noted the reference in the wide ranging description by Evans, our Shire-historian, as follows –

' ... the circular island, which will be seen in the middle of the pool in front of the banqueting house...'

Having read of an island, what must it have looked like?

Doubtful of direct access to Robert Plot's Natural History of Oxfordshire (1677), likewise referred to by Evans in the same Shire-historian account, we persevered. It is quite rare along the Quest to experience one of those 'Eureka' moments when one hits a resource of information that thrills the blood in satisfaction. In the early days, discovery of each primary association had been such, but the ageless endeavours of the Quest must be withering the poor old Author, for such thrills are becoming less and less frequent; but now here was one.

We are referring to the 'Enstone Marvels of Thomas Bushell' within the Gardenhistorygirl website of Arcady, of Master's Degree in Garden History, posted March, 2008; and to take the surprise a few thousand miles further, a lady out of the USA. It comes as no small shock to discover an American cousin who knows more about your back-yard garden than you do; especially in circumstances where we had gone to such lengths even to find it, Bushell's water-garden that is: and there it is, the sumptuous engraving of Bushell's waterworks of nonsense, derived from the work of Robert Plot; and noting furthermore ...

Robert Plot's 'Natural History of Oxfordshire' of 1677, the main documentary source for the Marvells, is now online (Google books).

We later discovered publication of the engraving of the Enstone Marvells in the 'Oxford Times'. It is replicated in the Author's 'Short Cut Gone Wrong' map.

Immerse yourself in a squirt of the Enstone Marvells: the greatest show on Mother-earth of its time; but since a wee wee tinkling of former grandeur. Thankful for the assistance of the USA, we settled for the song from the memorable film scene at the Forbidden Pool ...

> **'The rock and pool**
> **Is nice and cool**
> **So juicy sweet**
> **Our only wish**
> **To catch a fish**
> **So juicy sweet ...'**

Yet we are bound to foretell, Gollum appears to have picked up the habits of the shepherds of this part of Oxfordshire. Spend a penny with him in the caverns of The Mines of Moria; waiting, as he does there, over some distance, the relief of Lord Bledisloe's water closet ... and awaiting the convenience of our Volume II ...

One can perhaps readily call to mind a very young Smeagol airing the following ...

> **'1, 2, 3, 4, 5, once I caught a fish alive**
> **6, 7, 8, 9, 10, then I let it go again**
> **Why did you let it go ... ?'**

Gollum: ... not nearly scrumshus-s enuff and wriggling how we likes-ss it, my precious, that's-ss why ...

Binding of the Ring

'Bringing it All Back Home'

Hobbiton

> **'Looking out from Gloucestershire to Oxfordshire;**
> **And, by supremest lanscape-gardener's art,**
> **The lake below the eastward slope of grass**
> **Was made to seem a mighty river-reach**
> **Curving along to Chipping Norton's hills.'**
> (from Summoned by Bells; John Betjeman)

This is the view from Sezincote, a local ancestral home in the style of the Raj … 'Stately and strange it stood, the Nabob's house' … yet our focus is to be on the *hills* within the purview. Sezincote is but a mile from Bree and the same from Staddle, perhaps two from Archet, all of *Breeland*.

The movers and shakers (we must consult such derivation; and we have; the poem Ode: 1874, Arthur O'Shaughnessy) of the Shire live at Hobbiton; and likewise of our Mother-earth today: our current (at time of writing) Prime Minister, Mr. Cameron, lives in Chipping Norton or thereabouts …

…'so he went to [the Three-Farthing Stone] the Prime Minister's house, which is as near [the centre of the Shire] Hobbiton as no matter …

… and so, according to the Author, does Frodo, and Bilbo before him, and the rest of our cast of Hobbits. The Brandybucks' horn sounds in The Rings, the first time in over 100 years, at Weathertop. Not sounded a note this clarion call since publication of The Lord of the Rings, we now resound it loud and clear: the Author nominates **Chipping Norton** as Professor Tolkien's model for Hobbiton.

Whilst we are name-dropping (not unlike Professor Tolkien and 'Bagginses', whom we come on to recognise up the road ahead), one will have recognised Fletcher doing his Porridge in the Shire some years ago; indeed in Hobbiton …

[Ronnie Barker] would also realise one of his few unfulfilled ambitions, to run his own antiques shop. He opened it in Chipping Norton's High Street, christening it The Emporium.

Even today there is a Pub in Oxford called The Four Candles, near enough the Ashmolean Museum …

The eye-catching building next door but one to these premises is Oxford University's history faculty. It was originally the city's High School for Boys, which opened in 1881. The comic actor Ronnie Barker was a former pupil …

'Up on Housing Project Hill,
It's either fortune or fame ...'

The first inkling of Chipping Norton was the prominence of hills in its landscape. The main town sits on a hill (the greater portion of which is known as Rock hill) whilst the town itself sits in the shadow of its own 'Overhill'; which (and here we ask the Audience to suspend all belief for the time being) is the larger hillside of *Over* Norton.

The Author might be forever writing up the geography and history of Chipping Norton in the most minute detail; but to little point: Chipping Norton is well covered on the Web and so we assume that those interested in such details of our Hobbiton will engage themselves.

The Party Tree allusion is to the Author's mind so typical of the Professor, so Tolkienesque, that we are bound to share it; even though so many of the Tolkien Boys might wish to pound us into dust between pestle and mortar. Chipping Norton is the home of the humble Aspirin: in the days of the Professor, the cure-all for all kinds of ills, including that post-party hangover. These were the days pre-Paracetamol, Advil (in the US), codeine or any other of the vast range of pain-killer readily available today; so much so that the old Aspirin is today well out of vogue, except for heart problems where its beneficial blood-thinning properties are still recognised.

Edward Stone, a vicar from Chipping Norton in Oxfordshire, is generally recognised as the man who gave the first scientific description of the effects of willow bark. In 1763 he wrote a letter to the Earl of Macclesfield, then president of the Royal Society in London, in which he describes treating patients suffering from ague (fever) with 20 grains (approximately a gram) of powdered willow bark in a dram of water every four hours. Stone's interest in willows was due to the ancient 'Doctrine of Signatures' – whereby the cause of a disease offers a clue to its treatment.

According to Stone: 'As this tree delights in a moist or wet soil where agues chiefly abound, the general maxim that many natural maladies carry their cures along with them, or that their remedies lie not far from their causes, was so very apposite to this particular case that I could not help applying it; and that this might be the intention of Providence here, I must own, had some little weight with me.'

One of the famous Blue plaques denoting residence by those of note records the following:

The Revd Edward Stone 1702-1768
Discovered the active ingredient in Aspirin
whilst living here from 1745-1768.

And so not only do we have the hangover cure, we have its derivation from the willow tree; hence, we propose, the Party Tree in conception.

For those doubtful of the Professor's allusionary tendencies: from here to Rivendell ending our Volume I, from the Misty Mountains through to Fangorn Forest ending our Volume II, and right through and beyond the White Mountains the subject of our Volume III, we believe the Rings to be one long string of knots in the Professor's name-game playing by allusion('free association' might be the best description);and since we claim as much, we had better string along and untie as many as we can.

But the guiding light for our association of Chipping Norton must indeed be relativity of the position to our Bywater Pool. The Audience may check the OS maps to realise that the representation of Hobbiton and the Bywater Pool *in the Shire Map* is just about as close as one might get by way of easy illustration of the relative position of Chipping Norton and Neat Enstone. The attentive of the Audience will be heard to clamour: but everything is supposed to be mirrored *in reverse*; but not so here; precisely: the equally attentive of the Audience will recall our acknowledgement that the Shire Map presents anomalies the like of which we counter in attempting to solve our so-called Shire Map Enigma, in Appendix E.

The Professor had not to look too far from Chipping Norton to rename it. With no evidence whatsoever as to the veracity of source(the Professor always claimed to have forgotten the origin of the word 'Hobbit', also Hobbiton and its other derivatives), five or so miles north of Chipping Norton is the village of Bloxham, dominated by 'Hob Hill'.

A parting gaze into the distance from the heights of the two hills of Hobbiton; one to shine the light on another new high place of the Quest-

' … and on the higher land those cold grey streets, that perch like sentinels over the plains, Stow-on-the-Wold and Chipping Norton …

(By Thames and Cotswold, W.H. Hutton (1908))

Bear in mind that Stow on the Wold might be said to 'straddle' the dales below; and we saddle the already addled of the Audience with a question: as to the nature of a 'Staddle' stone; and, indeed where it might be, if not on the Ring-Maps, but within the text. 'Staddle' of the Professor's Index is but the turn of the page away; and, in turn, Archet and Combe.

There will be many at this early stage of the thought: the Author is lost in this world of Middle-earth in a most unlikely tale of association; but at least we have made a start: perhaps we make a better one (if we are to get this thing going at all) with the following –

'There was 'the unforgettable occasion in 1932 when Tolkien bought his first car, a Morris Cowley that was nicknamed 'Jo' after the first two letters of its registration. After learning to drive he took the entire family by car to visit his brother Hilary at his Evesham fruit farm. At various times during the journey 'Jo' sustained two punctures and knocked down part of a dry-stone wall near Chipping Norton.'

('J.R.R. Tolkien A Biography'; Humphrey Carpenter).

Rambling Man

There is much conjecture amongst the Tolkien Boys regarding the Professor's use of places in and around the City of Birmingham for his settings in The Rings. The Professor's first home in Sarehole is often mentioned. We waste no time on the matter, other than that, anagrammatically, it is an end in itself. Yet the place was dear to the heart of Professor J.R.R. Tolkien indeed …

'I could draw you a map of every inch of [Sarehole] … I loved it with an intensity of love that was a kind of nostalgia reversed. There was an old mill … a great big pond with swans on it, a wonderful dell with flowers, a few old-fashioned village houses, and further away a stream with another mill … it was a kind of a lost paradise and it was wonderful.'

(Ref: H&W)

No doubt much inspiration for The Shire, yet there is more of the reality to follow.

The Author learned of Bagendon, located 3 miles North of Cirencester, a town within the environs of The Shire. The Web tells of *Bagendon* …

This small pleasant village is situated in a quiet wooded valley set a little way back from a pleasant brook. There is some indication of its importance during the Iron Age as being a massive, well fortified capital of the Dobunni, the Belgic Tribe that once flourished here.

We must go some day if all is so pleasant and quiet.

The Professor would equally be aware, especially of its Iron Age heritage.

Wandering Star

Bagend and the Sackville-Bagginses

We offer in Buckland (RING M:II),via Vita of the Sackville-Wests, one fairly obvious derivation of the absurd family name, the silly '*Sackville*-Bagginses', but some hold Bagend and the family-name connected on other reasoning.

The 'Annotated Hobbit' of Douglas Anderson proffers a likeable intuition of the derivation. That writer tells us that the 'Sack' of

'Sackville' is a word-game joke of the Professor by means of the play against the 'Bag' of 'Baggins'. He also offers a linkage through the French Cul-de-Sac which is of course nothing but a 'bag-end'.

So plausible as to be incontrovertible for the Author, it would seem to follow that the Professor, being fully aware of the existing 'Sackville' name (he most certainly did not invent *that*) derived the 'Baggins' name and even 'Bagend' with the Sackville name in mind.

We refer further to Humphrey Carpenter's Biography of the Professor-

'In May 1923 Tolkien caught a severe cold which lingered and turned into pneumonia. His grandfather John Suffield, then aged ninety, was staying with the family at the time.

The old man lived for another seven years, spending much of his time with his youngest daughter, Tolkien's Aunt Jane. She had left Nottinghamshire and had taken a farm at Dormston in Worcestershire. It was at the end of a lane that led no further, and the local people used sometimes to refer to it as 'Bag End'.'

Precise identification of 'Bag End' is pointless and fruitless; an obvious invention in concept, if not name, very many authorities identify 20, Northmoor Road in Oxford (the Tolkien family home for many years) as the place correlation; especially for the supposed writing of the first lines of The Hobbit there.

We opened this RING MI with an apology for ideology rather than named places. No cook, and with no culinary knowledge whatsoever, the Author offers a taste of one he makes not earlier, but much later: perhaps 'Standelf' will suit to taste; if the Audience first makes it out on the Ring-Maps, that is to say. Not as easy to make out as we make it later. Which way to Standelf? Take the road to the Old Forest. Does the Ranger make any correlation between Northmoor Road and Standelf of the Ring-Maps? The Author foresees our own in and about the Old Forest, a New Place from there. And so we dwell on Northmoor Road later; and having dismissed precise identification of Bag End, we yet make further inroads.

In passing, the connection to Dormston of mention by Humphrey Carpenter is in the public domain, otherwise than by means of the Biography; there is mention on the Web. The Author knows little of Dormston, other than from a fleeting visit one calm Spring day in 2010. We searched for Bagend or any clue. Any local within our Audience will know instinctively of the abode of the Professor's Aunt Jane. At the far end of the village, perhaps hamlet more appropriate, we came upon a broken down old cottage, of the Red Riding Hood wolfish kind, all peeping-out secretive small windows, which might have had a farm behind. Too respectful of further inquiry, we consigned it to memory. At the nearer end of Dormston, we encountered a Double-Gate of erstwhile grandeur which certainly appeared to lead nowhere, but which was discovered by the Author (heart-pounding for the sense of dogs, guarding or biting, probably both) a grandeur-esque timber-framed Mansion of the Tudor variety, accompanied by grand Barns of the grand farming kind.

We came away from Dormston with no clue; but with a mental note of apology to the proprietor of said spooky cottage, and furthermore to the proprietor of said Mansion; perhaps they will accommodate us with an invitation, one day. We anticipate the invitation may not prove inviting, but appropriately enough, the reverse. At least we have apologised for the intrusion.

One final record of memory. The road leading into Dormston is skirted with many outhouses or 'sheds' in the Dutch Barn style; curved corrugated roofing in an arc from one side to the other. Like an eye half-open. These have clearly been here a very long time. We must admit to contemplation of the now-accepted shape of Bagend; as a tunnel burrowed into the hillside. The Professor sketched Bagend as such (see the sketches in 'the Annotated Hobbit'), and the Films give exactly the same representation.

We do so Rabbit on.

Incidentally, the spooky cottage called to mind the one in The Blair Witch Project.

Finally, we had noted the village of Bagendon without apology.

Apologies to the villagers there, too, for any intrusion.

We have just time, Gollum-like, to sneak in our discovery of 'Tolkien's Bag End'(2010) by Andrew Morton which we believe to refer to the place of our second visit; we shall be reporting further: when we reach Volume II we shall be looking back to the Bagend of Dormston in further detail.

Kinver Edge (Holy Austin) Rock Houses

'There's a hole in the bucket,
dear Liza, dear Liza,
There's a hole in the bucket,
dear Liza, a hole.'

The song has an (apparently Germanic) history longer than the cave holes.

This paragraph, written 2016, follows six years after the previous, and must be included for further invaluable insight into Professor Tolkien's models for the abodes of hobbits. Kinver Edge is in Staffordshire in England. These are cave-houses cut out from sandstone of Sahara origin and adapted to modern day use (since the 1770's)for contemporary basic working family needs: which have never been major, mostly food and shelter like the original cavemen; remarkably cool in summer yet warm in winter. There are doors and windows of wooden materials cut in holes into the natural rocks, which to all intent and purpose serve as the bricks the interior walls of houses. Most of the floors are tiled. The Archers' house has a groove a foot deep scooped out of the ceiling to accommodate the family Grandfather Clock standing on the tiled floor.

We went inside, but saw no telly ...

... but we did see the bottom of a crapper (so called in England, Victoria upon the Throne at the time), the level of brownstone (no tiles on it, but piles of it) below the outside farmhouse farmer-giles hole for it ... (there was no bowl, merely a hole through a bole: a throne opened in wood, as in *holes* in *boles;* some remembering we went through all that stuff in Bindbole Wood … yet not as *bowels* thrown open falling through the bottom far below into the earth: such faecetious humour privvy, out of respect for closet convenience, only to those sitting there, being WC but hardly PC except if he's done a big job before in the Yard and already on security camera, or in the Jungle with Ant and Dec and cameras watching every single movement) …

… which has a lot of the same stuff on it. Simon Cowell, who, it must be said, rhymes not with chyme but further down, a bowel full of it, is responsible for an awful pile, over and over again, regular through the year until his great gaping opening is closed, what with Strictly such a bind to his talent for producing so much of it …

(Yet *Miasmic* is one of a number he has made huge; amongst many others not quite so big over the years: the biggest through the talent shows before Simon's was Harry Caecum … it might have been on New Faeces …,or, indeed if none at all was coming through in the old days, Opportunity Block … s-ss …)

Perhaps you will go to Kinver one day and take a look up at the holes sitting up there on high in the rock and the wood.

The National Trust took over in 1989. The houses nestle in the apron (crochetted with holes like the game of Croquet, and thus Golf, if Bofur's hobbit joke … and yes it is in the book as well as the films … is still within your range) of the Iron Age Hill fort on Kinver Edge. It is well documented that Professor Tolkien visited these during their habitation, and there can be very little doubt Professor Tolkien will have had these in mind as doorways to hobbit-holes. There is even one built on site, and you will see the Author darkening that doorway, either in this Volume or some website linked to the Author. Britain Explorer (The original Hobbit Holes?) is way ahead of us …

Although the official biography of J R R Tolkien by Humphrey Carter (1977) does not specifically mention a visit to Kinver, there is a reference in a letter written by Mabel Tolkien while they were staying at Rednal that her sons spent almost all summer in the countryside and were taken out by Friar Francis. She cryptically mentions that they went for 'Tea in Hay' (a place) which may well be a reference to Iverley-Hay which is an area directly adjacent to Kinver.

Nothing is new under the sun: Los Hobbitses (derived of 'El Hobbit', the Spanish animated film version) are over in Espana, in hiding from the sun in Kyero in *your dream Spain cave house*. Some may also be lost in the cave houses in Cuenca, which is not a thousand miles away from Basque Guernica, where that many were lost and their houses reduced to caves of rocks, as the Picasso nightmare shows. The attack gained infamy because it involved the deliberate targeting of civilians by a military air force.

The horror of Guernica is in April 1937; six months later The Hobbit is first published.

> **'Democracy don't rule the world;**
> **You'd better get that in your head;**
> **This world is ruled by violence;**
> **But I guess that's better left unsaid.'**

Of course, Professor Tolkien had seen it all for himself in The Great War; so he turned to Fairy Stories.

> **'Over hill, over dale,**
> **Thorough bush, thorough brier,**
> **Over park, over pale,**
> **Thorough flood, thorough fire,**
> **I do wander every where,**
> **Swifter than the moon's sphere;**
> **And I serve the fairy queen,**
> **To dew her orbs upon the green:**
> **... I must go seek some dew-drops here ... '**
> (Midsummer Night's Dream of Shakespeare)

Gollum: ... Awffer Mas-sster away wivver Fairys-ss-ss-ss, precious-ss-ss ... an' furvver proofs-ss-ss ...

Chips

'Goodbye Mr. Chippy!'

RING M II:
Buckland

'I met one man who was wounded in love
I met another man who was wounded in hatred'

The captioned words may have us barking up the wrong tree, family ones that is, the Professor having done so many in explanation of the ancestry of Middle-earth.

The Author makes his apologies, but we must meet the Sackville-Bagginses.

The words evoke for the Author the trials, tribulations and trauma of family life. Take Alf Garnett's, and all their 'effin' ... for we all swear and blind on these occasions ... foibles; or, the Royle Family perhaps, very much at the *my arse* end of the social scale, the very opposite of that to which the Sackville-Bagginses aspire: Keeping Up Appearances, indeed.

Clearly 'wounded in hatred', their abiding emotion, they live a life of self-serving satisfaction, and schadenfreude, which raises its ugly Germanic head, with no offence intended, even if it is indeed Alf who is losing me bleedin' rag. The USA gets it, too, boasting Archie Bunker and what the Fokkers ... (who are really not *so* bad after all)... going on, all in the same bag and carrying the bagginses baggage of their own.

'Piddling Middle-class Fiddlesticks'

The Sackville-Bagginses do not appear in the Film version to any great impact, but do so to great effect in the BBC radio version. They come across as the cretinous, carping, unwelcome family member. We all have one. Other features are pomposity, priggishness and pretentiousness; and just to add another crude word we have not heard since our quest in The Hobbit: they are right pillocks.

With very little or no idea of the character of Vita *Sackville*-West, it is not at all for us to comment; but we do come to know something on the Quest of her caricature: that drawn by Professor Tolkien. Vita (who was still with us in the early Sixties) dug Hedges; privetly and publicly; as we shall see in our first exposure to what Vita Sackville-West was all about. We know of the Bagginses; what of the 'Sackville' line? We have already shared one view of the play upon the name, but some must surely (as did the Author before further inquiry) already have wondered how, where, and why Vita *Sackville*-West and the rest of her line came to feature in The Rings, and we endeavour to explain in the detail of our Portrait Gallegory at the Crossroads up the road ahead.

Take an Umberella.

We anticipate Vita's portrait with a question: can one conceive of 'Sackville-Baggins' without conception of the 'Sackville-Wests'?

Why else, indeed, 'Sackville'?

Middle-earth

The Professor includes material which at first exposure (at least to this Author) comes across as somewhat gratuitous and fatuous filling in of detail, hardly germane to the story at all. The Author declaims that on first reading he found such detail somewhat irritating and 'Walk On By' was crooning melifluously in our head.

We are told of Brandy Hall of the Brandybucks and the origins of Buckland. The Oldbucks changed their name to Brandybucks and built on the strip of land between the old River and the Old Forest. Brandy Hall has *three large front-doors, many side-doors and about a hundred windows*. It is described as its own independent country or a colony of the Shire. The main village of Buckland is Bucklebury; incidentally, not shown on any of the Ring-Maps.

Then there is *the Hedge*. The High Hay was built on the East side of Brandy Hall. It ran well over Twenty (20) miles all the way from the Brandywine Bridge. Whatever, does one suppose, is a 20 Mile Hedge doing in the midst of the terrain of the Lord of the Rings?

Ancient lands had ledges (we are to meet on the ledge somewhere about The Wilderness over the Misty Mountains way up the road ahead), possibly wedges (the doubtful will have to wait for the 'Naith' in Lothlorien)) but surely not *Hedges*?

Incidentally, the conspiracy unmasked is that of the other Hobbits having got together to go all the way with Frodo, as far as the Ring is to take him. They know all about the Ring and the adventures of Bilbo Baggins, and set out knowing all of this; to Frodo this was a reconnaissance trip with a view to his own great adventure later, probably alone.

Mother-earth

Buckland

There are two villages of 'Buckland' known to the Author, respectively in Oxfordshire and Worcestershire. We are to visit the second Buckland later upon the Quest. Those of long memory of our quest in The Hobbit may recall reference to *Buckland* House of the Welsh Marches, and we call in again there later in Volume II of our quest.

Barking Up the Wrong Buckland

Until the very latest stages (the month of publication) of the Quest, the Author was still in confusion between Buckland Village, of description next, and the area of the Shire called Buckland by Professor Tolkien. One had assumed the replication anything but coincidence, and so assumed they might coincide pretty much geographically, on the third assumption that the Secret Shire concept is well founded. Indeed at some points we accede 'Buckland' golfing *gimme* status for ease of putting it in the right place. It turns out (we think now) that the Professor simply borrowed the name from Buckland Village, whilst at the same time borrowed three more things, two so close together as being inseparable: the Tadpole Bridge perching over the River Thames above The Trout Inn on the way into Buckland; and, by way of derivation of 'The Golden Perch' tavern name, the history of

Buckland Village known only to those who know, like the Professor, or might learn of it on our Quest, like the Audience. All of this is up the road ahead (but not too far) and we add for the moment, only that the Professor borrows these allusions and gives them a home at Stock, for reasons which should become apparent. However, there is so much double-vision on this stretch of the Shire, we forewarn about the difficulty of opening your eyes completely; perhaps one will do, when in many cases there are two needed. For the moment, focus one eye upon Buckland Village and the other upon the Brandybucks Buckland. There are highwaymen robbers up the road ahead, at Bree, but in this instance, you will be looking like Ben (not Dick) Turpin, because the two Bucklands are to merge into more or less one and the same thing.

It turns out that Buckland Village finds home in The Marish of the Professor's maps, whilst the Brandybucks Buckland is a manor imagined across the waters of the River Thames via the Bucklebury Ferry: those of the Audience getting impatient and cross might sneak a peak at the Author's map 'A Short Cut Gone Wrong' for some more double-vision.

Smeagol: … Author Master's not any Professor, not any Gandalf, My Luv …

Gollum: … O No … can't get it all in, all in one go, O No … but best Awffer Mas-sster get on with it … We wants it! We wants it! We wants it! We must have **It** …!

We visit Buckland Village next, but return to the Brandybucks Buckland in 'The Golden Perch' with the tiddlers a tad further on, and again in 'A Short Cut to Mushrooms … Gone Wrong', before departing for The Old Forest, some ways up the road ahead with Samwise.

Buckland Village

Buckland is an estate village, created to house those working at Buckland House. The River Thames forms the northern boundary of the parish, just over 1 mile (1.6 km) north of the village. Buckland

House is a large Georgian stately home and the manor house of Buckland. It is a masterpiece of Palladian architecture erected by John Wood, the younger for Sir Robert Throckmorton in 1757. In 1774 Henry James Pye, Poet Laureate to George III, wrote a poem called Faringdon Hill. Part of the poem refers to Buckland:

> **'See Buckland here her lovely scenes display,**
> **which rude erewhile in rich disorder lay**
> **til Taste and Genius with corrective hand**
> **spread Culture's nicest vesture o'er the land,**
> **and called each latent beauty to the fight;**
> **clothed the declining slopes with pendant wood,**
> **and o'er the sedge grown meadows poured the floor.'**

It should be obvious that the succeeding paragraph was written well before the preceding ones and we do indeed *'offer explanation'* as next contemplated, up the road ahead. We are leaving the paragraph intact, not least because it holds true in relation to 'The Yale' ahead, and the Author is not minded to change it, even for you.

And so Buckland does have a counterpart on Mother-earth, in the area of the Old Forest, (The Wychwood, a golfing gimme), and remarkably for the Author, given by the Professor the *same name* in Middle-earth. This is entirely unique, and were we (as we are) trying to read Professor Tolkien's thoughts and mind, could it be that the Professor gives us an easy start in the exercise we now attempt upon the Quest? Granted 'Buckland' is a local enclave of the Shire, and Buckland is a village of Mother-earth, we really cannot *offer any explanation*, but that the Professor's focus upon Buckland is designed to facilitate the exercise. As such, the 'starter for ten' theory is the Author's only rationale.

The Author says much the same of 'The Yale' up the road ahead; another starter for ten: whilst in the context of the villages of Mother-earth in the area, behold the V two-finger sign of our quest in The Hobbit, this time directed across the English Channel … fighting on the beaches, fields and hills …

The Bucklebury Ferry is entirely another kettle of fish.

The Author is bound to foretell that we came upon the Bucklebury Ferry late on in the Quest. We were surprised … as Frodo by the Ringwraith there … as will be the Audience there … by the Author's pathway: a bridge almost too far; the ferry being no longer there at all: but its replacement bridge being very much so, and we shall all have to pay for it, in time and money, because since it replaced the Ferry, the bridge is one of the very few privately owned Toll Bridges left in England.

Light Finds the New Places We Tread: the Brandywine River and Bridge; Girdley Island; the Bucklebury Ferry; Stock: a First Flitch

The Brandywine River and Bridge

Gollum: … Long times-ss nun my po'try lyrrix so lyricals-ss, or my songses and dances-ss so awsssums-ss, precious-ss …

Smeagol: … Author Master be hearing uvver voices onner bridges up the roads ahead in Brandywines, My Luv …

Gollum: … No! Our-s It muss hear! Ourrs-ss muss It hear!! It mus-ss be hearing Ourrrs-sss!!!

(Whispers)
'We must have it. We wants it, we wants it, we wants It!'

… All uvver voices-ss Awffer Mas-sster muss shurrup about on his silly little questses … the precious rings-ss their filffy little neckses-ss allur same times wiv hobbitses-ss-ss …

Smeagol: … Good Smeagol always helps … an' thisser one wants helps so's no nasty hobbitses left to bovver us, My Luv …

> 'Well, I don't want no Short People
> Don't want no Short People
> Don't want no Short People
> 'Round here …'

Gollum: ... no more voices-ss, precious-ss, Smeagol do all po'try lyrrix so lyricals-ss, and songs and dances-ss so aws-ssums-ss, Awffer Mas-sster ... any more chances precious-ss songs and dances-ss, Awffer Mas-sster ... at Brandywines-ss? ... thisser randy one jess pines an' whines aller krafts-ssy lines ...

Voice Off (interrupts): ... it might be more accurate to say that Randy Newman *dra-a-awls* ... booked for a cynical appreciation of human nature, set in many places of the American Land of Dreams ...

'O'er the land of the free
And the home of the brave ...'*

Gollum: ... but what have Americans-ss voices-ss got to do wiv us—ss, precious-ss-ss?

Smeagol: ... We shall see O, yes, we shall see ...

Gollum: ... an' thisser *staggermental eucatastrophe* muss helps-ss show how Awffer Mas-sster awffuls-s descripshuns-s is-ss ...

Smeagol: ... Good Smeagol always helps!

We focus further upon the detail of the Shire Map to the west of the Old Forest; but marginally eastward of its association, The Wychwood in Ring M:III, following the Professor's Secret of the Shire. Because the investigatory work becomes so microscopic here, the focal point from which all else becomes visualised is indeed the relativity of The Old Forest. Even so, it is very easy to get lost in the Buckland area, as do the Hobbits, because there is no visibly integrated inerconnect, even less transport structure, ... you'd have to be a local to know it ... (all is secluded fens and dens where few lenses care to go, yet our site of *staggermental eucatastrophe* is indeed one) and the River Thames the guiding focal point. Most of the time you do not know where you are, relatively speaking, to anywhere else. No wonder the Hobbits get entirely lost here.

---

* *www.thames-path.org.uk/thames_northmoor_tadpole.html

' ... I'm lost on the river bridge
I'm all cracked up on the highway
and in the water's edge'

Apart from Brandy Hall, perhaps the most prominent features of the Brandybucks Buckland are the Brandywine River and Bridge to the North of the Hall, the Bucklebury Ferry marginally to the South of Brandy Hall, with the village of 'Stock' situated between the Bridge and the Ferry. The Ferry is (in the film) the scene of Frodo's memorable jumping feat from the Ferry landing, onto the departing wooden raft-like platform (not so much as a boat) with Sam, Merry and Pippin aboard, in narrow escape from the pursuing Ringwraith. There is no such drama in the text, with the Hobbits boarding the Ferry calmly enough, only to see a dark shrouded figure on the shore of departure ...

Our coming imaginings, some from the USA, of ferryboat structures on any grand scale, may be misleading. To this day, ancient ferries (the one at Hampton on the River Avon at Evesham, good for a Google, comes to mind; that one a bit like the Normandy landings craft on a tiny scale) were little more than floating wooden planks of stout doors, cut down flat to carry livestock, and to hell and high water the human personnel, far less worthy of worry than the market cargo. Little more than a floating raft, very often guided and glided along a chunky chain mechanism in the old days.

The Brandywine River and Bridge; Girdley Island

We shall soon be explaining more fully our conjecture (and so best assume so for the moment) that the Brandywine, otherwise the 'Branduin', equates to the great River of the Shire on Mother-earth: and that this will be the River Thames, following the Professor's Secret of the Shire; but this statement first requires refinement, by reference to what we presume to call the 'Brandywine-Evendim Waterway'.

The converse, for those not already with us, is that the Great River Anduin will be mapped ... (eventually in our Volume III) ... for the River Wye, which starts life as the Great River of Wilderland on our quest in The Hobbit; as the same is borne out by all our future associations; whether of Amon Hen, Amon Lhaw or, indeed, Tol Brandir (the Tindrock) in the midst of the Great River.

These associations are evident only from the greater perspective of the first of the Ring-Maps, as opposed to the Shire Map: the Ring-Maps show the flow of the Brandywine through the Shire, via the Brandywine Bridge and the Ferry, from Lake Evendim to the North. The River Thames itself does not take such path in terms of our associations on Mother-earth.

Astonishingly, (for the integrity of the Secret of the Shire), the Thames (or 'Isis') may be said to take such path by joinder into our ultimate association for Lake Evendim, (*and assume for the moment that Evendim lies in the environs of the town of Northampton*), by riverflows integral to our so-called 'Brandywine-Evendim Waterway': which are the Rivers Ouse and Ray.

The Brandywine-Evendim Waterway

> **'But I'd have you know that these waters of mine**
> **Were once a branch of the River Rhine,**
> **When hundreds of miles to the East I went**
> **And England was joined to the Continent.'**
> (The River Says; Rudyard Kipling)

This example of Victorian imagery might well have been in the thoughts of Professor Tolkien in drawing the line of The Great River of Middle-earth, the Anduin, of which more perhaps in Volume III; yet the process begins here.

As in Magic Mirror Maps and The Hobbit (and the Running River Running), we are to speak at length of conjoining two rivers of Mother-earth into a single waterflow on the Ring-Maps. The **Brandywine-Evendim Waterway** is to be our first example of such joinder. Those who followed our quest in The Hobbit will recall this as a familiar trait in Professor Tolkien's scheme of things, in particular for the Great River Waterway about The Carrock, the town of Ludlow.

The authority of Peter Ackroyd's 'Thames Sacred River' is sacrosanct on the Quest in that, qualified as the work may be in status of history of the Shire, the ambit of the work is so instructive in its vision of the River Thames that it merits navigation for oneself; and so our references are not appendicised, which could for some mean they might be missed, but cited within our text.

'The principal tributaries of the Thames are the Churn, the Thame, the Colne, the Leach, the Windrush, the Evenlode, the Cherwell, the Kennet, the Ver, the Wey, the Mole, the Medway, the Lea and the Roding. There are smaller rivers and streams that refresh and replenish the river – the Ampney Brook, the Gatwick Stream, **the Ray**, the Cole, the Blackwater, the Ock, the Lambourn, the Pang, the Loddon, the Wye, the Bourne, the Hogsmill and the Ember …'

We look upon the Windrush at length elsewhere (nearby Stock at the Barrow Downs), but for the moment we consider the *River Ray*; which we are to link with another river of substance in the area to its north, the Great Ouse: and once more Peter Ackroyd pours forth –

'Thames is an old name. With the exception of Kent it is perhaps the most ancient name recorded in England. It is assumed to be of the same origin as that of the rivers Tamar, Teme and Taff; they all may be derived from Celtic *tam*, meaning smooth or wide-spreading. *Isa* or *esa* are both versions of a Celtic root word meaning running water, as in the present Ouse … (Oxford is a corruption of Ousenford and Osenford). So we may construct a provisional translation for the Thames as running ooze.'

For the purpose of the Brandywine-Evendim Waterway, it is anything but coincidental that Peter Ackroyd's 'running ooze' is the Thames; the Ouse (running on) is identifiable as the Thames, and so it is *on the Ring-Maps*.

'The poplars are felled; farewell to the shade
And the whispering sound of the cool colonnade

**The winds play no longer and sing in the leaves,
Nor Ouse on his bosom their image receives.'**
(The Poplar Field; William Cowper)

There can be no doubt that the Professor will have known the derivation of the Thames name, and more especially that of Oxford, as explained by Peter Ackroyd,('Oxford' from 'Ouse') and we propose that the Brandywine is merely a cartographic linkage spawned from the etymological; Oxford sits on the Thames and as such the Ouse may be imagined a river feeding into it: which, indeed, is our supposition: that the Ouse joins the *River Ray* by the Brandywine-Evendim Waterway; in turn linking into the Thames.

We make no apology for a reminder …

'… the maps of Europe in the Third Age drawn by Tolkien to illustrate his epic show a continent very different from that of today in its coastline, mountains, rivers and other major geographical features. In explanation he points to the forces of erosion, which wear down mountains, and to advances and recessions of the sea that have inundated some lands and uncovered others.'
(Paul Kocher: 'Master Of Middle-earth'(1972))

Nor do we make apology for blowing our own trumpet up the road ahead, on the banks of the Withywindle, thus …

'History repeats itself; ironically, in the Prehistoric period, which we may imagine for the setting of The Rings, deep cut valleys would have become natural lake areas following the receding of the Ice Age: much of England would have consisted of the highest mountain and hilltops looming above vast flooded lakelands of water; and man has put the lakes back in places.'

The point here, however, is not the creation of man-made lakes, but what there is left of a once-existing watercourse after the Ice Age is receded. Some may recall, from our quest in The Hobbit, the ample evidence of Professor Tolkien's practice of drawing rivers conjoined where there is no clue of such joinder on the Mother-earth of today, with the Running River of The Hobbit prime example, but also 'the Great River Waterway' of the River Wye beyond the town of Ludlow.

In order to link the flow between Lake Evendim and the Brandywine, but on Mother-earth, we conjoin the flow of the River Ray above Steeple Claydon, into the Great Ouse, which by countless meanderings, broadly speaking (and some oousedles of Tolkienesque licence) reaches into Lake Evendim.

The route taken by the Great Ouse and which best matches the line taken by the Brandywine as shown on the Ring-Maps is, in turn, on the map of Mother-earth, northward of Steeple Claydon, through Padbury, Singleborough, Passenham, Lathbury, Newport Pagnell, Olney and Chellington to Coffle End; and thereafter … Wollaston, Great Doddington, and Ecton to Hardwick (Wellingborough) … to the shores of Lake Evendim: which is thus(for the Ranger) but an easy skim of a stone away: *and for all members of our Audience, subject our prior assumption of connection with the town of Northampton.*

It is the Author's view that the comparison of the line on Middle-earth, with all due allowance for many an island (such as Girdley's) of land intervening and requiring linkage by the imagination of waterflow, is remarkable in consistency. Indeed the great bulging curve of the Brandywine is accountable by the riverflows of Mother-earth comprising the Brandywine-Evendim Waterway.

Girdley Island

> **'In Xanadu did Kubla Khan**
> **A stately pleasure-dome decree**
> **Where Alph, the sacred river, ran**
> **through caverns measureless to man**
> **Down to a sunless sea.**
> **So twice five miles of fertile ground**
> **With walls and towers were girdled round: …'**
> (Kubla Khan; Coleridge)

The 'eucatastrophe' in all of the conjecture of the Brandywine-Evendim Waterway would perhaps best be trophied by rationale of, and association for, the *girdle* of 'Girdley Island'.

Now the Author has many times suggested (and will no doubt do so again) that a discovery was the last upon the Quest; but Girdley Island was indeed so; simply because we were, literally, thrown off course in looking for an 'island' in a river north of Oxford; and there was none to be found.

A trophy long sought by the Author on the Quest, the prize now sits in the midst of the Brandywine; the ultimate triumph of focus on the Shire Map; or at least our best shot at the trophy.

Peter Ackroyd leads our sub-aqua diving hunt …

'The Thames has many tributaries. There is good reason to honour them. The gods were meant to dance at the confluence of waters. The mingling of the tributary and the main river was deemed to be sacred. The site of entry was a holy place, guarded by the three seated goddesses who have been given the name of Matres … many are now buried; many are forgotten; many are today unhonoured and unsung…'

The sacred and honorific nature of confluence is soon to be fulfilled.

Emerging between the source of the River Ray and that of the Great Ouse (comprising our Brandywine-Evendim Waterway) is an area abounding with 'Claydons', meaning 'clay towns' of earthen production: Steeple, Middle and East Claydon; and last but not least, *Botolph* Claydon.

Some detail of St. Botolph is included in the Bureau of Shire-history in Appendix B; but the following is of note –

'… *permitted to chose a tract of desolate land upon which to build a Monastery, surrounded by water and called Icanhoe (Ox-island) …*'

Now the Author, for one, might easily imagine the waters of the Rivers Ray and Great Ouse conjoined by an ox-bow island in their midst, just as Girdley Island is sketched on the Shire Map; but what then of 'Girdley'? Each of the four Claydons inherits a 'lay' or 'ley' by name, and we conjecture that all four may be said to be bound together, as in a belt or gird, and thus 'girded' together in a 'gird' of leys; thus 'Girdley'. Girdle around the 'girdled' girdling Coleridge's Xanadu of Kubla Khan.

The Professor's awareness of so-called 'ley line' theory is examined further in Volume II, for such is indeed knowledge precious on the Quest.

But also to the final triumph, the trophy of trophies …

'The new comers were Wilfred of Ivanhoe, on the Prior of Botolph's palfrey, and Gurth, who attended him, on the Knight's own war-horse…'

(Ivanhoe, Sir Walter Scott)

From Icanhoe to Ivanhoe, and from Gird to Gurth, Girdley is by now ready association for Botolph Claydon.

Zooming out once more to the first of the Ring-Maps: the Brandywine flows down from Lake Evendim; as we imagine, on Mother-earth, that the Brandywine-Evendim Waterway flows from the area of the township of *Northampton* (thus a saintly gift for Volume II), but whose Lake Evendim must remain secret until the later Volume. We say more of Lake Evendim on the banks of the Withywindle, when light finds that river of The Rings about the Old Forest.

Thus most important for present purposes is that reference to the Brandywine River *on the Ring-Maps* equates to the Brandywine-Evendim Waterway giving rise, through the Oxford Canal system, to its confluence with the River Thames; yet again on the Shire Map, the Brandywine is covert association of the Thames.

Once we later shine the light on 'Stock' in RING M V (The Barrow Downs), we find the exact same process in reference to the Bruinen, the Windrush, having a second, localised name on the Shire Map: the Stockbrook.

The Brandywine Bridge

'Now, you courtly dames and knights,
That study only strange delights;
Though you scorn the home-spun gray
And revel in your rich array;
Though your tongues dissemble deep,
And can your heads from danger keep;
Yet, for all your pomp and train,
Securer lives the silly swain!'
(Fortunati Nimium; Thomas Campion:1567–1620)

We had forewarned that the notorious Mitford Girls have a place on the Quest ... and here they are ... *courtly dames and knights, That study only strange delights; ...*

There indeed exists on Mother-earth a Bridge over the River Thames, nearby the site we might expect for the Brandywine Bridge; the town of Swinford (in the area known as Eynsham) which bridges the River Thames, by Swinford Toll Bridge.

'Swinford' is inevitably 'Swineford' and thus the 'ford' for the 'livestock' of pigs; and hence a first allusion by the very name 'Stock'.

'To market, to market, to buy a fat pig, Home again,
home again, jiggety-jig. To market, to market, to
buy a fat hog, Home again, home again, jiggety-jog.'

The *Bucklebury Ferry* emerges from a duality: the predecessor of the 'Toll' Bridge of Swinford, of ancient history is formerly a *Ferry Crossing;* with local sources confirming such historical development:

Built in the 18th Century by the fourth Earl of Abingdon at a cost of around £5,000, the bridge carried pigs and other animals over the Thames, hence the name Swinford (a contraction of 'swine ford'). In return for the Earl's investment, King George III passed an Act of Parliament stipulating that the toll income would belong to the Earl and his 'heirs and assignees for ever'. The bridge was owned by his family until 1985, when it was sold for £275,000. The bridge's owner must provide a ferry in case the bridge is out of action.

He or she also has the right to seize the car of anyone trying to cross without paying.

In the history of swine crossing the Brandywine by Swinford Toll Bridge, the 'bridge' becomes interchangeable with its predecessor Ferry; and for our purposes, on Mother-earth, the Brandywine Bridge and the Bucklebury Ferry are one and the same, at Swinford.

Gollum: … es-ssept forrer Tadpoles-ss Bridge an' Trouts-ss Inn we's added later, Awffer Mas-sster . . you remembers-ss …?

Smeagol: … we always helps! … an' musnt forget Golden Percheses neivver!

We are sinking neither by the feeling that we have no Bridge and Ferry service separate one from the other in the vicinity on Mother-earth; nor sinking by the feeling that according to their position on the Shire Map, the Professor appears to have sketched them respectively to the North and South of Brandy Hall.

There is nothing in our historical researches to indicate that the Ferry spanned the River at a juncture any different from where the Bridge does so today, but clearly, for the purposes of the storyline of The Rings, if the Professor writes of separate locations, they will have been mapped so; or indeed vice-versa.

With plenty of booze to follow with the proprietors of Brandy Hall, in the meantime, Frodo is very nearly in the drink: and speaking of drink …

'At all costs we must keep you away from the Golden Perch. We want to get to Bucklebury before dark.'

The Author debaited a late candidate for the Brandywine Bridge (in distinction from the Ferry facility at Swinford) with a belated discovery, and what is more very close in the environs of Buckland Village of Mother-earth, and consistent with a journey onwards to a Bucklebury Ferry at Swinford: the 'Tadpole Bridge' hooks on over the Brandywine-Thames, whose main focus is renowned locally for 'The Trout' Inn; presumably an ordinary Pub in the Professor's day, today a fissure on the road of the smartest scale. It so makes one wonder how often the Professor filled his glass jar from here before taking himself, carrying his tiddley friends, filled from the brandywine, spangled over the dingly dells, splishing and splashing (like Gollum, Gone Fishing), paddling addled across the puddles, the sodden bogs, sunken logs and stickled-back locks swallowed by swollen Isis, all the way home on foot, more likely bicycle, to Waymoot …

Between Tadpole and Swinford Toll Bridge there lies the wooden Tenfoot Bridge, a Shire relic enough to make even hobbits feel tall. Cross it on the *staggermental eucatastrophe* website of our Index. It may well be Professor Tolkien spawned The Golden Perch from The Trout: and this is indeed the one that nearly got away; it being knocked on the head within a month before publication.

The Golden Perch …

> 'I went out to the hazel wood,
> Because a fire was in my head,
> And cut and peeled a hazel wand,
> And hooked a berry to a thread;
> And when white moths were on the wing,
> And moth-like stars were flickering out,
> I dropped the berry in a stream
> And caught a little silver trout.'
> (The Song of Wandering Aengus; W.B. Yeats)

Whilst the Professor places The Golden Perch at Stock, the perfect model showcase might indeed be The Trout nearby Buckland Village, perching on the Tadpole Bridge over the River Thames as it does; and from that aspect we see double once more: reeled in to the question … why swap the Tavern name for a species which is fishy in other senses; first because the Golden Perch is unequivocally a fish found only in Australia: what would be

112

wrong with The Golden Trout? Yet The Golden Perch is doubly doubtful!

The naturalist Richardson actually named the golden perch Datnia Ambigua and applied the specific name ambigua (Latin for 'doubtful') to the species because, as he states in his species description, he could not decide in which of two genera to place it. The key to the doubt might (and the mightiest of all challenges, or should it be a challenge to the Almighty) revert to the Professor's preoccupation with religious conflict: the Author's only visit to Buckland caused a doubt in our own mind for which church was the prevailing one in the historic village; for there are indeed two, each of some grandeur.

The Church of England parish church of St Mary the Virgin is largely a 12th-century building, with 13th-century chancel, tower and transepts and some minor Victorian additions. The main north and south nave doors are unusual in having a matching pair of Norman arches. In the chancel is a triangular locker containing the heart-burial (1575) of William Holcott of Barcote Manor. He was a staunch Protestant who only just avoided being burnt at the stake by Mary Tudor. After the Reformation, he became a zealous lay preacher, often gracing the pulpit in his 'velvet bonnet and damask gown … sometimes with a gold chain'.

St George's Roman Catholic Church is a Gothic Revival building, completed in 1848 for the Throckmortons of Buckland House. It has a chancel, north chapel, nave, south porch and western bellcote. Parish Masses at St. George, Buckland ended in June 2005, with Bishop Crispian celebrating the final Mass together with other local clergy on 29th June. St. George's church was sold in October 2005 and it is now a private chapel to Buckland House.

Perhaps, in the Professor's mind, Buckland was doubtful in a religious sense, both Protestants and Catholics operating side by side for centuries.

Gollum (sings):

*'I've been a miner for a heart of gold …
Keep me searching for a heart of gold
And I'm getting old.'

We searched long and hard for any significance of a perch that is golden … Yet it might not be straining the rod or one's creedulity to land yet one further catch: is not William Holcott in some senses on the perch of his pulpit, all shining in gold? We know for sure Holcott put his whole heart into the workings of the Church. Heart-burials are very rare (Thomas Hardy comes to mind), surely indicating a paragon(a Poly Gone Fishing below) of respect in the community; where of course, John Wesley was to follow a century or so later.

Smeagol: … Two parrots sitting on a perch. The first one says to the other …

Gollum: … 'Can you smell fish?'

'Bucklebury' Ferry

'And the heavy night hung dark,
The hills and waters o'er,
When a band of exiles moored their bark
On the wild New England shore …
There were men with hoary hair
Amidst the pilgrim band:
Why had they come to wither there,
Away from their childhood's land? …
Ay, call it holy ground,
The soil where first they trod;
They have left unstained what there they found –
Freedom to worship God.'
(The Pilgrim Fathers; Felicia Dorothea Hemans)

It may be forgotten that many of the Pilgrim Fathers were fleeing religious persecution.

---

*   Neil Young

We have sailed over to the Americas-ss-ss for a very good All American ferryboat waterpaddle; and for good reason enough: because the Bucklebury Ferry may have steamed here from over the pond ...

**'Others will enter the gates of the ferry
and cross from shore to shore ...'**
(Crossing Brooklyn Ferry: Walt Whitman)

We remain buoyant, well afloat: indeed goggling well over the gated waters, by reason that the Professor's games of seeing double have only just begun.

'Can horses cross the river?'

Of the pursuing Black Riders ...

They can go twenty miles north to Brandywine Bridge – or they might swim,' answered Merry. 'Though I never heard of any horse swimming the Brandywine.'

(A Conspiracy Unmasked)

Are we not searching for the resources of Professor J.R.R. Tolkien in creating The Lord of the Rings? The Bucklebury Ferry vaunts a daunting, haunting history to drown in, for which the Audience will require the assistance of the Web; more than there was in the Seventeenth Century to avail the victims of these rapid flowing waters ...

In the winter of 1636, some of the Welsh sheriffs were bringing up their Ship Money to Charles I and, 'as they were to be transported by Ensam ferry, by reason of the... tempest, & unrulynes of some horses & overloading of the boate, 3 or 4 were drown'd, £800 lost for a time, & 8 persons with some horses escaped by swimming.'

The Audience will understand that the Swinford Ferry (replaced by the Toll Bridge), being in Eynsham, will (in 1636) have been known as 'Ensam ferry.'

There is no doubting the quirks of England's history. Having passed through private hands any number of times, the Bridge last did so in 2009 at an auction price exceeding £1 Million; all income from the Tolls is tax free.

The *'Buckle'* bury Ferry calls now for the finnishing (but not yet final) curtain.

'Oh Steamboat Bill, steaming down the Mississippi,
Steamboat Bill, a mighty man was he,
Oh Steamboat Bill, steaming down the Mississippi,
Gonna beat the record of the Robert E. Lee'

Stock-bury may have been a more likely choice? There may be none of the Audience interested in such details, but the Author was … holding on for one darn cotton pickin' minute … aw, shucks … what might there be for us to grab ahold of, latch onto, and finally climb aboard in the swim of 'Bucklebury'?

We were unhappy to count all on the easy 'Buck' of *'Buck*-land' and *'Buckle*-bury' correlation; the obvious Dollar 'Buck' allusion: albeit perhaps connoting payment of money tolls for Ferry and Bridge? What of 'Buck' as Dollars as opposed to the 'Stock' of Shares?

' Out of the mud two strangers came …'
(Two Tramps in Mud Time; Robert Frost)

Bank on the best bet, yet bubbling under, drowning in literary history; all because it is now that the coin (penny or dime) has dropped like a stone to the bottom of the deep. A bridge and ferry in one and never the *Twain* shall meet: a mark for 'Huckleberry Finn'; Huckleberry: Bucklebury?

'I used to play at Pirates,
And sailed the seven seas…
I discovered the joys of reading,
And escaped the daily grind …
Then off again to America,
With Huckleberry Finn I did hide.'
(Imagination; Shaw)

116

The childhood reminiscences of George Bernard Shaw may remind us of those of Professor J.R.R. Tolkien: *Barrels out of Bond* in The Hobbit is, we have suggested, gangplanked on the pirate stories of *Treasure Island*, and possibly *A High Wind in Jamaica*: it may be conjecture, but to the Author's way of thinking, these parallels demonstrate that 'no man is an island' (John Donne), which is irrevocably true, except that, in the Author's view, Professor Tolkien has Jackson's in mind for the Bucklebury incidents: they *must* be crafted, drafted and rafted on the Big Muddy Mississippi; both situations invoke escape from enslavement of some kind: and as we suggest it is so, we mutter the Mantra of Middle-earth with freckles from under a speckled straw hat, through lips complete with straw for breathing underwater ... and (Chapter XII, Adventures Huckleberry Finn) – *yes, in facty, we would be in that same old town again* ... but not Cairo, our heroes intended destination ...

'Our ole raf"

Smeagol: ... do you say so, My Luv, do you say so ...?

Gollum: ... Gerron wivvit, Awffer Mas-sster ...

Smeagol: ... yes, indeed, My Luv, make haste! Time is short ... (grinning) ... a bit like wot hobbitses is like! ...

'Come-buckle to your paddle, and let's get along.'

Mark Twain's hero is a prong in Professor J.R.R. Tolkien's frame of buckle-words. Perhaps it is the Author who is bradawled; yet turn to the Bureau of Shire-history in Appendix B for many a Twain meet there: tales of Uncles Remus and Tom, welcome in a social history of the USA, down the river to the later ones of Huckleberry Finn. The Professor would have so enjoyed the play on 'twain' for duality. And in the second place, on a separate twain of thought, why the 'Brandywine' river? And so the Professor saw yer coming; another Tom in his cabin with all of the rest of us, sold down the river, taken for so many rides in his tales of the riverbank: well and truly succoured; yet help is at hand, by the tale of two more.

**'Dah you goes, de ole true Huck;
de on'y white genlman dat ever
kep' his promise to ole Jim.'**

Huck escapes from Pap by faking his own death, killing a pig and spreading its blood all over the cabin ..., Huck watches the townspeople search the river for his body. After a few days [hiding on Jackson's island], he encounters Jim, one of Miss Watson's slaves. Jim has run away from Miss Watson after hearing her talk about selling him to a plantation down the river, ... Huck and Jim team up, despite Huck's uncertainty about ... helping a runaway slave... Huck and Jim spy a log raft ... floating past the island. They capture the raft ...

(Web Plot Overview, The Adventures of Huckleberry Finn, Mark
Twain (1884))

Pigs and rafts and ever the twain shall meet by the Big Muddy.

"G-o-r-g-e J-a-x-o-n-there now,"

Quite apart from the pig and raft allusions, and no doubt a bridge too far for anyone's interest other than the Author's own, one of the high falutin' aims of the Quest is to encourage further research: here's some high falutin' yet deeper waters to dive in: *Brandywine* Spring is a spring falling hundreds of feet in Claiborne County, *Mississippi*; our US cousins will know that Jackson's Island, held by Huckleberry Finn and Jim, is the most celebrated river island in U.S. fictional history, except that it is no fiction: it sits in the middle of the Mississippi River.

**'When it was daylight,
here was the clear Ohio water in shore,
sure enough, and outside was the old regular Muddy!'**

Gollum (shaking head): ... Well, well, well, My Luv ... we never guessess ... so many *ss-ss-ss-es* ...

And so we guess that many a twain meet hereabouts; indeed, one might say, many thoughts are intertwined: quite apart(!) from the unification of the Brandywine-Evendim Waterway, the Bucklebury

Ferry and Bridge are (except for the tale of Tadpole Bridge) yet two from one; and perhaps also we hear more double-talk, by free association, with the Brandywine, and the pig and raft allusions, borne of 'The Adventures of Huckleberry Finn'.

Of course, this could all be mere coincidence.

Yet we are bound to remind you all of the Mantra of Middle-earth ...

'I fear you may be right that the search for the sources of The Lord of the Rings is going to occupy academics for a generation or two. I wish this not to be so. To my mind it is the particular use in a particular situation of any motive whether invented, deliberately borrowed, or unconsciously remembered that is the most interesting thing to consider.'

'Don't want no Short People 'round here'

Smeagol: ... how duz we feel about silly hobbitses, now My Luv ... the Master an' the Fat One seen plenty dangers over Brandywine Bridge and Bucklebury Ferry ... shudn't we sympafises, My Luv ...?

Gollum: ... yess, indeed ... Dreadful danger! Dreadful danger! ... iss plentys-ss more where that comes-ss from, my precious-ss-ss ... We hates them! They sto-o-ole it from us-ss!

We sneak (with Gollum) a glimpse through the trees to see more of what is to come in the Old Forest: maple trees; except that, for obscure reasons, we see less of them when we get there than we had hoped; which naturally caused us to wonder where they might have disappeared.

Now the Old Forest is an Ancient Royal Forest, and so to a final irresistible tie of the knot: our Nation (and many welcome guests from the others of Earth) is much spring-heeled by the Royal Wedding of William and Kate, April 29,2011; wedding us the most majestic of marriages: the Bride walks the aisle from the village of 'Bucklebury' in Berkshire; whether the Professor knew of the coupling is one for another tiara boom-de-ay; but a decidedly

119

deciduous dowry: we now know that the Bride is ahead of us on our Quest; for she has returned to Westminster Abbey the English field Maple trees that have inexplicably gone missing from Maple Hill in the Old Forest when we get there: at last the Royal Secret is out.

Gollum: (sings)…'Come on and kiss me, Kate' …(evil whisper) … we wonders-s that ship-shape s-ssister of her's likes a ride on *my* raft … O wot a s-sstern it got … ss-ss-ss … ?

Stock: A First Flitch

> **'What time I watch the darkening droves of swine**
> **That range on yonder plain.**
> **"In filthy sloughs they roll a prurient skin,**
> **They graze and wallow, breed and sleep;**
> **And oft some brainless devil enters in,**
> **And drives them to the deep."**
> (The Palace of Art; Alfred, Lord Tennyson)

We happen to be in the right place (and so, we think, thought the Professor) for the swine, and brainless devils going off the deep end. This author cannot resist a nudge, hint or clue from time to time along the way of our Quest; and we are to take stock of it all in the paragraphs soon to follow: but, saving your bacon, we are not quite ready to bring it home, but it's back in a switch to another flitch … up the road ahead for pigses of the second flitch …

Smeagol: … We guesses, yes, we knows … snowball's chance in Hell of Mordor we tells the secret names … Smeagol keeps all secrets, yes, … no squealer Smeagol, no, no … no names we tells … not yet … Follow Smeagol …

> **'This little piggy went to market,**
> **This little piggy stayed at home …'**

Gollum (cynical and mean): … and where is it going in the Shire with these names-s, we wonders-ss, yes we wonders-ss … where is the mob herding, we wonders-sss … droving to the funny farm, yes we wonders-s … yes, precious … all funny farm swill … for fat old major … but we wants them to know, doessn't we, my pre-e-ecious …? (shaking head) … No more names-s! No more games-s! No more secrets-s!

Smeagol: … Smeagol keeps all secrets, yes … Trust Smeagol now … trust Smeagol *still*?

Gollum(defiant): … Three it is-s … yes-s, indeed, Three … Three on the Farm … names of pigs-ess-ss …

… *Snowball … Squealer … Old Major* … is-s *Animals Farm* it is-s, My Precious-ss …

Smeagol: … and more filffy swine to come … yes, indeed … pigses of the second flitch at **Stock** … Follow Smeagol! … See what Smeagol finds …

Conspiracy Unmasked: The Brandybucks Buckland

… and before we overlook Professor Tolkien's borrowings from Buckland Village, we think the Professor rafted down the River Thames both Tadpole Bridge and the Trout Inn, bound together from there, to tie down the Brandywine Bridge and The Golden Perch at Stock, and indeed that fanciful fish name from Buckland Village too. It seems to the Author that the Professor could easily have mapped The Swan (easily renamed) at Swinbrook (with emphatic Mitford connection) into the story at Stock; … but that might ring the bell too soon …?

We must shout 'last orders' on this most winding inquiry (no doubt winding the Audience up as much as the Author), which we hope perhaps to straighten out further below:

Look for 'Where Lies the Professor's Short Cut Gone Wrong?' and 'Crossing the Bar (anduin)'.

Binding of the Ring

> 'Great praise the Duke of Marlboro' won,
> And our good Prince Eugene.'
> 'Why, 'twas a very wicked thing!'
> Said little Wilhelmine.
> 'Nay, nay, my little girl,' quoth he;
> 'It was a famous victory'
> (The Battle of Blenheim: Robert Southey; 1774-1843)

Brandy Hall; the Oldbucks and the Brandybucks

This battle was fought near the village of Blenheim, in Bavaria, on the left bank of the river Danube, on August 13, 1704. The French and Bavarians, under Marshall Tallard and Marsin, were defeated by the English and Austrians, under the Duke of Marlborough and Prince Eugene … The battle broke the prestige of the French King, Louis XIV; and when Marlborough returned to England his nation built a magnificent mansion for him and named it Blenheim Palace after this battle.

We speak now of the Marlborough Dynasty and Blenheim Palace in particular. Extracts of their history are in the Bureau of Shire-history in Appendix B.

Brandy Hall

Blenheim Palace sits in the centre of a large undulating park, a classic example of the English landscape garden movement and style. Through the park trickles the small River Glyme, and the Architect Vanbrugh envisaged this marshy brook traversed by the 'finest bridge in Europe'. The marsh was channelled into three small canal-like streams and across it rises a bridge of huge proportions.

In this setting the Bridge appeared incongruous, causing Alexander Pope to comment:

'the minnows, as under this vast arch they pass, murmur, how like whales we look, thanks to your Grace'

It should be made clear that the Author's metaphor of Plankton to Whales was, in all honesty, not derived here.

The plan of Blenheim Palace is basically that of a large central rectangular block. The central block is flanked by two further service blocks around square courtyards. The three blocks together form the Great Court.
There are many Stately residences of the area that might fit the description of Brandy Hall. Of course, Blenheim has hundreds of windows. So do many other great houses. The reference to three doors is intriguing: by virtue of the entrance in the central block, together with that at each of the two vast wings, it is supposed the Palace could be said to have three entrance doors.

The location of Brandy Hall/Blenheim Palace is a most positive factor.

Brandy Hall is built on a strip of land between an old river and the Old Forest. Blenheim is indeed just so: between the River Cherwell and the beginning of the forestation culminating in the Wychwood in Oxfordshire.

In addition to the proximity of 'Buckland' in Oxfordshire, one speculates whether Professor Tolkien makes an oblique reference to 'Bucks' as American Dollars, picking up on the transience of the family from Old Money to New Money.

Our earliest thought was that these associations might well be flights of fancy on our part, there being enough resemblances between the Marlborough/Churchill dynasty and the descriptions of the Brandybucks of Brandy Hall, to make them worth mention; to make them an inkling at the very least; *perhaps* an accurate association of ideas by allusion.

It was then that a change of name confirmed the association; in our view, ***without any further question***.

Does not the change of name from 'Oldbuck' to 'Brandybuck' echo that from **Spencer** to **Churchill,** of long history ...?

'... *George Spencer, became the 4th Duke of Marlborough at the age of nineteen ... We now have a change of surname because their son, George, 5th Duke of Marlborough, took the additional name of Churchill by royal license in 1817. The Churchill surname is interesting in its origin ... Burke's Peerage gives the family origin as coming from Gitto de Leon whose son was Wandril de Leon, Lord of Courcil. The name then changed from "de Courcil" to "de Chirchil" and ultimately "Churchill"...'*

(Churchill's Spencer Ancestry)

We now consider the association unequivocal: the Oldbucks became the Brandybucks, just as the Spencers became the Churchills; they live at Brandy Hall and Blenheim Palace respectively. The 'Spencer' heritage is apparently far less grand, being reference to the 'dispenser' of such as provisions. Lady Diana is, of course, originally, 'Spencer'; one for the family tree surgeons.

As for 'Brandy' Hall, we may have anticipated that the Vanderbilts were a U.S. family of Distillery wealth but, alas, that railroad leads us nowhere. Winston Churchill's passion for Brandy (and more or less anything else alcoholic) is, on the other hand, legendary. It is not difficult to find Web articles which question whether our great Wartime leader was Alcoholic. How else does one categorise a man who drinks Whisky at Breakfast and sometimes a bottle of Champagne at Lunch as well as Dinner?

In between all the other things he had to do, which after all were not inconsiderable, the Prime Minister relaxed with bricklaying. Albert Finney's rendering is the best the Author knows. Others have attempted, but on screen, for the Author, Finney's is a triumph. One assumes his rendition is accurate: 'KBO' or 'Keep Buggering On' replays itself as a Churchillian catchphrase. Likewise we have never forgotten the epitome of politeness of his response, when asked how he was:

'Thank you for asking, I am ...'

We Keep Buggering On.

The High Hay Hedge

'But if the arrow is straight
And the point is slick
It can pierce through dust no matter how thick'

Now Vita Sackville-West and her lifestyle and interests are beyond the scope of the Quest, but suffice to say she cut a unique figure for the contemporary day and age. Her lovers included Virginia Wolf. If one thinks the Author is prone to 'stream of consciousness' writing, one might try Virginia's Mrs. Dalloway.

Vita's other famed relationship was that with Violet Trefusis; which causes us to contemplate a conspiracy of the high-flying V's; but the Da Vinci Code did the 'V' sign to the last supper and on to breakfast; so we must await Violet in the Portrait Gallegory at the Crossroads up the road ahead. Amidst Vita's Romantic interludings, of which we gossip some more in our Portrait Gallegory, she became a literary figure of some fame and, perversely enough, or perhaps not, a scion of the architecture, layout and design of gardens and everything in them. Her design at Sissinghurst in Kent, developed alongside her husband the equally noteworthy (possibly notorious) Harold Nicholson, is the stuff of horticultural legend.

Their marital relationship is equally the stuff of legend.

Churchill's home, Chartwell, is a just a few miles away from Sissinghurst.

'Most writing is re-writing'
(Poet R.S Thomas)

We might raise inquiry whether Professor Tolkien may have cross-referenced 'High Hay' Hedge from the 'Fern Hill' of Dylan Thomas (… the 'house high hay …'), much admired in the day.

125

If the 'High Hay' connection of 'Fern Hill' is tenuous (but to the Author, ready and easy) then one re-echoes the question: what is a 20 mile hedge doing in the heart of the Professor's story, as the Hobbits approach the deep dark forest with the Withywindle running nearby? It really does seem entirely anomalous.

A formal hedge (and the Professor informs that the High Hay is tended continuously) is of its nature a man (or woman)-made edifice somewhat at odds with an otherwise entirely naturalistic setting. There are wild hedgerows, and plenty in the Oxfordshire locality, but these wander boundaries, boxing in fields, far from straightlined ornament: the Shire Map shows the virtual straight line of the hedge, certainly after Crickhollow: why illustrate so unnatural a line and shape? Perhaps because the Professor thought the whole concept of formalistic hedges, contrived to garden design: barmy, out of order and a push over the edge.

Vita Sackville-West dreamed of becoming a bit of a champion poet, but sensing failure, championed, Mirabile Dictu, Latin being quite appropriate in the Horticultural context, *Hedges;* to say nothing of whoever else's bit she champed on.

Hidcote Manor (once a candidate for association status, but now discounted) is a National Trust jewel not at all far from the environs of which we write. It is within 10 miles of each of The Barrow Downs, Bree and Weathertop. The magnificent gardens were developed by the American, Lawrence Johnson and were hugely admired by Vita Sackville-West, especially for what Lawrence Johnson did with *Hedges*. So much so that the Introduction to the Hidcote Manor National Trust literature was formerly (there being no date on our old copy, but, guesswork says maybe 1970) that written by Vita Sackville-West from an article published in The Journal of the Royal Horticultural Society, November 1949. Nowadays there is a small quotation on the back cover. In the Portrait Gallegory, we hear of Vita at work on the script: in nearby Broadway; when she wasn't at play with … the other high-flying V's: Violet (Trefusis) and Virginia (Woolf); but not necessarily in that order, of which more at the Crossroads.

The following is taken directly from the old National Trust literature:

'But in a big garden like Hidcote great skill is required to secure not only the success of the actual planting, but of the proportions which can best give the illusion of enclosure; the area must, in fact, be broken up in such a way that each part shall be separate from the other, yet all shall be disposed round the main lines of the garden in such a way as to give homogenity to the whole. At Hidcote this has been achieved by the use of hedges, with openings cut for the convenience of communication, rather than by the use of walls and gates; tall living barriers which do much to deepen the impression of luxuriance and secrecy.'

We do so wonder whether Professor J.R.R. Tolkien would have shared Vita's enthusiasm. The Author imagines that formal hedges were the very antithesis of Tolkien's rapture in nature.

Other similar commentaries on Vita Sackville-West's passion (for the moment for Hedges; there are reams about her others) abound:

Hidcote
Major Lawrence Johnson started the garden in 1907 when little grew on the property except a cedar tree and a strand of beech trees. At first he laid it out according to formal English designs, but then he went on plant hunting exhibitions to China and South Africa and his perspectives widened.
Vita Sackville-West admired Johnson's innovative ideas about hedges.'
There are many similarities between Lawrence Johnson's style of gardening to that of Vita Sackville-West's and her husband Harold Nicolson's garden at Sissinghurst. The major design features in both gardens are the series of secret garden rooms – walled or hedged enclosures that offer a sense of intimacy. Both garden designs considered the vistas, so that each path or alley through a lime walk or rose walk drew the eye to another garden view, a seat or a statue.

At a later stage ('the Old Forest'), Merry recalls a gap in the Hedge which the Hobbits pass through.

In passing, Bankers speak of a 'Hedge' in terms of a protection against risk, normally financial. The derivation is presumably 'hedging one's bets.'

'And though doubtful of biscuit,
I'm willing to risk it, …'
(The Song of the Mischievous Dog; Dylan Thomas)

We shall indeed risk it for a biscuit: the Author might just be prepared to hedge the bet that the Professor's High Hay Hedge is the fruit of a seed sown by Lawrence Johnson via Vita Sackville-West and the Thomas epithet; later on we drag Vita through the hedge; ever backwards.

We had hoped that Hidcote might boast something like Twenty miles of hedge; but it has just Four to this day. Yet the Twenty miles is readily explicable by reason that the Hedge must span the Old Forest: one presumes some twenty miles in the decades of the Professor's writing; but we may never know, for our researches did not extend that far; perhaps some Ranger will show us the way through the length of The High Hay Hedge, like Merry.

The High Hay Hedge may just be a Tolkien caricature cum satire of Vita's gardening propensities in words, pictures and, of course, maps. 'Parody' may be the best word, for the Professor uses it himself (in Letter number 190) in the context of description of the Shire; and as we foresee in the Portrait Gallegory.

We think 'may be' is under-hedging the bet: ask oneself once more; why is the silliest hedge – of silly shape, length and purpose (the point being it *has* no purpose) – included in the burgeoning tale of so much scale we would be silly to attempt description; other than for the fact that the Professor thought the whole idea lunatic, daft, and hideous in the extreme.

Vita's Hedges are, in the Author's opinion, bankable; of equal note and value for any of the Audience visiting the Shire, is *Kiftsgate*, marvellous garden setting all but next door to Hidcote.

Satirisation of contemporary persona (some Celebrity at last!!!) is an overlooked (not to say completely undetected) and, entirely for most, unexpected facet of The Lord of the Rings; but the Author believes we detect it here, with more to come through the Portrait Gallegory at the Crossroads up the road ahead.

The notorious Mitford Girls have a place on the Quest; six of them await us in RING M:VI: such very cute Burgessesque numbering: Anthony Burgess contrived the number of chapters in 'A Clockwork Orange' (published in 1962)to reflect the then age of majority at 21.

Vita is already there; as is she also, we contend, wickedly referred to by the Professor as such; in the Letters.

Winston Churchill may well already be in on the Professor's act; as we are to include his most famous speech in ours: and now for one more; of Hitler and the Nazis-

'We want no parlay with you and your grisly gang who work your wicked will.'

(And all Hobbit lovers will notice Winny's Celtic triplicities.)

We may not leave the Buckland area, home to Blenheim Palace and the Marlborough dynasty, without reference to the passion of our greatest War Captain in deed, and word and sound; holding it all together when all may have seemed hopeless and lost-

'Even though large tracts of Europe and many old and famous States have fallen or may fall into the grip of the Gestapo and all the odious apparatus of Nazi rule, we shall not flag or fail. We shall go on to the end. We shall fight in France, we shall fight on the seas and oceans, we shall fight with growing confidence and growing strength in the air, we shall defend our island, whatever the cost may be. We shall fight on the beaches, we shall fight on the landing grounds, we shall fight in the fields and in the streets, we shall fight in the hills; *we shall never surrender*, and if, which I do not for a moment believe, this island or a large part of it were subjugated and starving, then our Empire beyond the seas, armed and guarded by the British Fleet, would carry on the struggle, until, in God's good time, the new world, with all its power and might, steps forth to the rescue and the liberation of the old.'

'One for the Shire!' cried Aragorn.

The hobbit's bite is deep with sting, in a tight spot, underground in Moria … up the road ahead …

'A Short Cut to Mushrooms … Gone Wrong'

The following exposure of Professor Tolkien's design may be quite obvious to the Tolkien Boys, but perhaps not to the rest of the Audience; and, once again, the Author came to terms with it quite late in the day, actually only upon attempting to put together the Author's Map 'A Short Cut Gone Wrong'. One starts from the premise that on leaving Hobbiton, Frodo's ultimate destination is Rivendell, because that follows Gandalf's suggestion for the safety of the old road. The Tolkien Boys will know that Aragorn picks up on the hobbits' intending but mistaken 'short cut' route later at Weathertop, asserting that his own *never* go wrong.

'Why does Hobbitses
Languishes in the Marishes,
My Luvvs?'

Of the Brandybucks Buckland …

'And no wonder they're queer, … if they live on the wrong side of the Brandywine River, and right agin the Old Forest. That's a dark bad place, if half the tales be true.'
(Daddy Twofoot, A Long-expected Party)

After catching glimpses, Frodo decides to take a short cut through woods to avoid the road where the Black Riders are more likely to be encountered. His intending destination is Crickhollow, his new house where Frodo intends to rest at least overnight. To reach Crickhollow within the Brandybucks Buckland, the company must traverse The Marish in order to cross The Brandywine River at the Bucklebury Ferry. That route, rather than head for the Brandywine Bridge north of Stock, saves a quarter of the journey. Going straight, Frodo estimates the shortened distance some eighteen miles.

There is field after field of close description of geographical features following their cutting through dense woods, which may or may not be the extensive trees of Ditchley Park of our map, Churchill's secret hide-away in the War; chosen for the tree cover of its approaches, invisible from the air, the Germans may not even sight the mansion hidden within, let alone target it for damage: but the Audience will, indeed, through the clouds, and we happen to believe that the Hobbits came this way too: whilst our roaming may be a little over romantic here, there may be clues hidden in these parts ... if they are to be seen at all ...

'I will follow you into every bog and ditch' ... Their course had been chosen ... to cut slanting through the woods ... until they reached the flats beyond. Then they could make for the ferry over country that was open ... He soon found that the thicket was closer and more tangled than it appeared. There were no paths in the undergrowth ...'

Ditchley qualifies as the only concentrated barrier of woods before open country beyond, and it was chosen in wartime for its density and thick cover, even from the air. Reference to *ditch* strikes a line back to *rush* in the context of the Windrush, back in Magic Mirror Maps.

Yet one river-reference (slightly further southerly of the Evenlode, which for convenience we cross a little way further on) needs mention in particular...

"Why, this is the Stock-brook!' said Pippin.'

Reading forward our Second Flitch at Stock, this river we take to be the River Windrush. The Author's Map 'A Short Cut Gone Wrong' aims to show as much.

The Audience may need reminding of this quirk of the Hobbits' journey which is not at all readily deducible in the Professor's intent by looking at The Ring-Maps (nor the Shire Map) ... at least, not by the Author ... until one studies the text, paying close attention to the Professor's carefully chosen words, which are these ...

'... Pippin said: 'I hope we have not turned too much to the south ...'',

and a few paragraphs later ...

131

'… they now saw that they had, in fact, turned too much to the south …'

It becomes plain to see (not least from the Professor's repetitive words of how far they have indeed gone wrong southwards in direction) that the Hobbits head south from Hobbiton through The Marish, yet, unbeknown to them, much too far south of where they intend, only to realise they have made a mistake, and so then (taking in the scenery with Farmer Maggot) have to change direction northward of Maggot's Farm, to be taken by Maggot by cart to the Bucklebury Ferry, thence onwards to Crickhollow.

As queer as The Old Forest is to be, this turn on their heels, (if not a full 180 degrees) like soldiers on the march at the end of a column, is even queerer until one accepts that the Professor is following a route pre-planned around the Secret Shire: the reason being (in the Author's logic) that the Professor plans first, from Hobbiton,(under the guise of a visit to Crickhollow and then a mistake in taking that route) to take in the area of The Marish (being parts of Oxfordshire on the River Thames), then the Brandybucks Buckland (including, and this indisputably, Brandy Hall representing Blenheim Palace)and (not least because of its dread reputation for paganism, and, perhaps, witchcraft), then the Wychwood (of Mother-earth) and thence to head northwards to The Barrow Downs, of much the same reputation.

> **'… before the motor car, before the wheel,**
> **before the duchess-faced horse,**
> **when we rode the daft and happy hills bareback …'**
> (A Child's Christmas … Dylan Thomas)

The Nogood Boyo caroused these parts in the late 1930's (as we shall be hearing) and a sense of *daft and happy*, childlike, playful fun is (to the Author's mind) growing slowly in the story. Frodo and Sam and Pippin and Merry are but children on this early outing (but see how they grow up fast), and is it not *children* who get lost for no apparent reason …

The almost inexplicable wandering about irritates somewhat, tending to a wonderment about, perhaps, literally, wherever is all of this leading to? Then there is Tom Shippey's reminder of a necessary acquired familiarity with landscape, all building slowly towards the drama in The Old Forest. The true explanation may be that Professor J.R.R. Tolkien walked (from his Oxford base) the talk, drew a map, and then talked the walk in the text of The Lord of the Rings, and then ... left the travelogue behind him for us all to uncover where the Professor had as a matter of fact (and fantasy fiction) been on his travels ...

Gollum: ... Gerron wivvit, Awffer Mas-sster ...

Smeagol: ... yes, indeed, My Luv, make haste! Time is short ... (grinning) ... a bit like wot hobbitses is like! ...

'Now, little boy lost, He takes himself so seriously ...'

The detour (ostensibly to get to Crickhollow) southwards requires some rationale, given that Hobbiton to the Barrow Downs is as straightforward in Middle-earth as indeed it is on Mother-earth(Chipping Norton to The Rollright Stones); and the explanation is that the Professor clearly wishes to bring the sinister aura of the Wychwood of Mother-earth into the plan of Middle-earth.

In other words, if one is starting from Hobbiton (Chipping Norton), why go south at all if one is heading for Rivendell (Great Malvern of the Malvern Hills) ... Later in The Old Forest, the story implies that all of these wrong directions are part of the sinister pull of the Forest itself. It might even be that the One Ring is provoking this attraction into bedevilled territory.

What all of this demonstrates to The Author's own personal satisfaction is that the Professor is not haphazardly creating the storyline without plan for destination, but, literally following what there is and what he sees on the ground. We take comfort that The Atlas Queen of Middle-earth illustrates the same basic progress: we owe her work for the position of Maggot's Farm, having no idea how she wurzelled that one out in all this clodhopping hurly-burly.

'Time let me hail and climb Golden in the heydays of his eyes, ... Down the rivers of the windfall light.'
(Fern Hill; Dylan Thomas)

Many rivers come to the light, to bathe in it, and to flow on into the River Thames, the Brandywine cutting deep though The Marish. The Hobbits are bound to cross the Windrush: the Stock-brook of previous mention. Yet two more watercourses are mentioned on the short cut, *previous to crossing the Windrush ...*

'After some time they crossed the Water, west of Hobbiton, by a narrow plank-bridge. The stream was there no more than a winding black ribbon, bordered with leaning alder-trees... Soon it disappeared in the folds of the darkened land, and was followed by Bywater beside its grey pool.'

One may scan the 'Short Cut Gone Wrong' map to identify The Water as the River Glyme for consistency with one another and their watercourses. The proximity of the Bywater Pool at Enstone adds to this proper conclusion.

"You can come too,' said Frodo, 'and bring all the water-bottles.' There was a stream at the foot of the hill. They filled their bottles and the small camping kettle at a little fall where the water fell a few feet over an outcrop of grey stone.'

This may well be the Evenlode, not named by the Professor at this stage in the text, because it is to be named as the Withywindle a little later in the traverse of the Old Forest. The descriptive materials there indicate that the River is sometimes not much more than a brook or stream.

The Author suggests that if the rivers are right in identity terms, they are crossed in the order they would be crossed heading south on Mother-earth, exactly as in the story, namely Glyme ... Evenlode ... Windrush. The Professor stresses their misdirection south-east, but logically this might mean south-west on Mother-earth.

**'Where lies the Professor's
Short Cut Gone Wrong?'**

Smeagol: ... Audiences can find it for theyselves, My Luvv ...

Gollum: ... yess, precious, muss follow Awffer Mas-sster on Short Cuts-ss maps-ss ...

Smeagol: ... is difficult, we knows, wot wiv Stock an' Tadpole Bridges and Trouts Inns gets moved to Brandybucks Bucklands, My Luvvs... so Author Master reckon upper roads aheadses, My Luv ...

Gollum(smug): ... is-ss los-sst like nas-ssty noser Bagginses-ss atter Back Door in Goblinstowns-ss ... we dursn't expecks-s they's ever gonna finds-ss it, precious-s-ss ... los-sst, los-sst, ... los-sst Audiences-ss is-s, like my precious-ss-ss-ss ...

Blanket Coverage in the Parish

**'What's beautiful about it?' said Pippin, peering
over the edge of his blanket with one eye ...
Frodo stripped the blankets from Pippin ...'**

We think the Professor is grinning like a goblin gurner here, turning us all over with a giggle. Having just crossed the Evenlode, the township next most likely on the road is Witney ... world renowned for the quality of its blankets; the industry, emergent from Victorian times, synonymous with the wool trade.

Dylan's Blanketty Blank Verse in Oxford

'I want to be *good* boyo, but nobody'll let me ...'

But he generally enjoyed himself because he got to know some of the dons there. He wasn't popular amongst them, because they thought he was a bit of a wastrel, so he hung out in pubs and met students.
Thomas certainly lived up to his reputation for liking a drink or two, and was seen regularly at notable hostelries such as The Turf, The Gloucester Arms, The Trout and The Perch.

He would be surrounded by undergraduates eager to hear his stories, including the poet Philip Larkin and another future writer, Kenneth Tynan.'

(BBC News Oxford, 2014)

There is a pub called The Perch in the right area on The River Thames for The Golden one, but the Author prefers The Trout because you get a tadpole on top.

It was right around this area the Nogood Boyo turned the Historian A.J.P. Taylor into a gibbering wreck, forced to pull fully on any comforter near-enough; as well as turning his wife Margaret over a few times, or so it is said, and that is where the wet blanket comes into it; apparently Taylor made his bed and let Dylan lie in it, a right wet one from what one reads of his stuff, such as *A Personal History*.

Margaret had inherited money when her mother died in 1941. She spent some of it on pictures: a Sickert, a Degas, a Renoir, a Utrillo. They began to disappear along with crystal decanters and the piano. Recalled Taylor ...

'I might not have minded so much if it had not been for Dylan's boasting,'

Smeagol: ... wet blanketses ...?

Gollum: ... we'd have smuvverd that wino Nogood Boyo by thisser time ... Ach-ss ...

Smeagol: ... O yes, indeed, My Luv ... smuvverd him wivvit ...

The composer Elizabeth Lutyens was supposed to have heard Thomas say:

'I'll have to see if I can squeeze Maggie's left breast and get some money.'

Gollum: ... shudda squeezed the bowff of 'em an' plays-s *'dubbles-ss yer moneys-ss'* wiv that silly quizzesmas-sster Hooeey's-ss Green ... Ach-ss ...

Smeagol: ... on tellys in 1950's an 60's My Luv, Audiences dussnt knows it ...

The Nogood Boyo spun the Historian, wife rapt in a blanket, around him like a little finger. By the end Dylan had them both tucked up, yet again one might just as easily swap the first consonant ...

'I heard, long years ago, her call, but blew it back;
... Ah, not for me the windblown scarf, ...
The bicycle to the Trout, the arm-in-arm sweatered swing, . .
(Dylan Thomas, uncollected poem)

'Frodo reckoned they had eighteen miles
to go in a straight line.'

We cannot pinpoint the beginning of Frodo's short cut after the incident with the Elves; yet the distance from Chipping Norton (or Enstone of the Bywater Pool) to Swinford Toll Bridge is, in a straight line, anywhere between Fifteen and Twenty miles.

Crossing the Bar(anduin)

'For tho' from out our bourne of Time and Place
The flood may bear me far, ...'
(Tennyson)

'Long ago Gorhendad Oldbuck, head of the Oldbuck family, one of the oldest in the Marish or indeed in the Shire, had crossed the river, which was the original boundary of the land eastwards. He built (and excavated) Brandy Hall, changed his name to Brandybuck, and settled down to become master of what was virtually a small independent country.'
(A Conspiracy Unmasked)

If the Audience is wondering where all of this wandering leads us, it leads in fact to Professor J.R.R. Tolkien's own covert conspiracy. Hidden beneath the history of the Brandybucks Buckland there lies the hidden truth that its features derive from the other side of the Baranduin – Brandywine – River Thames.

Peeping onto our Portrait Gallegory miles and miles and months ahead … in writing to son Christopher in 1944-

'As for what to try and write: I don't know. I tried a diary with portraits (some scathing some comic some commendatory) of persons and events seen; but I found it was not my line. So I took to 'escapism': or really transforming experience into another form and symbol with Morgoth and Orcs … and so on; and it has stood me in good stead in many hard years since and I still draw on the conceptions then hammered out …'

(Letter number 73)

'Through throats where many rivers meet,
the women pray,
Pleading in the waded bay for the seed to flow
Though the names on their weed grown stones
are rained away,'
(In The White Giants Thigh; Dylan Thomas)

Perhaps the headstones look on the Mitford mob at Swinbrook.

Professor Tolkien has secretly drovered a piggy Animal Farm yard across the River Evenlode (Withywindle) to the Brandybucks Buckland, … one might say to join Old Major at Blenheim … in terms of the Mitfords At Home in Swinbrook, the mob morphing over into Stock; and moreover the Tadpole Bridge and the Trout Inn, across the River Thames (Brandywine) morphing into the Brandywine Bridge and The Golden Perch: and much more over in terms of broad association with …

… the Mitfords, upon the revelation that they belong together with their Spencer/Churchill cousins, and the Audience may research that connection (through Clementine Churchill, nee

Hosier) for yourselves: the first Lord Redesdale married a Hosier of the same family. The real pub in Stock (Swinbrook), The Swan, has a picture of both families together in a swimming party, at Asthall, the Mitfords' first family home, of recall in our Portrait Gallegory.

For you Lords, Ladies, maids and footmen, even (just like Bottomlie Grubbs, crawling in the swim, down below), you lowliest serfs amongst the Audience, doing something or other in one's sluice, the Shire of the Professor's day is where you will find yourselves in the reality show of a Downton Abbey of the Professor's times: from the decadence of the 1920's into the decade following, on into the stark contrasts of 1930's strictures of hierarchical society in England beyond compare, indeed anywhere else in Europe or planet Earth; and it took a depression and a war to change all that.

'My pathway led by confusion boats
Mutiny from stern to bow'

Of course, the confusion in geographic terms (between Buckland Village and the Brandybucks Buckland) is now explicable, because the Professor has half-inched (on the maps) the name of the Village, together with two of its features, Tadpole Bridge and the Trout Inn, together with the connotations of Swinbrook, and rafted them over the Rivers Evenlode and Thames, to join the Brandybuck Churchills; and now indeed we do hear dogs ...

'Grip! Fang! Wolf! Come on, lads!'

The Tolkien Boys will be baying for blood, for at this stage we still have plenty to prove, lads, or to be shown not proven at all ...

Smeagol: ... We shall see, O yes, we shall see!

When all is said and done, it takes a map to understand these anomalies and 'A Short Cut Gone Wrong' is our effort; probably gone wrong, even around the bend; or, dropping from the clouds through the trees, nuttier than squirrel poo; as, indeed, this may be ...

'Queer'

A world-famous Oxford story from a new angle: the essential role played by the River Thames in the creation of Alice's Adventures in Wonderland and Through the Looking-Glass.

It was on rowing trips with Alice Liddell and her sisters that Lewis Carroll (the Oxford don, Charles Dodgson) invented many of the tales which were later incorporated into his two books; it was on the river bank on 4 July 1862 that Wonderland had its birth; and it was from particular incidents on or near the Thames that Carroll drew inspiration for some of the best-known episodes.

(Publicity, Alice in Waterland; Mark J. Davies, 2012)

We have already introduced the 'looking-glass' connectivity with Alice, by the medium of the 'Jabberwocky' poem, and also now proffer this: (reference 'Alice, Huck and Tom') earlier …

Smeagol: … so's to mean hobbitses, My Luvvs …

'[the hobbits get] lost in The Marish in the approaches of The Old Forest on the exact same stretch of the River Thames … as a glimpse at the 'Short Cut Gone Wrong' should show …'

… and so, the hobbits boldly go where Alice has been before … on a waterside-trek, rather than a star-side one, albeit the Professor's exit from The Old Forest may remind of travel by time capsule … enter 'Lost In Space', up the road ahead. We should add that some of the Professor's favourite reading was 'science-fiction' … of which of course there are firmaments in The Lord of the Rings.

Perhaps also a parallel universe in that Professor Tolkien was to create a story based on the geography of places he knew so well; just as Lewis Carroll had done before with Alice: but adding maps of the 'Jabberwocky' poem kind, legible only back to front, as in the mirror.

Lewis Carroll and J.R.R. Tolkien are both Oxford Dons in love with their river-based Oxfordshire surroundings, so much so that they hide them in the scenery of their fantastical works; yet doubly fantastic upon realisation that the Oxford scenery is one and the same from Alice to The Marish of The Rings.

Meant to synthesise the goings-on in The Old Forest, 'queer' is a most unusual choice of word, which one might avoid these days for its connotations of sexual orientation; and indeed the word displays its vintage, because it would be so dated as to time-travel the user way back a century or so, to say Victorian or Edwardian times.

The word is indeed in continual use in Lewis Carroll's 'Alice's Adventures in Wonderland' and we believe Professor J.R.R. Tolkien may have adopted it from there, for use in The Old Forest: it being one of the originals of fantastical writing that we know. Is there any other comparable example of a nonsense world which nevertheless allows one to step inside it, believing it may exist? Truly a secondary world, born of suspension of belief.

There may be yet another; in 'A Clockwork Orange', where Anthony Burgess uses the phrase 'as queer as a clockwork orange': of which more juice from the blood orange in Appendix C ... real beautiful, My Luvvs.

From 'The Pool of Tears' ...

> *"Dear, dear! How queer everything is to-day!*
> *And yesterday things went on just as usual.'*

This is a truly lovely, wonderful, magical world because one escapes the cruel, pitiful, tragedy of everyday real life occurrence, which don't happen in the unreal world: unless one chooses to *write* it that way ... *Gollum, Gollum, Gollum ...*

From the closing paragraphs ...

> **'So she sat on, with closed eyes, and half believed**
> **herself in Wonderland, though she knew she had**
> **but to open them again, and all would change to**
> **dull reality ... and all thy other queer noises, would**
> **change (she knew) to the confused clamour of the**
> **busy farm-yard ...'**

And here now is the Author's werry own queer wally world.

Walrus Walter Below Stairs

**'I'm not strange, weird, off, nor crazy,
my reality is just different from yours.'**
(Cheshire Cat, Alice in Wonderland)

Bottomlie (pronounced 'Bottomlee') 'Walrus' Walter Grubbs was a strange fellow in many respects, not least physically. He sported a heavy Walrus moustache, hence the nickname, straight out of the Victorian or Edwardian era, like Lewis Carroll and Alice, but this growth was the result of deep trauma. The long moustache, below jawline level, masked a rather unfortunate pair of oversize incisor teeth which, if one were thinking on the dark side, brought to mind the Nosferatu, the vampire such as is embodied in Dracula. Now the Nosferatu (as the name translates in Latin) implies nocturnal activity only, and the same may be said of Bottomlie Walter Grubbs in the account that follows. It is commonplace that certain species of the animal, bird and fish kingdoms (fox, owl and such as dogfish) only come out at night, but that is nothing to do with their teeth, which must be false because birds do not have any.

The impression received was not unlike the legendary Mark Twain, whose look is iconic, and who we all know by now had a perchant for rivers and water, notably the 'Big Muddy' Mississippi, as even the surname of his huntin' shootin' an' fishin' hero, Finn, would tend to prove. If anything, Grubbs's growth was twice that of Twain. In his own words …

**'You can't depend on your eyes when your
imagination is out of focus.'**

Yet there was one further similarity. Any image of Mark Twain reveals the piercing, beady, almost boss-eyed gaze of a person on the lookout for something, and not knowing quite where it is: double vision, but this time myopic, rather than iconic; Bottomlie Grubbs suffered an equally curious squint which made him look as if he was searching the bottom of a private world, or indeed, globe, again rather like certain fishes, for instance the scavenger varieties. On one view, it may have been entire self-consciousness which caused Bottomlie to look down upon the moustache, which was so prominent down there, he could hardly take his eyes off it.

A child of the 1960s, the poor teenage Grubbs had suffered terribly at the mocking tones of the lyrics in John Lennon's 'I Am The Walrus', song and of course it didn't help that during that period Lennon was wearing one too …

'I am the walrus
Goo goo g'joob, goo goo goo g'joob …'

… which other cruel teenagers would verbally abuse him with, even in the street; Walter literally couldn't get a walrus out of his head, like Kiley Minogue, but without whiskers and those scary teeth; we cannot imagine how he suffered beside the swimming lake in the old woods, (not a modern day tiled pool at all) but very close to the wonders of nature where, apart from the occasional shout of derision, the young Walter always felt entirely at home, dipping, and dripping, in and out of the water, inspired as a very young lad by Frankie Howerd singing (which had caught on by 1949 in England, but was a number one hit in 1939 in the USA, the other side of the pond, as it were, because on this side at the time we had other fish to fry in France) … 'Over In The Meadow' (or sometimes called 'Three Little Fishes') …

'"Swim" said the mama fishie, "Swim if you can"
And they swam and they swam all over the dam
Boop boop dit-tem dat-tem what-tem Dee!
Boop boop dit-tem dat-tem what-tem Dee!
Boop boop dit-tem dat-tem what-tem Dee!
And they swam and they swam all over the dam …'

… but the written lyrics do not do it justice, and Frankie makes the place sound more like a fish.

The lad Walter was indeed so much inspired that the youngster, (who intended a career in service to the Aristocracy, so he had better learn to crawl) could swim underwater, length after length, around and around, which made the taunts of 'Fishface' a little more bearable because Wally couldn't hear them down there. Nor, of course, could *Walrus Wally* or *Walrus Chops,* as he was derided, be seen.

Below Buck Hill Manor: Grubbs Up

Bottomlie Grubbs the Butler, generally *Grubbers* above stairs, but to the younger members of the haristocracy 'Grubby', by way of sign of affection,(yet perhaps something to do with the particles of Shipphams fishpaste left over from breakfast, clinging on the big moustache like limpets), father a footman gone upstairs in the world, … dredges up from his leaking recess in a cubby hole down belowstairs, mud and sludge all over his plimsoll line, making a change from the swimming fins Grubbers mostly splishy-splashes about with in the water that floods everywhere down there below, like a waste-hole with no plug, to wash away the nasty smells of one's iffy, sniffy, staff and stuff … and drudgery his trade, trudges ever upwards, frogspawn and tadpoles in his pockets, a lit candle protruding from an empty tin of tuna strapped to Walter's sternum, with strong purple rubber bands from Pilates stretched around below his armpits, trayed up fishplates and knives balanced *Billingsgate Bobbin-like, other arm akimbo like Africa, on the mohawk mountain ridge of spiny hard skin crested over the top of his grubber head, nape of neck to mid-forehead, a bit fishy as one Doctor was of the opinion … but with the deepest disrespect in his heart, meaning to bite back this very night with a serving of poison, gruesomely and gloatingly mis-spelled *poisson* on the menu card, stuffed with Ricin, reduced from castor beans growing in the Buckland Bog, and brought back from over there by Algernon Lord Redesdale …(Algie the Bulge he was called behind his back and huge belly too, and nothing to do with any battle) … on his haughty cultural travels in foreign parts, now enters their Lordships' dining room to the call of 'Sua' (His Lordship's demeaning Tamil word for *pig*) which M'Lord uses merely to remind Grubbers of where he comes from and belongs, wishing poor Wally all imaginable ills before kicking Grubbers under the table so as to remind him not to forget he's a place …

---

*   Hat worn by porters in London's old Billingsgate Fish Market, God rest her Soul: Billingsgate Hats (1949) Youtube.

"Before you choose your wish son You better think first
With every wish there comes a curse"
(Bruce Springsteen)

That kicking gave Walter the blues like no one since ol' Wally Trout
on guitar, by no coincidence a Walter too, and with an album out
called *No More Fish Jokes*; but that was not at all a good sign for
a devout Christian such as Walter Grubbs, given what the butler
swore, which was *'Holy Mackerel'* leaping out of Walter's hairy
fishface gob with a gibber like a kipper slip-sliding from a box;
determined to redeem himself for the blasphemy, and to wash his
gullet out with some words watered-down, Walter cursed the Lord
of Buck Manor to *go take a running jump in the River …*

(to follow with the Hobbits, lost in The Old Forest)

Honnish, Boudledidge and Hitler Above Stairs

… and is there any sense on the Menu tonight …

(… to the chatter of pestering *honnish, bred from the class of
mouthed birds and sucklings, in pidgin-smidgen, frivolous english,

---

*   (*In childhood, the sisters developed a secret language Jessica Mitford recalled
in a biography of her sister Unity:*
*"Boudledidge grew up in a very primitive fashion. Pal was Bal, equals Baddle,
equals Boudle. Ch would be je; picture would be bigjure or bigjer; chair would
be jer. T was d, and it went from there of its own accord. We were starting it at
about the age of seven, and went on perfecting it until about ten. The language
had to go with facial expression, which was one of great sorrow, and the noise
was pressed out of the side of the mouth. 'Uuge and objegzionalbe' I called her,
and when we quarreled I would urge her to 'gommid id', meaning that she
should go and commit suicide – when she did, my mother reminded me of that,
as though I had second sight.*
*As for Honnish, that was a language between Debo and me. Kenoy is
Honnish for hen, so a phrase like 'in a woy kenoy' in Bobo's letters is a
borrowing, she would have been too old for Honnish, which was more an
accent than anything else."*
Unity Mitford: A Quest, David Pryce-Jones, Weidenfeld and Nicolson,
1976.)

145

… *wondair, … d-a-a-a-hling, Oh ee ees wondairful! …)

… to *taste* bolly luvvly bubbly, full to jowls jolly, to *smell*, gannet of fish-dish, plattered up posh-shape, to *see*, family all luvvly, our greedy tummy jubbly, and to *touch*, assbones jaw-jaw ugly, chump champions chomping …

… and to *hear* the final whisper of pidgin-smidgen-boudledidge, tailing off in a whimper of prayers unheard or ignored, and crying …

Heil Hitler!

… leading us darkly to Who's-Who's ironcross opinions, bitte union with Fritzy, unter Haw Haw jewbones uberlord lying, strangled gastrofried genocide to make their eyes water, what with *work making one free*, in Auschwitz, ashes and sackcloth…

… don't you agree, Grubbers, old fishface, as you lie low with the other pond-life, out in the cold …?

(pike-dives under kick below table) … cold, indeed so, My Lord …

(do remember, My Lord, as we bow, scrape, curtsey yet curse you below stairs … revenge is a dish best served *cold* …)…

… Yes, M'Lady … will that be all, Your Ladyship …?

Gollum: … Lordy, Lordy! … not to forget, precious-s, Prufessur Tolkkun is hearing all w-w-weerds-ss langwidges-ss in W-w-w-aymoots-ss-ss jess over Brandywines-ss-ss … see *Short Cut Gone Wrong* mapses …

… and so now … our saturated Audience sated of all honnish pidgin-smidgen senses and all boudledidge nonsenses … the final of toasts, the brandywine salutation of solution for meinhost …

Sieg Heil! Sieg Heil! Sieg Heil!

----

*   The House of Mitford; 2004: Jonathan Guinness

Achtung! Achtung! Achtung!

Smeagol: … dreadful, dreadful, *dread-fullest* danger, Author Master, Smeagol's fishbones shake to think of it, Author Master … and so it was to be, My Luvvs …

> **'The branch of the linden is leafy and green**
> **The Rhine gives its gold to the sea**
> **But somewhere a glory awaits unseen**
> **Tomorrow belongs to me …**
> **But soon, says a whisper**
> *Arise, arise, tomorrow belongs To me!'*

… and to worm me out of this struggling cabaret canteen of cutlery: nothing but a menial, modest, shallow road bridge leading over the Windrush into Swinbrook, a lowly entrance, limp like a wormlet lying low before The Swan, (and with no recognition by name so far as we know), nothing like a perch (and more like the straggling wriggle … 'lowly, slowly' … of Ted Hughes-worm-squiggle; emerging with badgers from the darkness ahead); and so Professor Tolkien brings the Tadpole Bridge and The Trout Inn over from the Buckland of Mother-earth and disguises them here in the Brandywine Bridge and The Golden Perch with the pigs at Stock, that is to say Swinbrook on Mother-earth; being the brook of the pig swain: which means that the ancient ferry (before there was any bridge) at Swinford Toll Bridge might well represent the Bucklebury Ferry on its own discreet (from any bridge) stretch of the imagination.

'This little piggy went home …'

If this rationale appeals to our Audience, it is remarkable how the migration bears comparison with the foundation of Buckland by the Oldbucks thence Brandybucks at Brandy Hall. One is so tempted to say (and we have once already) that the Professor drovered the Mitford mob home …

And am I falling off my own by suggestion that a 'Golden Perch' might suitably cage and capture the Mitfords in their semi-regal, lordly and haughty, high and mighty-minded posturings, towering

147

above the rest of us (like Herr Hitler) in superior beings of the Master Race?

Smeagol: … Farve's the worsest, musn't be too unfair on the rests of 'em … but Dianas an' Unitys no angelses neivver, Author Master … Bobo's werry *Uuge and objegzionalbe*, My Luvvs …

Gollum: … Fas-sshis-sst Pigs-ss all ovvem, the precious rings-ss their filffy little neckses-ss allur same times wiv hobbitses-ss-ss … in Germanys-ss upper roads-s aheads-ss … we promises-ss onner precious-ss-ss, yess we does-ss-ss …

Smeagol: … or maybe's they's be drownded before …?

Gollum; … an' that silly Bottomlie Grubbs-ss creechers got sumffing to do wivvit … inner creeps-sy Old Fores-st, not so far aways-ss now, Audiences-ss-ss-ss … better be no songs-ss-ss for Wallys-ss-ss …

Smeagol: … nor any poemses neivver … none poemses … Smeagol does all …

Anguish in the Parishes of the Shire

Time for song in departure from The Marish: warning of a thoroughly nasty and unforeseen turn of events off and on the old road ahead from The Old Forest to Rivendell …

> **'In rather vulgar lettering**
> **A very disgruntled group**
> **Have posted bills**
> **On the Cotswold Hills …**
> **There are bad times just around the corner,**
> **There are dark clouds hurtling through the sky …**
> **… prepare for depression and doom and dread,**
> **We're going to unpack our troubles from our old kit bag**
> **And wait until we drop down dead.'**
> (There Are Bad Times …; Noel Coward: 1952)

RING M III:
The Old Forest

'I'll walk to the depths of the deepest dark forest'

One commentator (Massingham, Wold without End, infra) speaks of the once vast extent of the Wychwood, to the west of Oxford and far, far beyond, and it is at the Council of Elrond that Elrond shares what must be regarded as one of Professor Tolkien's perceived tragedies in nature …

'… of the Old Forest many tales have been told: all that now remains is but an outlier of its northern march. Time was when a squirrel could go from tree to tree from what is now the Shire to Dunland west of Isengard. In those lands I journeyed once, and many things wild and strange I knew …'

For the record ('Y Viva Espana'), we place Isengard in the northern Spain of Gondor.

The caption line is self-explanatory. The deep darkness is relieved by Tom Bombadil and Goldberry. We meet Tom for the first time here in the Forest, and we are to meet them, very much to the Author's distraction, once again, and again, and again; it is we (a personal opinion) who are relieved when they finally leave the scene; but we say more of Tom and Goldberry up the road ahead at The Barrow Downs.

Middle-earth

'Make me thy lyre, even as the forest is: …'
(Ode to the West Wind; Shelley)

The account is in Chapter 6, the Old Forest.

Fatty Bolger is a fifth Hobbit. He leaves now. Merry finds a brick-lined tunnel through the Hedge leading to an iron-barred gate. They have now officially left the Shire and are on the edge of the

Old Forest. Fredegar is mentioned. Fredegar is an easy corruption of Tredegar, a Welsh valley mining town. One supposes the 'Eager Fred' elision was of amusement to the Professor.

The portents of the Forest are all ominous. Explicitly, the trees do not like strangers. The woods are at one stage described as 'abominable.' The trees once attacked the Hedge. The Hobbits put the offending trees on a bonfire: Bonfire Glade is a wide bare circular space encircled with trees like a wall. The trees surrounding the Glade are denser and thicker. It is at once to the Hobbits 'dreary' but also 'charming' and 'cheerful' after the closeness of The Forest.

A tree crashes down once they resume their path.

This is hinted as deliberate.

The path is climbing upwards when they come to a setting which is levelling out. They have reached a green hilltop, with no trees, metaphored as a bald head above the thick forest fringe beneath; like (the Author's words) the Monk's tonture.

The Hobbits can see the line of the Withywindle River and, also the faint lines of The Barrow Downs in the distance: the Downs have a 'sinister' reputation amongst Hobbits, like the Forest.

They cannot see the East-West Road.

Going Wrong Still

The drift south and east (as opposed to the intended northerly direction) which first went wrong through The Marish, is picked up once more …

' … they had lost all clear sense of direction, though they knew well enough that they had long ceased to go northward at all. They were being headed off, and were simply following a course chosen for them – eastwards and southwards, into the heart of the Forest and not out of it'

A huge Willow Tree engulfs Merry; the others rescue him by means of fire: Tom Bombadil to the rescue.

The two notable specifics are the Bonfire Glade and the bald-headed hill.

Mother-earth

> ...' **What if my leaves are falling like its own!'**
> (ibid.)

Lost in Space

Before we enter the Old Forest, and before we overlook the further relevance of the fiction about the pull south-east, we can perhaps confirm our theory of why the Professor creates the story so: answerable by the Hobbits' directional, once escaped from the Old Forest with the help of Tom Bombadil; thus ...

'Then suddenly the trees came to an end ... They stepped out from the Forest ... There was Tom Bombadil's house ... behind it a steep shoulder of the land lay grey and bare, and beyond that the dark shapes of the Barrow-downs stalked away into the eastern night.'

The Rollright Stones would be easterly but northwards from the edge of the Wychwood.

Our sub-heading 'Lost in Space' is deliberate: trees do not suddenly end at the forest edge nor does one step out of the forest in any normal sense. These are not naturalistic descriptive features at all. Perhaps the Professor creates a literary time-capsule (of evil) in which all sorts of strange and queer things may develop, rather like the Doctor's Tardis; who knows?

Smeagol: ... We doesn't know, and we doesn't want to know ...

Gollum: ... Gerron wivvit, Awffer Mas-sster,... Audiencess missing me already ...

151

Smeagol: … *us*, My Luv, it is *us* Audiences is missing …

Yet we now know a lot more about fantasy worlds, such as that of Alice in her 'queer' Wonderland.

Down On The Ground

The West Oxfordshire District Council's list of Scheduled Ancient Monuments cites the following at Monument Number 21774: Pair of Bronze Age Barrows situated on Maple Hill in Wychwood Forest. Further, from the Heritage Search afforded by the Council online: consists of 2 barrows located on the highest point of Maple Hill … Bowl barrow 2350BC – 701BC.

We immediately presumed that Maple Hill was to be of interest, because, from our quest in The Hobbit, the Professor borrows barrows … by the barrowful … for our many sitings on our quests: which, interresting, indeed it proves; but first …

Light Finds the New Places We Tread: Crickhollow, Newbury, Standelf, Haysend and the Withywindle

Crickhollow

**'It's easier to fool people
than to convince them that they have been fooled'**
(Mark Twain)

We had already to our satisfaction shared the affinity of 'Crickhollow' with 'Crickhowell' in Wales, but that has its own Welsh heritage: Crughywel: we translate 'Crug', the vowel pronounced 'ee', the 'Rock' of 'Hywel', a Welsh prince.

The 'Crickhowell' of Wales paints a dramatic picture in Volume II of the Quest. The Author is unable to resist the temptation to have the Audience preview the 'Tower village'; but that preview will require the Welsh Dictionary and a map of the environs of Crickhowell.

Not to tease, look for 'Tretwr' and a little insider-knowledge: the Professor dwelt hereabouts in writing The Rings; and the further gem, at yet another *'Buckland'* nearby: Buckland House in the Welsh Marches, familiar from our quest in The Hobbit, and to be revisited in Volume II.

Weird, but a reality; not unlike the Old Forest.

'Crickhollow' and 'Newbury' are part of the Professor's ubiquitous word name games by allusion, which were to remain amorphous over so many of the Author's wasted hours of confustication … a hangover from The Hobbit; yet anonymous until we stopped fussing about choice of words; and kept things simple; in the cerebral sense: empty headed.

We would not have snapped out of our confustication but for the relativity of the location of both to Brandy Hall (Blenheim Palace) and the Brandywine (River Thames) upon the Shire Map. This was a case of plotting from the Shire Map on to the OS map of Mother-earth for places relative to Blenheim . We eventually settled upon Wotton and Hollybank: the word-play being tortuous and open to further conjecture, even ridicule; yet it is the Author's best inkling.

'Crick' 'Hollow' ('Only fools and horses work')

'Crick' is as pain, as in 'pain in the neck'; 'hollow' is as in 'wooden' as in 'empty-headed': thus 'Wotton' denotes empty headed pains in the neck. We had in our Portrait Gallegory, already identified a safe candidate for 'Lobelia Sackville-Baggins' within the 'vacant' society, the veins and vains of pre-World War II society in England, meaning Vita Sackville-West), seemingly observed and abhorred by the Professor; just as nature abhors a vaccuum; another empty space. Madresfield, (revisited at Rivendell), may have played a part as the Professor looked down from the heights of the Malvern Hills, and we pay them a visit some miles off in the distance.

The Professor will no doubt have full in view the Mitfords, sometime considered National, not Treasures, but Disasters. Churchill bangs Diana up, with husband Oswald Mosley, in prison for not God's sake but for the sake of Adolf Hitler: Nazi admirers, sympathisers, and indeed advocates of the form of fascism dictated by Hitler and Mussolini of Italy that must have Professor Tolkien, and others the like of George Orwell, quaking in their boots: speechless at the perceived madness of thought, word and deed; indeed of a whole attitude to fellow mankind.

The 'no doubt' in terms of the Mitford Sisters evolves to positivity within our Portrait Gallegory, where we identify a definitive correlation between Wootton and the Mitford name; all through the medium of the 'Mitford Letters', which we read with some intrigue there: a glance ahead with the Rangers ... Diana Mitford and her fascist Lothario, lover and leader cum husband live in Wootton Lodge before their imprisonment by Winston Churchill for most of the last War.

'the very biggest spotty dog you ever did see'

We conclude that Diana Mitford and Oswald Mosley are in the mind of Professor Tolkien for the empty heads of the Wotton name: we conclude that the Woodentops (a famed children's puppet show in England) have a place in Crickhollow.

We rely upon old authority for the logistical connection-

WOOTTON, a village, a parish, and a hundred, in Oxford. The village stands on the river Glyme ... The manor belongs to the Duke of Marlborough. Woodleys and Hollybank [form parts of the manor].
(John Marius Wilson's Imperial Gazetteer of England and Wales, 1870-72)

In reality the childlike nature of the Mitfords' existence may be best understood by reference to a game called Follow My Leader or Simple Simon Says where the game-players follow the instructions of The Leader (Diana's epithet for Mosley), or Simple Simon, or else are taken out of the game. It might have been logical to extend the game to Germany for Follow My Führer or Achtung Adolf.

Newbury

We assume that the 'bury' of Newbury derives from the 'Holly' of Hollybank (a wordplay used by the Author, a long way forward at Caradrhas where we are to ask that 'holly' be berried in the mind for future reference), whose 'bank' is, we believe a knowing reference to the nature of the hill at Wotton and so at Hollybank. The Author could not conceivably have known this kind of thing; but there is no doubting the Professor would have known; and so we contribute from the Web-

A Wotton Hill style enclosure is a small square or rectilinear defended site dating to the later Iron Age – broadly speaking the 1st century BC to the 1st century AD. They are characterised by **single banks** *and ditches of a substantial scale, often augmented by stockades and elaborate gateways... the majority being located in Northamptonshire... There are very few examples of Wotton Hill style enclosures in England. Less than ten sites have been recorded, although this number is likely to increase...*

There is presently a stunning photoshot of Wootton Hill on the Web... *Image Title – Wotton Hill is topped by a walled enclosure.*

And so we deem the 'bank' of Hollybank to be a 'new' later vestige of the 'Wotton Hill' style of enclosure; experts may differ for here fresh Light Finds a New Place indeed. Thus 'Hollybank' may be converted to 'Newbury'.

Wootton and Hollybank coincide pretty well geographically with Crickhollow and Newbury.

One day we shall go looking for a bank in Newbury.

Standelf

**'What is this life if, full of care,
We have no time to stand and stare.'**
(Leisure; W.H. Davies)

At this instance we perceive agreement with our old colleague Bill Ready whose mention of the spy-glass required for poring over the Ring-Maps we first heard back in our Genesis. There is some of the Professor's 'cunning devilry' with 'Standelf' of the Old Forest. We made first mention, way back within our dialogue of 'Bag-end' in RING MI, of ubiquitous reference in the Annals of the Wise and the Great to 'Northmoor Road'.

On the Eastern edge of the Wychwood on the map of Mother-earth lies the village of 'Northmoor'; now 'Northmoor Road' is forever indelibly associated with number 20 of that Road; the Professor's family home for many years, from which address numerous of the Letters are written; and living brick legend for the Tolkien Boys: for whom such legend has it that the Professor wrote the words of the childrens' story which started it all: the opening line of The Hobbit; so much legend that the Tolkien Boys recite it verbatim to this day.

The postal town for Northmoor is that of 'Standlake' and we believe the Professor may have simply converted the 'lake' to 'elf' for a reason which, (not unlike an elf), is not immediately apparent, except perhaps that Northmoor (Road) is where all the Professor's business with elves first began.

At one stage, we were reading 'Standelf' as 'Scandelf' and mused over 'Here's Gandalf' but left it there, bemused. We remain unimpressed by other theories presented in such regard; some on the Web are of other etymological sourcing, but we stand by our own; which is in fact best borne out by comparison of the position of Standelf/ Standlake with the positions of Stock, Brandy Hall and Crickhollow on Middle-earth against those of Swinford, Blenheim Palace and Wotton on Mother-earth: in much the same direct northward line.

Haysend

'Where is the boy
Who looks after the sheep?
Under the haystack
Fast asleep ...'

By allusion to the High 'Hay' Hedge, 'Haysend' at the southern
extremity of the Old Forest, that is to say the lower end, is a sheer fit
for 'Lower End' of the Wychwood of Mother-earth. 'Lower End' may
not show on the OS map, but it is here, and local maps will confirm as
much. The Author knows 'Lower End' from the time we went a' calling
on Lord Rotherwick in the Wychwood: we visit Lord Rotherwick; only
to be disappointed, for one must make an annual appointment.

The Withywindle

'My word, you do look queer!'

"That,' said Merry, pointing with his hand, 'that is the line of the
Withywindle. It comes down out of the Downs and flows south-
west through the midst of the Forest to join the Brandywine below
Haysend ...'

By reason that our association of the Old Forest and The Wychwood
are in the Author's mind incontrovertible, it follows that there is
really only one candidate for association with the Withywindle:
this must be the switch off the River Evenlode, throwing a (hardly
natural)line off its main course, wandering through the Cornbury
Park Estate of Lord Rotherwick via several successive channels
darting down off the Evenlode Valley: north-east to south-west to
join the Brandywine River; which as our future researches will seek
to establish, can only be the River Thames.

We reserve our position on 'channels' pending further spadework,
which means lots of digging about for the history of their labours.

Curiously, the flow of the Withywindle pretty much follows the flow
of this(hardly natural) branch of the Evenlode on Mother-earth,
when one might have expected a reversal process(of the Secret of

the Shire) to run the opposite diagonal. This is in fact nothing new (to the Author) of the Professor's scheme of mapping: the Shire Map Enigma has, in the Author's contention, copious instances of whole areas juxtaposed within the Map, yet displaying features within such area corresponding with their lay-out on Mother-earth.

On Mother-earth the main course of the Evenlode does indeed run on to join the Thames, but as such there is no congruence between the Shire Map and the reality of Mother-earth; again this comes as no surprise at all to the Author, the Shire Map being a can of worms hooked up with innumerable wriggles, niggles and wrinkles of eyes squirming nearby in the swim of the Withywindle: Deephollow, Willowbottom and Rushy to name but three of our debate.

The difficulties of worming out derivations in the names of Deephollow, Willowbottom and Rushy follow well (in Volume II) after this Volume I; but the Rangers may like to reflect upon the Professor's Secret of the Shire to cast their own net; and ultimately, we *do* land *all three*.

'There are snakeses, wormses, things in the pools.
Lots of things, lots of nasty things ...'

And after all of the binding (withy) and winding (windle) of the River of the Old Forest and our minding where we are, the Fourth of the Wise and the Great serves to muddy the waters ...

'As for the sudden striking description of the Withywindle in chapter 6, with its drowsy late-afternoon sunshine and through it winding lazily 'a dark river of brown water, bordered with ancient willows, blocked with fallen willows, and flecked with thousands of faded willow-leaves', it would not do so badly as a description of the stream that runs down to join the Thames at Oxford, the Cherwell – a 'very apt name' says Ekwall's *English River-Names,* meaning probably 'the winding river'.'

'The tender Evenlode that makes
Her meadows hush to hear the sound
Of waters mingling in the brakes,

And binds my heart to English ground. A lovely river, all
alone,
She lingers in the hills and holds
A hundred little towns of stone,
Forgotten in the western wolds.'
(The Evenlode; Hilaire Belloc)

It must be said that Web photoshots of the Evenlode might equally
match the description, notably the dirty brown ditch water and
trailing willows; not forgetting that 'withy' of itself implies the
willow, notably from the 'Witham' of Bindbole Wood.

Yet as much as Tom Shippey dewithies our windle ...

The origins of the waters currently working this stretch of the
Evenlode, (through the Cornbury Estate and the valley of the
Evenlode), are buried somewhere in history, but available for
research for those interested in such details. A small shovelful to set
us on our course –

*The 2nd Earl of Clarendon inherited Cornbury from his father in 1674, and
continued the interest in landscaping developed by his father. He had a stone
bridge built over the Evenlode to form a new approach to the house from the
north east side; prior to this the avenues suggest that the main approach was
from the north west.*

Other vestiges of the mid Seventeenth Century are in the Bureau
of Shire-history in Appendix B; which brings us to the Grand
Vista: the chain of reservoirs set in the valley of the Evenlode,
and as we suppose, the Withywindle, of whose origin we are yet
to find a clear view. What we can see (the full history is murky)
of the current layout comprises a series of man-made narrowing
reservoir lakes, visible for all to view on the OS Maps; and
even better to share on the right Website (Geograph: Reservoir
Cornbury Park) which has shots of the reservoirs stretching into
the distance. There is also a shot (Geograph: Wychwood marshy
waters) of presumably what there was before human interference.

Marshy ditchwater fenland, wild and running. The generosity

of such contributors permit us all to share a view of what (we conjecture) Merry was looking at.

History repeats itself travelling, naturally, backwards in time: ironically, in the Prehistoric period, which we may imagine for the setting of The Rings, deep cut valleys would have become natural lake areas following the receding of the Ice Age: much of England would have consisted of the highest mountain and hilltops looming above vast flooded lakelands of water; and man has put the lakes back in places.

No doubt the Professor has Merry looking back on the river valley in pre-history.

Professor Tolkien repeats his own history in another sense; a yearning for the natural state of things, before 'human interference'; we think it most likely that the Professor would have abhorred the construction of a reservoir network, (even Centuries before), where nature once literally took its own course; and here we interfere inhumanely with our own future; a work of words directly from our Volume II:

' ... there is something of a pattern of Lakes flooded by man in the works of Professor Tolkien: quite possibly now [Evendim] Reservoir; and we are to learn of the flooded lake adjacent Caradrhas; and pretty conclusively (for the Author) the 'Lake Town' of 'Esgaroth' in The Hobbit; the Elf-jewel of a clue for any Ranger of the Audience still with us but meaning to progress into Wales; an association we aim to share, if ever we get that far...'

Hence, with the Professor's wry smile, we point with Merry's hand at the Professor's line of poor vision ...

' ... The Withywindle valley is said to be the queerest part of the whole wood – the centre from which all the queerness comes, as it were...'

In the view of Professor J.R.R. Tolkien, so queer to interfere by man-made reservoir with the perfectly created work of Mother Nature.

Waterworks for godsworks, indeed!

*My word, you do look queer.

Binding of the Ring

The Professor has written of his own association with the Wychwood, one of family lineage, in writing to son Christopher, thus in Letter number 95-

' ... the origins of our peculiar people ... For barring the Tolkien ... you are a Mercian or Hwiccian(of Wychwood) on both sides...'

(And which also tells us something of the origin of the worship of 'Wicca' and Wiccan worshippers, as we seem to remember we did on our quest in The Hobbit).

'Tolkien' is the untraced strand in a line which, on the maternal side, is (from Letter number 165) of Worcester of the Shire –

'I am in fact more of a Suffield (a family deriving from Evesham in Worcestershire) ...'

A lovely coincidence, for much of the writing of the Quest derives from Evesham County Library.

Other absorbing features of the Wychwood came to us late in our researches, by this time having visited the Forest with a degree of success which might have been bettered-

The Oxford Cotswold villagers at Leafield exercise their right to enter Wychwood Forest each Palm Sunday to make Spanish Water. The reputedly miraculous spring water of Wychwood was mixed with Spanish liquorice and lemon to make a cure-all to last the entire year. Bathing the eyes in Holy Water – rainwater caught on holy days, such as Easter and the many Saints' day – was always particularly valued.'
                    (Folklore of the Cotswolds, June Lewis-Jones (2003))

---

*   Stanley Holloway

We found out for ourselves. We come on to explain that, not being Easter, we were unable to explore the Wychwood to the degree we wished. We decided to take what we could from the Ordinance Survey Map of the area. We were astonished. To the North of the line of the approved Oxfordshire Circular Walk there are extensive clearings, of no particular shape, well marked in pale Green on the Map. The Key signifies that the pale Green identifies a National Park and Area of Outstanding Natural Beauty. The Darker Green surrounding it identifies Woods and Forests.

Lo and Behold, one sees just below the line of the approved Walk that there is a circular area of less density, as such distinguished by a shading of pale Green, as opposed to the darker Green. It has upon the Map the signage of a Bird Sanctuary.

The incredibly helpful and efficient Geograph website identified the clearing from a large scale OS map. It is called Newhill Plain. There are many fine photographs of the Wychwood and its surroundings on the Geograph website.

To the South West is an area of the same pale Green, again circular and about the same size as the first clearing. This is Maple Hill.

Returning now to Newhill Plain, we were fair flummoxed to discover that this apparently innocuous patch of Green has a notorious history. The Audience is pre-warned that the account of Newhill Fair takes some time; but then again the Fair itself endured over Centuries; until it eventually outlasted its welcome; and whose raucous history is potted in the Bureau of Shire-history in Appendix B.

All's fair game in the Forest, so we leave with an extract from another website:

The original Forest Fair began in the late 18th Century and was held at Newhill Plain Cornbury but ceased in 1856 because of 'drunkeness and debauchery'

We leave the Wychwood in the earnest hope that the account of the affair at Newhill did not bore the Audience, not so much 'out of your tree' but at all. We depart with bells ringing in our ears. Does the name Wombwell (of the menagerie of exotic beasts) ring any bells with anyone but the Author? After all, it is not that far from 'Bombadil', but the Audience is free to suggest we pull the other one, because of what it's got on.

To date we have nothing about a Bonfire. But Fairs do have pig-roasts and they can easily get out of hand, especially when there are so many trees about. In any event, the Professor creates fire of his own in the Wychwood, Sam using fire to extricate Merry from the clutches of Old Man Willow here.

The Wychwood Forest might readily be supposed identifiable as the Old Forest without more, simply by reasons of geographical position; the discovery of Newhill Plain and Maple Hill are considered conclusive by the Author for purposes of association with the Bonfire Glade and the bald hill; and association of the Wychwood follows as night follows day: but beware the night in the old Wychwood; for there is mystery, magical and mystic … and … *Mammon* …

No man can serve two masters: for either he will hate the one, and love the other; or else he will hold to the one, and despise the other. Ye cannot serve God and Mammon.

(Matthew 6:19-21,24)

If only we had the permission of Lord Rotherwick to roam the Wychwood on best behaviour, promising to be good and … not to sneak about like we did the last time …

Rambling Man

'Well, the Lone Ranger and Tonto
They are ridin' down the line …'

The Rangers must stand by their Kemo Sabe … (quien lo sabe; the all-knowing) … through the Old Forest; indeed a loan one is to silver us with bullets any time now; perhaps the 'Ranger' Strider is borne of the Professor's wandering about the Wychwood.

We may know more by Easter.

The Wychwood Forest is in the ownership of Lord Rotherwick and the woodlands are closed to visitors throughout the year, with one exception. As a local informed us, Lord Rotherwick permits the public to walk the Forest on Palm Sunday, the only day of the year when this is allowed.

According to one source as of the time of writing, in late Summer 2010, there has been a spate of thefts. These have been rather getting on His Lordship's wick and the Rangers who protect the Forest have to be wary and watchful of who and what comes in and goes on.

It is not for us to make any observation about His Lordship's policing policy. Visitors with the wrong motives would wreak havoc in these dense woods. The obvious and immediate threat would be fire (a risk inflamed in the Old Forest of The Rings), let alone thefts which are reported from the various business enterprises that have been developed within its perimeters. The Forest is also an ancient Deer Park.

These businesses have the well-being of the Forest at their heart. A number are designed to welcome the public into the Forest by means of outdoor courses for all age-groups.

We dread that one might become judgemental in the matter. Being outsiders it is none of our business; and it would be none of our's even if we were local. We offer the opinion that such security policy seems necessary, sensible and fair, balancing the potential risks against the legitimate means of exploration available. The Author has acknowledged there is much obsequious sneaking about in the Old Forest: we hope to get invited another time because we can't make Easter.

One is reminded of Brian in Python's The Life Of. He was 'a very naaawty boy'; and so once was the Author. Having chosen one that did not have 'Private' or any other forbidding writing on it, the Author climbed a Five bar gate and set out for Maple Hill. We walked a mile or so through dense woods, following a clear pathway with Tractor tyre marks as its fringes. We saw one young Buck which scooted off, calm and unalarmed.

We were wrong about the Tractor tyremarks, as it turned out, or transpired. The Author merely perspired.

We turned left on a similar path, assuming we were skirting Maple Hill. Having left the Road at the Gate, we were now nearly back on it having walked the two sides of a triangle.

O No! Triangles, Pentangles: the Blair Witch Project…

Near the Road, perhaps a mile on the Road from where we started, we came upon two sizeable big–top shaped tents; we should like to say they were hidden and camouflaged into the background of trees, but truthfully they were white. Mind-boggled by who might be stretching out in the woodland so ostentatiously, and their reasons and legitimacy, we hastily hastened our Deliverance out of there.

Duelling Banjoes twanged, arrows flew and it was we who quivered.

We jogged back towards the Five bar gate.

These days we get tired jogging the memory.

'Hi Ho Silver Away …'

Halflingways back, we were ambushed by the only Ranger (other than for Strider, and those of the Audience) who had troubled us all day. He shot like a silver bullet up another track which was masked from view until we were cornered. Given a bit more time, we may have hidden in a bush or up a tree. There are plenty. This lone Ranger rode a powerful Quadbike, not a Tractor, but still a mighty steed. It was not Silver, but Green. Camouflage no doubt.

The Ranger shot from the hip and lip in unison, riddling the Author with a few bullet-pointed questions; he slickly silver-tongued his way into our motives: How had we got here? Why were we there at all?

He marshalled us to 'make your way off' His Lordship's private land. The Ranger was not at all pleased to see me.

The Author deftly fired back a few shots of his own.

Was it possible to access Maple Hill, how big a hill was it, and were there Maples like Canada?

The Ranger spat back 'No', 'not very' and 'a few' to my crazed line of fire, so we called it a draw and the Author hit the road, scouting for another confrontation, maybe a duel, maybe in the sun for a change.

But not without three final cunning, muffled, parting shots; murmurings about Totem Poles, Teepees and Tomahawks.

The Ranger clearly knew Maple Hill well but the same did not apply to any local we met. One young mother, who had given us the information about Lord Rotherwick's walking regime, lived within a half-mile at Lower End but had never heard of Maple Hill; let alone seen it.

We did eventually encounter a Tractor; with a Farmer on it, on Hatchings Lane, which bisects the Forest. As one does, we got stuck behind it on a narrow section. His replies to our questions fell on deaf ears, but that was because he wasn't very willing to turn the Engine off. He did eventually but we were no better off, because neither had he ever heard of Maple Hill. He offered some comforting suggestions about footpaths and Rangers, but we had had quite enough of them by then.

We came to a realisation that nobody had ever heard of Maple Hill because nobody had ever seen it. Not because of Lord Rotherwick's walking restrictions, but because it is buried, or rather, barrowed, out of sight, behind a high treed skyline. Hopefully some are Maples, but we may never know.

Just why is Maple Hill a 'bald' hill for Professor Tolkien, when the Mother-earth name so much suggests a tree covering?

> **'Iago Prytherch his name, though, be it allowed,**
> **Just an ordinary man of the bald Welsh hills,**
> **Who pens a few sheep in a gap of cloud ...**
> (A Peasant; Poem: R.S. Thomas)

We really had no idea until we derived an allusion in Wales, researching the geography of The Hobbit. There we find Mynydd Moel (the Bald Mountain), which at 3,000 feet has no tree covering, just bare rock and scant grass. Mynydd Moel is literally bald; of trees, in any event. There lies an allusion and likewise for those interested in such details, a small clue of the geography of The Hobbit; for it is our belief the Professor transposes the descriptive name: for the easy reason the Professor most certainly knew Mynydd Moel and its environs; and so now will the energetic Ranger come to view The Lonely Mountain of The Hobbit.

We must assume the Professor had in mind the ancient days before the advent of the Maple in the Old Forest, for by the same token we assume that no trees were there when he wrote of the 'bald hill'. We came away, having got so tantalisingly close but never having seen the cut of the Hill's knapper.

Hang about (til Easter).

We never thought to anticipate the Crucifixion like a Birthday or Christmas.

Easter.

We'll be back.

There is yet further Gollumesque sneaking about here. In truth we are aiming for a Lordly invitation to view Maple Hill, whose sad omission we have chronicled like so many Heeps of Uria.

If our association or association has credence, then presumably there were no applicable restrictions in Professor Tolkien's day.

Carpe Noctem (Night Fishing)

'Do you think I've gone round the bend?'
(The Mad Hatter, Alice in Wonderland)

... That same night, very dark already, Bottomlie, fed up to the back of his great incisors, decides immediately to fill the gap in his life, by accepting the engagement with friends mooted (on one's way to Oxford) for some time. Old Walrus Chops was going to a reunion. Walter slithers like a fish out of water would (all wobbly slimy jellied eel style) down the endless stairs to the bottom of the well which lay below his leaky chubby hole lodgings, and dreams of a voyage for getting there, maybe a boat by night ...

... and to dream, of all imaginable creature things, of turning into a cat, and a captain too, once, upon a seasidetown time and tide, having a portrait painted up (for some book or other about the Ring lost in a river of the Shire) of proud-as-a-sealion Bottomlie Walter Grubbs, himself ... in jack tar porthole collar, jaunty cap and *'haul on the bowline'* rope-tuned braiding, of all imaginable jolly roger sailor things ... and sailing away in his dreams on the high seas: to hear a distant voice recognisable from an old catnap, of all imaginable familiar things, under an imagined wood, words out of a liquid world, indeed as whitfurrows waves northerly in the distance there ...

Blind Captain Cat climbs into his bunk. Like a cat, he sees in the dark. Through the voyages of his tears, he sails to see the dead ...

... as shall Walrus Walter this very same night ...

... but our hero holes his boats, and turns to swimming for it. The sodden butler (which M'Lord had indeed once called Grubbers) swam for what seemed hours towards the old wood which was his destination, and underwater all the way, not seeming to take a single breath as he swam along. Someone would be lighting a fire to signal the meeting point in the glade deep in the woods.

'You're mad, bonkers, completely off your head.
But I'll tell you a secret.

All the best people are.'
(Alice, Alice in Wonderland)

Bottomlie sloshed out of the water on the riverbank and shimmied, this way and that, through the dense trees surrounding the Bonfire Glade of the Old Forest. Bottomlie 'Walrus Wally' Grubbs began to feel like he was some kind of big fish; but not in a small pond, because we've gone past that, at the Bywater Pool, if you remember.

There in the Bonfire Glade stood His Lordship in all His Regalia, Master of Ceremonies, in the centre of a crescent half circle; and facing the Master on the outer crescent were all Walter's old familiar friends. Walter took his station amongst them. Was there to be demonic ritual, the coven of covens, a unified gathering of the clans from all parts of the Kingdom … ?

(… but there was no sign yet of the cranky Sturgeon or the bloater Salmon'd from over the border to the north, who must have gone their own way, ignoring any reunion, let alone the old one in the first place …)

'Welcome, my fine fisherman Piscean friend; Grubbs up!'

His Lordship tossed Walter a small piece of pinkish flesh, which might have been a piece of fish, but was, in fact, not; and Walter responded with chortling applause, and clapping like a sea-lion on a platform in the circus in the old days …

**'And they shall be broken in the purposes thereof,
all that make sluices and ponds for fish.'**
(Isaiah 19:10)

(… *a waste-hole with no plug, to wash away the nasty smells of one's iffy sniffy staff and stuff* …)

It was in fact a man's big toe, not a fishfinger but a fishcake scavenged from the foot of the Lord of Buck Hill Manor, indeed the foot kicking the pig under the table that night Walter lured his Lordship into the river with a curse. His Lordship had collapsed into the river very soon afterwards, complaining of severe stomach pains, and some family members suspected Salmonella, for she was always about, splashing aquabiotically in somebody's guts; and many of the family not altogether well themselves. There was very little left of His Lordship of the Manor, his other toe with the rest of him in the belly of a fish, not unlike Jonah.

> **'Imagination is the only weapon**
> **in the war against reality'**
> (Cheshire Cat, Alice in Wonderland)

All because Bottomlie 'Walrus Wally' Grubbs is no pig, for kicking under the table or anywhere else, but from birth a shape-shifting Catfish familiar, indeed scavenger captain, come to worship His Lordship in the Bonfire Glade of the old Wychwood ... Walter's gills are hidden wavering lesions, slits through a skin of scales in the soft throat area, well concealed behind the long Walrus moustache, somehow grown even longer than when you last saw Walter look down upon it ... Yet this is no Lordship known to Man. Walter has assembled in the Old Forest before their Most Worshipful Lord of Shapeshifters and Familiars, in the company of all the frogs, toads, snakes, cats, rats, foxes, rabbits and even the odd badger still left, with all other sundry creatures, shapeshifters and familiars of witches, sitting in an arc like Noah's.

Bottomlie 'Walrus Chops' Grubbs enjoyed the left-overs from his fellow fish-familiars' feed on the Lord of Buck Manor and, quite franky howerdly, flipped over announcement of the next dinner engagement at the Manor, hoping it too would go even more swimmingly for the scavenging catfish captain that is Bottomlie. Perhaps there would be a river bird could be written into his own private menu card for once ...

Smeagol (sings; Joy, Teddie and Babs Beverley):

> **'Sisters, Sisters**
> **There were never such devoted sisters**
> **Never had to have a chaperone, no sir ...'**

Gollum (dark, grim; licks lips):

'I needs to keep my eyes-ss on Her-r-r ...'

FIN

Wandering Star

**'Very old are the woods; ...
... Sing such a history
Of come and gone ...'**
(All That's Past; Walter De la Mare)

As foretold, beware the night in the old Wychwood; for there is mystery, magical and mystic ... and ... *Mammon* ...

No man can serve two masters: for either he will hate the one, and love the other; or else he will hold to the one, and despise the other. Ye cannot serve God and Mammon.

(Matthew 6:19-21, 24)

The discussion of Witchcraft in our Cauldron of Appendix C takes further shape in the area of the Wychwood; not forgetting that the shenanigans of James Pennethorne Hughes were the rage in Oxford of the time of the Fairyseeker, notably also the time of the Professor. So much so that we christen the University town Oxford-Under-Wychwood, an epithet which may well be stretched in terms of the activity of Witchcraft, but plainly not so in terms of comparative geography: the Wychwood has always cast its shadow over the area; and the Author is about to enter that dark shadow ... with the Audience cowering beside ...

**'Who knocks? ' 'I, who was beautiful
Beyond all dreams to restore,
I from the roots of the dark thorn am hither,
And knock on the door.'**
(De La Mare; tbc)

We may already be feeling something out of the ordinary might be going on through the sense of disturbance hidden in the words of

Professor Tolkien. Hints that trees are falling according to an evil design, and the aura of malevolence of the trees and of the forest as a live, contrary, being are all about …

> **'Who speaks? ' 'I – once was my speech**
> **Sweet as the bird's on the air,**
> **When echo lurks by the waters to heed;**
> **'Tis I speak thee fair.'**

One senses antipathy within the Old Forest … Professor Tolkien forewarns of the 'sinister' reputation of The Barrow Downs, of itself in ancient days within the forest skirt; and the Author now forewarns of some very unlikely goings on in the area: we hint in our Cauldron of Appendix C at bloodletting upon Weathertop, and all readers of The Rings will know that Frodo is near fatally stabbed there by the Morgul blade of the Nazgûl King; we are to speak of the Witch Rings of Bretforton in the proximate area and, to name a third, we speak especially of Long Compton whose dread reputation persists to this day …

> **'In gloom groped a hope-wearied hand**
> **Over keys, bolts, and bars.**
> **A face peered. All the grey night**
> **In chaos of vacancy shone;**
> **Nought but vast sorrow was there – …'**
> (The Ghost; Walter de La Mare)

The aura of evil attaching to the Wychwood area is long recognised, and we say so specifically in the early days of the writing of The Rings; for we have the following testimony of H.J. Massingham in 'Wold Without End' published in *1932* …

> **'On your left and on your right**
> **In the day and in the night,**
> **We are watching you.'**
> (Auden; tbc)

'My own view differs from that of my friend, W. Force Stead, who wrote a long and most interesting poem on the district in a

172

volume (The House on the Wold) published in 1930. He clearly recognised its "Unhallowed emanation," but attributed its cause to the "something sinister that hangs over any heathen or pagan countryside," and *it is a singular fact that the Wychwood area was not Christianised until centuries after the rest of the Cotswold.*

But to assume that a pagan locality is ipso facto a diabolised one is to my mind altogether too naive and conventional a reading of the enigma – even granted that there can be something diabolical about a decaying and overripe paganism. All the same, I preferred to examine the more secular evidence. Only a fragment of the immemorial Wychwood Forest now remains in the neighbourhood of Finstock and Leafield. But up to 1863 its dimensions extended from Swinbrook and Woodstock, below Finstock, to north and west of Charlbury. In far more ancient days it reached beyond Rollright, in north-east Cotswold, but the enclosing of its more southerly range did not begin until the mid-Victorian period. Thousands of its great trees were felled, thousands of acres of heath and copse grubbed up and fetched under the plough, so that in a few years all but the present remnant was uprooted.

What is wrong with that country, so I concluded, is that it ought to be forest, was meant to be forest, and now fails, owing to the arbitrary act of avaricious man, to be forest.

It disobeys the primary law of its being; it is false to itself; it longs to say "forest," and only mews a feeble "pasture and cornland." Its spirit is dead, or so mutilated as to have assumed a perversity of expression out of key with its destined life.

Perhaps the conscious human mind manifests this dumb sense of outrage in its own awareness of something macabre in the very air about the scene. Or, if you are an animist, which I certainly am not, and like to put it in another way, the violated spirits of that aged forest have taken their revenge for their eviction and the desecration of their shrines by putting a curse and an evil spell upon the cultivated land that has recently taken its place.'

**'But do not imagine we do not know
Nor that what you hide with such care won't show**

At a glance.
Nothing is done, nothing is said,
But don't make the mistake of believing us dead:
I shouldn't dance.'
(The Witnesses/Two; W.H. Auden)

Gollum (Tim Burton's Joker; Jack Nicholson): … ***ever dance with the Devil …***

Even the redoubtable Author is spooked by this of the Old Forest; and so we fly further as fast as our broomstick will carry us …

No man can serve two masters: for either he will hate the one, and love the other; or else he will hold to the one, and despise the other. Ye cannot serve God and mammon.

(Matthew 6:19-21, 24)

Here they both be …

'When the green field comes off like a lid
Revealing what was much better hid:
Unpleasant.
And look, behind you without a sound
The woods have come up and are standing round
In deadly crescent.'
(W.H. Auden; ibid.)

'Unpleasant'

… By a Witch Tree on Weathertop, in the shadow of The Last Bridge, in the glades of the Trollshaw Hills and in the deluge of the floodwaters of The Ford, we shall there indeed find the Evil One, the wheel of fire still rolling onwards … onwards to the Land of Mordor … where the shadows lie …

'This wheel's on fire
Rolling down the road
Best notify my next of kin
This wheel shall explode …'

174

RING M IV:
The Three Farthing Stone

'I've walked and I've crawled on six crooked highways'

Highways require a marker; we have contemplated six, but at least we have a corner stone of Four Shires, but read on, now down to that magic number three.

Middle-earth

It is fairly easy to get lost on account of the Three Farthing Stone; on account of the Four Shires Stone; on account of it now marking just three Shires.

There are only two references to the 'Three-Farthing Stone' in The Rings; we know so from the Professor's Index of 'Things'. The Professor makes no mention of it on the Hobbits' journey outwards and ultimately to Mordor; but it is a marker upon their return from Mordor and thence to the Shire.

Both mentions are within the trauma of 'The Scouring of the Shire'. The first is oddly casual, of a group under guard walking tiredly through the Shire-

'At the Three-Farthing Stone they gave it up. They had done nearly fourteen miles with one rest at noon…'

The casual speech is a minor example of the Professor's intimacy of internal dialogue. The inference is that we have already seen and know the Three-Farthing Stone, having been with the Hobbits to the Shire before, with the implicit but rhetorical question of why would the Professor bother to tell us any more about it: it simply *is*.

The second is especially emotive, that is to say, looking far forward, if one is attuned to the emotion of the Majesty of the Lady Galadriel at Lothlorien; and to the emotional majesty of the serenity of

Lothlorien: the Lady Galadriel's parting gift to Samwise Gamgee of those remaining of the association of the Ring upon departure from Lothlorien: boxed and gifted 'Mallorn' tree dust-seeds; the Author sows his own seeds of the Mallorn tree at Lothlorien; for us they come to fruition there, far away and further on.

And so to Samwise Gamgee-

"But I'm sure the Lady would not like me to keep it all for my own garden, now so many folk have suffered,' said Sam … Sam planted saplings in all the places where specially beautiful or beloved trees had been destroyed, and he put a grain of the precious dust in the soil at the root of each. He went up and down the Shire in this labour; but if he paid special attention to Hobbiton and Bywater no one blamed him. And at the end he found he still had a little of the dust left; so he went to the *Three-Farthing Stone*, which is as near the centre of the Shire as no matter, and cast it in the air with his blessing …'

Now the Four Shires Stone is a dead-ringer for the Three-Farthing Stone in association terms, except that the severe anomaly of the Shire Map raises its ugly head once more. Before another difficult pairing raises his ugly head by the end of this RING M III, we simply restate that whilst for the moment we nominate the Four Shires Stone in association for the Three Farthing Stone of the Rings, it may be so in *conceptual* terms, but cannot in all truth be so in *comparative geographical* terms: for it is in the wrong place on the Shire Map, were we to apply the Professor's Secret of the Shire.

Nevertheless, by virtue that we would have no means of solving the Shire Map Enigma without, we must first visit the New Places(each of Frogmorton, Whitfurrows, The Yale, Brockenborings and Scary, for those wishing to pre-consult the Ring-Maps) on which we are to shine some new light: without association for the New Places, the Shire Map Enigma would be insoluble; and the enigma may even yet remain so.

The Author is of the belief that, quite frankly, the Professor chose to meet the Stone *coming back,* lest its association with such as

The Barrow Downs and Bree of Mother-earth should make the discovery of the Secret of the Shire too ready and comfortable for his audience.

At least, such is the conjecture of the Author.

Mother-earth

The Four Shires Stone is on the junction of the A44 with the Great Wolford Road and is recorded on all decent maps. The Stone is a large stone monument which reminds one of the first of a pair of imposing entrance gateposts leading to a grand country estate. We guess that it is 15 feet high and perhaps four feet on each of its four sides. The pillar is made of dressed Cotswold stone topped off with a ball finial. Into each of the four faces of the monument is stone-carved a County or Shire name: Gloucestershire, Oxfordshire, Warwickshire and Worcestershire.

The Worcestershire face has a further inscription: THE FOUR SHIRES STONE.

Light Finds the New Places We Tread: Frogmorton, Whitfurrows and The Yale; Brockenborings and Scary

Frogmorton

> 'With their lithe, long, strong legs,
> Some frogs are able
> To thump upon double-
> Bass strings, though pond water deadens and clogs.'
> (Bullfrog; Ted Hughes)

This inkling was spawned somewhere between the name of the former residence of H.M. the Queen Mother at 'Frogmore' in Windsor Great Park and the 'Moreton' of Moreton-In-Marsh, our association of Bree. This association lies, as a matter of fact, between.

Why more Frogslegs, we hear ye all a' croakin'? This final leap of faith was derived from a chance footnote in the writings of Paul Kocher, referencing the poem 'The Mewlips' amongst the verses of Tom Bombadil, a separate (but once more inexorably linked) publication of verse by Professor Tolkien. The reference is to the 'marsh of Tode'. Whilst the Kocher footnote expresses absence of detectable link (unless with 'The Dead Marshes') to The Rings, what of Moreton-In-?

And so we take that big leap with the webfeeted amphibians; and what a Web we spawned: Toad-Marsh: Moreton-In-Marsh: Frog-Moreton; Toad and Frog: Witch familiars or, for the uninitiated, the 'pets' of the Witches called upon to aid the invocation of spells. The Audience may spot a short excerpt of the lore of witches' familiars, within the Bureau of Shire-history in Appendix B.

> **'... Why do I find**
> **this frog so interesting as I inspect its most secret**
> **interior and make it my own? Do these weeds**
> **know me and name me to each other have they**
> **seen me before do I fit in their world? ...'**
> (Wodwo; Ted Hughes)

In the Author's holey-in-the-toad opinion and more song, 'Froggy Went A Courtin' And He Did Ride': to the ancient Witchcraft of Long Compton. The long history of Witchcraft at Long Compton is with us about Weathertop: Witchcraft belongs in Long Compton and so, too, frog(s) and toads about Moreton: and in sound, kneedeep in the marshes here, geographically for its placement on the Ring-Maps.

'Needeep'

Jumping to the question: did Professor Tolkien really spawn this Web?

The Author's exhausted whisper before we croak it: with the memory of the Oliphant, we honestly believe the Professor Mastodon the word to a rebirth. The Oliphaunt makes a slow

178

return in our Volume II; something of a tusk to remember that the Oliphaunt makes appearance in the Rings: proudly recited by Sam in The Two Towers: where Sam humbly 'speaks poetry' as the Professor tells. Why bring the elephant into our Quest? This is not the Circus: indeed not, but those interested in such details may find Websites to suggest that the ancestry of the frog is rebirthed in the Elephant; which is why one never frogets!

Our final parting shop: much retail activity of Moreton-In-Marsh is in the late-night 'hopping about Todenham Road.

Some witches are considered *ugly*, perhaps recognised in a simile heard by the Author only in Wales … 'ugly as a bucket of slugs' … Some witches are considered *mad*, perhaps recognised in a simile heard again by the Author only in Wales … 'mad as a box of frogs' … but I heard this tale of madness from the The Nobel Voice, On The Road Again, (Bringing it All …) …

> **'Well, I wake up in the morning**
> **There's frogs inside my socks …**

I shan't spoil it for you, but the next rhyme is 'icebox'.

Whitfurrows

> **'Mark where the pressing wind shoots javelin-like,**
> **Its skeleton shadow on the broad-backed wave!'**
> (Modern Love; George Meredith)

Our starting point is the definition of 'Tew', which as a noun may mean a rope or chain for towing a boat; and as a verb, to tow along, as a vessel. The image, of itself, visualises the wake of movement through water, hence waves and, by visual association, furrows: inevitably white ones.

The Author had considered the visual allusion on our own part, only to have it confirmed by real experts. In the 'wave and furrow' instance we apparently have an example of the perfect pun; because there is no semantic or functional overlap between waves and furrows, there being pure picture play and reliance upon only visual association. Now the theory of puns is full of details of interest for many, and for those interested refer to the Web (Puns: Hempelmann and Samson) which is where we grooved out the wave/furrow wordplay; tew words so great on the Author's crest.

And so with furrowed brow, we wave to Whitfurrows from Great Tew; which already had a place upon the Quest: we had in any event meant to be a Rambling Man to Whitfurrows within RING M: V (The Barrow Downs).

Great Tew is thus our unequivocal association of Whitfurrows, the most quintessential rustic village of which our future rambling tells.

> **'The river of God is full of water: …**
> **Thou waterest her furrows,**
> **thou sendest rain into the little valleys thereof:**
> (Psalm 65)

The Yale

> **'Well, he puts his cigar**
> **Out in your face just for kicks'**

The association here is so straightforward, we class it alongside 'Buckland' as Professor Tolkien's 'Easy Guide to Middle-earth'; except, of course, that the rest of the guide-book is not at all so easy to follow.

The connections between the paramount (along with Harvard) University of North America and Winston Churchill are such and so many and varied that one might suggest the Professor renders The Yale for the village of 'Churchill' far too ready an association.

Yale supports the Churchill Foundation which sponsors Scholarships to Churchill College in the University of Cambridge. Indeed, connection harks back to the very earliest days of an illustrious career, tantamount one supposes to one of the most ever

scrutinised; and admired by our US cousins …
From the New York Times; December 14, 1900 …

Winston Spencer Churchill, M.P., the young English war correspondent, received an enthusiastic welcome here tonight. Mr. Churchill arrived in this city at 4 o'clock and was immediately taken in charge by the Yale undergraduates, a committee of whom, headed by Capt. Gordon Brown of the Yale football team, showed the visitor about the college. Mr. Churchill was later entertained at the University Club, where hundreds of undergraduates met him.
This evening Mr. Churchill lectured before the university set at the Hyperion, among whom was Lieut. Gov. Woodruff of New York, and was receive with much applause, Dean Francis Wayland of the Yale Law School, whose guest Mr. Churchill is, introducing him. Mr. Churchill's talk was mostly of his own experiences in escaping from Pretoria a year ago yesterday, and of his flight to Delagoa Bay. Mr. Churchill spoke feelingly of the bonds between England and America.
He was given a reception at the graduates' club later in the evening.

No doubt Professor Tolkien's South African birthright will have made him a follower, we do not necessarily say admirer (but suspect so) from early days. The admiration of the USA was clearly reciprocated, especially so when the compliment is expressed in terms of one's abiding passion-

'Meeting Franklin Roosevelt was like opening your first bottle of champagne; knowing him was like drinking it. '

We suggest that The Yale is the unequivocal association of Churchill in Oxfordshire, through our Winny: confirming the more than obvious reason for nominating a Shire nameplace that of a famed American University.

The position relative to Frogmorton and Whitfurrows merely reinforces the association; but with this caveat: mind the position of Churchill to the south of Whitfurrows (Great Tew) on the Ring-Maps; on Mother-earth, Churchill is due south of Long Compton, our nomination for Frogmorton. We previewed difficulties with certain anomalies of the Shire Map. Once more, such anomaly is the subject of our attempt to solve the Shire Map Enigma in Appendix E.

181

Brockenborings (etsetera)

'I warn you, if you bore me, I shall take my revenge.'
(Letter to C.S. Lewis)

This latest new place emerged, the first but not the last time we shall be boring the Audience in a daear (*dire*) emergency, by reason that we looked for a brocken boring relative to Frogmorton; and Shipston-on-Stour emerged to the light, breaking through to the north of Long Compton; indeed snouting out its emergence much where the Author had trusted it might be, consistent with the Professor's Secret of the Shire.

'Badger' is sometimes mochyn *daear* (the pig of the earth, reverting to the old Welsh way of picture-painting, perhaps familiar from 'Magic Mirror Maps'), but whose other name is *Broch*, hence also the 'brock(en)' origin in language. The word 'daear' resurfaces at Tharbad below, in the first root of a haven (dredged of earth) for boats at Gloucester; up the road ahead.

The Welsh word *daear* (more or less *dire*, yet a worse hole to be in ... *die – aaargh!*) is relevant for any number of mountains from molehills, (not least because those skulking, skulping, scrapers are clocking around the block with brock down the borings in a milkwood this very night) and it is a word to bring us all down to it: meaning *ground* or *earth* in Welsh, and, so, fitting tight and snug our emerging game of words, with all emergencies evolving of earth-moving experience, and notice the voles at it too. We suppose that the concept of a boring emergency is *antithesis* worthy of a look in the dictionary to see what it means, day or night.

'Badgers' Bottom'
('stinking to high heaven')

Of mention because it is the name of a cider local (Hayles Farm) to the Shire, also because it shares some attributes of the skunk, but especially for its prescents high in the middle of the air up the road.

Brockenborings has set within it a pest (so culled by some) of Mother-earth; whilst to our US cousins the skunk will be familiar stench, 'brock' comes as the unwelcome surprise of our country pile in the Shires of England; and so welcome home Brock the Badger ...

Missing or Dead

> 'And the badger in its bedding
> Like a loaf in the oven.'
> (The Warm and the Cold; Ted Hughes)

... bumper-badged butchery, dead still and counting, the bone blood and meat of black and white roadkill, is skewered tonight red raw on the grill; but this night without father to set warm for dining; 'cos the cubs of the clan are missing their Dad, dead meat in the van: and dead right they are crying ...

> 'An infant crying in the night
> An infant crying for the light
> And with no language but a cry.'
> (Tennyson; tbc)

... we must look for poor pa, spread out all over (sick), one too many faux pas down the lane gassed under ...

> 'Gas! Gas! Quick, boys!'
> (Dulce et Decorum Est★)

... or nil'd by mouth, muzzled barrels for nostrils, back home late for a fate the worst ever ...

> 'Of them who running on that last high place
> Leapt to swift unseen bullets,...'
> (Spring Offensive★)

... and, so, Dad's never back to fill the cete of honour or his plate with the kids again ...

> 'For by the hearth the children sit
> Cold in that atmosphere of Death, ...

**To see the vacant chair, and think,
'How good! how kind! and he is gone.'**
(In Memoriam; Tennyson)

Gollum: ... ***Gorblimies-ss! ... Crikesey Moses-ss! ... Hhheeeaavenses
above ...!*** Now Awffer Mas-sster got The Lord Alfreds-ss emerging
from the setts-ss ... an' poor soul Wilfred Owens-ss★ ... who's next,
we wonders, yes we wonders-ss?

Smeagol: ... O, yes, My Luvvs ... many sets of badgerses in childruns
litterachures ... an' Brock reely is so nice an' frenly creachurses ...

Gollum: ... Badger's wild inner windy Woods of Willows-ss ...

Smeagol: ... Ol' Brock is down Watership Downses ...

Gollum: ... an' Trufflehunter hunts inner Narnias-ss ...

Smeagol: ... but have all to leave their comfy armchairs for good,
My Luv ...?

> *... all charming characters beyond compare,
> in the countryside's hateful love affair ...*

' ... TB or not TB, that is the question ...'

The Author has no valid perspective on the question of the fate of
Badgers, but I debate whether Professor J.R.R. Tolkien would ... as
to their cruel hate by some ...

**'Lowly, slowly,
A pink, wet worm
Sings in the rain:
'0 see me squirm ...'**
(Worm; Ted Hughes)

... food for thought (and badgers), the jury is out; the verdict
variable, veriform like the worm ...

Smeagol: … wiv plenty of wriggles room for everyone, My Luvvs …

In Memoriam (Tennyson)

'Tho' Nature, red in tooth and claw
With ravine, shriek'd against his creed'

… and so, blood and guts it has been so far, and recurdling ready for respilling: but, before, a sunnier run down the tramlines, bearing in mind that after three setts, the run is over and the game's up; as at Wimbledon, whose white lines may yet return to upset us:

'Penalty point, the Author, for abuse of sets …'

Directly north of Frogmorton lies the township of Shipston-On-Stour. Now we thought to christen the town 'SOS': quite appropriate in the sense of imminent danger; for way ahead at Lothlorien we glimpse for the first time ever the motor traffic sign warning …'Beware Badgers'… (and in Wales, Christmas 2016, 'Beware Otters Crossing'), but with no indication which, we badger-bumpers or Brock, is supposed to be bewaring.

'Beware Badgers'

… in a no-nonsense, mind your manor moody …

'Toad's … a hopelessly bad driver, and quite regardless of law and order. Killed or ruined— it's got to be one of the two things, sooner or later. Badger! we're his friends — oughtn't we to do something?'
   'Well, *then*,' went on the Badger, '… we'll take Toad seriously in hand. We'll stand no nonsense whatever. We'll bring him back to reason, by force if need be. We'll *make* him be a sensible Toad …'
(The Wind in the Willows; Kenneth Graham)

'The blood and the guts they're gonna make you swoon!'

Just as many of us have never seen a skunk of Loudon Wainwright III's memorable lyrics and tune, so too some of us may never have seen a *Badger*. This bore home to the Author on a visit to the Shire by an American friend, who had never set her eyes on the creature: very much like the Author one dark, dark night …

'How do you run from what's inside your head?'

… no door-knocking Brock but boring-down breakneck, eyeball to eyeteeth, mandibles and molars, blazered black badger, white tie and tailed: squinting-sprinting, blinding-sight shape-shifter, shaggy-dog bed blanket,(sighs of your mattress), growling king-size, churring and purring, heading quick homesick, downhome-subterranean … my dread danger dreams …

(rolls over in nightmare … *Well, I go to pet your [badger] I get a face full of claws … I got a hole where my [genitals] disappeared … Then you ask why I don't live here Honey, I gotta think you're really weird …*)

… my basement blues, my heartbeat hammers, me creeps and willies, O my seedless grape goolies, lockjaw genitals, meat and two veg, sprouts with bloodspots, spoiled beef and carrots; grasping, gasping, gaping crown jewels in a Hampton caught Henry, Carry On Screaming … then out comes the red stuff, O my brothers, *real beautiful* … horrorshow over; movie credits: badgers called Munch (sound) and Molar (first grip) and Mandible (second grip) …

Smeagol (reads): … *In 19th century Europe it was not unheard of for parents to threaten their misbehaving sons with castration or otherwise threaten their genitals … and is a phenomenon Freud documents several times. In this same period, … others in America and English-speaking countries offered to Victorian parents circumcision and in grave instances, castration of their boys and girls as a terminal cure and punishment for a wide variety of misbehaviours (notably masturbation) and ills, becoming very popular over time …*

(… *Author Master, is reality sometimes queerer than dreams an' screams? … does Smeagol do dreams? … does they ever come true, Author Master?*)

Smeagol: … wakesy wakesy, Author Master … muss leave the wasp factory til nextime we's on the road again …

'Quick, quick, quick, quick … slooow …'

… as a fox trots by, I must wake up … to tell the Audience that the Author was, indeed, once charged at by a badger …

Smeagol: … Smeagol's bones shake to think of it! Dead, dead, dead, dead slooow nooooow …

> **'… Who in that land of darkness and blind eyes**
> **… O who will tell me where**
> **He found Thee at that dead and silent hour?**
> **What hallowed solitary ground did bear**
> **So rare a …**
> (The Night; Henry Vaughan)

(… lair … Vaughan's reference is to God, but Brock is King of the Heavens this night) …

The amenity of Shipston-on-Stour may be observed as of the comfortable traditional style, even may we say of the most set … (end of first) … in their ways; yet most interresting and above all, down to earth. This is an environment which, in a world whose cyber technology speeds cerebral contiguity ever closer and faster spinning, takes us back to the common or garden terrestialities of a slow and somnolent stillness this time of day; presumably ever ready for the energies of the right time of the twilight zone; set … (end of second) … your watch for the coming, inveterrably, longer, night-life.

'The houses are blind as moles (though moles see fine to-night in the snouting, velvet dingles) or blind as Captain Cat there in the muffled middle by the pump and the town clock, the shops in mourning, the Welfare Hall in widows' weeds. And all the people of the lulled and dumbfound town are sleeping now …'
(To begin at the beginning: … of the night … Under Milk Wood; Dylan Thomas)

Quite familiar to the Author for its central marketplace setting, we trust not to put their environment down with the comment that whilst in our experience relatively slumbersome during daytime dreamscrapes, we suspect the entire catchment a veritable jet, which is black, set … (end of third) … of activity by a lack of light by night; only the wariest of watchers may be awake to half-see the dark rooms hosting not only their family's sporty tunnel ballgames, but also their cousins' antics fantastic, clapped eyes on only by their shy supporters, peeping from behind their hiding place …

> **'Because the Badgers are moving the goalposts.**
> **The Ferrets are bending the rules.**
> **The Weasels are taking the hindmost.**
> **The Otters are downing tools.'**
> (Carole Ann Duffy)

(… and the Rats have broken the banks ten years ago …)

> **'… and Federer breaks all records our era;**
> **and Serena, sweat, net, and serves next a sister…'**
> **(… ets-ssetera, ets-ssetera, ets-ssetera,…)**

'Game, set and a *match*' cries the Author in triumph: only to have the match awarded against us for yet further abuse … we went under all mourning that day, in the depths of our darkest depression … we slept tirelessly the following night, even though tossed by dreaming white lines up the road ahead … we emerged awake during the darkness of night, hawkeye bright headlights blinded us like lazers … more white stripes spread all over Wimbledon Common … end of the final set … End of match.

Upsetting for a time …

Gollum (red headband, tennis racquet, smashing grass): … you *cannot* be *se-e-e – rr – iouss-ss*!

But then let us take you to the tiebreak.

Smeagol: … yes, My Luvvs, what does badgerses mean to us …?

'Brock' being as safe as may be and, for want of any other conception of double-meaning, we assume the Professor has in mind the badgers boring through the darkened delvings. Thus Brock in borings or, even borings broken, as we shall hear.

Our old friend Brock being interrminably but covertly at home here, we scraped for the Professor's allusion; we dug deep, and came up with a profundity ...

'The charities founded by will of Richard Badger, proved at London 7 December 1907. This testator bequeathed for the benefit of the poor of certain parishes in this county, and in the counties of Warwick and Gloucester, a considerable sum which has been invested in the following railway securities, now held by the official trustees: ... This parish is entitled to one-fourteenth part of such income, amounting to £55 16s. 2d. yearly, for the benefit of the poor; this is distributed in meat and coal; also to one-twenty-first part, amounting yearly to £31 4s., which is applicable to the Church Restoration Fund ...'

(British History Online)

Shipston is a beneficiary.

... return from Horsefair, past Sheep Street and ... down Telegraph Street ... The horse trough is one of two given to the town by Richard Badger ... [along Church Street]... further on the right is the Ellen Badger hospital founded by Richard Badger in 1896, in memory of his wife...'

(Shipston on Stour, Heritage Walks)

Our delvings through Shipston on Stour reveal that the town is in its history dominated by the presence of the Ellen Badger Hospital, which indeed is situate on Badger Crescent. 'Badger' is a name recognised and revered in the community of Shipston.

We do not discount that the 'Brocken' element may once again sustain the Professor's tirade against the abuse of nature; with absolutely no reason for suggesting that progress in these parts is different from any others of Mother-earth, the breaking of badger runs would no doubt horrify Professor Tolkien; for, it seems, the

189

Professor abhorred the pace of traffic in any mechanical progress, even to the extent of any new road building.

The sun is about to break for Brock, broken by light …

> **'Light breaks where no sun shines …**
> **And, broken ghosts with glowworms in their heads…**
> **File through the flesh where no flesh decks the bones…'**
> (Light Breaks Where No Sun Shines: Dylan Thomas)

I have broken the poet's full words down, cutting lines out and in between … the Nogood Boyo won't mind I hide some of his earth in the Tir … (teeer) … another nice Welsh word for 'earth' … but by now we have bored the Audience quite deep enough through the earths of Middle- and Mother- … indeed to teeears …

… and so Professor J.R.R.Tolkien shall have the last word, beset with Badgers as he was in The Adventures of Tom Bombadil …

'Out came Badger-brock with his snowy forehead and his dark blinking eyes. In the hill he quarried with his wife and many sons. By the coat they caught him, pulled him inside their earth, down their tunnels brought him.'

Plain to see that the Professor's taste in poetry lies away below the levels of the modernists, and we shall see how upset about it indeed he was in our Portrait Gallegory at the Crossroads up the road ahead, where brock is in the good company of the Mitford Moles …

Screaming back to the foxes of our trot earlier, those ready for foxes, but no badgers in The Lord of the Rings, will have overlooked this …

'He waited for an opportunity, when the talk was going again, and Tom was telling an absurd story about badgers and their queer ways …'

> **'They are young, they are tender, they are nice.**
> **Eat them, eat them.'**

Gollum: ... an' Hufflepuff an' all badgers-ss rolling outer Hogwarts-ss ... the precious ruffled wiv 'em, an' we shuffled wiv 'em, an' we scuffled wiv 'em, and then, yes-ss, indeed, my precious-ss-ss, we's muffled an' truffled 'em so luvvly an' scrumshus-ss-ss, ... nice an' tasties-ss, Audiences-ss ...

Smeagol(wistful): ... yes, we remembers we done the very same wivver stewed rabbitses, thasser long time under bridge waterses gone by now, My Luv ...

Gollum: ... *Coneys* the Fat Hobbit calls 'em, precious-ss...

Smeagol (reminisces): ... Of Herbs and Stewed Rabbit, so it was, My Luv ...

Smeagol: ... any more my po'try lyrrix so lyricals-ss, in Brockenborings, Author Master?

Gollum: ... Ha, Ha! No, say-ss Awffer Mas-sster, 'cos we already had Tennis on ...

Scary

> **'Ride a cock-horse to Banbury Cross,**
> **To see a fine lady upon a white horse;**
> **Rings on her fingers and bells on her toes,**
> **And she shall have music wherever she goes'**

Some claim reference to Elizabeth I in the well-known nursery rhyme.

The township of note, to the north of Oxford, is that of Banbury; as the centre of the Cromwell English Revolution, the Puritan-lead, often violent, revolt against the Catholic Church may well have been enough to 'scarify' the Papist populace.

'Wowee! Pretty scary ...'

'Scarify' may sound as if a Disneyesque concoction between 'scare' and 'terrify', but its usage is of decent age: for instance in R.D. Blackmoore's 'Lorna Doone'(1869). It also appears in The Adventures of Huckleberry Finn.

During the period of the Reformation Banbury had three crosses: The High, Bread and White Crosses.

In the late 16th century Banbury's inhabitants were recorded as being "far gone in Puritanism". Consequently the ruling clique of the council ordered that at least two of the town's crosses, the High Cross and the Bread Cross, be destroyed.

Just after dawn on the morning of 26th July 1600 two masons began demolishing the High Cross, with a crowd of at least one hundred men looking on. When the spire fell to the ground Henry Shewell cried out jubilantly, "God be thanked, their god Dagon is fallen down to the ground." The Bread Cross and the White Cross were destroyed in the same year.

With perhaps sufficient for present purposes, we must add that 'scarify 'in the sense of scar or mark may allude to the practice of marking buildings with an arrowed cross to record significance for the marking of ancient tracks, recognised by some, such as Alfred Watkins; ultimately confirmed by the Cross of any crossroads such as that at Banbury; beyond our scope here, this being a subject in itself, the book of Alfred Watkins('The Old Straight Track'(1923)) remains the bible of all such theory, today popularly called the theory of ley lines; but, for those interested, the Author has seen Web articles with good photoshots of such ancient marks, in particular carved upon Churches.

We hesitate at this stage to share our thoughts of ley lines, some of which may become knowledge of some value, nay precious, upon the Quest.

Banbury is notable for such as the Professor, the staunchest of Roman Catholics, being one immersed (one realises the fullest depths alongside the Mirrormere in our Volume II)in the struggle, sometimes suppression, of the Religion throughout history.
We trust that the position of Banbury is sufficient to give association for Scary.

Some will recall the plotting of the route through the Wilderland in The Hobbit, which took in so many religious sites the victims of The Reformation of King Henry VIII.

Binding of the Ring

We must await rationale of the Shire Map Enigma in order to set to rights their relativity to Evendim and Fornost, whose position is indeed acrossways on Mother-earth: Brockenborings south(-east) of Fornost, Scary south(-west)of Evendim: by the medium of our 'Centre Shire Window' of the Enigma; by that window of the Shire Map, the towns home to the Badgers and the Crosses, fall *not* to be reversed relative to Northampton and Birmingham; the latter indeed being the finding of our light upon Fornost, and everything to do with fur.

The placement of Brockenborings has much impact upon our solution of the Shire Map Enigma: the difficulties of consistency with the Professor's Secret of the Shire resulting from close analysis of the Shire Map. The same may be said of Scary as of Brockenborings; and they become a pair in our thoughts just as, in the Author's vision, Frogmorton and Whitfurrows are paired; as the Audience will perceive, Scary forms something of a focal point of the north east frontier of that four sided area which, (other than Scary), has Brockenborings, Frogmorton and Whitfurrows as the other three focal points of the territory. It is as if the four frame a 'Centre Shire Window' upon Middle-earth: and so it is to be with our solution of the Shire Map Enigma; noticing that the relative positions of these four are much as their counterparts of association are to be found on Mother-earth, and so **not** reversed by the Professor's Secret of the Shire.

To revert to the Three Farthing Stone.

There had been so very little to say: not only in the public domain via the Web, the naming of the Stones of Middle- and Mother-earth are so similar, with recognition of a reduction from Four Shires to Three Farthings, as to be definitive.

193

Except, that is, for the Shire Map once more.

In many ways the Four Shires Stone had been the lynchpin of the Quest; surely incontrovertible, in describing the Professor's Secret of the Shire in our Genesis, the Author chose the relation of The Barrow Downs to Bree; far more apparent as a base assumption would have been a choice of the Four Shires Stone in relation to Bree.

Or so we had thought; and then we discovered the anomaly of the Shire Map, which crushed our previous thought of a straight association between the Three Farthing Stone and the Four Shires Stone into so many chippings, we sought out Norton for Aspirin.

Clue-leaver as ever the Professor, so too the plankton Author; the anomaly of the Three Farthing Stone may prove easier for those prepared to exchange 'Shires' for 'Farthing'.

A 'Three Shires Stone' for anyone?

The Audience will not be required to do any climbing (as does old Stinker) to view the Four Shires Stone: the Web has many fine photoshots; in which one may even look for the missing Shire.

A short explanation, within the Bureau of Shire-history in Appendix B, may assist the missing Shire search: but that may be confusing, even for the Author sitting here in the Shire that went missing. As we understand it, the district of Evenlode, formerly a part of Worcestershire adjacent the Stone(but for historical reasons remote from the rest of Worcestershire, from which it was 'detached'), became part of Gloucestershire in 1931,with the result that the Stone no longer fronted any remnant of Worcestershire, but the remaining three Shires only.

Rambling Man

Our review of the Stone meant, so we thought, that we were done with the immediate vicinity.

To our amazement, within a quarter mile of the Stone, adjacent to the lay-by we turned into in order to head the other way, we glanced some kind of Memorial Garden.

Guesswork suggests it is the equivalent of 400 square metres (as if 20 x 20 Metres) but it is by no means square; more triangular. Within it lies a marbled headstone dedicated to Paul Temple (1964-1994).

The only Paul Temple the Author heard of was the fictional Radio and Television detective created by Francis Durbridge. Apparently the character became a huge star of T.V. in Germany. A colleague here recalls that in fiction Paul Temple one time retreated to a place of his in nearby Broadway.

The rest, meaning any connection with the detective, including the date references, remains a complete and utter mystery.

Go take a look.

Wandering Star

Having wandered so far for the Three Farthing Stone, only not to find it conclusively by reason of the Shire Map, and not unlike the Hobbits returning from Mordor: we gave it up, at least until we solve the Shire Map Enigma in Appendix E.

'Actually the Shire Map plays a very small part in the narrative, and most of its purpose is a descriptive build-up. It is, of course, based on some acquaintance with English toponymical history...
(Letter number 190)

For, of course, the 'Three Shires Stone' is of its own special toponomy: and a history whose acquaintance the Author makes in the course of our Quest; one, so it turns up, in Appendix E, that is most welcome indeed: for it might, just might, ring the true label of the Three Farthing Stone.

Smeagol: ... see anyffin', My Luv...?

Gollum (perched upon finial, summit, the Four Shires Stone; shielding eyes to distance): ... no sign, my precious ...

Smeagol: ... Three *Shires* Stone ... we heard the name once ... But what does the name matter to us, My Luv?

Gollum: ... We shall see,... O yes, we shall see ...

Smeagol: ... Long ways to go yet, My Luv ...

Gollum: ... yes, my precious-ss-ss ... long, very long ways to go yet ... *to* Awffer Mas-sster's Appendics Eeeee ...

RING M V:
The Barrow Downs

'I've been ten thousand miles in the mouth of a graveyard'

Not *so* many miles for Frodo, this long journey may be related to the number of times one might walk around the stone-circle of our association; and certainly into the mouth of a Graveyard.

Middle-earth

'Scarce images of life, one here, one there,
Lay vast and edgeways; like a dismal cirque
Of Druid stones, upon a forlorn moor,
When the chill rain begins at shut of eve,
In dull November, and their chancel vault, The Heaven
itself, is blinded throughout night.
Each one kept shroud, nor to his neighbour gave
Or word, or look, or action of despair.'
(Hyperion; John Keats)

The Hobbits set out from the house of Tom Bombadil, for the Barrow Downs to the East. This evokes the Secret of the Shire. On Mother-earth one is travelling West from the Wychwood Forest towards The Rollright Stones.

Thankfully (for some) they say farewell to Tom and Goldberry.

They travel many hills undulating up and down. They imagine they have cleared the Downs but looking Eastward, they see in the distance a range of imposing hills; their description is capped in the following words:

'crowned with green mounds, and on some were standing stones, pointing upwards like jagged teeth out of green gums ...'

(Professor Tolkien's work is identified by many dental analogies:

there is another extraction upon The Trollshaws and yet another in Rivendell).

They come upon a flat saucer shaped hollow circle at the top of a hill. In the middle stands a great standing stone in the shape of a guardian finger or warning.

They sleep, awaking to the great stone casting a long shadow.

Soon they are upon the island of the hollow, shrouded by fog all around.

They are within a Hall of fog, which has created walls and a roof over them.

They fall within a chilling trap.

It is all cold.

They venture down off the hill in single file. Down an endless valley, towards a gap in the hills that is the north-gate of the Barrow Downs.

Two huge standing stones loom above Frodo in the darkness. They stumble blindly towards them, uphill.

Frodo reaches the top of a ridge and there is no response to his cries for the others.

He falls. There is a tall dark figure above him with perhaps two eyes and a grip strong and cold.

The Barrow-wight takes Frodo and the other Hobbits, or they are somehow taken, into the Barrow. He sees the other Hobbits bedecked in jewels and treasures.

Frodo hacks off an arm that has fingers walking towards Sam around a corner of the Barrow. Frodo severs the arm at the wrist and his sword splinters in the act.

The Hobbits are rescued by Tom Bombadil once more.

Mother-earth

'And today on the downs,
In the wind, the hawks, the grasses,
in blood and air,
Something passes me and cries as it passes,
On the chalk downland bare.'
(Up on the Downs; John Masefield)

Again just off the A44, the Rollright Stones are well sign-posted. The Rollrights are some 100 metres into a field now owned by The Rollright Trust. Their layout is identified by a Trust Notice Board. A nominal fee is payable. The stones look onto the unobscured view of the rolling landscape of unending hills. The description 'Downs' would not have occurred to us, but it is indeed most apposite.

The circle of stones is much wider than one might expect. Its width would probably be something the equivalent of one and a half cricket-pitch lengths, some 30 yards. There are also many more stones than one first imagined. There are over 70 counting each individual piece of stone, understanding that some stones are clumped together making precision in counting impossible. The largest is the height of an average man. The smallest protrudes perhaps 6 inches out of the ground.

There is a full description on the Web of the identifications attributed by Archaeologists to the stones. However, note the local descriptions here and also those offered by the Author.

Across the road some 250 yards into a field stands probably the most impressive stone of all. Larger than any of the circle, it must stand 8 or 9 feet tall. This is the so-named King Stone. We have to say that, looking upon the stone as an upright human body, the curved arching effect of the latter side of the upper torso did indeed remind us of a man arching his back in horror away from impending terror. This follows the legend that the stones are persona turned to stone by witches.

Alternatively,(although admittedly the image had not occurred to us before reminded by the Professor's words), the shape might well be reckoned a finger bent in dreadful warning; all the more sinister when one has no knowledge of the object of the pointing finger. The guardianship aspect tends to the inference: be very wary, there is something here under protection and something else ready to protect it.

The 'Whispering Knights' are yet a separate group of four tall stones, topped off with a large, almost horizontal one which may have moved over the ages. This group is surrounded by protective railings. The Whispering Knights being in the nature of a 'portal dolmen', we were very nearly thrown by the two great Stones that Frodo finds, nearby the north boundary of the Barrow Downs, just a stone's throw away. The feature that is often missed in relation to the site of the Rollrights is the Barrow in the field to the East of the Circle. At its simplest, a Barrow is a prehistoric Burial Ground.

Ironically we were enlightened as to this by the story of Middle-earth, and then went off to discover the correlation on Mother-earth. This equates with the usual pattern of our discoveries, but in this case we had already appreciated the association of the Barrow Downs with the Stone Circle of the Rollrights, yet the Professor had gone further. He makes mention of two very large standing stones near to the north-gate of the Barrow Downs.

Neither the King's Stone, nor the Whispering Knights might qualify, for obvious reasons from their description.

> ' ... I have watched
> Thy shadow, and the darkness of thy steps,
> And my heart ever gazes on the depth
> Of thy deep mysteries. I have made my bed
> In charnels and on coffins, where black death
> Keeps record of the trophies won from thee,
> Hoping to still these obstinate questionings
> Of thee and thine, by forcing some lone ghost
> Thy messenger, to render up the tale
> Of what we are.'
> (The Spirit of Solitude; Shelley)

To the North-East of the Circle there is, or apparently was, a further example of what is known as a Portal Dolmen. This is a burial mound or Barrow, whose entrance takes the form of two(or admittedly, or even typically, more) stone supports without necessarily a third piece lying across to form as it were a lintel. In 1764, William Stukeley visited the site of the Rollrights and saw the remains of a round barrow, nowadays ploughed or eroded away. We do not profess expertise in the subject of Portal Dolmens. The foregoing is our understanding.

More to the point, it is an analysis consistent with the Professor's two great standing stones, and that is sufficient for the Author's purposes.

We remind that we are not conjuring, but conjecturing.

It seems to the Author no coincidence that upon discovery of these two stones, Frodo and the others become interred in the living nightmare of burial within the mound and the horror of the Barrow-wight.

A further inkling not only of the Professor's knowledge of the Rollright Stones, but moreover his tendency towards allusion to geography; on this occasion in terms of 'Farmer Giles of Ham' nevertheless consider the following-

'This is a definitely located story (one of its virtues if it has any): Oxfordshire and Bucks, with a brief excursion into Wales. The places in it are largely named, or fairly plainly indicated ... The incident of the dog and dragon occurs near Rollright, by the way, and though that is not plainly stated at least it clearly takes place in Oxfordshire.'
(Letter number 116)

As ever, what might be plain to the Professor causes the rest of us years in the finding.

The diligent of the Audience will pursue the diligence due to the website 'Standing Stones in Oxfordshire'(Celia Haddons), whose details of the many, perhaps connected, system of standing stones in this area and beyond are nothing short of miraculous; outweighed only by the tonnage of the stonework that comprises these many miracles of prehistoric man.

Light Finds the New Places We Tread: Stock

Stock: The Second Flitch

> **'... This little piggy had roast beef,**
> **This little piggy had none,**
> **And this little piggy cried**
> **wee wee wee wee all the way home ...'**

Time for more double-talk; and double-difficult, too: even though we may have pigged out at Swinford, swine crossing the Brandywine by the Swinford Toll Bridge, formerly Eynsham Ferry and, by our reckoning, having counterparts in the Brandywine Bridge and the Bucklebury Ferry.

Gollum: ... es-ssept forrer Tadpoles-ss Bridge an' Trouts-ss Inn we's added earlier before, Awffer Mas-sster .. you remembers-ss ...?

Smeagol: ... we always helps! ... an' musnt forget Golden Percheses neivver!

In terms of the Swinford Toll Bridge and Ferry facilities, it is written in history that we have one or the other, but not two: sure footed thus far, we are about to double-up on the trotters with two cuts at 'Stock': Swin-*ford* and now Swin-*brook*. For those who doubt Professor Tolkien might ever have pigs' trotters on his mind in the vicinity, we are soon to meet 'Trotter' at Bree: for such is the Professor's original name for 'Strider', who is of course, Aragorn, King. For those in two minds about 'Trotter', we meet him for the second time in the Portrait Gallegory at the Crossroads up the road ahead: in the guise of a hero-figure of Professor Tolkien's own, the oft mentioned Roy Campbell.

In so many ways, the Author would have much preferred to shine a light and tread to Stock in the vicinity of Bree, there being there numerous Redesdale, Mitford and pig and fascist connections such that in many ways,(some might say, just so the family of mention), they belong together.

> **'Oh!' said the engine driver,**
> **'That's not fair.'**
> **'Oh!' said Piggy,**
> **'I don't care.'**

However, Bree has in its own right so many new places spoking from it, that we must find the light of Archet, Combe and Staddle of Bree-land in the course of a trip to the market-town at their hub. This accolade being awarded by the Professor to Moreton-In-Marsh; which only goes to show how times have changed. As well thought of as is Moreton today, the first and third (Chipping Campden and Stow on the Wold … O yes they are …) lay claim to far greater superiority in terms of location, location, location: being the best blurb the Author might make-up or -over at date of exchange, without the double-talk claptrap of the velocerealtor, here, there and everywhere else you may get yourself raptored.

The Estate Agent is a very hungry place.

Combe, the middle of the three, lies where one might expect, in a deep valley; without the pretensions of Archet and Staddle, we had better add what a comely valley village it is; or else when we next go to Blockley, there may be no coming back.

The Stockbrook

'Why, this is the Stock-brook! 'said Pippin.'

We have chosen this single line of dialogue, happily for two reasons. First (and also check the rest of the paragraph) it reads like the voice of Satnav, indicating precisely where we are on the journey; very much harking back to the comment of the Fourth of the Wise and the Great, that characters of The Rings 'speak like maps': whose very purpose we may now come to realise in taking up our Quest.

Second, and here the Audience will accuse the Author of splitting hairs; but in this case: words. Here, in the text, 'Stock-brook' is hyphenated, but not so on the Ring-Maps. The Author's conjecture is that such representation facilitates the disclosure of 'Swine-brook'; thus Swinbrook on the River Windrush.

Now if, as is our contention, 'Stock' may allude to both Swin-*ford* and Swin-*brook,* then each may be supposed to be sketched by the Professor on Middle-earth by reference to some discernible point on Mother-earth. We have the Brandywine Bridge and the Bucklebury Ferry for the 'Stock' of Swin-*ford*: what feature of the Shire Map might associate Swin-*brook*?

It will be seen that the 'Stockbrook' is the river flowing through Stock and into the Brandywine on the Shire Map.

The Professor may not have sketched the Bruinen (Windrush) by that name on the Shire Map; but if 'Stock' equates to 'Swine', we contend there is not too much of a stretch in the imagination of the Professor's dualism to suggest that the Stock-brook represents but another name for the River on which Swinbrook lies: the Windrush; otherwise, and alternatively, the Bruinen on the Ring-Maps.

Swinbrook is a famed focal point upon the River Windrush. Quite apart from the self-evidence of the OS maps, Ancient lore confirms the confluence of the Windrush with the Thames ('Isis') –

Isis, having received Windrush, passeth downe to Einsham, in the Saxon tongue Eignesham , a Manour in times past of the Kings, seated among most pleasant Meadowes, which Cuthwulfe the Saxon was the first that tooke from the Britains, whom he had hereabout vanquished, and long after Aethelmar, a Noble man, beautified it with an Abby.

(Historical notation of Campden, 1610, from The Stripling Thames, Fred Thacker)

Recalling from Swinford and its Toll Bridge at Eynsham ('Einsham') that 'Isis' is a traditional name for the River Thames, then the Windrush, too, feeds the Thames.

Again from Campden,1610:

Isis, from thence over flowing many times the flat and low grounds, is first encreased with the brooke Windrush, ...

It seems that the Windrush is originally known as a 'brook'; even today the river is in some places very little more than a mere brook, stream or rivulet.

This is to prove not the only instance upon the Quest by which the Professor uses a river-name (Stock-brook) in order to associate the name of a place upon that river: Swin-*brook*. There are similar examples up the road ahead in 'Mitheithel' for the township in fact the site of The Last Bridge; and also, as we are to suggest in Volume II, in 'Thistle Brook' of the Shire Map.

In doing so, the Professor may well have in mind the sometime (but unusual) practice in England's history of naming towns for the name of the River on which the town is sited, or as the River was historically known, often by reason of the name of the peoples that occupied its banks; of which the best example is 'Tuckborough' of the Green Hill Country on The Shire Map. The Audience will need Appendix E (Shire Map Enigma) for any rationale of *Tuckborough* and the Green Hill Country.

To summarise, the concomitant is that the Windrush has two different names, depending on whether one is contemplating the general Ring-Maps: for the Bruinen; or the Shire Map: for the Stockbrook.

Returning to the main question, if one accepts(if one accepts any at all) *only* Swinford in allusion for Stock, then some rationale for the name of the river 'Stockbrook' is wanting; and the Author, for one, is left wanting any other. We shall have to leave the fact that the Stockbrook is drawn to flow out of the Green Hill Country, for the Shire Map Enigma in Appendix E.

The further allusion is the stock one of 'Fascist swine'.

Swinbrook is of notoriety from some distance beforehand, and again up the road ahead, once we open the Door through the Portrait Gallegory at the Crossroads. England might wish, but fail, to ignore the baggage of certain of the Mitford sisters; a number with a ferryload (first loaded at Swinford) of baggage, two with associations with prominent Fascists: Hitler, Mussolini and the home-grown Oswald Mosley. 'Swinbrook' is irrevocably an association of the Mitford dynasty. Today on Mother-earth there is hardly anything but their memory, including the graves of four ... Nancy, Diana and Unity ... we very nearly wrote 'three' forgetting Pamela, no distance away on the other side of Swinbrook Churchyard ... of the 'Mitford Girls'. A curious, but not necessarily inexplicable, separation; of which more in the Portrait Gallegory at the Crossroads up the road ahead.

As we shout 'last orders' on Swinbrook for the night, the last surviving Mitford Sister, Deborah, Duchess of Devonshire, retains the Mitford presence as Landlady of Swinbrook's only Pub(lic) House, the Swan Inn; but that is for another day at the Crossroads.

By the time of this publication, Deborah has just shouted 'Last Orders' for the very last time. We just have time for another one ... to resume the tale of *Snowball, Squealer* and *Old Major* ... from Animal Farm in our first flitch at Stock ...

Animal Farm (First Edition August 1945) is originally entitled A Fairy Story:

Years pass, and the pigs learn to walk upright, carry whips, and wear clothes. The Seven Commandments are reduced to a single phrase: 'All animals are equal, but some animals are more equal than others.' Napoleon holds a dinner party for the pigs and the humans of the area, ... Napoleon announces an alliance with the humans,... and reverts the name of the farm to 'Manor Farm'. The animals, overhearing the conversation, notice that the faces of the pigs have begun changing. During a poker match, an argument breaks out between Napoleon and Mr. Pilkington when they both play the Ace of Spades, and the animals realise that the faces of the pigs look like the faces of humans and no one can tell the difference between them.

An awful lot of Mitford was not supposed to sound the way it did, and neither (with all due respect) was this letter …

Deborah to Diana in prison, August 1940:

Muv writes saying one can write to you at last, oh I do so long to see your cell. I haven't seen you or your pigs for such ages that I've almost forgotten what you look like what with one thing and another …'

Binding of the Ring

The consistencies between The Barrow Downs and The Rollright Stones will speak for themselves, not forgetting the relationship is recognised and written up on the Web; and also the perfection of their location for the purposes of our Quest.

We believe that the Film Makers are on to the association between The Barrow Downs and The Rollrights. Take a look in the foreground of the scene where, having pillaged Farmer Maggot's cabbages and carrots, the Hobbits fall down a steep embankment, finding Mushrooms at the bottom.

Nothing but Rocks and Stones.

Here we might add reference to the Fonstad Atlas; it being quite uncanny how the visual representation of the Atlas matches the Barrow Downs of Mother-earth, notably in the specific terms by which we describe the association of The Rollright Stones: the placing of the two great standing stones in the diagram of the Atlas was the spur (as of a bone) to our knowledge of a Portal Dolmen in the vicinity; of which we find not a ghost anywhere but that by the ancient William Stukeley.

Rambling Man

And so to Whitfurrows.

Some 15 miles away one eventually drops into the village of Great Tew, once one finds it. It is tucked away at the bottom of a leafy dell in mid-Oxfordshire. It is not be confused with Little Tew, which is roughly tew miles away.

Tew is pronounced Chew and is apparently derived from old Anglo-Saxon, meaning *row* or *ridge*.

It is the quintessential English rural village, a veritable paradise for those to whom the traditionally idyllic rustic life is meat and potatoes, probably because that is all there was to eat in those days. Perception is indeed everything and such is how the village is most likely to be perceived. Most cottages are reddish-brown-amber bricked, and thatched. Quaint and pretty if one likes that kind of word.

Asleep is another word.

If one regards London (or New York) or any City life as one polarity then this is the extreme end of the other one.

It is a seriously splendid Tew for those who are connoisseurs of the brand. The following should encapsulate the feel. An enterprising resident has copied the form of the Highway Code signage, nailed it to a long thin woodlog and planted it in the roadside.

In black writing on a white background within the customary red triangle, we are warned:

SLOW KITTENS!

One of the attractions within Great Tew is the marvellous Falkland Arms. Oak beams and benches and flagstones everywhere. The Inn or Pub has a massive history. The Falkland Islands were named for the then incumbent Lordship.

Never before had we been invited to a pinch of snuff or claypipe of tobacco with our measure of ale. We supposed that this was the first time ever in our lifetimes we would be offered such facilities, so we eschewed the opportunity in order to postpone the pleasure for another time.

There are a lot of mugs hanging in the pub. Not hanging 'out' or 'about'(too early for locals) but up on the ceiling. Earthenware or China ones. Hundreds. 'Too many to be counted' said the Barmaid, having tried a count but getting dizzy with the effort of looking heavenward and moving from row to row. Either she was on the Cooking Sherry or had just walked The Rollright Stones.

A sorry Belgian tourist was gagging for a beer. He had only out of date Sterling £20 notes or Euros. The barmaid refused both. We were the only three in the bar. He couldn't get a drink other than for ourselves, an open tap for thirsty tourists. We let him suffer a while, then bought him a drink. In return we accepted the pitiful amount of Euros he had in coinage. He guzzled the drink and we inquired as to whether he was driving. He said he was.

We told him he'd had enough and if he wanted another we only had Euros on us.

Wandering Star

**'... Wherever nature led; more like a man
Flying from something that he dreads, than one
Who sought the thing he loved ...'**
(Tintern Abbey; Wordsworth)

The Author loves Nature well enough; but the jury is hung (albeit from trees) in the case of Tom Bombadil and Goldberry.

Unlike the Rollright Stones, which may speak for themselves in association of The Barrow Downs, Tom Bombadil and Goldberry cannot speak for themselves and we must do our best on their behalf; which leaves us a little better than dumbstruck: this pair is something of a double mystery; so much so, the film makers omit them entirely. We exfoliate their luxuriating foliage in so far as possible, considering their nature most unnatural.

In Chapter 8, Fog On The Barrow Downs, the Hobbits set off from the house of Tom Bombadil.

The character of Tom Bombadil was once indeed a complete mystery to the Author. He is at once unbelievable, simple and childish in a fairytale fashion, smug, irritating and downright frustratingly silly-gnome like. That is a personal opinion. He bowls along, does magical, mystical things at the right time and then just disappears, usually not before sharing one of his musical delights with his audience.

This is perhaps a disparagement too far. It had occurred to the Author that, conscious of the Professor's cunning, the verses reverberating through the Rings have some kind of hidden clue or message within them, probably to date not yet revealed or deciphered. On the other hand, maybe the Professor just liked to play with meters and rhymes.

A confessional once more. When the verses manifest themselves, the Author slips them and wonders what he might have missed.

Own up, out there.

Bombadil's Goldberry, an elf-woman who lives in Tom's house is an extraordinary glamour puss, or Pussy Galore, so much so that one ends up with visions of Tinkerbell, Marilyn Monroe and Madonna or Kylie, all in one.

Even the name 'Goldberry' would seem not of Tolkien's usual calibre. It has no inherent quality of language, etymology or history. Goldberry sounds like a product, possibly a bar of chocolate or confectionery. A Tart, possibly. That is unless Tolkien was gifted with true prescience and foresaw the celebrity obsession (we very nearly wrote 'culture') of modern day. We imagine Goldberry could well be the portent of a Mrs. Beckham to come. Where that leaves 'Goldenballs' is with the Stars.

Goldberry is the only ringer (dead or alive) for Celebrity in The Rings and we broadcast the following Celebrity News bulletin: the global Cerebrum is 'Dead, Dead, Dead' (the Nogood Boyo) and deadened with celebrity fix. We are overdosing. We prescribe not 'Hello' but Good-bye and riddance. Hail Travis de Niro in his Taxi to drive it off the streets, newspapers and T.V., purging all known orifices of the filthy lucre of the ludicrous.

All of the superficialities of Goldberry's nature become entirely kitchen-sinked by the Professor who tells us that Goldberry does the housework. The Author's own view of Goldberry is that the Professor was so distracted elsewhere that in the meantime he had Goldberry do the washing-up.

It is the Author's sincere opinion that until Professor Tolkien hit upon the real focus of his tale in The Rings (which, after sketching the Ring-Maps, meant onwards from The Barrow Downs to Bree, and the advent of Strider), he was very much feeling his way by means of his other work, 'The Adventures of Tom Bombadil'. Commentators (such as Bill Ready)and other critics are wont to point out the 'flaws' in the Lord of the Rings; and we do so agree with reluctance, in the instance of Goldberry, who seems to spend an awful lot of her time mopping them, even sporting a Mermaid like lower torso, like Darryl Hannah in Splash, which Goldberry does once and again getting in and out of the bowl of water she appears to glide in; not unlike the goldfish who we conveniently forget in 3 seconds; but we can't.

Is she Superwoman, Supermum or even Supernanny and if so, where are the kids? We have really struggled with what is going on when Tom Bombadil appears. We know that so have many of the Tolkien Boys. Goldberry simply mystifies us: the whole episode of Goldberry's presence seemed to us wholly incongruous with the qualities of the remainder of the narrative. We notice the Films make no reference whatsoever, so maybe we are not alone, after all.

By way of justification for such adverse comments: Gandalf is a Wizard and does magical and mystical things, yet somehow is believable. At first sighting, Tom Bombadil takes us as a caricaturised gnome out of the back garden.

We leave this section with yet further conjecture. Professor Tolkien plotted, crafted and schemed this great work over many years, so we are bound to accede that the character must have some, possibly special, significance.

Since we first wrote the foregoing somewhat critical words, a few shafts of sunlight may have broken through and we may have some inkling of Tom. This is hardly within the scope of the exercise in geographical matching we set out with, but in a very real sense, The Green Man is everywhere. We use the terminology The Universal Green Man; and in the Bureau of Shire-history in Appendix B, the Shire-historians give an account of the Green Man, whether in the Shire, or indeed anywhere.

We cite the work of Randel Helms (Tolkien's World (1974)) for discriminating analysis. Helms in turn refers to the work of Northrop Frye (Anatomy of Criticism) …

'Tom Bombadil is Tolkien's version of the … one romance character who can 'elude the moral antithesis of heroism and villainy' pervasive in romance, one of the 'spirits of nature … [who] represent partly the moral neutrality of the intermediate world of nature and partly a world of mystery.' Tom's 'moral neutrality' is attested by Gandalf, when Elrond ponders whether he should have invited Tom to the Council[of Elrond[. He would not have come,' says Gandalf for such matters as the Ring and the battles fought over it 'have no power over him.' Even if he were given the Ring itself, 'he would soon forget it, or most likely throw it away.'

Finally, the words of the Professor himself, markedly as intriguing upon this subject as all others: from the Preface to The Adventures of Tom Bombadil, a separate volume of verses written by Professor Tolkien and involving Tom:

'The subject matter may be on the surface, light-hearted or frivolous, though sometimes one may uneasily suspect that more is meant than meets the ear.'

Just so the Professor of Tom Bombadil and Goldberry, we have banged on at length, even to other continents, in hopeful anticipation of enlightenment; whilst we remain of the belief that the Professor was merely warming up, warming to the tale of the fate of the Hobbits which gets hot at Bree, and hotter with bloodshed at Weathertop, we nevertheless re-echo the voice of the Professor which will not go away, ever ringing the infernal bracken bursting bells of Tom's green garden ...

' ... more is meant than meets the ear.'

The theories of the Universal Green Man may hopefully provide some ease of meaning to our uneasiness with Tom; and as such we include a number, reference RING M:V in the Bureau of Shire-history.

To return momentarily to our Cauldron of Appendix C of the Quest, in terms of the findings of James Pennethorne Hughes and the theories of the fairies: Tom Bombadil may be one of the Fairy Little People discovered by the Fairyseeker in the undergrowth, or rather as we recall, in the swamp: from the very beginning the Author was of the impression that Tom Bombadil was the Leprechaun of Ireland and its legends.

> **'... much as I love them,**
> **I'm always kinda' glad**
> **when they go away ... '**

We take much solace from this Randy Newman plaintiff song of when Tom Bombadil and Goldberry enter the scene.

Lucretius

The description of the severing of that crawling arm will for so many of you bring back to mind the work of the Roman poet, Lucretius. Since Lucretius is well out of Copyright, and since the Author was fated to go excruciatingly through it (in Latin) once upon a time in ancient history,(1972), we thought to give the Audience a small Corpus; in translation, and here now is what we suffered all that time ago.

Lucretius doctors on about the Body being severable whilst still retaining Soul. He provides the example of the snake, which when cut up continues to wriggle in its various sections …

'And since we mark the vital sense to be
In the whole body, all one living thing,
If of a sudden a force with rapid stroke
Should slice it down the middle and cleave in twain,
Beyond a doubt likewise the soul itself,
Divided, dissevered, asunder will be flung
Along with body. But what severed is
And into sundry parts divides, indeed
Admits it owns no everlasting nature.
We hear how chariots of war, areek
With hurly slaughter, lop with flashing sickles
The limbs away so suddenly that there,
Fallen from the trunk, they quiver on the earth,
The while the mind and powers of the man
Can feel no pain, for swiftness of his hurt,
And sheer abandon in the zest of battle:
With the remainder of his frame he seeks
Anew the battle and the slaughter, nor marks
How the swift wheels and sickles of ravin have dragged
Off with the horses his left arm and shield;
Nor other how his right has dropped away,
Mounting again and on. A third attempts
With leg dismembered to arise and stand,
Whilst, on the ground hard by, the dying foot
Twitches its spreading toes. And even the head,
When from the warm and living trunk lopped off,
Keeps on the ground the vital countenance
And open eyes, until't has rendered up
All remnants of the soul.'

Tell that to the Knight in Monty Python and The Holy Grail, we mused.

Even better than Lucretius is the tale of the Highwaymen; Tom, Dick and Harry. We have not made this up; that would be false pretences and daylight robbery. These robberies are at night time.

Tom, Dick and Harry

'Tom, Dick and Harry Dunsdon were of a respectable Fullbrook family and when they had turned to crime on the highway they favoured the Bird in Hand Inn at Capps Lodge, just outside Burford. One night they attempted a break-in at Tangley Manor as a change from holding up stagecoaches. When Dick put his arm through the shutter of the front door to grab the key it was seized by a couple of the Manor staff and the local constable, who had been tipped off by someone who had overheard the brothers' plan. The men inside the hall swiftly tied Dick's hand to the iron handle. Then they 'recoiled in horror as the cry 'Cut, cut' came from outside, followed by piercing screams and Dick's arm falling through the door shutter to swing on the handle inside. A pool of blood was all that was to be seen outside as the sound of galloping horses died away. Dick presumably died from the effects of having his arm severed so dramatically by his brothers, as he was never seen with them again. That is, not in the flesh – reports of a ghost appearing by the gibbet tree close by the old inn where Tom and Harry hung in chains after being hanged at Gloucester in 1784 specified that it had but one arm.'

(Folklore of the Cotswolds, June Lewis-Jones (2003))

We cannot resist the contemplation that the Professor knew of Tom, Dick and Harry. Indeed it is proven-

' ... I'd drown you in stuff, like Tom, Dick and Harry.'

(Letter number 98)

Tom, Dick and Harry Dunston are not just any old tom dick or 'arry about the place. One is lead to conjecture about the relationship between this threesome and Bert, Tom and William, the less than shining bright Stone Trolls of The Trollshaws. Our conjecture may be misconceived, for there are three very dozy, dull and dark models for the Trolls up the road ahead, once eventually we find them.

Friendly Locals and Germans

Within the circle of stones, we were circumferenced by a charming couple who many times walked the circle, counting. We counted three times they encircled us in the middle.

'How many?' we asked.

'Never the same any time' they responded.

By which they meant that according to local legend, no matter how many times one counts, the number will never be the same.

They also helpfully explained that the circle represented The King surrounded with an arc of The Witches. They also mentioned Fiddlers turned to stone by the Witches, some distance away. None of the official notice boards (of The Rollright Trust) mentioned Witches or Fiddlers (Knights whispering, yes, but no Witches or Fiddlers) so again we were left to wonder what the Hell was going on.

On a second visit which included the Whispering Knights we came upon a couple of friendly Germans. They told us all about the legend of Witches flying about on broomsticks. Not that they knew the word but the gesturings were more than sufficient. We told them that was a load of boloney. We were struck rigid when they inquired in cliched germanic hyper-clinical fashion:

'Vat ist Boloney?'

'Sausage like Frankfurter' we replied.'American sausage.'

They seemed to dislike the U.S.A. coming into the argument, this possibly having happened to them once before, and said 'we prefer English.'

That was all until we asked where they were from: 'Hamburg' came the reply. The retort was easy meat and so obvious we resisted it. For a short time, admittedly. You couldn't make it up, could you? We honestly haven't.

RING M VI:
Bree

' Where the people are many
and their hands are all empty
Where the pellets of poison are flooding their waters'

Bree is the focal point of the life of four villages in the vicinity. They are defenceless to the weaponry of the Nazgûl or Ringwraiths who first reveal the force of their venom at Bree. Merry is the initial target of their force.

Middle-earth

Bree-land is a group of four villages including Bree. There are Staddle, Combe and Archet on the edge of the Chetwood. Bree comprises 100 stone houses. There is a deep dyke with a thick hedge on its inner side. It has a road causeway, with two primary gates.

The Inn of the Prancing Pony has three stories with many windows. It fronts the road, but with two wings running backwards on land cut out of the slope of the hill. There is an Arch leading to a Courtyard between the two wings. There is a door way under the Arch with a few broad steps up. The main bar help is a couple of characters called Bob and Nob.

The intention is to travel Eastwards even as far as the Misty Mountains.

At one point, Merry is strangely conventional and traditional in his speech, minding the others to mind their 'P's and 'Q's; the Professor's purpose may be to put us on our guard; albeit despite countless attempted theories (for instance, on Wikipedia), nobody has the definitive explanation of the usage.

At a later stage, Frodo announces to his audience that he is thinking of writing a book, at which the gathering within the Inn is astonished.

The Hobbits and local Breelanders lose complete interest when Frodo does not show any sign of writing the book 'on the spot'.

The Author so knows the feeling.

> **'The winds were wither'd in the stagnant air,**
> **And the clouds perish'd; Darkness had no need**
> **Of aid from them — She was the Universe!'**
> (Darkness; Lord Byron)

Strider senses that there are temptations over the Ring coming from outside. At one point an elongated version of 'Hey Diddle Diddle' complete with the cow jumping over the Moon is sung with much hilarity and appreciation by the crowd. Yet all is darkness inside …

> **'Close up the casement, draw the blind,**
> **Shut out that stealing moon,… '**
> (Thomas Hardy; tbc)

For no readily apparent reason, Frodo causes himself to disappear by putting on the Ring. The Author came to realise belatedly that the force field of the Nazgûl is sufficient to force Frodo to put on the Ring, so that he may be found.

> **' … Within the common lamp-lit room**
> **Prison my eyes and thought; …'**
> (ibid.)

With apologies if such was obvious from the outset to the Tolkien Boys and other readers; the Professor's intent became clear from the BBC Radio version, in which the Nazgûl are heard to scream, manically-

'Put On The Ring!' many times over.

We are told that one swarthy Breelander is very suspicious.

There is much 'muttering' and private talk with Barliman Butterbur, the landlord.

This Chapter very much concerns the hobbits' doubts about Strider, and who and what he is and wants. Sam is especially cynical and suspicious.

It is revealed that Strider overheard that Frodo is Mr. Underhill; also that Black Horsemen have already passed through Bree and that Strider knows who they are.

(It is Tolkien folklore that when fame had reached him, Professor Tolkien was accustomed to book himself into such as holiday accommodation, indeed, as 'Mr. Underhill').

The essence of what Strider says is that the Hobbits need him and they are not aware how much this is so: for instance they will never get to Rivendell now, on their own.

Butterbur intervenes, telling them that Gandalf had left a letter for Frodo. The letter says, in the landlord's words, that Black Men are looking for a Mr. Baggins, not Underhill.

Strider tells these Black Riders are indeed from Mordor.

The letter invokes them to make for Rivendell.

Sam continues his taunting of Strider who exclaims that if Strider wanted the Ring, he could have it there and then.

He also adds that he will be making for Weathertop.

There is talk of their regret at missing Gandalf, and reference to their last meeting on First May, Mayday.

Merry announces the Black Riders are upon them and there is reference to 'Black Breath.'

> ' ... Let dingy details crudely loom,
> Mechanic speech be wrought: ...'
> (Shut Out That Moon: Thomas Hardy)

Mother-earth

On this rare (we think unique on the Quest) occasion, the description of the Mother-earth location becomes so entwined with that of Middle-earth that we link them in the Binding of the Ring section.

Light Finds the New Places We Tread: Archet, Combe and Staddle

We choose a random Web rendering (there are copious) of a description of the villages of Bree-land, simply in order to reserve the actual descriptive words of the Professor, of each of the villages, for ourselves.

*Bree is a fictional village in J.R.R. Tolkien's Middle-earth, east of the Shire. It is the chief village of **Breeland**, a small wooded region near the intersection of the main north-south and east-west routes through Eriador. Breeland is the only part of Middle-earth where Men and hobbits dwell side by side.*
The name 'Bree' means Hill, according to Tolkien, referring to the fact that the village of Bree and the surrounding Breelands are centered around a large hill. There are three villages in Breeland in addition to Bree proper.

***Staddle** is populated entirely by hobbits, making a living from light agriculture, of pipeweed, primarily. Staddle is on the south-eastern side of Breehill, sitting south of Combe and Archet. It is the only of the villages (other than Bree itself) visible from the Great East Road.*

***Combe** is populated primarily by Men, with some hobbits, all of whom make a living from agriculture. Combe is situated on the borders of the Chetwood and on the edge of Breehill, between the villages of Archet and Staddle.*

***Archet** is the furthest north. Located in the Chetwood, it is populated primarily by Men.*

We aim to work North to South.

Archet

'High on arched field I stand Alone: the night is full of stars: Enormous over tree and farm The night extends, And looks down equally to all on earth.'
(Christmas 1940; Philip Larkin)

First paragraph, 'At the Sign of *The Prancing Pony*' ...

'... Archet on the edge of the Chetwood ...'

Contrary to the web source, Archet is not 'in', but 'on the edge of' the Chetwood. As if Chipping Norton does not have enough to say for itself on our Quest, then Chipping Campden heightens the clamour. Well (if not the best, indubitably ceding pre-eminence to Broadway, the residence of the Author) known of Cotswold Villages, much more so than Norton, whose inferiority is well noted by the superior beings of Campden (even though Hobbiton boasts a nearby resident Prime Minister), Campden is one fine town full of all that is fine: people and towering (like the one in Broadway, but which Campden hasn't got) above all, fine architecture: we are to meet the Archetypes later in losing, only to regain, the Precious; those are prominent Archaeologists, but these are architects, simply of course because they designed Campden in architecture of the finest; not forgetting Broadway has many fine buildings of its own.

We shall come back to the beauty of Broadway on a short-cut gone wrong with Strider in the approaches of Weathertop; but for now we shall have to be making do with Chipping Campden. We have walked the main street of Chipping Campden so many times, one might say one was bored of it; but we present many dissenters.

Chipping Campden has become known for its unusual and attractive High Street, said by G.M. Trevelyan (most famed of the Historians of England) to be ...

'... the most beautiful village street now left on the island'.

Granted we lifted the approbation from the Campden Tourist Board literature, who might well be expected to thrive on such historical accolade, yet the following really made us sit up straight, to correct our arch stoopidity –

Pevsner described Chipping Campden as 'the best piece of townscape in Gloucestershire, arguably one of the best in England'.
*Chipping Campden is one of the loveliest small towns in the Cotswolds and a gilded masterpiece of limestone and craftsmanship. The main street curves in a shallow **arc** lined with a succession of ancient houses each grafted to the next but each with its own distinctive embellishments.*

Not only do historical voices trumpet dearest Campden, but the modernists so love it too. But, seriously, having walked Campden High Street so many times, only now courtesy the modern voice, did we realise that the street forms an unbroken 'arc' or **arch**, or if one were within the refinery of Bath, a **crescent**.

Campden, of itself, signifies perhaps an ancient 'winding valley' and 'Chipping'(also of Hobbiton) most usually a 'marketplace', yet 'quarry' might be imagined; but we think that the *arch* of Archet is well founded, cast in stone and evocative of the famed architecture of Chipping Campden; to say nothing of the construction of its renowned marketplace.

Having denigrated Campden merely for sense of fun (we really do quite like the High Street, though Broadway's is higher in our estimation), we must all now cow-tow to the grandeur of the town's central market: if you want arches, and butter from cows, then here's the place.

The ancient Market Hall was built in 1627 by Sir Baptist Hicks for a cost of £90.00. It was for the purpose of giving shelter to the local market selling cheese, butter and poultry – not wool as is sometimes thought.

An impressive edifice the like of which is seen rarely in England (the townships of Tetbury and Ledbury house two more)it is a covered market with tiled roof, whose walls are formed by a series of open arches on to the High Street in which it forms an island between the two avenues which pass either side. Each Arch is twice the size of the average front door, very much like the size of the typical English Church door; thus most impressive arches; fourteen of them: five on both of the road sides and two at each end: arched indeed.

In fact 'arched' open windows, and such description, of itself, imparts to the Author the pronunciation of 'Archet' envisioned by the Professor: not as we were accustomed to say 'Archette', whisking us fleetingly to France; but just as in 'arched window';and again, as in the opening line of our opening poem: the archedness of the Market Place may well have been sufficient for the Professor in the designation of 'Archet', without reference to its shapely High Street.

As common as is the speech of the Author in description of Chipping Campden, there follows the finale of the Market Place-

Each corner of the building has a pediment, and each gable had a window which is now blocked up. The side arches have stone ballustrades and the floor is paved with stone.

In summary, Campden boasts arches for all to see; and from the arch-capital of the Cotswolds, namely Broadway, whose jewel of the Hills status our village retains to this very day, we recognise an underarching, indeed lesser, claim to pedigree of Chipping Campden.

The Author has no doubt overdone a gentle mockery of the sense of self-aggrandisement amongst the residents of Chipping Campden; but, then again, give life in the Upper High Street of Broadway a glance for the superior being: one may never again after look higher up to a street.

After you, Marmaduke; the Author inhabits a hobbit-hole here.

Combe

> **"'In the lonely barton by yonder coomb**
> **Our childhood used to know," '**
> (The Oxen; Thomas Hardy)

First paragraph, 'At the Sign of *The Prancing Pony*' …

'Combe in a deep valley a little further eastward …'

It is the essence of Combe that it nestles at the bottom of a valley: the name speaks for itself with equivalence in Anglo Saxon, but most readily for the Author for whom the 'Cwm' of 'valley' is in the Welsh blood.

The village of Blockley is our association here: for whilst in the days of the Professor, Blockley might well have occupied the valley bottom, it seems to have grown like Topsy, being all up and down each side of the surrounding hillsides; even the locals acknowledge that a trip through Blockley may be a bit of a roller coaster ride.

All Topsy and Turvy.

Geographically, it is indeed on the perifory of the Batsford Arboretum (for the Chetwood) yet as a matter of truth it is equally on the fringes of Bourton Wood (for the Midgewater Marshes), with Blockley one's most likely destination.

Blockley is south of Chipping Campden, but northerly of our Staddle, thus indeed 'between the villages of Archet and Staddle'.

Staddle

'Boots and Saddles'

First paragraph, 'At the Sign of *The Prancing Pony*' …

'… there was Staddle on the other side of the hill …'

The word may be unfamiliar to those who have never had the opportunity to sit fairy-like on a Mushroom; or at least one imagined in stone, for 'staddle stones' are those mushroom shaped stone 'stools', for want of a better word, so customary in view anywhere in the Cotswolds. Yet their origin is as utilitarian as a place for sitting;

for sitting upon the stones of old were the grain or hay storehouses and barns, raised above ground level in order to deter such as rats and other vermin. Occasionally one sees a farm outbuilding with the stones in situ, but rarely these days: they are far more usually items of decoration in domestic gardens.

'Staddle' is not to be confused with 'straddle', nor 'saddle' with which there must surely be etymological connection; but we are yet to get to the bottom of that: the Author would gladly hedge the bet that the next time we hear talk of such stone, we hear speak of 'straddle stone': a common or garden misgnomer.

Whilst we muse over country bumpkins, the Author is quite serious in the revelation that whenever we refer to Stow-on-the-Wold, we habitually wordplay 'Stow-On-The-Waddle': no doubt an illustration of how excessive country air, or apple-juice, or pipeweed, is liable to addle me out of it: the saddle, that is. The very easy elision from Stow-on–the-Wold to *Staddle* demonstrates just how addled.

'Stow' and 'Wold' simply mean a stockade on the rolling hillside; and so our best inkling of name derivation remains our 'Stow-On-The-Waddle'; our only excuse being that if it crossed the Author's mind, the Professor would have crossed there thousands of light years before.

It is true, of course, that Stow sits atop the surrounding hills and may be said to staddle them in the *staddle stone* sense.

But wait; this name culture appears to be spreading; to which intent follow the account of The Battle of Stow-on-the-Wold; that in the Bureau of Shire-history in Appendix B. Strange that the Battle should take place at a location which *straddles* the Road of mention in the historical account. Less strange that it should take place on a hill to the northwest of Stow-on-the-Wold.

Now those approaching Stow from the north, along the A429(the Fosse Way), cover the first section over the Bourton Downs, and truth to tell one is less aware of a hill in elevated position than a straight but steady climb onward to the town. This is thrown in sharp relief if one takes the narrower road (B4077) out of town through Upper and Lower Swell (already an indication of losing height) to Ford and Temple Guiting; which might be a descent to Hell, other than for the most picturesque shaded road valley tunnel of imagination; and so Stow is definitely elevated, and on the top of a hill, depending upon one's approach; confirmed by Wikipedia–

Stow-on-the-Wold is a market town and civil parish in Gloucestershire, England. It is situated on top of an 800 ft (244 m) hill, at the convergence of a number of major roads through the Cotswolds … Given its exposed spot on the top of Stow Hill, the town is often referred to with the couplet "Stow on the Wold, where the winds blow cold and the cooks can't roast their dinners", but there is no source for this. It may be a corruption of the rhyme connected with Brill in Buckinghamshire.

At Brill on the hill
The wind blows shrill
The cook no meat can dress
At Stow-in-the-Wold
The wind blows cold
I know no more than this.

The descent into Hell was purposeful, for Stow became one hell hole for many Royalist forces following the Battle of Stow on the Wold; another helpful Web source–

In 1646 a Royalist army under Astley marched through the region in a desperate attempt to join up with King Charles at Oxford. They were brought to bay at Stow by a Parliamentary force. They fighting was fierce, and deadly; the Royalists were routed, and over 1000 imprisoned within the church.

It is said by some that the hopelessly wounded were finished off by decapitation.

So great was the slaughter that it was said that ducks were able to bathe in the pools of blood that formed on the street leading away from the market square. This is said to be the origin of the street's name; 'Digbeth', for 'Duck's Bath'.

We close our musings of Stow-on-the-Wold for Staddle with a number of supportives-

'Besides Bree itself, there was Staddle on the other side of the hill...' (first paragraph, 'At the Sign of *The Prancing Pony*').

The 'Brill' connection excites the comment that Professor Tolkien has been quoted to the intent that the name 'Bree' is itself a corruption of the 'Brill' of the rhyme; and so the pairing of Bree and Stow also by the ancient rhyme.

Once more unto the breach of our Civil War:

'There is more to St Edwards than this memory of conflict; take the time to walk around the outside of the church to the north side. There a small door peers between two massive old tree trunks. You almost expect a gnome to peek around the door any minute.'

This last being from the same Web source as the references to the Battle of Stow-on-the-Wold in Appendix B, that author should be engaged alongside us on the Quest; simply because we had already years ago drafted in the uncommon sight of this door at St. Edwards Church, Stow, for the entrance door to The Mines of Moria, yet still so far up the road ahead; we greet all with welcome there in Volume II. As of writing, a Web search for 'Yew trees St. Edward's Stow' reveals a magnificent shot of the door through the trees. We cannot imagine there is another such as this on Mother-earth: except, perhaps, for that the subject of Holman Hunt's 'The Light of the World', a larger scale version of which was for many years on view at St. Paul's Cathedral in London, by way of illustration of Revelation 3:20 ...

'Behold, I stand at the door and knock; if any man hear My voice, and open the door, I will come in to him, and will sup with him, and he with Me'

Our very last thought upon 'Staddle': Stow balances on the hilltop atop Bree and the rest, as does a Gnome, Elf or Fairy on its bottom.

Binding of the Ring

Moreton-In-Marsh has become connected with the Tolkien mythology, and Bree in particular, in the minds of the Tolkien Boys for a number of reasons:

'To begin at the beginning,...'
(Under Milk Wood)

The Quest took us off on our adventure (in the very first place) by reason of the correlation between Bree and The Barrow Downs: being opposite in direction in Middle-earth, that is to say Moreton and The Rollright Stones. Moreover, Moreton is in the right place geographically in relation to The Rollright Stones and the Three Farthing Stone, which are (at least in the case of the former, there being anomalies in the Shire Map in terms of the latter) described earlier here as 'givens' for association. Our statement, of course, assumes the Professor's Secret of the Shire. It will be recalled that it is from Bree onwards that problems of association occur.

'I began to think vodka was my drink at last. It didn't taste like anything, but it went straight down into my stomach like a sword swallower's sword and made me feel powerful and godlike.'
(The Bell Jar, Sylvia Plath)

Moreton houses 'The Bell' Inn which it is known was frequented by Professor Tolkien on his visits to his brother Hilary in nearby Evesham. The Bell has on its wall an Article headed 'Barliman Butterbur in the Bell' which was of no little assistance in our Diddle Diddle of Bree, and our Quest generally. The Bell fits very well Professor Tolkien's description of The Prancing Pony, where the Hobbits first meet Strider or Aragorn as he turns out to be. This encounter is the precursor to the action at Weathertop, which is why their geographic relation becomes of such relative importance.

One of the Tolkien Boys of the Author's acquaintance came high kicking in here; for he regaled the Author with the tale that the drinkers for whom The Bell is their local spoke to our acquaintance of the old days when a Pony was often brought in to share the atmosphere of the Pub. He did not go on to say that the Pony shared the Beer which caused the 'Prancing'; the Author has dreamed that one up: but yet the Author recalls some tale or other of a dog accustomed to pubcrawl with his Master who ended up dancing; if we ever find the Dog, we shall be bound to report him not missing, but thankfully found.

> **'The curfew tolls the knell of parting day,…**
> **… And leaves the world to darkness**
> **and to me.'**
> (Elegy Written in a Country Churchyard; Thomas Gray)

Turn to the right hand outside The Bell and ones sees The Curfew Tower, which is in front of us standing on the corner of Oxford Street. It is shown in the 'Short Cut Gone Wrong' map.

The Curfew Tower dates from the Sixteenth century. It was also used as a local temporary gaol.

On the front of the Tower building is a replica board of mainly road (Toll) charges.

From the text of The Rings-

'The gates were closed at nightfall; but just inside them were small lodges for the gatekeepers.'

Moreton in Marsh is a curfew town and still retains its curfew tower.

> **' … and the highways were streams of people, and the ditch**
> **banks were lines of people. Behind them more were**
> **coming. The great highways streamed with moving people …'**
> (Chapter 21, Grapes of Wrath; John Steinbeck)

It emerges that Bree is at the intersection of the Great East Road and the Old North Road. Moreton is equally at a crossroads: that of the A44 (represented as the Great East Road), and the A429, running south to Cirencester, and northward to Warwick.

'For Bree stood at an old meeting of ways; another ancient road crossed the East Road just outside the dike at the western end of the village, …'

Market town or *market right* *is a legal term, originating in the Middle Ages, for a European Settlement that has the right to host markets, distinguishing it from a village or city.*

In pre-19th century England, the majority of the population made their living through agriculture and livestock farming. Most lived where they worked, with relatively few in towns. Therefore, farmers brought their produce to informal markets held on the grounds of their church after worship. Market towns grew up at centres of local activity and were an important feature of rural life. As traditional market towns developed, they featured a wide main street or central market square. These provided room for people to set up stalls and booths on market days. Often the town erected a market cross in the centre of the town, to obtain God's blessing on the trade.

The meeting of ways would have established Moreton's place as a centrepiece market down from the days of the Agricultural Revolution. No other town of Breeland has such central focus: Moreton is a general market town; on the whole the rich breelanders gained wealth from the wool trade in the other Breeland towns of Archet and Staddle.

RING(+):

At the Crossroads of Bree

Preview

'While the sisters' enduring reputation owes much to their originality, forceful opinions, and good looks, the turbulent times in which they grew up provided the catalyst for their highly publicised exploits. The decade leading up to the Second World War was one of ideological extremes and, like many of their contemporaries, they were drawn to radical politics which they saw as the answer to Europe's ills. Their belief spanned the political spectrum, from fascism, Nazism and communism, to socialism, Gaullism and Conservatism, politics dividing the family as sure as religion had done in former centuries, political absolutism replacing religious absolutes. The causes they took up were closely connected with the men who embodied them, with the difference that Unity and Jessica chose men whose politics corresponded with their own natural ideological tendencies, while Nancy and Diana's political beliefs were sustained by the men they loved.'

'I went down to the Crossroads ...
I'm standing at the Crossroads ...
Believe I'm sinking down ...'

By some measure the most deliciously delinquent headbanging live electric guitar solo the Author ever clapped ears on, one to licks of cream over, we determined to hear it at our Crossroads: **Robert Leroy Johnson** (May 8, 1911 – August 16, 1938) is an American singer and musician in the blues tradition. One may note that The Hobbit is published in the year before Johnson dies, and that seeming irrelevance comes into its own up the road ahead, underneath The Misty Mountains in Volume II.

We hit collision course at the Crossroads, both physical (over halflings way through this Volume I), geographical and indeed historical, upon the Quest. The crossroads of the earth is that of Moreton-In-Marsh or Bree; that of history is that of planet Earth; reaching a tipping point, a fulcrum or pivot, in the times we speak of now: the two decades pre-War: the 1920's and 30's. And, it must be said, this ground of earth breeding its own special spring off stock. Our Audience may regard our associations of personality (and there are many upon the Quest, as our previews of our Portrait Gallegory will have indicated) as mere tourist information and no more.

The following from Letter number 73 is expanded more fully much further on in the Portrait Gallegory, in description of the Professor's attempts at writing before turning to such as The Hobbit and The Rings-

'I tried a diary with portraits (some scathing some comic some commendatory) of persons and events seen ...'

And so this is not territory wholly unfamiliar to Professor Tolkien.

We view primarily the Mitford dynasty but include the Marlborough line of the Churchills, Vita and other Sackville-Wests; and more, such as the Sitwells, Betjeman and Waugh in the same contemporary vein; even George Bernard Shaw casts a glance from the Misty Mountains. We discover a model for Aragorn; Walter de la Mare makes an appearance, and we exhibit the new wonderboy poet on the block, Dylan Thomas, making exhibitions of himself, private and public, in his own uproarious style.

These we regard as part of the social history of The Shire back in the day of Professor Tolkien's writing of The Rings; and its effect upon the development of the story, we alone may judge. As such, the Author comes on specifically to reject any charge of irrelevancy of these matters in the creation of The Lord of the Rings: they do matter. It matters not that they may be new, but it should that they be applied, like paint.

It is the Author's view that the events of The Rings would not have appeared in the story as they do, were it not for this setting on Mother-earth, both geographical and human. For instance, this perspective is fundamental to an understanding of the 'Scouring of the Shire' chapter. Indeed, it is arguable that 'Stock' can have no allusive meaning *except for the Mitfords at Swinbrook*.

As of general applicability to the Quest as the following may be, we chose to record it now in terms of the theatre of the Professor's writing:

'There is no special reference to England in the 'Shire' – except of course that as an Englishman brought up in an 'almost rural' village of Warwickshire … I take my models like anyone else – from such 'life' as I know …'

(Letter number 181)

We are doing our best to illustrate the models of the physical earth; but now include some of the lifeblood of Mother-earth. We are bound to realise the nature of the socio-political environment in England at this period in history (the 1920's and 30's, and into the 40's), and, more to the point, the one in which the Professor was living and writing The Rings. The forces of fascism, communism, democracy and of other political doctrinal systems were vying for the power that control brings.

The foregoing was the Author's clumsy attempt to paint a historical picture, but 'The Mitfords Letters Between Six Sisters'((2007), edited by Charlotte Mosley) does it so much better, we open our Door through the Portrait Gallegory with the synopsis provided in the Editor's Note, previewed in the 'Preview' of our Portrait Gallegory; perhaps difficult to comprehend of the decade succeeding that sometimes known as the Roaring Twenties, highlighting no doubt the gaiety in relief at the end of the First World War, gratifying the upper echelons with the highlife of fashion, style and glamour, to the delight of the socialite who had it all: whilst the champagne corks popped in all the right circles, there bubbled for the lowerlife socialist beneath a cauldron of dissension that fomented into a second World War.

"I was a miner
I was a docker
I was a railway man
Between the wars …
I kept the faith and I kept voting

---

*   Billy Bragg

Not for the iron fist but for the helping hand
For theirs is a land with a wall around it
And mine is a faith in my fellow man ...
Build me a path from cradle to grave
And I'll give my consent
To any government
That does not deny a man a living wage ...'

'... the king went on a tour of the depressed mining villages of South Wales. He saw the Merthyr Tydfil Labour Exchange, and made a detour, not on his schedule, to see the Bessemer Steel Works at Dowlais. Where 9,000 men had been employed only a few months before was a desolate scene of wreckage, with hundreds of men sitting on piles of twisted metal and the rubble of demolished factory buildings. Seeing their king they stood and sang hymns. The king stood bareheaded and said grimly:

'These works brought all these people here. Something must be done to find them work."

If the vivid description by A.N. Wilson ('After the Victorians' (2006)) reminds nobody but the Author of the fate of the Tower of Orthanc, they may be right: for we may be looking at the Tower of Barad Dur in Mordor.

Letter number 213:

'I love Wales (what is left of it, when mines [etc.] have done their worst),...'

One observer in Volume II happens to say so ('Merthyr' to 'Mordor' does have something of a ring about it), but his most valuable revelation is to be that Professor Tolkien spent some time, writing The Lord of the Rings, no distance from Merthyr Tydfil.

A.N. Wilson is speaking here of the visit of King Edward VIII, one which achieved 'almost instantaneously legendary status'; but, of course, the King went on to become his own legend in the company of Mrs. Wallis Simpson. Filmgoers will have tasted the party nonsense in the frolickings of the King, abducted in favour of Mrs. Simpson, who dealt a great many blows in furtherance of alliance, so one hears; but at the end the King abdicated: merely another word for letting someone else get one off for another job without too much fuss; and in any event, the failed King is present, with great affection, in the Mitford Letters.

And if we are all so entranced by The King's Speech, we shall all be equally charmed by the intimacy between the Mitfords and the erstwhile King.

Nancy to Diana, December 1945

'The Colonel rang up & says the Windsors are giving my book to everybody for Xmas, which tickles me very much ...'

Diana to Nancy, June 1966

'We went over to the Dook ... [... teased for not buying land around Buckingham Palace in order to prevent intrusive photography ...] ...

Dook: 'You mean the crown should have bought the land? Couldn't *afford* it, that's why."

Diana to Deborah, August 1980

[following reference to a corpse] ... Put one in (a photo I mean) of Dooky.'

The abdicated King's pro-German tendencies are well documented; hardly surprising when the Dook is hanging around with the fascist Mosleys for company, Dooky. And so we trust we set the scene for what is to come. Yet a most 'vibrant and hugely enjoyable portrait of an age'(the Observer) has already been painted by A.N. Wilson(in 'After The Victorians'), where he shares a vision of the lives and times; the first his own perception of the sympathies of the Abdicated King, then that of Nancy Mitford in her own right; but we do not say of any ideological affinity, but merely a relationship.

The sober and objective view –

'It is a poor sort of memory which only works backwards, as the White Queen says to Alice, and the 'fascist' sympathies of King Edward VIII did not extend to condoning any of the Nationalist Socialist programme – though the Nazis were very keen indeed to exploit his name in their propaganda.'

To the imaginings of the naughty lady, Nancy Mitford, with an introduction by the historian-

'... there is no secret about the fact that when the new King Edward VIII was living in exile as the Duke of Windsor, he made friends with Sir Oswald and his wife ... Twelve years after the war, Sir Oswald's acerbic sister-in-law Nancy Mitford wrote to a friend from Paris: 'The Mosleys ... and the Windsors are literally never apart. They want us all to be governed by the kind, clever, rich Germans and be happy ever after. I wish I knew why they live in France and not outre-Rhin.''

A.N. Wilson needs no approbation here but, just so the Mitford Letters, the historical account is fascinating insight into the times and lives contemporaneous with Professor Tolkien and the writing of The Rings, and which the Author ventures to suggest have no little impact upon the Professor's story and, perhaps covertly, especially the maps.

Several of the characterisations of the Portrait Gallegory appear in a Chapter called 'The Silly Generation', and furthermore throughout the historical account, and we share a little more further on; but those with a taste for tales of Royal scandal, no doubt titillated by those of the abdicated King, will revel between the sheets in the 'Love in the Suburbs' chapter: this particular chapter of history is so majestically frisky and fruity, not to say fruitful, those wishing to dig the real dirt will be bound to join in the games of King Edward VII (Dooky's father)and read of the exploits of many of our flying V's: Vita, Violet Trefusis and Virginia Woolf, both of whom Vita has knowledge, clandestine carnal.

The prurient voyeur who would like to, but can't, need not fear; for the Author does the business for you through the keyhole in the Door; the Author fully understands that some of us will roll over to The First Exhibition mounted/showing in The Portrait Gallegory within Appendix D for the very first time; as it were, verging on the vallance virginal. Scandal at last, we contrast the 'notoriety' of the Mitfords, yet Vita Sackville-West is once again and forever in hiding; if not behind the Hedge: often in her bushes.

Yet for bawdy banter brazen at the other end of the social scale in the early 1930's, such as in the Music Halls and saucy seaside postcards, this is hard meat to beat from local yokel Joe …

Down in the fields where the buttercups all grow,

Oh, Mary Green loves me and I love her true,
We blush when we meet like all true-lovers do,
Beneath the plantation where cool meadows run,
We spoon in the dark and we have lots of fun,

Down in the fields where the buttercups all grow;

Oh, Mary she thought I was bashful and slow,
But she changed her mind when I let myself go,

Down in the fields where the buttercups all grow;

Me girl climbed a gate and said turn your head Joe,
But I'd a stiff neck so we let matters go,

Down in the fields where the buttercups all grow …

Me girl friend and I went behind a haystack
When a bumblebee flew down the small of her back
I saw what had happened and in my distress
I shoved me right hand down the back of her dress,
Me hand down her back when she struck me a blow
I didn't know that bee was so far below,

Down in the fields where the buttercups all grow …

A cow lickin' Mary's face tickled her so,
She thought it was me and said, 'Don't slobber Joe'

Down in the fields where the buttercups all grow ...'
(Charlie Higgins; 1931)

When you get to know them, you might try to gauge the reaction of such as Farve and Muv Mitford.

We are *not* amused.

The Mitford Letters

In the meantime, we predicate a much deeper look at the letters exchanged between the six Mitford sisters by a neat extract, from the Mitford Letters, summarising a number of the geographical associations that we have made to date, and some new ones-

'When the letters begin, the family had been living for six years at Asthall Manor, a seventeenth-century house in the Cotswolds, which the sisters' father, Lord Redesdale, had bought when he sold Batsford Park, a rambling Victorian pile that he had inherited in 1916 and could not afford to keep up. Before the First World War, David Redesdale, or 'Farve' as he was known to his children, lived in London where he worked as office manager for The Lady, the magazine founded by his father-in-law. Life in the country was far better suited to this unbookish, unsociable man, whose happiest moments were spent by the Windrush, a trout river that ran past Asthall, or in the woods where he watched his young pheasants hatch. Unluckily for his family, country sports did not exhaust his energies, and Asthall, which the children loved, was not to his liking. In 1926, they moved to Swinbrook House in Oxfordshire, a grim, ungainly edifice that Lord Redesdale had built on top of a hill near Swinbrook village.'

For the moment, store Batsford Park in the woodshed; we cut the light to the wood there, at the Chetwood; and we return to Swinbrook (recalling our second flitch at 'Stock'), after Asthall and Batsford.

Asthall

Asthall is a pretty village between Minster Lovell and Swinbrook, the lost Church of Widford not far in the distance. The Church is lost to anywhere and anybody else in the most strange manner and is worth a look on the Web; for we are to return to look for it in Volume II. Asthall Manor received an unwelcome guest in the shape of the Author in the summer of 2011, poking about where we shouldn't down the private drive in his customary workmanlike Dive Definitely-Disgusting gorblimey trousers, with the temerity to approach the front-door when his place was clearly the tradesmans' entrance at the back; to be gently shooed away from disturbing a family lunch at the dining table of a size grand enough to fit Farve, Muv and all of the Mitford girls, together with respective partners(Adolf merely a twinkle in Unity's eye and fanatically active elsewhere at this early stage of proceedings)around; and come to think of it, we suspect that once upon a time they did. Our later jolly to Swinbrook recalls that the Churchills were sometimes company here at Asthall.

Batsford

Redesdale (from the family origins in Yorkshire) is the Baronial title; Redesdale Manor is sited in the Gloucestershire village of Batsford; thus Batsford Park. Moreton-in-Marsh (of our Bree) is annexed to the Manor and Park both geographically and metaphorically. No doubt the Redesdale dynasty would have regarded the town as an annexure of the Manor. Still today one of the town's hostelries is The Redesdale Arms; the Town Hall, the Redesdale Hall. Batsford Park houses the Manor and its grounds for the greater part the Batsford Arboretum; and so, emerging from the woodshed, from Park to Arboretum, the Rangers may press ahead to the Chetwood.

The essence of Redesdale Manor and Batsford Park are completed by its own Estate Church within the grounds, centuries of Redesdale and Mitford history within.

The Mitford parents were notoriously right wing pro-England traditionalists of the most conservative reactionary kind, but even they appeared to balk at the Fascist tendencies of two of their daughters, at least in public; subjugated only in the case of Farve, to an indiscretion kept ominously discreet, until later times(and so too our's, later in our Portrait Gallegory), that Lord Redesdale was covertly fiercely anti-semitic as much as Diana and Unity, two of his extraordinary daughters, proved overtly so.

For the uninitiated there were altogether six Mitford sisters (Nancy, Pamela, Diana, Unity, Jessica and Deborah),whose notoriety owed itself to their glamour, romance and controversy in politics; their notoriety extended across the pond to the USA, in the most stark terms, as we shall observe in anticipation of our Portrait Gallegory.

The Author becomes weary of their 'notoriety' and all other derivations, but it is assuredly the best word we have found so far: 'scandal' and all other derivations being far too modernistic.

Nancy, also an author, was a leading novelist and socialite of the day.

Diana married the leader of the British Fascists, Sir Oswald Mosley.

Unity went one further and became the friend, some claim girlfriend, of Adolf Hitler; there have even been claims that Hitler fathered a child by herr: but the Boys from Brazil are surely adequate imagination of the Shekelgruber family line: Cut the Dogs.

Jessica, communist in instinct, ironically spent much of her life in the USA.

Deborah restrains herself and becomes Duchess of Devonshire.

Pamela was relatively subdued in her activities, most noteworthy for witty contribution from distance.

If one struggles with the import of Fascism, the Author recalls from one of our researches of the Mitfords, the comment of one of the sisters of her belief in the maintenance of a 'slave' class in society; possibly Unity, we may be wrong; but we trust the Audience gets the picture in one crack of the whip.

Mosley led the Blackshirts, the British Fascists, reviled for the riot in London's East End, when his special brand of fascism, directed against the Jewish community, went anything but kosher: blood everywhere. The British Fascists were modelled on the Blackshirts of Mussolini's Italy. The Plaque at Cable Street is shown in the 'Short Cut Gone Wrong' map.

Unity joined the Nazi party and is photographed in swastika'd Nazi uniform. Unity Mitford was a villain of the day; as close to Adolf Hitler as anyone might care to get, apart perhaps from Eva Braun. Little star of wonder Unity (is reported to have) shot herself in the head the day England declared War on Germany. So run the usual reports, but, beguilingly, we are to receive other news from the USA. She survived but never really recovered.

The most profound of ironies, Unity is born in Swastika in Canada.

For the Author, their spectre casts a very dark shadow over the pre-War history of rural upper-England: something dark, fearsome and foreboding in the inhuman nature of a class coming to terms with change: even today, the shame of their neo-Nazi outlook, from Farve down to certain of the sisters, provokes a tremor of dread, not unlike the unhealthy air which hangs over the Old Forest Wychwood back in the day, one so disturbing that one shudders, preferring to turn a blind eye, to the indiscretions of some of their number; at least amongst those who know; lending a voice to those who refuse to come to terms; yet again …

Smeagol: … We doesn't know, and we doesn't want to know …

We are bound to peer into the gloom at their places and their beings …

241

Swinbrook

Just a few miles away from Moreton-In-Marsh is the village of Swinbrook. We meet the sisters all along the Quest; but we record the burial of four of the sisters in the Churchyard here; the visit is a poignant one for those familiar with the family history: so parochially English of convention, their fame spreads overseas.

All the while our US Cousins are looking on in wonder and amazement at the antics of the aristoclasses of England; it is to the States that we turn to advertise the idiotsyncracies (and I know I used that before in The Hobbit) of the eccentrics at home: those resorting to the 'Mitford Letters' will find the following, of the 'American Weekly' (1946) more from which we are bound to disclose on leaving the Portrait Gallegory, with a final shot in the dark in the already heady tale of the Mitford Sisters ...

'Those Mitford Sisters ... The Aristocratic Mitford Sisters Traveled, individually, This Way and That, With the Perverse Hand of Fate Guiding Them Into Channels That Brought Embarrassment to Their Parents.'

There is so much to say of the Mitford Girls that we shall do our worst: our Portrait Gallegory sets out to paint a fuller picture; and against the criticism that these are words wasted upon the Quest, having nothing whatsoever to do with the Shire of Professor Tolkien; *we reject it*: not least because (in the Author's most humble conjecture) some parts of The Rings (geographical and literal) are comprehensible only against the backdrop of events within the Shires of Mother-earth contemporaneous with the Professor's writing of The Lord of the Rings.

Accompanying the image of Unity Mitford on the cover of News Review (1937), 'The First British Newsmagazine', under the banner(sic) 'NAZI-LOVER THE HON.UNITY FREEMAN-MITFORD ... but for 'certain difficulties' a German ...'

... and the following from the Mitford Letters ...

'Unity on the cover of a news magazine, November 1937.Hardly a week went by during the 1930's without one of the sisters making headlines'.

Professor Tolkien commences to writing the Lord of the Rings in 1936.
Thus a challenge thrown out to those who may refuse to countenance our Portrait Gallegory.
Perhaps the best introduction to the Portrait Gallegory is the sense of change affecting the lives participating in these times.

The Audience will see through here, (and we have already depressioned us with one or two), some very badly-drawn boyo sketches of the Author's own; but we leave it better to the masters of history, and a painting of 'The Silly Generation', (in which, in passing, it is the Sitwells who appear the height of sillybillyness), in more impressive impressionistic style:

'Shaw was giving expression to a widespread view among intellectuals that something had happened, not just to convert audiences in London, and not just to England, but to Western civilisation in general. Whether the war had caused or promoted or only reflected this something was incidental to the fact that it had happened: Western civilization had gone down the drain ...'
('The Silly Generation', After the Victorians, A.N. Wilson)

As indicated previously, and further in Appendix D, there is to be a truncated version of our Portrait Gallegory to be followed up on return from Mordor in the context of The Scouring of the Shire: this will be in Volume III, if there is to be one at all.

RING M V:II:
Weathertop

'I saw a black branch with blood that kept drippin"

**'This wheel's on fire
Rolling down the road
Best notify my next of kin
This wheel shall explode ...'**

The darkness upon Weathertop is pierced with blood.

In this RING M:VII of Weathertop, we choose to *retrospect* the Chetwood, thence the feature that intervenes it and Weathertop, namely the Midgewater Marshes; and we just have time to retell an account of a short cut that went wrong on the way.

And so we stress (as indeed we are with Weathertop looming) that we look whence we have already come on Middle-earth; as indeed we aim to show on Mother-earth.

Light Finds the New Places We Tread: The Chetwood; The Midgewater Marshes; Broadway in the Dark

The Chetwood

**'Nought but vast sorrow was there –
The sweet cheat gone.'**
(The Ghost; De La Mare)

The Professor's name games are very rarely as apparent as we contend in relation to the Chetwood, for possible as may be a connection of Ancient Celtic derivation, we cheat these in favour of a straight deal: noting also the Cheetwood of the Manchester area, we contend that Professor Tolkien merely had in mind the circumstance of the creation by my Lords Redesdales, of Batsford Park and its developing Arboretum.

A little historical commentary discloses the cheating sleight of hand –

The stature and backbone of Batsford Arboretum which we see today was no more than a dream when its creator inherited the Batsford Estates from John Freeman-Mitford in 1886.

During the 1860s Algernon Bertram Freeman – Mitford (later 1st Lord Redesdale) travelled widely in oriental Asia as an attaché to the foreign legation. He was deeply influenced by the landscapes in China and Japan and became fascinated by those plants that he found there, especially the bamboos. Whilst in Japan he became a respected expert on the politics and culture of the country.

Upon inheriting the estate Algernon Mitford, known as Bertie, demolished the Georgian house and rebuilt a new mansion between the years 1888 and 1892 as well as rebuilding many estate houses. However, it was not until 1890 that Bertie was able to turn his attention to the gardens.

His influence was most radical almost erasing all traces of the original layout. He created a 'wild' garden of near natural plantings inspired by his observations of plant groupings in the Japanese landscape. He was able to create a garden which allowed him to explore his ideas combining conventional parkland with a garden landscape. He had become an accomplished and respected plantsman and a great authority on bamboos. Most of the major trees, many of which are most unusual, were his original plantings.

He also created one of the foremost bamboo collections of the time and some of these still live on today …

We shall never know what Professor Tolkien might have thought of gardens *'erasing all traces of the original layout'*, indeed whether such wood was cheating nature.

The Chetwood of Batsford Arboretum is precisely where it should be on Mother-earth, subjecting the Ring-Maps to the Professor's Secret of the Shire: west of Moreton-In-Marsh, intervening Bree and the Midgewater Marshes on the Ring-Maps.

Midgewater Marshes

**'The mosquito knows full well, small as he is
he's a beast of prey.
But after all
he only takes his bellyfull,**

he doesn't put my blood in the bank.'
(The Mosquito Knows: D.H. Lawrence)

... They were far beyond the borders of the Bree-land, out in the pathless wilderness, and drawing near to the Midgewater Marshes.
The ground now became damp, and in places boggy and here and there they came upon pools, and wide stretches of reeds and rushes filled with the warbling of little hidden birds. They had to pick their way carefully to keep both dry-footed and on their proper course. At first they made fair progress, but as they went on, their passage became slower and more dangerous. The marshes were bewildering and treacherous, and there was no permanent trail even for Rangers to find through their shifting quagmires. The flies began to torment them, and the air was full of clouds of tiny midges that crept up in their sleeves and breeches and into their hair.
'I am being eaten alive!' cried Pippin. 'Midgewater! There are more midges than water!'
'What do they live on when they can't get hobbit?' asked Sam, scratching his neck.'

'Ain't it hard to stumble
And land in some funny lagoon?'

We would never have considered a forest in candidature for association with the Midgewater Marshes, except that we looked for something of Mother-earth relative to the position of Moreton-in-Marsh (Bree) and Batsford Arboretum (Chetwood) according to the Professor's Secret of the Shire; yet, knowing of the existence but never thinking to go in, we were to land up (but down) in a 'funny lagoon' within Bourton Wood.

This association was singular amongst the others; it came late when the general layout of the associations was all but overviewed, and we were filling in the gaps of our supposed knowledge. With no pre-knowledge whatsoever of the layout or nature of Bourton Wood, we were by now so confident of the trail revealed by the Secret of the Shire that we fully expected to find the Professor's resource.

The density of Bourton Wood is approached through any one of several gates along the B4479. The best approach is by the one

246

opposite the turning to Batsford and Aston Magna. From this gate, take the 2 O'clock diagonal track that plunges ever downward to the depths of the valley floor; but from this point one has no idea what might be waiting there. At this stage, one expects a level playing field for our game of hide and seek.

'My clothes are wet, tight on my skin,
But not as tight
as the corner I painted myself in ...'

From any other access gate, there are many interweaving paths (many straight) beaten or trodden up and down within. *Down* is apposite if one enters by one of these interweaving paths, for on our first visit, (indeed entering by one of such paths) it was only following a relatively steep slide of a treacherous (and muddy) downward slope that we found our hidden bog valley: one arrives on the upper rim of an escarpment wholly unexpected in mid-forest, being one side of a long deep valley, cut there by the water of a stream that flows beneath the undergrowth and tree cover, such that it is sometimes out of sight. Either side of the stream is wetland we declined for the sake of dry feet. The 2 O' clock diagonal is far easier if ever you go looking.

It is the like of the floor of a jungle rain forest. A complete boggle of growth outside the norm in the typical English forest, this secret bog valley is filled with strange flora, bull rushes, water grasses and reeds, some of which were unknown to us; one we first thought to be indeed bamboo.

Perhaps the answer is blowing in the wind; from Batsford Arboretum. The Author's first thought was Professor Challenger of The Lost World of Conan Doyle. Our companion muttered about Greystokes Tarzan; and the Swiss Family Robinson.

We can but assume the cleft valley operates as a cloche trapping moisture with tropical greenhouse effect, fitting two galoshes well.

'Gosh!' muttered our companion, not for the first but a third time.

It is true to say that the terrain was boggy rather than marshland, but Professor Tolkien would have known what this might be like after heavy rain; and in very hot summer months. At the time of our first expedition, we had had no rain for weeks. We cannot avoid the harrowing thought that for the Professor such terrain may have evoked the trenches of World War I. In adverse conditions, the valley would be serious impediment to any progress.

But it was the Midges that were missing in action. There were plenty of insects in flight, but no swarms of the annoying, irritating, biting kind; the like of which if ever one visits the Western Highlands, is likely to provide any number of unwanted souvenirs: itching join-the-dots eruptions reading a postcard from Scotland if you are not too busy with the Calamine.

A tiny (like their smaller members) of their natural history has insected itself within Appendix B; and our US cousins may be familiar with 'punkies … no-see-ums', whilst others not.

The Author is bound to tell that the Midgewater Marshes is the most hidden reality in the den of a jungle; let the kids loose in here if you ever get to show it to them: once you get them in, you will never get them out of there.

'I've got you under my skin …'

A helpful old scout who had walked the Wood mostly every day over the last 20 or 30 years had ears and eyes to the ground: in the last 10 years or so the Midge hazard is all but dismissed by pesticide.

'I've got you deep in the heart of me …'

The Midges woe begone, many projects in the conservation of nature are gone overground, evidenced by the countless 'hides' built for observation, some veritable tree-houses on stilts with ladders up; and here's a proof, which we include for reference to marshland habitat …

A study in Bourton Woods, Gloucestershire, England, found that nestboxes were used by Marsh Tits in successive years in only 20 % of cases.

Whilst the Audience may have no interest in such details, the Author was, fleetingly, in the Marsh Tit, whose nesting preferences bring us nice and cosy back into the heart of Bourton Wood's dense undergrowth of fern, nettles, woodland grasses and rushes, with foxglove and cow parsley on the fringes, and all other diverse marsh-borne entanglements beneath a high, high tree cover; so much home to them, the marsh tits eschew new fangled nestboxes for the tangles of the chewed rush sprung mattress; Spring being their favoured time for sprogging one's offsprings; with basement bedstead in the bowels of mother nature for a womb: there would surely be frogs and tadpole tiddlers riddling a blind birth ... just like 'Fern Hill', all so lovely and watery ...

'Time let me play and be
Golden in the mercy of his means, ...
... And the sabbath rang slowly
In the pebbles of the holy streams.
... And playing, lovely and watery
And fire green as grass.'

The poem will bring aged 9 back to most of you ...

**'I would sacrifice anything come what might
For the sake of havin' you near...'**

Looking far ahead, the Author speaks of 'eucatastrophe' within Lothlorien, but the Midgewater Marshes comes near, but only if there's none come too close to callsign.

**'There's an Airforce station, somewhere tucked away
Where it is exactly, we're not supposed to say.
The C.O. and the A.C.O. were always very kind
It's name is quite misleading, life never is a bind ...
At Much-Binding-in-the-Marsh, ...'**
(BBC Radio)

Have we not told that we are in Much-Binding-In-The-Marsh!

There can be little doubt Professor Tolkien would be familiar with this scatty radio show.

Insects will have consumed our scout all his ears in the woods. Whilst he thought he had heard of The Lord of the Rings, he had missed the name of its author; 'Tolkien'? he buzzed. We owe him much more than these cheap shots, though ever by arrow of desire to thank him for a contribution; knowing as we do, so busy in Bourton Wood, he will never read this account of this most sublime arc of England's green and pleasant land.

'Don't you know, little fool, you never can win?'

A final nail in the coffin (of the Midges) was hammered in construction of the Wartime Aerodrome that caused the disappearance of the greatest area of Marshland in the memory of the locals of Moreton-in-Marsh. The Aerodrome is these days replaced by the Fire Service Headquarters; but memories are vivid enough for the storage of its local history within the Bureau of Shire-history in Appendix B: thus are we fully fulfilled of the Philleypools.

We conjecture that some of the vivid description by the locals would warrant identification of the Midgewater Marshes, so much better perhaps than our Bourton Wood; nevertheless, we are sticking in the marshlands of the Wood for association; not only because otherwise we would miss the old scout who was indeed in his place there, and he will be still: if not, then moving somewhere about, scouting; and equally so because the old Aerodrome site, well to the east of Moreton, is out of place in terms of the Professor's Secret of the Shire: but Bourton Wood is in perfect position; which is not to miss the eventuality that the Midges of the old Marshlands were of use in the Professor Tolkien's mentality ... but even the Professor must surely, sometime, wake up to reality ...

But each time I do just the thought of you makes me stop Just before I begin ... cause I've got you *under my skin* ...

'My cuts, short or long, do not go wrong'

Get Thee behind Me Satan is a plea yet in vain echoed from our Cauldron of Appendix C, for we venture off the straight and narrow:

we are in a wold gone wrong. By the scheme of things, perchance our penance is in preparation and lies at Weathertop.

We shall see.

It was at this point, in the approaches of Weathertop, that we took a short cut with Aragorn that did go wrong; and, as a matter of textural accord, Aragorn speaks of such 'short cut' upon the approach of the hobbits to their most fateful of heights, namely Weathertop.

There are more than abundant potentialities by way of choice for likely sites of association on the route of the Quest. Perhaps we should mention one, in part in order to vindicate the choice of another site as Professor Tolkien's most likely association in fact.

'You told me that Broadway was waiting for me ...'

We had long considered the Broadway Tower as a potential association for Amon Hen. This association is overtly in the public domain, as Web resources reveal. The famed Tower has a magnificent range of views over, some say, thirteen counties stretching in the distance into Wales.

There is a full history of the Broadway Tower on the Web. The Tower is known as a 'folly' of the Earl of Coventry, apparently built by the Earl for the pleasure of his wife in such position for the ready view of its lighted Beacon from the distant Coventry.

Once the abode of the doyen of the Arts & Crafts movement, William Morris, the Tower may be viewed by the Public upwards its lighthouse-like spiral staircase, all the way 200 odd feet up to its battlement shaped galleried summit. Without a Web view, the Audience may be assuming that like most towers, the Tower is round in shape. Its shape is a peculiarity, for its facades are three, which makes for a triangular shape in section from above. The Author for one has never before seen a like shaped tower. It is a most impressive sight dominating the Broadway escarpment and skyline, hundreds of feet above the village below.

If one prefers to delve like Gimli below the elevated privilege of The Earl and his visionary spouse, go down for the wartime Nuclear Royal Observer Corps bunker, 100 metres from the Tower pinnacle. Fifty feet down a narrow iron ladder, the Author moled over how times had changed since Earldom lost its cached. Now we were underground spying out for Zeppelin missiles directed from several hundred miles further away than Coventry. Subterranean excavacations must be arranged through Gimli or other authority: Dwarves only.

But no, the cavern has nothing to do with The Mines of Moria, whose transitory 40 miles Gwahir might easily make out on the horizon; Caradrhas is visible to the naked human eye from here.

Unless our eagle-eye has missed it, Professor Tolkien does not specify the carved Eagle upon the Seeing Seat of Amon Hen. Yet the image, captured on film where four carved stone eagles adorn the Seat, is just right. The eagle has the apposite telescopic quality of vision. One examines the Eagle connection and discovers that in the Coat of Arms of the Earl of Coventry, who had the Tower built, the Eagle is inherent. Eyrie enough, but Gwahir might be getting us carried away. The Broadway Tower sits on the middle of three Cotswold hills (Middle as opposed to Fish Hill and Snowshill) whilst Middle-earth has two hills of relevancy: Amon Hen and its fellow Amon Lhaw which are expressed to have Tol Brandir (the Tindrock) sited between them.

Eventually, the Broadway Tower gave way in our association to a seeing point more applicable so far as concerns description and, specifically, location. If our theories of the Professor's Secret of the Shire are to have any credence, then the Broadway Tower is simply in the wrong place for candidature. It overlooks the gem of Broadway village and even in the distance our associations for the Trollshaws and Rivendell, but it does not overlook our association for the Anduin, as Amon Hen must.

Frank Millet and the Americans

Visitors to the churchyard on Snowshill Road, Broadway, may have missed an interesting Latin inscription as they passed under the lychgate. It was carved as a tribute to the famous artist Francis Davis Millet and loosely translated it reads:

"In tribute to Frances Davis Millet a man of excellence in the arts and in literature. He met his death with fortitude as the ship Titanic sank whilst still giving hope to those who feared for their lives. His dear friends sought the dedication of this memorial in fond memory of his treasured fellowship."

Millet's most famous painting is, perhaps, Between Two Fires, which, like many others of the period was executed in the 14th Century Abbot's Grange in Broadway. With the help of William Morris, Millet salvaged the Grange from complete disrepair and it became his studio for many years. Millet was host to a small group of artists, including Americans, who congregated in Broadway at the end of the 19th century, including John Singer Sargent whose painting Carnation Lily Lily Rose is famed for its Broadway setting. Millet was born in Massachusetts, USA, in 1846. He graduated from Harvard with a degree in literature and became a correspondent on the Russian-Turkish War 1877 – 1878. He lived both at Farnham House and Russell House as well as Abbots Grange, which was his studio for many years.

In April 1912 Millet booked a first class passage on the maiden voyage of the Titanic en-route home to the United States. She sank on 15 April having struck an iceberg. Millet was seen helping women and children into lifeboats.

His body was recovered and he is buried at East Bridgewater, Central Cemetery, Plymouth County, Massachusetts.

The Lygon Arms

The Lygon Arms of Broadway is a world renowned hostelry dating centuries back. The Lygon is of the Madresfield connection, more fully revealed on the outskirts of Rivendell. American and other celebrities once thronged here. The Guest Book is apparently scintillating with stardom: Marilyn Monroe, John Wayne, Taylor and Burton etc.; one day we hope to write something about it; but first we shall need to be offered sight of it. We already have a working title for the concept: provisionally entitled ...

'The Deluded Honks (Diana Mitford) meets Kit her Leader (Oswald Mosley) at The Lygon Arms for a *private assignation* (language of the upper crust) or *quick and dirty jump or bunk-up* (language of the Welsh Valleys, or anywhere else who likes their crust without especial sophistication, Yorkshire's puddings coming to mind) with Vita Sackville-West hyper-critical (inter alios) of the Hedges, for they should be straighter than they are: more like a stiff Scotchman, if you follow the straightlace of Her Majesty and Mister Brown, (or perhaps it was his straightlance) who ever missed the iron-centre of her Prince Albert, it is told ... whilst somebody called Thomas is making a nuisance of himself, by urinating where no Good Boyo would and being sick in the same place.'

Our favourite story of John Wayne comes from an old timer of these parts. Whenever he rode into Town, the most famous Cowboy of all time stood every child of the Village ice-cream from the vending van on the Green. The old timer ought to know; he was a child at the time.

Gable Clarke

The Author has yet to review the Lygon Arms Guest Book; he would first search for Clark Gable; with no idea whether Clarke Gable was ever on Broadway, nor in it, we know that Gable Clarke was. Gable Clarke is one of the most famed citizens of Broadway; known for his rustic look and ways; many written works about Broadway contain his photograph and wisdom. Both now long Gone With The Wind, we do so wonder whether Gable the actor was ever in Broadway. It is not going to matter after all; the actor's real name was (William) Clark Gable ... but, breaking news, Gable Clarke's was not: Frank Clarke of Broadway was rechristened for the actor. Quaint enough, but not so ticklish as putting ferrets down your trousers, which Gable (of Broadway ... *not* Clark Gable ... but who, we hear, had plenty of fun ferreting in dark holes without his

254

trousers) did for the American tourists; to be bought his beer for the day, all day. The Author's source reveals that Gable (of Broadway) drank 27 pints of beer one lunchtime, and still thirsty did another 27 the same evening. And after that, Gable went drinking.

You might like to watch the boys ferret legging on the web.

Gable Clarke's photograph adorns The Crown & Trumpet here; and my mate Broadway Bob tells me Gable was rather full one day, so sat on the small bridge nearby, fell asleep and backwards into the River: upon getting out, Gable went back to the Trumpet to dry out with a drink.

A Lygon Footman (indeed, Footman, complete with green waistcoat and sometime Top Hat) mate of the Author thought to make a few quid by hiding behind a bush and snapping a photograph of Paul McCartney and his daughter Stella at the Hotel, maybe for sale. Macca saw him and offered him two choices for his immediate future. One involved keeping his job. As for the film negative: Here Comes The Sun: one more time.

Buckland

We have mentioned in connection with Buckland, Oxfordshire, that there is a further Buckland in Gloucestershire and we go there now; one and a half miles from Broadway. The Web relates-

This beautiful secluded village nestles beneath the Cotswolds escarpment at the foot of Burhill. It is thought to have the oldest rectory in England, with an impressive timbered hall that dates from the fifteenth century. John Wesley preached in the church of St. Michael, the east window of which contains some splendid 15th Century glass, judged by some to be the nicest in the Cotswolds, and reputed to have come from Hailes Abbey at the Dissolution. William Morris attended church services here when he came to Buckland in the 19th Century and was so impressed by the glass that he personally paid for its re-leading.

The Web carries mention of Iron Age fortifications upon the hills above Buckland, with a number of Archaeological finds; and the Author became intrigued by the map-find of 'Burhill', which may possibly once have indicated a 'burning hill' or otherwise a Fire beacon hill.

Broadway is no genuine association in our terms, and yet we are bound to accolade it a worthwhile site, or my mates here would never forgive me. Special thanks to Karen and Natalie Wilde for support and Andy Smith (the Broadway Orc) for being the voice behind the counter …

Smeagol: … even when we's not lissnin'…

The unhappy shape of Weathertop is clearly visible from the promontory of the hill of Broadway Tower, just a few miles away to the North East; in many ways the view is the best available from any perspective, and we aim to show it to the Audience, for its weird sliced top is to shape our thoughts forever after.

Amon Hen, Amon Lhaw and the Tindrock all await Volume II.

Amon Sûl is lurking at no distance now.

Be sober, be vigilant; because your adversary the devil, as a roaring lion, walketh about, seeking whom he may devour…

(I Peter 5:8)

Men (such as Gable of Broadway) are not always so in these here parts; albeit *sometimes* vigilant …

…as in the Covid lockdown periods, filmed by Gary Thompson on https://youtu.be/jzv486jbPw8

WEATHERTOP (REVISITED)

Middle-earth

'One day you'll be in the ditch, Flies buzzing around your eyes, Blood on your saddle … Idiot Wind …'

256

The Audience will know that we are come upon the Hill of the Wind … Amon Sûl …

'It's Alright Ma (I'm only Bleeding)'

There is evidence of the Black Riders. A horn like fire sounds from a hilltop. It is apparently the Brandybucks' horn, not sounded in over 100 years. Crickhollow resounds with horns. Strider speaks of the Dark Times. The horses bolt as a result and only Merry's ponies are left.

Strider elects to leave Bree by the main road. Accused by Sam of taking a shortcut, Strider retorts …

'My cuts short or long, do not go wrong.'

They draw near to the Midgewater Marshes. They see lights leaping from distant hilltops. The hills are now undulating and rising to some 1000 feet, by means of a track which is plain on the ground. Strider tells that there are no barrows on Weathertop.

Professor Tolkien's description of Weathertop is rudimentary, with mention of grassy and rocky sides and a steep climb on one side over a bridge-like stretch of grass, upwards to a hill crowned with the remains of a ring shaped structure. Within the ring is scorched earth, possibly from an attack on Gandalf. The remaining ring structure looks like a broken crown. One is left with imagination of a cut-off, thus flat, hill.

Arguably, in terms of Mother-earth comparable, such a ring of visible crown-like stonework would most usually be flat, especially given the evident burnt nature of the ground: who burns a fire on undulating ground? The feeling is one of empty desolation and bleak creepiness, especially with the impending attack of the Ringwraiths or Nazgûl.

Weathertop's shape is depicted this way on film, but is a mound of rock with banks of grass. Meon Hill is virtually all grass. The film version makes far more of the ruined stonework, including broken statuary.

When attacked by the Ringwraiths, Frodo feels a pain like a dart in his left shoulder. On film this is a severe, life-threatening, sword wound of a Morgul-blade inflicted by the Witch-King of the Nazgûl, before Aragorn charges the evil spirit off with fire, a terror to all Ringwraiths.

Mother-earth

'Rough wind,that moanest loud
Grief too sad for song;
Wild wind, when sullen cloud
Knells all the night long;
Sad storm whose tears are vain,
Bare woods, whose branches strain,
Deep caves and dreary main,—
Wail, for the world's wrong!
(Dirge; Shelley)

Meon Hill is some 6 miles south of Stratford Upon Avon. It forms part of a small range including Dover's Hill. It has a height of 627 feet (according to the vista map at Dover's Hill) and circumference of 2.5 miles …

'… they could now see a line of hills. The highest of them was at the right of the line and a little separated from the others. It had a conical top, slightly flattened at the summit …'

The Professor's text caused us to emphasise this paragraph, whose description was written quite a few years before we were stunned by the congruence of the Professor's words, found much later.

Smeagol: … isser troof, Audiences …

… It is irregularly conical in shape. The most unusual feature of the Hill is that it appears virtually flat on the top, as if the top of the cone had been sliced away by a great sickle. This platform shape is explained by the fact that at some point it was an Iron Age hill-top fort.

The upper fringe of Meon Hill has some bare rocky patches but essentially grass covers the rest. There is much tree growth in particular to the south-west aspect and upper third of the circumference. The very top is virtually free of tree growth except for the so called Witch Tree amongst a very few other scattered specimens. The immediate impression is of something rather odd protruding into the skyline. This may be the aura of the anomaly itself or may be the natural result of the weird history attaching to the area in general and Meon Hill in particular. Meon Hill sticks out of the skyline like a sore thumb or in this case, throat, neck and ribcage; we may yet cut in a shoulder: that of Frodo.

The shape of Meon Hill has become for the Author, iconic; this was so from the date we first saw it, many years ago, when the cone-shape first suggested itself: another fine closer (than Broadway Tower) view of the sliced off cone is from the Stratford Upon Avon side, at Lower Clopton. We took this view of Meon Hill fifteen years before we became aware of any association between Middle- and Mother-earth; and we do not mean here, of Weathertop: we mean any association *at all*; and we first wrote of it another five years later: haunting is not the word: which is omenous; sufficient to mis-spell all one's frolicking about up it.

Leave aside for the moment the image of the body butchered and bleeding; for we sail upon a canvas of far greater force in this wind; one spliced by H.J. Massingham in 'Wold Without End' published in 1932. The Audience may recall mention in RING M:III for its strange tales of the Wychwood. There can be very little doubt that Professor J.R.R. Tolkien knew this work, a leading 'guide-book' (but not so called way back when) of the Professor's very own shire.

'And we passed to the Isle of Witches and heard their musical cry ...'
(Voyage of Maeldune; Tennyson: tbc)

Ship Ahoy!

'... flat-topped Meon Hill with its earthworks faces the sea-like plain in which are Evesham, Worcester and Stratford. The

Cotswolds look on Meon and Meon looks on the plain. Once a sea, it remains one in the eye's vision with the trees for the dark surges of the waves and Meon a pediment for some vanished statue of a Cotswold Cortez …

… Meon Hill puts out among the tree-billows like a square-rigged galleon, and well out in the deeps the Malvern Isle irrelevantly rides …'

Quaint enough for a sea-scene, Massingham should perhaps not have admired the admiral Armada, but have painted 'The Pequod' of Captain Ahab, for there is a Moby Dick of a whale for the harpooning; no distance away at The Trollshaws of The Rings. The Rangers may already have captured Bredon Hill on their Treasure Map; the 'stranded whale' of the Cotswold sea-plain. We lock Bredon Hill away in the Pirate Captain's Treasure Chest and sail away with it to further buccaneering seaventures; we spyglass the Trollshaws our next port of call.

Amon Sûl: the Hill of Wind: the wind is here; and there will be blood, and much before Frodo's time is come, but there are no eyes who see to tell …

Now to be deadly serious …

> **'Why should I let the toad *work***
> **Squat on my life?**
> **Can't I use my wit as a pitchfork**
> **And drive the brute off?'**
> (Toads: Philip Larkin)

Gollum: … *frogs-s … toads-ss … pitchforks-ss* … **by the pricking of my fumbs-ss, sumffing wicked this way cumms-ss …**

Smeagol: … pitchforkses, My Luv…?

Gollum: … *Ends life, kills laughter* … time's up soon, weird, wayward sisters of Wusstershires-ss-ss … dead, dead, dead, human forms-ss of Witches-ss-ss … O, yes-ss … soon enuff … My Precious-ss-ss-ss … an' make a start on Valentines-ss-ss Day…

The Wages of Sin is Death

'My love, she speaks like silence
Without ideals or violence …
Valentines can't buy her …'

Smeagol (in recall of Shakespeare's witchcraft):

'Fair is foul and foul is fair,
Hover through the fog and filthy air …'

Meon Hill was the site and scene of the so called 'witchcraft' murder of Charles Walton in 1945. Charles Walton was found murdered on the night of 14 February 1945 (St. Valentine's Day) at a farm situated on the slopes of Meon Hill. The foremost Police Detective of the era, Robert Fabian, was asked to lead the investigation into Walton's death but failed to gather sufficient evidence to charge anyone with the murder. The scene was a shocking one because the murderer had slashed Walton's neck open with a trouncing (or bill) hook, and driven the prongs of a pitchfork either side of the neck, pinning Walton to the ground in a special way, allowing the blood to flow into the ground. A cross had been carved with the bill hook on Walton's chest, with the implement then being buried into the ribs.

Unbelievably, released quite recently before publication, *steveponty. com* has pictures.

'I stumbled to my feet
I rode past destruction
in the ditches,
With the stitches still mending,
'neath a heart-shaped tattoo
Renegade priests
and treacherous young witches
Were handing out the flowers
that I'd given to you …'

There are to be ditches, stitches … and witches … up here on Meon Hill …

A number of the accounts of the circumstances attending the murder are to be found in the Bureau of Shire-history in Appendix B: *not for the faint-hearted* … hold your breath. The Author evokes the witchcraft of *two* Charles Waltons:1885 and 1945.

We have said all along that Meon Hill gives us the creeps.

We are not alone.

'Deaf to the Welsh wind now …'
('The Malverns'; W.H. Auden)

We reach a new level in the language of The Rings, suspending the suspense of the wicked goings-on at Weathertop: in order to suspend us all from a rooftop in Wales, taking a special journey for the vexed question of how the name Amon Sûl is derived, and equally so, how it might be pronounced. We start from the premise that nobody (apart from Professor J.R.R. Tolkien up there above the rooftops) really knows, given the difference between the pronunciation in the Film (Aragorn's 'Soool') and the BBC version (as to rhyme with 'bull') … and however else you may have heard it.

The one guarantee is that our own will be as nothing any of the Audience will have heard before; simply because it assumes a Welsh provenance: yet it must be readily acknowledged there is nothing to say the Professor's intention with *pronunciation* was that it followed Welsh.

'The answer, my friend , is blowing in the wind …

The Author is, having first found them, to consider Amon Hen and Amon Lhaw in Volume II, but for present purposes, what of Amon Sûl, the Hill of Wind of Weathertop; blowing in the wind without a keyboard circumflex (^)over the vowel 'u'; the circumflex it *should* have *properly* represented: blame this keyboooooaaard for omission. Even if our publisher's format *will* properly represent the circumflex, we shall leave this paragraph intact; simply to draw attention to the matter.

The Audience may recall the Professor's explanation (in Appendix E) of the Quenyan 'Amon' as 'Hill'; plural 'Emyn'. Oddly, and of no significance whatsoever, 'Emyn' in Welsh means 'Hymn'; no doubting our Welsh ancestors went up there on high for Choir practice.

Amusingly enough (for the Author) the ^ is in the Welsh language a 'To' curiously (for the Author) with no ^ over the 'o' even though its pronunciation is fairly long, such that until we rechecked the Welsh Dictionary, we had always assumed there was one; it is in fact pronounced not unlike the 'Tor' of the Derbyshire Peak District; also we understand of the High and Low Tor of the vicinity of New York City.

'To' in Welsh means 'Roof'; just what we need in the wind. There is in Welsh no other word covering 'circumflex'. Yet the 'To' is at least picturesque: we shall no doubt get slated for that in Wales.

We went off on the 'To' not only to shoot the breeze with the Audience amidst all the cloud of just how 'Sul' should be pronounced, but for those interested in the Professor's use of the Circumflex. Enough to make even the sane man jump, we suspect there will be no queue forming off the end for this particular flight of the Professor's parachute; but hang it; let's skydive-

'... the use of the circumflex in other languages such as ... Dwarfish has no special significance, and is used merely to mark these out as alien tongues... '

(The 'other' languages of mention are those *other than Sindarin*, the foregoing citation succeeding the next quotation from Appendix E, specifying the use of the circumflex *in Sindarin itself*.)
And so, as we are to hear, the circumflex in Sindarin indicates a very long vowel sound, but in all other cases, has no particular significance.

(In passing, it may be borne in mind that 'sul' is without more in Welsh pronounced 'seal': sanctity itself for the Welsh speaker who prays so once a week; Dydd Sul being Sun-day in Welsh; the order of components reversed, 'Dydd' meaning 'day'. Any day of the week, 'Amon Sûl' has nothing to do with 'Sunday', whose Welsh equivalent we share merely for indication of its pronunciation: the 'Sul' of Sunday may be spelt in the same way, yet do remember 'Amon Sûl' bears the Professor's circumflex).

So what of the significance of the circumflexed 'u'?

The Welsh language never circumflexes the 'u' vowel; were it to do so, 'Sûl' might well be something like the 'siiirl' of 'Sirloin' steak or, beating it a stretch further, 'soool' as does Aragorn in the Fellowship of the Film Trilogy: assuming the usual vowel sound beaten to death.

And so here we take initial comfort (towards our serial derivations of the circumflexed 'Sûl') from the Professor's Appendix E-

'In Sindarin long vowels in stressed monosyllables are marked with the circumflex, since they tended in such cases to be specially prolonged … [as explained, by way of footnote, in 'dûn' and 'rhûn' [with circumflexed 'u'], respectively 'west' and 'east']'

One (there are alternatives) Welsh word for 'wind' or 'breeze' is 'awel'; hence *(and especially with the benefit of anglicisation, conquering all soon)*, in preference over '(b)ull' (BBC)…'oool' (on Film)… or 'iiirl' (the Author's steak), perhaps we stretch a wingspanned earphone to 'ooowl', like the wise old bird?

We may well be in a position to hear where the 'S' sound may originate, there being a place of Mother-earth for guidance: 'Llansawel' of the Carmarthenshire of West Wales; the Windy 'church' or 'village'. The 'Llan' of church (or village) calls in Welsh for a soft 'S' for comfort of speech before the 'a' vowel. In other words, 'Llanawel' is a awkward one (hear what a awkward one, indeed, it is) for the Welsh tongue; it cries out for an 'S' for comfort of speech.

As does 'Llan', so 'Amon' ends with the hard 'N' consonant; and so Amon 'Sooowl'(representing a very long and flat 'sawel')is at the very least within earshot of the Welsh ear.

In this rendering, the Anglicised pronunciation of Llansawel is a mighty ally: butchering the 'll' sound, and without the phonetic input of the Celt and ignoring vowel strength altogether, we might hear Clansowl ... The Englishman speaks of 'Llansawel' as something like 'Clansowl'; and we really cannot get into the front end (double 'll') here; but which is intrinsic to our derivation of 'Amon Lhaw' in our quest in The Hobbit.

**'Ah but I might as well
try and catch the wind ...'**
(Donovan)

Amon S ... ooowl ... (of the wise old) is as close as the Author is going to get in our contention for the Professor's intended pronunciation; yet ever with acknowledgement that pronunciation might not be intended to follow Welsh, apart from word derivation.

Thus Amon Sooowl(as in wise old) is our preference, bearing in mind that our suggestion is but conjecture in any event: yet we do suggest that the derivation from 'awel' is no longer blowing in the wind: the circumflexed 'ul' is derived from 'awel' with the lenitation 'S' prefixed.

The marginal change to 'Amon Soul' does not put the wind up us too much. Either option is some distance from Viggo Mortensen's manner of pronunciation; but then again whooooo knooows hooow the Film makers schoooled 'Soool'.

We have reheard the BBC Robert Stephens version, to rhyme with 'bull'; but are dull (yet another) to that sound, having no reserves of bull, Welsh or other, to clear it up. 'It' comes in many colours, and consistencies; so if you feel like hearing it being done, listen to it sung by one of our masters of song: make you so damn happy (another hit), be doing number ones, no matter how many times you do doo. Hit (with prefixed 'S', one more time in the ancient Welsh tradition) on the artist (who laid the dead skunk about Brockenborings)and get covered in it; the Author saw him do it, live: May 22, 2011; played the guitar, banjo and piano all his bearing down ways through performance. Loudon calls it (coloured not up, but down, for consistency), the Shit Song.

Amon Sawel: too far out for some?

Ah well: Llansawel is a fair wind away from Chicago.

> **'We stood in the windy city, the gypsy boy and I;**
> **We slept on the breeze in the midnight ...'**
> (Donovan)

Binding of the Ring

Making a match between Middle- and Mother-earth, as we are, (and of much comfort to the Author in the integrity of the Quest), the simulation of Weathertop in the Fonstad Atlas is so accurate, we swear the author must have been here to Meon Hill; it really is so very close a picture; except of course that the Atlas Queen has (presumably) never visited the Shire to see for herself.

Bloody earth curdling

We found nothing and nobody of amusement upon Meon Hill. The Author learned too late (as in the Wychwood) that one needs the farmer landowner's permission to go atop Weathertop. We had already been atop. We found a grassy curving, not entirely flat, summit with thistles the most prevalent. The top feels about as desolate as one could imagine, despite the miraculous views for many miles around. In perfect honesty, the Author could not identify the 'Witch Tree' but some scout has posted a decent photograph on the Web, together with a synopsis of the Walton murder.

The Author is obliged to mention the anomaly of the route to Weathertop, because it has significant implications for the purposes of our Regaining the Precious in knowledge of ley lines, somewhere up the road ahead.

We receive some support for the anomaly of the diversion from the main track within the text of The Rings itself. Chapter 11(A Knife In The Dark) contains the following words of Pippin, curiously linking in with the short cuts of Aragorn(one that goes wrong, to Broadway, of which we have already spoken)-

'Our last short cut through woods nearly ended in disaster.'

Aragorn then-

'... led the way quickly down towards the wooded valley.

His plan as far as they could understand it without knowing the country ... was to steer *as straight as he could* over the wild lands to Weathertop Hill. In that way they would, if all went well, cut off a great loop of the road, which further on bent southwards to avoid the Midgewater Marshes. But, of course, they would have to pass through the marshes themselves ...'

The loop below Chetwood is clearly shown on the Ring-Maps. The company passes through the Chetwood instead; and the Marshes. Aragorn picks up the geography-

''That is Weathertop,' said Strider. 'The Old Road which we have left far away on our right, runs to the south of it and not far from its foot' ...

Strider is keen to point out that Weathertop is some way off the road: one might bear in mind the anomaly of the passage by Weathertop for future reference: for we delay our thoughts on the science of ley lines until somewhere up the road ahead.

> **'Like one, that on a lonesome road**
> **Doth walk in fear and dread,**
> **And having once turned round walks on,**
> **And turns no more his head;**
> **Because he knows, a frightful fiend**
> **Doth close behind him tread.'**
> (Rhyme Ancient Mariner; Coleridge)

The descriptive associations of Weathertop and Meon Hill are reasonably congruous, but the attack on Frodo by stabbing must surely qualify as a clear linkage. Professor Tolkien would undoubtedly be fully conversant with the Walton murder. Quite apart from his avowed interest in all spiritual matters, and of course The Rings is strewn with Witch references, this was the leading news story of the day appearing on the front page of all the major newspapers. The case involved the renowned Fabian of the (Scotland) Yard. The witchcraft comparables and the methods of piercing the torso uncanny … We obviously cannot be certain that Frodo's hurt was allusion to a real death, but there can be no doubt about the possibility, or even probability, of the Professor's application; and (within the 'Precious Regained' of our quest on the road up ahead), we speculate upon the stage of writing of The Rings when the Walton murder occurred.

The villagers about Meon Hill at the time of the Walton murder built a wall of silence; and ever since. Locals today know something; we have spoken with some but we say no more, not least because they will not.

The Author is determined to uncover more of the truth of Weathertop, and what Professor J.R.R. Tolkien may have known or suspected, but for the moment it is beyond earthly powers …

Rambling Man

Dover's Hill

It was the site of an informal olympic games (yes, Olympic Games) in 1622. It represents the most vivid outcrop of the Cotswold Edge exposed much earlier, whose oolite limestone substrata are mined all along the escarpment for the yellow stone for which the Cotswold Hills are famed.

Long Compton

*"Sheer coincidence you said, Synchronicity'

The Author hops the web back to Frogmorton of RING M:IV and the Village of Long Compton, and therein mention of *two Charles Waltons* ...

Located 4 miles NW of Chipping Norton [Hobbiton] *and 4 miles NE of Moreton-in-Marsh* [Bree].

This attractive Cotswold stone village stretches out along the A3400 between Stratford-upon-Avon and Chipping Norton to the very foot of the long hill (occupied by the Rollright Stones) that climbs up over the Cotswold edge, across the county boundary from Warwickshire into Oxfordshire. The village has a cheerful inn, many trim houses and cottages, and an Anglo-Saxon church (the core of which is 13th-century), St. Peter and St. Paul, whose handsome perpendicular tower looks westward over a large bumpy field which was probably the site of the original ancient village. The church's lovely south porch is approached by a yew-lined path leading from a delightful 17th-century cottage on 'stilts' with lynch gate.

The village in bygone days was notorious for witchcraft. Local belief in the power of witches continued until well into the 20th-century. In 1875, a Long Compton man slew one old woman with his sickle because he was convinced that she had caused the debilitating pains and cramps in his legs. Tradition says that in the 6th-century St Augustine visited the church and raised a man from the grave. '

Such is Frogmorton, of so many frogs, toads and familiar to Witches ...

... and a *first Charles Walton* ...

'I'm Dead ... But I Don't Know It ...
He's dead, he's dead ... I didn't know !'
(Randy Newman)

---

*   Loudon Wainwright

Ebrington

'Hickory Dickory Dock,
the mouse ran up the clock ...'

Very close to Meon Hill (and also to Hidcote Manor of the Sackville-West connection) is the small village of Ebrington. It becomes somewhat tiresome to adjectivise the villages of the Cotswolds; one becomes road weary with 'pretty' 'delightful' and 'charming' all of which they most undoubtedly are.

There really is no substitute for seeing the Shire for oneself.

Ebrington is notable for the Ebrington Arms pub, the lively heart of the village, and St. Eadburgha' s Church: St. Eadburgha was a desendant of King Alfred; she was sainted for her piety. The legend has it she was given a choice between Riches and the Bible and chose the latter. The Author knows of two Churches dedicated to St. Eadburgha. The second is the Twelfth Century marvel between Broadway and Snowshill in Worcestershire.

The Ebrington Church is distinctive by reason of the work of Robert Thomson, the Mouseman. Yorkshire has many more examples of his famed work in the carving of mice upon wood. Many pieces of furniture have the trademark mouse (typically 2 to 3 inches long) or mice carved not into the wood but in relief raised above the wooden base. They scurry everywhere in Ebrington Church, including the Rood Screen.

In passing, the Broadway St. Eadburgha's has a Thomson church mouse of its own. One will need to attend a Service to catch a glimpse. This mouse is at all other times confined to the safety of its hole and home out of sight and reach. It is normally to be found crawling up the Paschal Candle. The Author ought to know because his missus gifted the Memorial to the Church.

Of more than thirsty interest is the Greene Dragon Pub at Cowley. One may need the instincts of the Gloucestershire Girl Guides (who are headquartered nearby; indeed that is the first signal that one is nearby) to find it, but it is well worth hacking around for a couple of hours if the Guides are away with Arkela. The Bar has 55 Thomson mice but you will never count them all. Not unlike the Rollright Stones for unaccountability. There is even one on the oak gate outside.

Wandering Star

> **'When shall we three meet again,**
> **In thunder, lightning or in rain?'**

It need hardly be mentioned that Meon Hill is but 6 Miles from the Stratford upon Avon base-camp of the Witches of Macbeth. Stratford is itself replete with all manner of spooks and ghost stories. The Author might one day take one or two of the Audience to an old haunt of the Author's, where the proprietor speaks of the Ghost of a Victorian gentleman who regularly sits down in one corner.

The Mickleton area in which Meon Hill resides has a folklore history of Witchcraft. The nearby village of Bretforton has a curious feature. It has one of the very few public houses owned by the National Trust. This has a long history that is worth investigating in its own right. The Inn is The Fleece, locally known as 'The Ark' perhaps because of its quaint shape which might look a little ark-like, assuming one knows what an ark looks like. There is the most impressive collection of pewter plate imaginable. Without wishing to be period – date or time accurate (this not being the Antiques Roadshow), it is real Oliver Cromwell eating style …

Startling are the so called 'Witch Rings' which lie in front of each of the two public fireplaces at the Inn. One fireplace is dated 1670. These are circles of white, two on one fireplace and three on the other, painted into the hearth of each. They are not merely painted; but circles grooved into the floor around a raised centre and painted around in a circle, each 8 inches in diameter; quite apart from the shape, why white one wonders?

> *Is there any body out there?*
> **… who knows of Witch Circles … ?**

They were for the purpose of warding off witches and other evils, as the pub literature tells. Quite why a witch would be coming down the Chimney is beyond us, but that is our ignorance and the Witch Rings are indeed there.

The Audience will well remember that Charles Walton is done to death primarily with a trouncing/bill hook, otherwise called a sickle or scythe. The latter were apparently a panacea for witches …

Mr. Louis Foster Edwards, of Harlech, recalling the memories of many years ago, offers the following evidence:--

Scythe-Blades and Fairies. – 'In an old inn on the other side of Harlech there was to be an entertainment, and, as usual on such occasions, the dancing would not cease until morning. I noticed, before the guests had all arrived, that the landlady was putting scythe-blades edge upwards up into the large chimney, and, wondering why it was, asked her. She told me that the fairies might come before the entertainment was over, and that lithe blades were turned edge upwards it would prevent the fairies from troubling the party, for they would be unable to pass the blades without being cut.'
(The Fairy-Faith in Celtic Countries, by W.Y. Evans-Wentz, (1911),

**'How can I cut these binding cords?
How can I break this damning spell? …'**
(Shaw; *tbc*)

As our Appendix C attests, the methods for the judgment of guilt in witchcraft were numerous, pins for bleeding, and also 'sacking': where the victim was tied inside an old sack, sometimes leather, but most commonly for wool, which may be stitched together to accommodate the poor soul. Strange to say, our guide that day showed us several kinds of old wool sacks, commonplace in the vicinity, especially in the lee of sheep grazing Meon Hill over so many centuries; and the thought of being put in the sack, sometimes with animals to liven things up, did indeed rather stick in the memory, if it serves us well. The judgement was even more perverse: if the witch drowned, she was innocent. If she survived the water, she was guilty.

> 'Have I offended Lucifer's Hordes?
> That they swarm from deepest Hell.'

The darkness of the door of ignorance has been enlightened. Witches were feared to infiltrate by chimneys in Victorian times. Read the dark poem of Mary Coleridge …

The Witch

I have walked a great while over the snow,
And I am not tall nor strong.
My clothes are wet, and my teeth are set,
And the way was hard and long.
I have wandered over the fruitful earth,
But I never came here before.
Oh, lift me over the threshold, and let me in
at the door!

The cutting wind is a cruel foe.
I dare not stand in the blast.
My hands are stone, and my voice a groan,
And the worst of death is past.
I am but a little maiden still,
My little white feet are sore.
Oh, lift me over the threshold, and let me in
at the door!

Her voice was the voice that women have,
Who plead for their heart's desire.
She came – she came – and the quivering flame
Sank and died in the fire.
It never was lit again on my hearth
Since I hurried across the floor,
To lift her over the threshold,
and let her in
at the door.

The word 'witch' is absent from the body of the poem, perhaps to suggest we might be speaking of all women who might, in all innocence, be susceptible to the charge; she need not scream 'I am a Witch' to be thought so. The Author has taken the layout of the Poem, with the 'door' of each stanza staggered to the next line for effect, from 'Witch Words' edited by Robert Fisher (1987), because of the powerful effect of doing so, tending to the open-ended question whether she will indeed be let in. Moreover, it tends to resonate the dread of the voice of the last stanza: that the Witch will invade the chimney and hearth unless she *is* to come in through *the door*. The absence of the exclamation at the end indicates the inevitability of the visitation and the voice's resignation to it ...

> **'There was a wicked messenger ...**
> **When questioned who had sent for him**
> **He answered with his thumb**
> **For his tongue it could not speak, but only flatter.'**

... one has heard, even recently, of some very strange goings-on up there on Meon Hill, ... talk of grown men and women wearing the heads of animals upon their shoulders ... and the oldest friend to some, (but not to anyone the Author calls a friend), has indeed been there, ... and, believe me, this friend who gorges on a grudge against goodness, who devours all, and who carries a manic curse for the corruption of mankind ... is summoned to go there again ... for witchcraft, murder and bloodletting are not unknown on Weathertop; but the murderer is, and may be destined to remain so ... who knows?

> **'Upon a bank, easeless with knobs of gold,**
> **Beneath a canopy of noonday smoke,**
> **I saw a measureless Beast, morose and bold,**
> **With eyes like one from filthy dreams awoke,**
> **Who stares upon the daylight in despair**
> **For very terror of the nothing there.'**
> (Gloria Mundi: De La Mare; *tbc*)

> **'Mercy Me, Master'**

... for the old friend is summoned to go to the old house by the Witch

Tree on Meon Hill some night soon, perhaps tonight: the Messenger will be answering the door ... and it will most likely be the night of St. Valentine's Day because of what is going on inside of that house ...

Voices over Shire (rumbling, misgiving chant)-

'Thunder on the mountain, heavy as can be ...
the hammer's on the table
the pitchfork's on the shelf
For the love of God,
you ought to take pity on yourself.'

Voice (Inside; Dark Speech) '... It is I, the Messenger bids thee welcome ... we have been expecting you for quite some time ... old friend ... Come ... Come ... Come ...'

Smeagol ... where is it messenger's come from, My Luv, an' where's taking us to ...?

'Beyond the horizon, 'neath crimson skies ...
Through countries and kingdoms and temples of stone
Beyond the horizon right down to the bone ...'

Smeagol: ... *right down to the bone,* Author Master ... ?

' ... a messenger came ... from Mordor: a horseman in the night ... The Lord Sauron the Great, so he said, wished for our friendship ... And he asked urgently concerning *hobbits,* of what kind they were, and where they dwelt ... For Sauron knows ... that one of these was known to you on a time ... find this thief ... and get from him, willing or no, a little ring, the least of rings, that once he stole ... '

(Gloin, Council of Elrond)

Smeagol ... **So why do those demonic faces glare at me?**

(Demonic Faces: G. Bernard Shaw)

Witch (Dying):

'Someone hit me from behind ...
Through this weary world of woe ...
No one on earth would ever know ...'

RING M VIII:
The Last Bridge

'I saw ten thousand talkers whose tongues were all broken'

Any number of silent tongues are set in stone upon the roof of the Church whose township at last reveals The Last Bridge.

Middle-earth

The index to The Rings provided by the Professor is to the point, there being one only to The Last Bridge; but such reference is one so crammed full of relevant detail, we are bound to cite its relevant features-

'We have now come to the River Hoarwell, that the Elves call Mitheithel … There is no way over it … except by the Last Bridge on which the Road crosses …'
'What is that other river we can see far away there?' asked Merry.
'That is Loudwater, the Bruinen of Rivendell,' answered Strider. 'The Road runs along the edge of the hills for many miles from the Bridge to the Ford of Bruinen. But I have not thought yet how we shall cross that water. One river at a time! We shall be fortunate indeed if we do not find the Last Bridge held against us…
They hurried along with all the speed they could make, and after a mile or two they saw the Last Bridge ahead, at the bottom of a short steep slope …'

Mother-earth

We follow Strider's advice and traverse one river at a time; but in fact two, the Mitheithel and the Hoarwell combined. We shall be crossing the Bruinen at, where else, but the Ford of Bruinen. If the Audience is lost, we plot the Bruinen or Windrush up the road ahead at the foot of The Trollshaws.

We cannot but resist whetting the appetite of the Rangers, for that 'short steep slope' is very familiar to the Author: the hill on the Broadway Road (B4632) out of the town that is home to The Last Bridge: comb through the Wikipedia file of Winchcombe, and all its links; do look out and up to the grotesque 'gargoyles' of St. Peter's Church; but there is yet one link missing: how to find The Last Bridge? A tour of Winchcombe discloses no major bridge to speak off; at least at first sight: but there is, or *was*, one.

This following is a tale not of two cities, towns nor villages, but of *Three* bridges; we have emphasised the threefold for the threesomes in our Cauldron of Appendix C: we warn the Audience of a proclivity in this regard. Likewise we have mentioned how we went wrong at Broadway, for its Tower, and we were, if one remembers, serially at cross-eyed purposes in our quest for Hobbiton, where Oxford first caught our eyeball: well, we are afflicted not once, but twice, more in failure of 20/20 VISION …

A similar peradventure occurred in relation to The Last Bridge. We went through three (even four) permutations before settling finally upon our preferred candidate. It became our preference for association with The Last Bridge especially for because it tied in with our conclusion of the Mitheithel (or Hoarwell) and also the Bruinen, whose confluence is shown just to the south of The Last Bridge on the Ring-Maps. Many will recall our citation of the River Windrush for the Bruinen by easy transference of the Welsh 'rush', Brwynen; but there is much more to do with the Bruinen before we make a match, as we attempt at the foot of the Trollshaws.

We precede our ultimate association by reference to the two other bridges which crossed our mind in terms of The Last Bridge; *our third being the last and definitive*. We consoled ourselves in the knowledge that this area (to the south and east of The Trollshaws) is swimming with rivers and rivulets and thus an everlasting number of bridges of varying size and importance. Ironically, our first in contention was in our earliest draft account: *The* Last Bridge. We have elected to leave the account intact because this little bridge is a treasure of beauty, the rustic idyll in our memory; before we drown in reverie, we cannot resist that we have left in our initial account as written.

Unabridged.

Bridge at Ford

We discover the river ford of 'Ford'; a bridge crossing over the Windrush River, in a suitably southern but *easterly* position for the purposes of the Professor's Secret of the Shire. A minor bridge these days, over a winding country road, the Bridge at Ford nevertheless has great antiquity and charm; for country people and ways, it would no doubt be of much further significance as a crossing in the days of the Professor.

For those affording a trip to Ford, the bridge has the most charming fairy-glade stretch of water, Windrush or anywhere, that the Author has ever had the joy to set eyes upon.

Having acknowledged our perceived misconception here, the Rangers might like to wander the area for our ultimate association, being some 3 miles away, and of itself a bridge within the nearby vicinity.

Eckington Bridge

Now this is a major bridge in the area straddling the River Avon, on a rounded oxbow like curve, midway in distance between Upton on Severn and Evesham, the source of great Tolkien family connection, even to this day. A serious contender for its real presence, five spanned arches over a wide stretch, perhaps 100 Metres; yet we realise that Eckington Bridge, being marginally west of Bredon Hill on Mother-earth, is on the wrong side of the Trollshaws to fulfil our concept of the Secret of the Shire.

Even so, Eckington Bridge is worth a look on the Web in its own sturdy right.

The Mitheithel: Unbuilding the Bridge

'Oh, a dainty plant is the Ivy green,

279

That creepeth o'er ruins old!'
(Charles Dickens)

The Footbridge is a little bridge somewhat lost in the annals of the history of Winchcombe; but we must yet review that history for a derivation of the 'Mitheithel'.

It will have become self-evident that a surfeit of bridges, without the focal point of nearby town or village, might lead to confusion; and we have been: but we were struck by a flash of intuition in the inkling that the river 'Mitheithel' must have a Professorial, nay Tolkienesque, build-up, and so we began to take the construction of it apart, brick by brick.

The first brick was built from the Welsh Dictionary, from an intuition that 'eithel' might be a derivation separate from the 'Mith' root: by way of *elision,* increasingly familiar to us from our quest in The Hobbit. The build down is destructed from the Welsh word 'eiddew' for *ivy:* phonetically, 'eyethew', so long as we take care that the sound of the Welsh 'dd' is understood.

Now 'th' of 'Mitheithel', which in both instances we are accustomed to sound hard, indeed as in 'both', does not equate at all, phonetically speaking, with 'dd' in Welsh, which sounds softly as in 'wi*th*' and '*th*e' … or, indeed in ei*th*er of *th*ese or *th*ose, and as also in *th*an, *th*at, *th*en, *th*ey and *th*us, tending to prove what a commonplace sound it is.

Yet 'eiddew', might well, by a hardening of the sound from one language to another, be heard to correlate: for we must open our ears to hear whether the Professor will have doubled-up the *second* pronunciation with the *first* of the double 'th' of Mitheithel; and so the second 'th' will be pronounced not as the soft 'dd' of the Welsh meaning for 'ivy', but hard in both, and indeed as in 'both': phonetically, 'Mitheithew', 'th' hard in both cases: 'eith' derived from 'eidd' of 'eiddew'.

'Ew' of eidd – ew sounds as in the yew tree (but with 'y' silent); and the Professor takes secateurs to lop off '(y)ew' at the end of the branch and engrafts it 'eith-*el*'.

Our destruction is thus: Mith – eiddew; Mith – eithew ('th' hard in both places); and finally, 'Mith – eithel'.

'Soft' and 'hard' will not be the professional linguist's method of indicating sound, but the Author shan't bodder beyond this; for it is the Author's only theory, method or pathway for our thoughts thought through.

After all the tongue-twisting, 'Mitheithel' is, for the Author at least(by now becoming fairly used to the Professor's patterns in the creation of place names by elision),a relatively easy derivation of 'eiddew', the Welsh word for 'Ivy'.

'Mitheithel' is born of ...

Before we take the myth out of the 'Mith' of 'eithel' (now representing the Welsh ivy, 'eiddew'), so what of 'Ivy' about The Last Bridge?

The second brick was foundationed on the Ivy Castle of the township of Winchcombe. Not within our knowledge, and we submit only within the purview of very few eyes such as those belonging to Professor J.R.R. Tolkien, the Web has become the all-seeing eye of our Earth –

Documentary evidence indicates that there was a castle at Winchcombe east or north east of the town. It appears to have been adulterine, constructed 1140-44. Leland writes 'There was a fortress or castle right next to the south side of St Peter's. A very long time ago there was a church dedicated to St Nicholas in the eastern part of the town, but it was ruined long since. This parish church, (according to documents at Winchcombe Abbey) was later known as Ivy-castle, and its site is now occupied by a few poor houses and gardens. Gatehouse suspects that the reason for the name Ivy-castle is that when the old building fell into ruin, ivy grew up its walls. The last Prior of Winchcombe told me that he had heard of a fort or castle once existing in the east or north-east part of the town.

And so how to Ivy into league with 'Myth'? Our research of the area disclosed The Mythe area of nearby Tewkesbury, which might have been enough for most of our followers, yet better still disclosing that 'Mythe' in Old English means the joining of two rivers. Yet to nominate a River, now we need two.

> **' ... I hear arising**
> **from lanterned gardens sloping to the river ...**
> **The high thin rare continuous worship**
> **Of the self-absorbed.'**
> ('Here on the cropped crass ...' (infra); Auden)

Chosen for the way the town indeed plunges down a slope to the river, such that flooding is indeed commonplace; yet self-absorption is a pour pun already used onwards at Rivendell.

The River Isbourne is a pretty little river, often overlooked in transit through Winchcombe: a statement readily explicable by virtue that it runs shyly below the steepish hill on which the township sits, via Sudeley Castle(no connection with the Ivy one, yet Sudeley of some note on the Web but whose walls there is insufficient time to scale here), by three coy little bridges of no specific stature or name: the Isbourne so sheepish that in crossing the bridges, one fails to realise that the River flows beneath; we bleet, sheepishly enough, that one of the roads under which the river meanders is Sheep Street.

And yet it is the little River with a proud boast: the River Isbourne is the only river in England to flow north for its entire length. It emerges from a spring on Cleeve Common (nearby Cheltenham) and joins the River Avon at Evesham, more or less directly North of Winchcombe.

Our contention for the Mitheithel, especially for the line of its flow by comparison with the Ring-Maps, and the fact that it flows through the town of the old Ivy Castle (and the important transference from the Welsh 'eiddew'), is by several strands of association, the River Isbourne.

And thus 'Mitheithel' is born of Isbourne.

The second river of 'Myth' connection flows below the road ahead.

Light Finds the New Places We Tread;
the River of Bruinen

Of note previously (linking the Rivers Ray and Great Ouse), Peter Ackroyd reminds us-

The Thames has many tributaries ... many are now buried; many are forgotten ...

The River Windrush is the second of our two Rivers of 'Mithe' connection; except that these two do not as a matter of exact fact connect; yet the source of the Windrush is so close to the flow of the Isbourne that it meets the Author's requirement full well. Both rise in the area known as Seven Springs, such that they may freely be associated, and for our purposes connected. The Professor clearly knew the Windrush intimately, for its associations are all about us in this Volume I, notably for Swin-brook and the Stock-brook, which recalls our contention for the Windrush on the Shire Map.

We have, for the time being, exhausted the tale of two Rivers, the Mitheithel and the Bruinen, but we must yet give further rationale to the flow of the Bruinen; and we are to do so when further light shines upon the River: that will be from the foot of the hill shown on the Ring-Maps as The Trollshaws. The tale of the Bruinen is yet incomplete until we go further up the River Bruinen: from The Trollshaws.

Incidentally, we make nothing of Greyflood nor Loudwater yet; others might; but they may be simple alternatives to the waters we have been drowning in thus far.

Bridges and Tears

> **'And like those waters rushing**
> **Among the wooden piers,**
> **A flood of thoughts came o'er me**
> **That filled my eyes with tears'**
> (The Bridge; Henry Wadsworth Longfellow)

Gollum: … *They cursed us. Murderer they called us. They cursed us, and drove us away. And we wept, Precious, we wept to be so alone …*

The Author promises tears by the end, perhaps your own, for much depends on the appeal of evil that dwells in your heart: for the judgment of guilt is (like all else) up the road ahead …

Smeagol … where will it end, My Luv …

Gollum: … Fords-ss Bruinens, precious …

Smeagol … when will it end, My Luv …

Gollum: … Valentines-ss days-ss, precious …

Smeagol … how will it end, My Luv …

Gollum: … the Second Coming, precious … and a promiss is a promis-ss, is a promiss-ss-ss, precious-ss-ss …

Binding of the Ring

The *Last* Bridge

But why might the Footbridge be called the *Last* Bridge? One would have assumed it was the last in geographical terms; but, no, we believe the Professor alluded to it as the 'last' for historical reasons. These became apparent the very first time we walked the Footbridge of Winchcombe. Quite frankly, having ridden over it countless times by motor transport, we walked it for the first time in Summer 2011 and the reason for the Professor's nomenclature was here for all to see, on its iron commemorative plate:

THIS BRIDGE WAS COMPLETED IN APRIL 1984 TO REPLACE ONE DATING FROM 1899 PRIOR TO 1950 THE RIVER WAS FORDED WITH A FOOTBRIDGE FOR PEDESTRIANS

Prior to 1950, the Professor would have known the crossing of the River Isbourne by bridge on foot. We thrilled to the thought that, just as so many other sites along the Quest, Professor Tolkien stood here and looked upon the same bridge, or rather, its predecessor.

The stalwart Eckington Bridge is far more of a *last* bridge in terms of destination west on Mother-earth, onward to, say, Cheltenham; but this was the last pedestrian *foot* bridge, of which the name speaks for itself. We had made a mental note of a walk on foot before we came to see the Footbridge for ourselves, the name having imagined itself in our mind as an ancient of the type.

Gollum: ... issn't no footbridges-ss from riverbanks-ss to riverbanks-ss left now ... iss there, precious-ss...?

Smeagol: ... Author Master ...?

> **'Indeed, it seemed a hidden enemy**
> **Must lurk within the clouds above that bank,**
> **It strained so wildly its pale, stubborn eye,**
> **To pierce its own foul vapours dim and dank;**
> **Till, wearied out, it raved in wrath and foam,**
> **Daring that Nought Invisible to come ...'**
> (Gloria Mundi: De La Mare; *tbc*)

The one bridge that immediately springs to mind is the Mathematical Bridge over the River Cam in Cambridge in Queens College of the University: now that is a heavy duty sore sight of scurrying scoundrel eyes orcing over a bridge of the mediaeval kind; except that it dates from just 1749. The Footbridge of Winchcombe will have been nothing so grand, but the Cambridge one strikes a picture. Worth a look on the Web for its (absence of) nuts and bolts, we may just imagine the last Orcs, (joints and necks of nuts and bolts spawned on the sordid banks of a poet), swarming over the last bridge to the last battle ... or, as Aragorn doth wonder ... perhaps to *find it held against us* ... by other forces ...?

Voices over Shire (whooping, gloating applause)–

'I'll burn that bridge before you can cross …
They'll be no mercy for you once you've lost …
If I catch my opponents ever sleepin'
I'll just slaughter them where they lie …
All my loyal and much-loved companions
They approve of me and share my code …'

We shall endeavour to locate a photograph of the old Footbridge, and will have shared it if we did. Its significance is marked on all Maps, including those of Ordnance Survey: 'Footbridge' is marked on all maps as if a distinct vicinity of itself; not merely to mark the site of the Bridge, but as a focal point of Winchcombe. We challenge the Audience to suggest the same phenomenon elsewhere; we came up with the Ironbridge area of Birmingham, but we think instances rare enough.

The Footbridge does indeed cross the Isbourne on the Broadway Road out of Winchcombe and yet indeed it does slide beneath the road at the bottom of a 'short steep slope'. One really does fail to notice the River flowing beneath the B4632.

We recall the Professor's abhorrence of mechanical process, to the detriment of nature, even as to motor cars and roads, which makes the Professor one of the first of the Green Party that we may acknowledge; but this awakening was borne to us last of all; yet at last: upon reading the signage of the Footbridge of Winchcombe.

'In Venice among the canals he found himself 'almost free of the cursed disease of the internal combustion engine of which all the world is dying."
('J.R.R. Tolkien A Biography' by Humphrey Carpenter).

Rambling Man

Hoarwell

Voices over Shire (gibbering, jarring psychobabble)-

286

**'I'm gonna make you come to grips with fate
When I'm through with you,
you'll learn to keep your business straight ...'**

We have a second river-name to deal with; the Hoarwell. Much depends upon which of the Ring-Maps one chooses to look at, for the bracketted (Hoarwell) sometimes appears as the name of the river by other Ring-Maps ascribed as the Mitheithel; but for the moment we are looking at the zoomed-out version forming the North-West section of Middle-earth, the one divided into four quarters. Whilst we know from Strider that the Mitheithel and the Hoarwell are one and the same, the relevant of the Ring-Maps tends to show the Hoarwell as the river which unites the Mitheithel and the Bruinen; and so, can we make anything of Hoarwell downstream? To repeat, we make nothing of Greyflood nor Loudwater yet; others might; but they may be simple alternatives of purely descriptive nature.

As a matter of entire conjecture, but here beyond into the realms of speculation, we advocate the town of Cirencester for association with Hoarwell. Once more the Professor would be naming a river for the main town upon it, just as Mitheithel for Winchcombe. Now the latter stem of Cirencester is of 'caester', meaning old Roman Town; yet what of Ciren, or as we hear it, 'Siren'. There is the easy derivation of 'hearing' the siren, hence hear well or conceivably, Hoar-well. The Sirens of Greek Mythology were by their female allure wont to entice sailors literally onto the hard-rocks. It crosses our mind (but we hardly risk share her with the Audience, as a Siren consorted with by the Professor) that the colloquial meaning of a woman who is a 'siren' speaks to her attractive but dangerous allure: and we say no more of the 'Hoar' of Hoarwell, except that all old Roman towns had a well. We shall speak no further of the 'Hoar' of Hoarwell but we expect to pay the full price, in terms of frosty response, for calling any girl so crude.

**'If ever the devil's plan was made to torment man
It was you, Jezebel, it was you ...'**

Smeagol (of Jezebel): ... her dressing in finery and putting on makeup led to the association of the use of cosmetics with *painted women* or prostitutes ...

Gollum (sings; mimics The Nobel Voice): ... Jezebel the nun she violently knits-ss-ss-ss ...

Lest any observer shudder at the possibility of such crudity on the Professor's behalf, we call to mind the observations of the Fifth of the Wise and the Great (Isaacs) upon the 'Halfast' of the Professor's creation; all so long ago in our quest in The Hobbit.

For those in disgust with the mere intuition that the Professor may have walked this street, the Author's impression is that the Professor was the complete clinician in terms of etymology, philology and any other 'ology that concerns words. Words are simply words, devoid of the emotive nuance of any word to thrill the blood. If the Audience is to think the Author overdoes the male chauvinist (and contra-feminist) doctrine implicit in our rendering of 'Hoarwell', and indeed the fastidiousness of a clinical approach, read the Professor's Letter number 43 for a theoretical upon the female of the species. The Author sincerely believes that were we to print any of it, we would lose half our Audience; assuming we have an audience, and assuming half is female; but assuming the Ladies would take offence in the first place: where sincerely none is intended.

Voices over Shire (gibbering, jarring psychobabble)-

' ... I'm gonna wring your neck ...
You can take your clothes put 'em in a sack
You goin' down the road, baby and you can't come back.'

Speaking of offences, everything in the garden is rosy in the fairy world, except that things do once upon a time fair very eerie in fairy tales, and in such as this Quest of ours when Randy Newman is in a little criminals mood...

'A window breaks
Down a long dark street
And a siren wails in the night ...'

Abberline to Lusk:

If I may say so, Sir, a most befitting description of the circumstances of the latest killing in the East End ... November 9, 1888 ... She was said to be fluent in the Welsh language ...

'The body was lying naked in the middle of the bed, the shoulders flat, but the axis of the body inclined to the left side of the bed. The head was turned on the left cheek ...

The breasts were cut off, the arms mutilated by several jagged wounds & the face hacked beyond recognition of the features. **The tissues of the neck were severed all round down to the bone ...**

Gollum (sings): ... and the wind ... cries-ss ... **Mary** ...

The Winchcombe Imp

Those of the Rangers wishing to know more, might search under *Edwin Russell, Winchcombe,* for reference not only to the history of the town, but also to Professor J.R.R. Tolkien, and something about Gargoyles and a Winchcombe Imp, whatever and wherever those may be.

Our combing of Winchcombe very nearly over, we might just share a few extra old peculiars of Winchcombe Heritage, selected from local history paperwork available at the marvelous St. Peter's Church here; whose complete treatise is set in the Bureau of Shire-history in Appendix B by way of historical note.

On a further hysterical (we do our best) note, extracts from the local literature provide three points of special interest in Winchcombe ...

Chancel screen ... Impish head of Master Carpenter...

Gollum (St. Peter's Church Roof): ... Imps-s ... Imps-ss ... wot about Imps-ss-ss?

Smeagol (down from roof; inside Church, gazing at Chancel screen): ... Winchcombe Imp, My Luv ... Winchcombe Imp ... is in Holy screen of Church of St. Peterses ...

Gollum (gazing): … yes-ss, … looks like us-ss, it does precious … and we's bin' winking one eye for many, many Centuries-ss … (scratching head) … why's we all alone here precious-ss … why jest only one of Imps-ss …?

Smeagol (heading back to rooftop): … come … come … see what Smeagol finds …

40 grotesques around the church: some may be of those responsible for building the church.

Smeagol: … see, see what Smeagol finds … many looks like us, My Luv … many, many looks like us …

Gollum (nodding approval): Yes-ss, indeed precious, they all looks-ss like meeeee …

Smeagol: … like us my Luv, like us … (whispering; to hisselfs): … yes—ss, I means like us-ss … Hhaaaaa … the Precious go gets a gargle … one or two inner Cupboard …

The ghost of a 12 year old girl is supposed to haunt The Corner Cupboard Inn … dating back to 1550 …

Gollum (later): … not seen no ghosts-ss yet, precious-ss … praps we bes-sst stay all night … yes-ss … less 'ave another one, eh, my precious-ss … yes indeed, … less' have another one …

(Drunk In Recitation)

   'Come to us, O come, come' in the stormy red of a sky'
      (Voyage of Maeldune; Tennyson)

(sudden scream)… Lit'l red girlsess, lit'l red girlsess-ss … dreadful danger Awffer Master dreadful danger …

(much later; very merry; pleading)

... Master, Master ... any chances precious-ss songs and dances-ss ...?

(much, much later; very, very merry; sings):

> ' Ho Ho Ho to the bottle I go
> Heal my heart and drown my woe
> Rain may fall and wind may blow
> But on a high roof I will lie
> And let the licker go gargling by
> Winchcombe Imp 'n' Gargoyle, Oi
> Ach-ss ... gollum ... gollum ... gollum ...
> ... croi oi ...'

(After: The Drinking Song of The Rings)

Voices over Shire (whooping, gloating applause)-

> (... They approve of me and share my code ...)
> '... I practice a faith that's been long abandoned
> Ain't no altars on this long and lonesome road ...
> The suffering is unending
> Every nook and cranny has it's tears
> Up the road around the bend
> In the last outback, at the world's end ...'

'But this is terrible!' ... 'Far worse than the worst that I imagined from your hints and warnings... What am I to do? For now I am really afraid. 'I am sorry,' ... 'But *I am frightened* ...'

Strike Up The Band

> **'We're Sergeant Pepper's Lonely Hearts Club Band
> ... We hope you will enjoy the show ...'**

RING DI:
The Trollshaws

'Where black is the colour, where none is the number'

Our caption evinces the darkness of the episode at The Trollshaws; and that our company finds none of the Trolls they had feared; only reminders of their presence from the journey of Bilbo Baggins in The Hobbit: Stone Trolls.

> **'In summertime on Bredon**
> **The bells they sound so clear;**
> **Round both the shires they ring them**
> **In steeples far and near,**
> **A happy noise to hear.'**
> (Bredon Hill: Houseman)

Houseman's two shires will be Worcestershire and Gloucestershire.

Gollum: ... we warnss you all be ye ready lis-sst'nin' very *un*-happy stone silences onner steep hills upper head, Audiences-ss-ss ... we warnss you all ... no goods-s to say the precious dursnt *warns-ss-ss* ...

Not the first and not to be the last time upon the Quest that we have ordered our labelled sections out of their usual sequence,(a spin we get into once more in switching to Swanfleet before the swashings about Rivendell)we chose first to cut the light to new places, before we examine Middle- and Mother-Earth and their associations; because of the substantive connection between our perception of the flow of the River Bruinen and the statements we have made in RING M VIII with regard to the meeting or 'Mythe' of the two rivers Isbourne and Bruinen: there we saw fit to imagine a joinder where there is none in fact on Mother-earth today. We repeat that liberty for we are about to take it once more, in order to illustrate our own view of how the Professor drew the Ring-Maps, consistent, of course, with the Secret of the Shire.

And for those of the Audience with long memory (in fact from the

292

Genesis of the Quest), we have yet to find *The Golden Valley* from the 'Rhudaur' of Welsh.

Light Finds the New Places We Tread: further of the River of Bruinen; Rhudaur

The Windrush(Bruinen and Brwynen)

'Green grow the rushes O!'

We make no apology for a reminder of an important principle underpinning the Quest ...

'... the maps of Europe in the Third Age drawn by Tolkien to illustrate his epic show a continent very different from that of today in its coastline, mountains, rivers and other major geographical features. In explanation he points to the forces of erosion, which wear down mountains, and to advances and recessions of the sea that have inundated some lands and uncovered others.'

(Paul Kocher: 'Master Of Middle-earth'(1972))

If the Professor thought it appropriate to dispense with the stretch of an English Channel, it may be not too much of a stretch(of the imagination)to sketch (and stretch) the flow of a river or two beyond our present imagination.

Likewise, Peter Ackroyd reminds us –

'The Thames has many tributaries ... many are now buried; many are forgotten ...'

If the Professor thought to con-join in the Ring-Maps, for a first and a second time, two rivers(the Ray and the Great Ouse, and the Isbourne and the Windrush) which are in fact not, at least visibly; then he might do so a third time; and we happen to believe that the Professor has, with the Windrush itself; for in our view the Professor has drawn the Bruinen rushing on past and to the East (on the Ring Maps; but which would be West on Mother-Earth) onwards and through Nin In Eilph by the waters of the Churn, and thereafter the Chelt; whereas on Mother-earth the Windrush does not in fact extend its flow through the line of the Churn and Chelt as imagined; but what a close study of the Maps of Mother-earth *does* reveal is that the **contour** of the Windrush flows like the stream of dream into these rivulets, running through and beyond Cheltenham; and this, indeed, is how the Author believes the Professor drew the Ring-Maps. By such imaginary extension of the Churn and Chelt, the Isbourne and the Windrush would indeed flow respectively (as the Mitheithel and the Bruinen) West and East of the Trollshaws, as the Professor shows them on the Ring-Maps, those compass-points respectively reversed on Mother-earth.

The exercise is very much like that in the example of the Brandywine-Evendim Waterway, and is easy enough from the OS Map for those interested in such details: simply trace the flow of the rising of the Windrush joining into the flow of the Isbourne, but also extend the flow of the Windrush into the Churn and then the Chelt: reverse the tracing and we have pretty much the lines of the Bruinen, Mitheithel and Hoarwell represented on the Ring-Maps. As ever, we do not claim so exactly, but the relative position of the Trollshaws and The Last Bridge convinces the Author (at least) of Professor Tolkien's methodology.

Rhudaur

The Audience will see the name bisected by The Trollshaws.

Simplistic enough a build from the Welsh language, comprising two words :'Rhyd' and 'Aur' (pronounced 'rheeed' and 'eyerrr', as best we can convey the sounds), meaning Ford or Valley of 'gold' and thus the 'Golden Valley' of Gloucestershire whose extent runs through Stroud, Chalford and beyond to include some five valleys, sufficiently feted that we have included a stretch of the valley in the Bureau of Shire-Historians, with specific reference to Chalford as a focal point.

Its tribute In Memoriam-

'Where Industry and Beauty once lived in peace'

Those interested beyond the account in the Bureau of Shire-history in Appendix B may take a look via the Web down the Golden Valley through the BBC lenses of 1982.

If the association of The Trollshaws proves unequivocal by virtue of the proof in hiding above Bredon Hill (we are to claim it is 'as good as it gets' in association terms), then the correlation of 'Rhudaur' and the Golden Valley proves that it sometimes gets even better.

Middle-earth

Chapter 12 of The Rings, The Flight to the Ford, begins with the aftermath of the attack of the Ringwraiths at Weathertop, then tells of the Trolls and otherwise of the 'sullen hills' of The Trollshaws, moving on then to the flight, as Frodo is chased down by the Nazgûl.

One may need to bear in mind that the Film trilogy omits the incidents of The Trollshaws more or less altogether; there is brief reference by Sam, which we mention. Apart, the company leaves Bree and moves straight to Weathertop and the wounding of Frodo; the flight to the Ford follows immediately in the film of The Fellowship of the Ring; in the Professor's story of The Rings, The Trollshaws intervene; no doubt the Film omission was by reason that the Stone Trolls assume prior knowledge of the journey of Bilbo Baggins, who had first encountered the Trolls in The Hobbit.

(The foregoing 'brief reference': the extended film versions do make reference through Sam Gamgee, who makes a remark about Bilbo's Trolls, with some large stone rather 'Buddah' like figures standing in the background; and of course The Hobbit films play them out in full).

We take up the Professor's tale in The Rings.

Sam and the other Hobbits find Frodo lying face down with his sword underneath him. Strider fears the deadly wound of the

Morgul blade and advises bathing the wound with hot water. Frodo has been pierced by the point of a long thin knife, with a dagger-like hilt. Aragorn looks for Athelas, a healing plant. Frodo feels that his arm is useless.

They now head South, crossing the Great Road, but into a more wooded area. The Road takes a wide bend northward. They hear a cold voice calling and also answering back. They enter a *cheerless* land of brush and stunted trees. They walk for a day, and are altogether four days from Weathertop. On the fifth day, the ground rises slowly. They come to the Last Bridge. The find of a Green Elf-jewel gives them hope. They find ancient stone walls and towers in ruins.

They travel southerly to the Road. After five days they see a huddle of wooded hills.

The description is one of 'sullen hills'.

The Oxford English Dictionary definition of 'sullen' is instructive: 'bad tempered and sulky,' with origins in the senses 'averse to company' and 'unusual' from Old French.

Our Audience will have to take the Author's word for the fact that this reference and exposure of meaning was discovered well after our first impressions of Bredon Hill were thought through and put down on paper, within the 'First Visit' of our 'Wandering Star' section.

According to Aragorn they are too far North for Trolls. It is concluded that there are no Trolls here. They encounter high land: dark edges broken with many bare points like teeth of a blunted saw. They find a pathway leading to a door hanging on one hinge. This they decide is a Troll hole. It is filled with bones ...

Suddenly, but not sullenly ... even where we are indeed, the Professor illuminates –

"There are trolls! Pippin panted. 'Down in a clearing in the woods not far below ...'... They halted suddenly on the edge, and peered through the tree

296

trunks, holding their breath. There stood the trolls: three large trolls. One was stooping, and the other two stood staring at him ...'

As perfect a description to be found, of what there **is** to be found: peering through so many trees ... at the top of Bredon Hill ... when stone still during daylight, they are indeed come to life ...

Mother-earth

'When Bredon Hill puts on its Hat, Men of the Vale beware of that'

So runs this commonplace saying in the Vale of Evesham, of which Bredon Hill forms part.

The Professor comes to speak of 'sullen hills'; the 'hat' reference is clearly to 'that' of ill weather, the Vale of Evesham being predominantly agricultural and market gardening land, with perhaps its most revered produce that of Asparagus or locally 'Sparrow Grass': incidentally, if ever any member of the Audience pays us a visit, the local pronunciation is 'Eevursham' so please do not think that we are in the wrong place.

The weather reference is that The Hill, shrouded in Mist, Fog or Cloud is apt to be wearing its hat.

The Author cannot resist his own nod in the direction of J. Pennethorne Hughes, our Fairymaster of our Cauldron of Appendix C, who declared the fairies and perhaps trolls wore green or brown or red hats or hoods: if the cap fits, wear it.

Included in this parish are the village of Bredon, which stands on a plain at the south-west base of Bredon Hill on the left bank of the Avon.

The slope of the land is from east to west, and at Bredon Hill to the north-east, in Bredon's Norton, the land is 700 ft. above the ordnance base. The highest point in the detached part of the parish, Cutsdean, is Cutsdean Hill at 1,000 ft.

One Web resource –

In the northern portion of the parish, near a wood called Aldwick Wood on Bredon Hill, are **some** *stones of a curious shape called the* **King and Queen Stones**.

It will not (unlike the Stone Trolls, as we are to discover) have escaped the notice of our Audience that we have permitted the King and Queen Stones pre-references, prior to our revelation of the truth of them; for these pre-references are misleading, as we are also to discover: notice for the moment the reference to 'some' and (by implication) 'two' stones in the foregoing paragraphs. Many later references specify 'two' stones.

The reticence of their number matches their reluctance to be found at all.

In the meantime, there is historical account of Bredon Hill and the Stones within the Bureau of Shire-history in Appendix B; not overlooking another metaphor of the Hill; that of the humpback of a Hippopotamus wallowing in the flat surface of water; nor forgetting to count *how many* are spoken of by our Shire-historian there.

We must remind the Audience that the Professor has already left his own clue; in the text of The Rings:

'… three large trolls …'

We are bound to mention that Bredon Hill was once also a Beacon Hill. The Packer authority tells us so-

'A description of the hill would be incomplete if it failed to record that, following the precedent set at the 1897 Victorian Jubilee, the Coronation of King Edward VII was celebrated by the erection near the Tower of a huge Beacon Fire … some 800 or 1000 of the inhabitants of the villages round Bredon Hill, bearing lighted torches, proceeded to a central point, and forming into a procession marched to the site of the fire …'

Bredon Hill must have been wearing its Hat that day; for it all fizzled out-

'The festivities connected with the celebration were sadly marred by heavy rain.'

Poplars

'**Far in a western brookland**
That bred me long ago
The poplars stand and tremble
By pools I used to know.
There, in the windless night-time,
The wanderer, marvelling why,
Halts on the bridge to hearken
How soft the poplars sigh.'
(Houseman)

Revisiting the poplars by the Ouse of Thomas Cowper, Houseman likewise shares a nostalgia in these lines, which incidentally they seem always to be; in The Cotswolds at least: most often on the ridges of hills; and if there is a deeper explanation, the Author is not aware of it. Rarely single, Cowper sings their praise as shelter from wind, and sun, here also when Bredon Hill has not got its hat on. We have visual testimony of their linesmanship in the painting 'Bredon Hill' by Alfred Parsons; one speculates whether this and Houseman's may be the same: but we have already commented how common a sight is the line of poplar trees ...

Smeagol: ... very poplar in The Shire, My Luvvs ...

Rambling Man

Along with Meon Hill which is downright spooky, Bredon Hill warrants a visitation in the spirit it deserves. Bredon Hill is a locally well-known sight from any vantage point East of it and looking westward to the Malvern Hills. It stands proud some 10 Miles before, as a precursor of bigger things to come, the Malvern Hills. It is some 1000 feet to the top. Its circumference, to the extent one can measure these things without the benefit of accurate science, is 9 or 10 miles. It never ceases to amaze the length of circumference which the height supports. The look of it would never suggest such figure.

However, it is large for a 'hill' and we have no idea whether it tends to qualify as a 'mountain', but that may give us an inkling of its presence. If Meon is a small hill then Bredon appears a very, very large hill. It has an extremely odd bloated whale shape, as the descriptions we have read do indeed verify. Please believe the Author, the Hill is a most uncommon sight. The Author has never seen such a stranded whale of a hill.

Bredon Hill has a scattering of small villages dotted whether on the fringes of its lower circumference, whilst none actually in the top half or two-thirds (the Westmancote of mention being, possibly, the furthest upward the hill of any dwellings) of the vast ranges of the hill, such that other than by real endeavour, one cannot say one is near the top. The villages are connected by minor roads like secret interconnecting warrens.

We drove in turn through Elmley Castle, Kersoe and Ashton under Hill, linked by the narrowest of by-roads. Elmley Castle appears to have had a Royal visitation on August 20, 1575. Queen Elizabeth's visit is commemorated here, which is quite astonishing some 500 years later considering all the intervening Monarchs. Probably none of them ever came.

And so back down the time tunnel to the Sixteenth Century, where and when some light dawns on the Royal visit. We have noted that Bredon has been a beacon hill; as we look forward to the Beacon hills of the Malverns, the spine tingles in the prospect that the line of fire formed the backbone of England's defensive warning system as far back in time as the threat of invasion by the Spanish Armada; albeit the Spanish invasion did not materialise until 1588 in the Anglo-Spanish war (1585-1604): yet, if the Spanish were not worrying Elizabeth at this time, her Scots cousin certainly was; though not history of the Shire, Appendix B reminds us of unhappy families of the day.

> **'A silent man in life's affairs**
> **A thinker from a boy**
> **A peasant in his daily cares**
> **A poet in his joy'**
> (The Peasant Poet; John Clare)

The peasants will have given the Queen a rousing welcome; and they are still with us centuries later.

'"Round Bredon Hill," are to be found, very much in their original condition, quite a number of rural retreats, with their thatched, gable-ended cottages, and black and white timbered walls, inhabited by homely peasant folk; and so far as outward surroundings are concerned one might easily imagine oneself living in the 16th instead of the 20th century. Probably Elmley Castle, with its historical associations, combined with its isolation, is far and away in advance of its neighbours in and artistic and old-world sense.'
(Round Bredon Hill, T.H. Packer (1902))

We saw no peasants. We will recheck that text; one would not use such terminology today: perhaps he said 'pleasant' and it was the Author's transcription that was poor. The Author points out that the 'homely peasant folk' may have been 'round' Bredon Hill in 1902; but those cottages are, on the whole, now the province of wealthier folk.

Elmley Castle has its own Hill Lane. The Church is that of St. Mary the Virgin. The road to Kersoe is walled by buildings either side, and narrow as a barn door. We were confirmed in our impression by the following reference in 'Bredon Hill & Its Villages', Rev. R.H. Lloyd (1967)-

'The road to Kersoe leaves the village of Elmley through what is known as the Hole in the Wall and proceeds due east.'

We were hoping Kersoe had something to do with a curse but our researches proved futile in this regard. Kersoe sits in what (at least in some parts) is called a box-end valley to be regarded as a cleft into the mountain. The cleft at Kersoe is the smallest of vales, but the idea is the same. The cleft shape disappears into the hillside and there is no way out of the depression except upwards the hill.

On another occasion we drove in the south-westerly aspect of the hill. The old part of the village of Bredon has many perfectly presented thatched cottages alongside the imposing Fox & Hounds pub. The Church of St. Giles is not to be missed. Dock Lane takes you down to the River Severn, at this point some 20 metres wide. Many pleasure boats use this stretch.

One cannot imagine any of these belong to peasants.

Onwards into Kemerton, on one of whose buildings there still reads:

'Landaus Waggonettes & Hunters For Hire': they will be justifiably proud to have preserved it.

The first of a number of roads within the villages of Bredon Hill called 'Hill Road' runs uphill from the War Memorial.

Next into Overbury whose Church is dedicated to St. Faith and has served the community for over 900 years. The Bowl of the Font is 12th Century, its stem 14th Century. It has remarkable Turret-like windows. There is a water stream to cross (no pun intended)in the grounds to reach the Church and a series of 5 Gothic-arched seats as memorials to local notables.

Two other places outside Bredon, but near enough-by, are worthy of mention.

First, Offenham which is noteworthy by virtue of its own Maypole. The Author cannot remember having seen one before and if he did we have forgotten it. We know of no other. Wikipedia is mighty when one needs information about Maypoles …

Offenham village is noted for its 64 ft maypole, the tallest of only six permanent maypoles remaining in England. On May Day there is maypole dancing, morris dancing and the crowning of the Queen of the May. It is not known for how long Offenham has had a maypole but the tradition dates back to medieval times.

Wandering Star

'I thought I could hear the curious tone
Of the cornet, clarinet and big trombone
Fiddle, 'cello, big bass drum
Bassoon, flute and euphonium
Far away, as in a trance
I heard the sound of the Floral Dance ...'

We are reminded ...

... a maypole is a tall wooden pole erected as a part of various European folk festivals, particularly on May Day, although in some countries it is instead erected at Midsummer. In some cases the maypole is a permanent feature that is only utilised during the festival, although in other cases it is erected specifically for the purpose before being taken down again.

Primarily found within the nations of Germanic Europe and the neighbouring areas which they have influenced, its origins remain unknown, although it has been speculated that it originally had some importance in the Germanic paganism of the Iron Age and early Mediaeval cultures, and that the tradition survived Christianisation, albeit losing any original meaning that it had.

A Morris Dance is a form of English folk dance usually accompanied by music. It is based on rhythmic stepping and the execution of choreographed figures by a group of dancers. Implements such as sticks, swords, handkerchiefs and bells may also be wielded by the dancers. In a small number of dances for one or two men, steps are performed near and across a pair of clay tobacco pipes laid across each other on the floor. The origins of the form of dance appear uncertain or disputed.

It is commonly thought of as a uniquely English activity, although there are around 150 morris sides (or teams) in the United States. The people of Bredon Hill are immersed in the tradition. 'Round Bredon Hill'(T.E. Packer (1902)) informs us-

303

'At Elmley Castle May Pole Day was always held on May 29th, and it was usual for the villagers to decorate the May Pole with flowers and carry it from house to house, while the children joined hands and danced around it singing-

'All around the May Pole we will trot,
See what a May Pole we have got,
Garlands above and Garlands below,
See what a pretty May Pole we can show.'

Blow me down coming so soon after the Phallic symbolism of our Cauldron of Appendix C. Note the Web reference to 'erection' of the Maypole; three times. The Maypole is by oral tradition the height of Phallic symbolism; size matters: the bigger the better.

To complete the Maytime extravaganza, we must mention the Mummers. Mummers' Plays (also known as mumming) are seasonal folk plays performed by troupes of actors known as mummers or guisers (or by local names such as rhymers, pace-eggers, soulers, tipteerers, galoshins, guysers, and so on), originally from England, but later in other parts of the world. They are sometimes performed in the street but more usually as house-to-house visits and in public houses. There are regular performances of the dances and plays throughout the Cotswold villages. Seemingly Pagan they are not to everyone's taste, but are apparently harmless fun, at least these days.

One often sees a horse's head amongst the Dancers' paraphernalia. While we are at it, the subject-matter reminds one of a strange custom still obtaining in parts of Wales; the Mari Lwyd, of which we spoke in our quest in The Hobbit.

Our friends from the USA may find interest in nearby Wickhamford. Wickhamford Manor is a 16th Century Manor House whose lakes and circular dovecote were mentioned in the 1086 Domesday Book. Penelope Washington, cousin to George Washington, first President of the United States, lived and died here. The tiny church of St John the Baptist houses her engraved tombstone dated 1697 bearing the Washington Coat of Arms (2 stripes and 3 stars) – the origin of the American flag.

One Henry Washington is known to have been a loyal Cavalier in the English Civil War. Washington was a descendent of Sir William Washington of Northampton which is the same family as that of George Washington, the first US President. A memorial in Wickhamford Church states:

"Sacred to the memory of Penelope, daughter of that most distinguished and renowned soldier, Col. Henry Washington".

Binding of the Ring

> **'The King was in his counting house**
> **Counting out his money;**
> **The Queen was in the parlour,**
> **Eating bread and honey.**
> **The maid was in the garden,**
> **Hanging out the clothes,**
> **When down came a blackbird**
> **And pecked off her nose ...'**

Blood is drawn on The Trollshaws for the first, but not the last, time, considering where we are and with killers about, but we don't know where and we don't know when; but aren't we beginning to guess ... *why* ... if not *who* ...?

The 'sullen hills' attribution should not be overlooked; the Author felt the same way as, ostensibly, the Professor in his writing of The Rings.

In addition we have the location of Bredon Hill, which is where according to the Professor's Secret of the Shire one would entirely expect to find The Trollshaws.

The finding of the King and Queen Stones and association with the Stone Trolls of The Rings is just as about 'as good as it gets' in terms of association. This association is a certainty once the Author reveals the nature of the inhabitants of Bredon Hill; for we can be stone-cold certain Professor Tolkien knew their abode.

'Now, for what the Audience has all been waiting for ...'

'Swiftly walk o'er the western wave,
Spirit of Night!
Out of the misty eastern cave,
Where, all the long and lone daylight,
Thou wovest dreams of joy and fear
Which make thee terrible and dear,-
Swift be thy flight!
(Night; Shelley)

The Trolls only come out at night, if your memory serves you well
... and you knew that you would meet again, turned grotesque
statuesque in The Hobbit, yet turning up here in stone, Tolkienesque
on The Trollshaws.

'I would not feel so all alone
Ev'rybody must get stoned ...'

For the sake of memory, the Author records that, as of the date of
writing, we have made two visits to The Trollshaws, and the first
following records our memory of the first ever visit. The Author
records his experience twofold, for the second visit proved far more
successful, and in terms of the Quest, stone cold sobering. One
might say the Author got stoned twice, but it was only once in fact;
yet countless times since.

Let us venture to one view of the dream of the fairy life ...

'O! I hear the tiny horn
Of enchanted leprechauns
And the padding feet of many gnomes a-coming !'
(JRRT, to be continued at Rivendell)

*Everything in the garden is innocent in the fairy world, except that things do
once upon a time fair very eerie in fairy tales, such as this Quest of ours, where
lurk some naked presences of mine enemies ...*

We might go straight to the second visit, and yet the first visit is perhaps worthy of its own first impressions of the Author; and so one quotes oneself:

First Visit

> **'I think, that if I touched the earth,**
> **It would crumble;**
> **It is so sad and beautiful,**
> **So tremulously like a dream.'**
> (Clown in the Moon; Dylan Thomas)

… or Nightmare …

'It has a scattering of small villages dotted whether on its lower circumference, whilst none actually in the top half such that other than by real endeavour, one cannot say one is near the top. The villages are connected by minor roads like secret interconnecting warrens.

That is the point of the place: unless you are a real local and know all the twists and turns, to a stranger the hill is virtually impenetrable. You simply don't know where you are, even at the lower villaged levels. Correction: the Hill is impenetrable unless one is prepared to walk. Even then the paths upward are secretive except to those who know.

The approach roads seem to be conspiring against one getting anywhere and certainly not anywhere towards the top where one might get a view outward. The upper third appears mostly rolling farmland with tracks known only to those who know. It is easy to get lost even within these narrow geographic confines. There is a genuine sense of being closed in and trapped, apart from the minor relief of a village at last.

The Author is forever justifying a *later* discovery; sincerely *after* the foregoing paragraphs were written, the Author happened to be reading over Chapter 12 of The Rings, our company amidst the 'sullen hills', and we came upon, not Trolls, but this-

'The hills now began to shut them in ...'

The hobbits, albeit with Aragorn, were cossetted in this place under darkness; and shuddered.

We visited in bright sunlight so the Devil only knows what this place would be like at night. Personally we would be terrified to be on one of these upward tracks in the dark without a clue for what's about, apart from something, well, *strange* or *different* and *very scary*.

It is not simply for the benefit of this account we say that even by motorcar we sped downward a high hedged track between fields of equally high crop; we were eager to get out, off and away from here. For a cosy local field trip it can be a God forsaken place with, at least to the sensitive soul, tremors of some other presence in the undercurrent of emotion; perhaps in the undergrass. We are not exaggerating for the purpose: we sensed something else; and were uncomfortable with the discomforture. Some weeks after the visit, the writer asked his companion for a reaction to the place and how she had felt about it, without any indication of his own:

'Anxious' came the swift and untutored reply.

Another colleague expressed the same dread, on an entirely separate visit, made many years earlier.

'Dashing the fires and the shadows of dawn
on the beautiful shapes,
For a wild witch naked as heaven
stood on each of the loftiest capes,'
(Voyage of Maeldune; Tennyson)

(breathe deep)

I seen a witch once. In Bromsgrove it was. She had the very face of a witch. Gnarled and black-a-vised, and ageless old. And warts on the wrist of her ... ' ★

Morose with the menace of the macabre.

Brooding on the ancient allure of blood in paganism, witchcraft ... or *ignorance*.

The movie The Wicker Man synthesises the sick sixth sense, at least for me: there are some creepy places, traditions, ways and ghosts of old, about; never mind the peasants, sickles, scythes, knives, hammers and pitchforks handy, who wouldn't think twice iffen *the eye* be put on 'em ... strangers is come, forrun bodies and minds and ways differen' to ours own, upsett'n us shirefolk an' all ... things could as well get ugly ...

'Reckon as you'm from another planet,... Do, and all. Ghost, or some 'at. Bloody zombie ...' ★

... or a witch in ... human ... form ...

... *'there s'll be some fun, else, in this orchard, afore night fucking come ...'*

JIM: Get rid on him.

GINGER: Don't go putting no bloody eye on us.

ALBERT: Chase him.

GINGER: Make sure he don't find no way back again ...

TAFFY: ... Don't cross them, Paddy. That's all I say. You'll be all right. Don't you worry.★

Voices over Shire (howling, growling drone)-

'the hammer's on the table
the pitchfork's on the shelf'

One of order moving into a different and secret field or realm. It could be, of course, that I am influenced by the folklore attaching to the Hill, and even by the Tolkienesque sensitivities of it, in the same way as it was suggested in relation to Meon Hill; but that is part of this exercise within the Quest: it is a challenge for others to discover what they may detect of spirits in this dead end, much as I did.

'... who looked so fine at first,
but left looking just like a ghost ...

There is sure to be more than the Stone Trolls of The Hobbit that we meet again up here on Bredon Hill: if your memory serves you well. This may not have been Professor Tolkien's fascination. There is more than enough in terms of Archaeological interest to satisfy the keenest of tastes. Stones and barrows everywhere, but not the Stone Trolls we craved.

There is apparently a great deal more upward in the concealed undergrowth. We never found them and our inquiries led nowhere with no live person able or willing to point us directly to the famed or possibly absent King and Queen Stones of Bredon Hill.

(You'll be all right. Don't you worry...)

... plunges hayfork into ground about body's neck, hauls on its handle to crush neck ... They gather round head with their knives. They cut it away ...★

What we did happen to find were old wool sacks lying on the hillside, of a kind we had seen before, about Weathertop.

'I marvelled at the power, strength, and rage
Of this poor creature ...
While twilight faded into darkness deep,
And he who watched it piped its pangs asleep.'
(Gloria Mundi: Walter De La Mare)

'Son, this ain't a dream no more, it's the real thing'

Our second visit proved the anomaly of our first visit and impression; for we discovered a source of authority which instructed us where to look for the Stone Trolls. This gave us the most excellent map-indication of how to find the Stone Trolls of the peradventure of

Bilbo in The Hobbit, and the adventures of Frodo and his company in The Rings.

One searches not for any of the villages of ease to find described so far, but for the so far unremarked village of Westmancote; indeed, the upper level of that small gathering (we do not say 'village') which is, by our authority, designed 'Upper Westmancote'.

(We noted later that T.E. Packer had mentioned 'Westmancote' in his writing over a Century ago.)

The Author acknowledges that he never gave Westmancote a second glance on our first visit. Joy of joys, we unearthed the Stone Trolls. We commence our short trip with the warning that we expected to find two or more typical 'marking' stones, perhaps the size of average Milestones.

How misguided one may be.

The discovery was made having wasted a good half-hour trundling beyond the bower of their covert prehistoric glade, which is in fact just twenty minutes' walk onward from 'Upper Westmancote'.

The Author imagines a stony silence for his relation of how, not knowing where to find the Stones, he was sent onward by a helpful mis-guide, onwards to the summit of Bredon Hill, and the 'Elephant Stone', yet another prehistoric stone up there on the Hill. We met him on the way back, he all apology, and saying –

'sorry to mislead you, the King and Queen Stones are down there on your right, just below that bank of trees; we sent you to the Elephant Stone ...'

Of Stone Trolls and Their Number on Bredon Hill

**'You'll remember you're the one
That called on me to call on them ...**

You knew that we would meet again
If your mem'ry served you well ...'

The Author retraced his steps, very nearly broke an ankle in slip-sliding his way below the bank of the visible tree-line, across the traverse of a very steep glade, whose reward was there; the 'King and Queen' stones, unearthed.

Now, as our authority of mention clearly testifies, there is a misnomer in the Royal duality. The traditions attaching to the 'King and Queen Stones' are (just as the Stones) unequivocally misplaced, for there are very clearly **Three** stones upon this secret site.

One has learned of the tradition of passing through the supposedly major King and Queen stones, but the gap between those two is matched by the gap between the middle stone and the albeit somewhat smaller(by comparison with the other two)*third* stone.

For future reference, the folklore tradition of a couple passing between the King and Queen Stones is that they will marry. Presumptively male and female in the days of yore, we have no idea how their Majesties cater for civil partnerships in the present day.

The Stones comprise a trio and there is absolutely no doubt about that fact. We speak of stones as if of the stepping variety in one's garden. Believe the Author, if you will, these stones are indeed as if stone giants, some 15 to 20 feet in height; they are three out-standing stones; yet one is, as already indicated, smaller; a good deal squatter and mis-shapen compared with the other two.

We came away with three pieces of knowledge, entirely satisfying to us for the purposes of our Quest.

First, these stones were brought and placed here by prehistoric man; or so thought the Author until he met with a second ancient of mention soon. They stand and stick out on this earthen bank of the glade like three sore thumbs; there are no other stones of any comparable size noticeable anywhere nearby; a few broken boulders, but nothing large. These stones have not emerged from beneath the earth as our early source (Packer) seems to suggest. The Author concludes that that writer could never have seen them; indeed the Author's mind boggled at how deep their proportion *beneath* ground must be in order to support their massive evidence *above* ground.

Late upon the Quest, the Author came upon 'Historic Worcestershire' (W. Salt Brassington 1894); which seems to agree with the Packer source that –

'... they bear no sign of human interference, and appear to be simply natural rocks denuded and perhaps displaced by landslips or the falling in of a cavern roof ... '

Outvoted two to one, the Author remains nevertheless of the persuasion that the stones do not belong here naturally. Equally pertinent is their substance; the second authority (Brassington) continuing-

' ... two great masses of white oolitic rock composed of fragments cemented together by a siliceous liquid; around them in ruinous disorder lie boulders of the same kind of rock ...'

The Audience will have noted two further departures from the Author: a further mention of just two major stones, and reference to other boulders in the vicinity; now there are unequivocally three stones, and the Author saw no others of substance. A lot may have changed in over a Century; but not their number, which is a curiosity of both Brassington and the later Packer.

The Author had indeed noticed the strange mixture of materials comprising all three stones: rather like mis-shapen beach pebbles of the largest size in a binding mix of concrete, and not at all the pale yellow as of the Cotswold stone, but rather pinkish or terracotta in colour. In attempting description, the Author had also thought of a cake or pudding mix, but had been beaten to it in terms of the general Geology of Bredon Hill, by the Reverend R.H. Lloyd in a work entitled ''Bredon Hill & Its Villages'(1967),as follows-

'Geologically, Bredon Hill is like a layer cake. It has a cap of Oolitic limestone, a base of Lower Lias clay, with Middle and Upper Lias formations between … The whole of it was originally laid down in shallow seawater, and has subsequently been forced up. The oldest rocks are about 150 million years old.'

Some will recall the Nogood Boyo's *anemones* protruding from the Cotswold Edge.

And of the Stone Trolls themselves-

'These two remarkable objects are made of Oolitic material … They are rather grotesque to look at, and because of their position give the impression that they have been moulded by man. There is not the slightest mark of any artificial sculpture upon these stones, but as there is a fissured passage between the King and Queen, as well as between the King and the adjoining mass of rock on the other side, it is probable that there may have been a superstition practiced here.'

Despite the original mention of 'two' objects, the Author took comfort that we had not been deluded in our threesome of rock 'mass'; but even the Reverend Lloyd is mixed up about the origin of the Stones, whether here by force of man or nature.

Given the understanding that the Rollright Stones had clearly been placed by human effort, we were altogether further mixed up by the footnote to the previous Brassington comment that the King and Queen Stones were in their natural position-

'It is worthy of remark that the Rollright Stones belong to the same geological formation'.

Is it not at least conceivable that they form some kind of marker between the Rollright Stones (Barrow Downs) and, say, Herefordshire Beacon atop the Malvern Hills? That is the view of several commentators, for what it may be worth (very little, yet enhanced by some knowledge of ley lines); and I do, indeed, believe, Professor J.R.R. Tolkien: because The Professor has the hobbits, guided by Aragorn, walk it through the Shire, with some (perhaps explicable) anomalies, Weathertop being the main one.

Our second piece of knowledge, after we began our first of three, some time ago: the Professor had walked the same path and climbed down the same glade.

Third, in his description of the Stone Trolls in The Rings, the Professor was, without question, looking at the King and Queen Stones of Bredon Hill; for there is a third stone, which is indeed the third of-

'... *three large trolls. One was stooping, and the other two stood staring at him ...'*

'No man alive will come to you
With another tale to tell
But you know that we shall meet again
If your mem'ry serves you well ...'

One need only be here in order to know; our final threesome: for any of the Tolkien Boys; for any lover of The Rings; for any lover of The Hobbit: go to this glade upon Bredon Hill – it is a mystical, magnetic, magical place – one where the Professor has, undoubtedly, been and felt the magic.

For those of the Audience for whom a call upon the Stone Trolls will never be a possibility, be assured that a Web search under King and Queen Stones, Bredon Hill, reveals a lot more about the Hill and the Stone Trolls, including many marvellous photoshots, with several impressive ones of the Trolls: Geograph's are superb, but still fail to capture the size of the stones.

But also be aware that there is not a photograph taken by, or otherwise known to, man that does justice to the stature of the Professor's Stone Trolls of Bredon Hill: only seeing is believing these stone monsters.

'... And there was nothing more to tell

You knew that we would meet again
If your mem'ry served you well … '

We share the latest front page news of Bredon Hill:

On 17 October 2011 Worcestershire County Council announced that Worcestershire's largest-ever hoard of Roman artefacts, including around 4,000 coins, featuring 16 different emperors, had been uncovered.

Quite a thought that these stones were here before the Romans.

We leave with the photoshot of the Professor which most aptly conveys the steep banks of the glade of the Stone Trolls; that delivered by Lord Snowdon as the cover of Paul Kocher's 'Master Of Middle-earth'(1972): this is a picture of serenity in nature; and thus we depart in stony silence.

But we leave with yet a few old bones to pick over …

Gollum (pleading): … Awffer Mas-sster, Awffer Mas-sster … any more chances precious-ss songs and dances-ss …?

Voice Off: … What *about, pray?* …

Smeagol: … Trolls, Master, but this time our po'try lyrrix so lyricals-ss, …

Voice Off: … O *Very* well …

Gollum (nodding, enthusiastic; in Recitation):

> **'But harder than stone is the flesh and bone**
> **Of a troll that sits in the hills alone …**
> **… And Troll do care, 'cos he's still there**
> **In a block of stone set by Wizard flare …**
> **Troll's old seat is still the same,**
> **And to sit beside, two more Trolls came!'**
> (After 'The Stone Troll': The Adventures of
> Tom Bombadil: J.R.R. Tolkien)

316

Wheels Afire

In a literary context, the Wheel of Fire may refer to the chain of tortuous or dire consequences that result from a single action.

Daniel 7.9:

'... his throne was fiery flames;
its wheels were burning fire ...'

The Wheel of Fire is part of the Aristotelian reading of a tragedy, which includes the central flaw within a character.
The Wheel of Fire is most commonly applied to the protagonist within a tragedy (i.e. the hero) and may aim to provoke sympathy from the audience when the hero falls from grace (this purging of emotions is known as catharsis), though it also adds dramatic interest to the performance.

Perhaps the *single action* is Bilbo's sparing of Gollum in The Hobbit, arising from pity; also by Frodo in the Emyn Muil and to be repeated by Sam on Mount Doom later in The Rings, who therefore is by survival alongside Frodo, also beneficiary of good intent in similar fashion ...

Smeagol: ... Ha Ha! Same ways, likewise, Samwise, My Luvvs ... Audiences shurely remembers ...

'Sam's hand wavered. His mind was hot with wrath and the memory of evil. It would be just to slay this treacherous, murderous creature, just and many times deserved; and also it seemed the only safe thing to do. But deep in his heart there was something that restrained him: he could not strike this thing lying in the dust, forlorn, ruinous, utterly wretched. He himself, though only for a little while, had borne the Ring, and now dimly he guessed the agony of Gollum's shrivelled mind and body, enslaved to that Ring, unable to find peace or relief ever in life again. But Sam had no words to express what he felt.'

We must await Volume III of our Quest to identify the central flaw in the characters of The Rings, and which (get your most stalwart helm on for many a battle of we Christian soldiers) involves a struggle with the Seven Deadly Sins.

Sauron A Sinner

**'Lord over Nature, Lord of the visible earth,
Lord of the senses five;'**
(The Palace of Art; Tennyson)

… for whom nothing is ever enough, whose Deadly Sin may be Gluttony, when indeed we reach Volume III …

Smeagol: … *He'll eat us if he gets it, eat the whole world* …

Of course, Frodo falls from grace, in that, ultimately, our hero chooses not to destroy the One Ring, but keep it for his own fulfillment, yet it is then that *Providence* raises the finger … of fate … for it is the essence of Providence that Good must overcome Evil …

Smeagol: … Whew! … this quest getting deeper an' deeper, My Luv …

Gollum: … an' much mores-s of Awffer Mas-sster Providens-ss at The Councils of Elronds-ss-ss, precious …

**'I've been walking forty miles of bad road
If the Bible is right,
the world will explode …'**

Gollum: … wait til we gets Audiences-ss to places-ss deeper still … down b'low in *Moria* … forty miles baddes-st bad road ever under them Misty Mountains, precious-ss …

**'The ghost of electricity howls in the bones of her face
Where these visions of Johanna
have now taken my place.'**

Gollum: … wait 'til we gets Audiences-ss to places-ss deepest still … down b'low in *Gehenna* … wait for Vollum, Vollum, Vollum III, precious-ss … Hells-ss is-ss called on allur both erffs, … my precious-ss-ss-ss …

318

And of those visions …

'People wandering from one corner of a loft to another, doped, drunk, half-awake, fast asleep, no point to the next breath, let alone the next step.'

Absurd; and so says Albert Camus up the road ahead in …

Gollum: … Vollum, Vollum …

Smeagol: … **Three,** My Luvvs …

Gollum: … pon-ssey pretenshussnes-ss … s-ssum froggy philossuffer of the abssurd, we wonders, yes-ss, we wonders-ss …

> **'This wheel's on fire**
> **Rolling down the road**
> **Best notify my next of kin**
> **This wheel shall explode …'**

This Wheel's On Fire (The Nobel Voice)

In 1968, a version by Julie Driscoll with Brian Auger and The Trinity …
With its use of distortion, phasing, the evocative imagery of the song's title and
… flamboyant dress, this version is closely associated with the psychedelic era
in British music.

Strike Up The Band

> **'Sergeant Pepper's Lonely Hearts Club Band**
> **… We'd like to thank you once again …'**

---

*   'Afore Night Come' is a David Rudkin play of 1962 whose violence
    may come back to haunt us, even up the road ahead. *In the play Rudkin*
    harks back to a pagan era where the crops were fertilised by human blood. cf.
    Walton murder.

RING E:I:
The Ford

'And the executioner's face is always well hidden'

'For this was on seynt Volantynys day'
(Chaucer)

The faces of the pursuing Ringwraiths are black hollows. Murder at Weathertop failed; whosoever remains intent on the final execution of Frodo and possession of The Ring.

Middle-earth

'And after ev'ry plan had failed
And there was nothing more to tell
You knew that we would meet again
If your mem'ry served you well ...'

We learn that Strider knows Rivendell and Elrond's house there. The Tolkien Boys will be aware that Aragorn was brought up here, falling in love with Arwen. As of previous mention by the Author, they feel as if the hills are shutting them in. They enter a long valley. There is heavy rain, but they can see Hills with 'many bare points like the teeth of a blunted saw'. We recognise the reference to 'Hills' as those of the Misty Mountains in the distance.

Glorfindel, a high ranking Elf who lives in the House of Elrond mounts Frodo onto his white horse. They ride a long, flat mile, seeing in the distance the Ford of Bruinen.

They are chased hard over the mile by the Black Riders, until great white horses in a 'plumed cavalry of waves' mow the Ringwraiths down with the waters of a torrential wave. We learn later, from Gandalf at Rivendell, just how the saviour torrents of water came to be summoned.

Mother-earth

'And now the bridge hangs tottering
Above the boiling tide ...
And like a horse unbroken,
When first he feels the rein,
The furious river struggled hard,
And tossed his tawny mane,
And burst the curb, and bounded,
Rejoicing to be free;
And whirling down, in fierce career,
Battlement and plank and pier,
Rushed headlong to the sea.'
(Horatius at The Bridge; Lord Macauley)

The imagery may become more focussed, even localised to Upton-on-Severn, by the end, for we are nearing it by virtue of a message scrolled from Mordor ... yet notice how this imagery fits for the deluge engulfing the Nazgûl riders such that (*after* Equus, Peter Schaffer) horse and wave *become one beast* ...

Upton-on-Severn is best known for two things:

... its bridge or ford over the River Severn; large rivers need big strong bridges: and here is the metal plate on the bridge, of the year 2000, to tell its own tale ...

UPTON UPON SEVERN CIVIC SOCIETY

This steel cantilever bridge with a main span of 200 feet was designed and built by Worcestershire County Council and opened in 1940 was one of the last riveted construction to be built in England. It replaced an 1864 swing bridge situated approximately 120 yards downstream of this point

... of flooding, because the River Severn runs right through its midst at a point of maximum fluviality on its long course. The local Inn, the (formerly White) Swan is festooned with photographs of its long history of suffering by the waters of the Severn, to the extent the walls are marked with the levels reached by the waterline over the years. We are speaking of serious, existence-threatening flooding here, not a drop in the bucket: the record levels are in tens of feet marked on the wall (the Author meant to check; but ironically The Swan has now been closed by consequence of the high waters) and The Swan stands on its banks already some Ten feet above the regular water level of the River.

'High tide and the heron
dived when I took the road'
(Poem in October; Dylan Thomas)

There is one further force of nature to be reckoned with at Upton. The Severn Bore, further described in the context of the Severn itself, causes a mini-tidal wave or micro-Tsunami to surge up and then down river from its sources to its Estuary from time to time when the conditions are right. The bore is apt to deluge the surrounding fields and countryside.

Flight to the Ford

Professor J.R.R. Tolkien carries the chase forward ...

''Fly!' he called. 'Fly! The enemy is upon us!' ...

'Ride forward! Ride!' cried Glorfindel to Frodo...

'Ride on! Ride on!' cried Glorfindel ...

... At once the white horse sprang away and sped like the wind along the last lap of the Road. At the same moment the black horses leaped down the hill in pursuit, and from the Riders came a terrible cry ... It was answered; and to the dismay of Frodo and his friends out from the trees and rocks away on the left four other Riders came flying. Two rode towards Frodo: two galloped madly towards the Ford to cut off his escape. They seemed to him to run like the wind and to grow swiftly larger and darker, as their courses converged with his ...'

Voices over Shire (howling, growling drone)-

'the hammer's on the table,
the pitchfork's on the shelf'

The Black Rider on the lead-horse carries the Master of Mordor's Scroll of Command to the Messenger of Mordor ... the second of the Ringwraiths bears a trouncing or bill hook, sickle, scythe or knife ... the third a pitch-fork or hayfork ... and the fourth ... a hideous hammer, also wool sacks, icons of the Shire ... the devices, tools and envelope in use by the Nazgûl for despatchment unto death, and to follow their Master's Command ... this being their latest sacking in the Shire by their cruellest of methodologies ...

... (or, at least, so far as concerns the deaths one *supposes* to be the work of the Nazgûl ... at scary Weathertop, the horror of the sirens at The Last Bridge, and on the sullen Trollshaws) ... for there is a Reprise to this flight to The Ford ...

Hunting the Witch

'At that moment Sam *felt a tremor in the ground* beneath him, and he heard or sensed a deep remote rumble as of thunder imprisoned under the earth. There was a brief red flame that flickered under the clouds and died away.'

The failure on Frodo at Weathertop provokes the wrath of the Master of Mordor ...

'Not so long and wide the world is,
Not so rude and rough the way is,
That my wrath shall not attain him,
That my vengeance shall not reach him!'
(The Hunting; Song of Hiawatha: Longfellow)

Yet, even now, all that is left in the waters of The Ford after the deluge are the ragged robes, shredded riding tack, shattered swords and other weapons for the malefaction of the Ringwraiths... cruel

323

hook or sickle, pagan pitchfork, dastard war hammer cast in Minas Morgul for the breaking of doors … heads if knives should fail … simple wool sack envelope for the spoils … except for a single parchment manuscript floating on the river tide … the Scroll bearing the command of the Master …

Scroll of Command

'Thou shalt not suffer a witch to live in the Shire in human form. All such witches are seduced into the power of the One Ring, as have been the Ringwraith-Nazgûl at my command, and these witches must be deemed to know its proximate whereabouts. Hunt them down, make inquiry of them by any means necessary, and bring to the Dark Lord of Mordor the head of all such witches and purveyors of magick, sorcery and other delinquency within the Shire, lest their knowledge fall into the wrong hands; but above all, though he be not proven such, bring to the Dark Lord the naked neck and head of the hobbit, one Baggins, who bears the One Ring, as it is supposed by the spies of the Dark Lord. Bring the head, divested of the One Ring, within a woollen envelope-sack of that little rat-land Shire, such that all who dare venture into Mordor shall know and fear its provenance. Meet with our old friend, upon the height of Amon Sûl, to assure success in the hunt for this one ring, of little import to your Dark Lord, a mere bauble of My Kingdom of Mordor, as the messengers of the Dark Lord have told before.'

Smeagol: … why's come Weathertop for meeting Messenger of Mordor …?

Voices over Shire (screaming, screeching, cackle)-

> **'This is how I spend my days**
> **I came to bury, not to raise**
> **I'll drink my fill and sleep alone**
> **I pay in blood, but not my own …'**

Gollum: … who's ol' friend, pre-e-e-cious-ss-ss-ss…?

Voices over Shire (seering, roaring devourment)-

'The Second Coming! Hardly are those words out
When a vast image out of Spiritus Mundi
Troubles my sight: somewhere in sands of the desert
A shape with lion body and the head of a man,
A gaze blank and pitiless as the sun,
Is moving its slow thighs, ...
And what rough beast, its hour come round at last,
Slouches towards Bethlehem to be born?'
(The Second Coming; W.B. Yeats)

Be sober, be vigilant; because your adversary the devil, as a roaring lion,
walketh about, seeking whom he may devour...

(I Peter 5:8)

It is the lion who walks the earth: the evil stalking devil, preying
upon those vulnerable. The Dylan lyrics are never simplistic (often
with conscious literary allusion) and all I do, for now, is roar on with
the Mantra of Middle-earth and the notion that Professor Tolkien
played much the same game ...

For the moment, the Author will offer only this, as I walk the long
road to Mordor alone, where some of the questions may become
revelation, much more likely with a helping hand ...

'Ain't talkin', just walkin'
Who says I can't get heavenly aid ...?'

Catharsis of One's Tragic Tale of Wicked Witchcraft

Flight To The Ford (Reprise)

Voices over Shire (whooping, gloating applause)-

' ... They approve of me and share my code ...
... I practice a faith that's been long abandoned ...'

… there is no certain evidence, for nobody surely knows … there being the misdeeds of killers, of sundry *code, practice* and *faith*, all abroad in the Shire and elsewhere on Mother-earth of historical and international record … yet perhaps some unrecorded, for there may well be more whose precise circumstance we know very little or nothing about over so many countless centuries … it may even be that old Annie Turner is *a witch in human form* … and even reverting unto Biblical times where the circumstances of Judith's decapitation of Holofernes remain open to serious question, indeed, in the Rubens, and several others, the sack-envelope device is entirely visible …

Gollum (sinister): … that Rubens-ess-ss allways sne-e-e-aking about when heads-s iss rollings-ss, precious-ss-ss … yes-ss, allways sne-e-e-aking … yess, precious-ss-ss, wots-ss about John the Baptistses-ss-ss … already heads roll-ss-ss-ss at Wevvertop … an' onner Larss Bridge … an' inner Rudkins-ss plays *Afore Night Comes-ss* … whos-sever nexsst, precious …

'Well, Abe said, *Where d'you want this killin' done?* God said, *Out on Highway 61'*

… and, *quaere* in more recent times, a complimentary *code, practice or faith*, may well have transcended the United States of America, what with Grant Wood's 'American Gothic' (1930) considered, in the unequivocal opinion of the Author …

… Yet another interpretation sees it as an old-fashioned mourning portrait … Tellingly, the curtains hanging in the windows of the house, both upstairs and down, are pulled closed in the middle of the day, a mourning custom in Victorian America. The woman wears a black dress beneath her apron, and glances away as if holding back tears …

… as evidential in malice and evil intent, the eyes telling us all we need to know about … what Pa can do with a pitchfork … and, turning with the eyes of Ma (if mother she be), fixed on some human form on the horizon heading for … *our Church* … **come and join us, come and join us**, brother, all welcome … rest thine poor head down here, our brother awaited so long …

Ma: … I means to look after it …

Pa: … Ma means *thee* … *Ma* gonna look after *thee,* awright … brother … (I see such sin in thisser critter, Ma …) …

Smeagol: … Audiences wants know of horror the sirens … The Last Bridge … My Luv …

Gollum(whispers): … is-ss probly las-sst one canonical fives-ss-ss-ss … Jack the Rippers-ss-ss-ss …

Smeagol: … We dursnt know and we dursnt want to know …

Killer (writes)-

… Catch me when you can, Mishter Lusk …

Voices over Shire (howling, growling drone)-

' the hammer's on the table
the pitchfork's on the shelf'

Wheels Afire

'I begin to see it in my mind all the time,
like a great wheel of fire'
(The Land of Shadow)

So, what more of the 'wheel of fire'? Not at all obvious from the few references in the text of The Rings, we shall look into the wheel once more, in some depth, at The Council of Elrond, where the members of the Audience may take a first look for themselves, at Rivendell …

Smeagol: … we knows, yes, we guesses …

Gollum: … Audiences-ss is los-sst … like Bagginses inner ours mountains-ss of mis-ssts-ss … they durstn't know … so's aways in Councils-ss we makes the nassty rollings red tongues-ss wot turns inner circles-ss, … stop: **dead** …

Smeagol: … Oo! Oo! We knows, yes, we guesses … Author Master stops dead in his trackses …

Voices over Shire (whooping, gloating applause)-

' … They approve of me and share my code
I practice a faith that's been long abandoned
Ain't no altars on this long and lonesome road …'

The essence of our drama is retold in Appendix C (A Cauldron of One's Own), namely how Druids (priests derived of the once upon a time Faerie Realm, but we are not going there, beyond what's input the Cauldron) were Pagan, worshipping the earth as mother and all nature, the sun, the moon, the stars, the weather and especially lakes and trees, which amounts to adoration of a then current vision of the power of rebirth and growth of that which, O druid brethren, is uniquely alight before us …

'A drift of smoke
Glitters with fire and hangs, and the skies smoulder,
And the lungs choke.
Once the tribe did thus on the downs, on these downs burning
Men in the frame.'
(Up on The Downs; John Masefield)

Yet in the earliest druidic practice, human sacrifice, by fire or otherwise, was accepted in order to adore the worshipful earth; later critics accentuated the other indicia of the worrisome witchcraft wicked, all deadmeat in the Cauldron of Appendix C now; which, *as a matter of fundamental principle*, is not so at all; there exists witchcraft of the purest intention, purpose and result; indeed, the Author has many good friends who teach it: come on over to Evesham in the Shire, some time, bringing your high hat for a cuppa frog spawn tea …

'It's Alright, Ma, it's only Witchcraft'

The established Church sought to centralise worship and avowed the 'wickedness' of any number of the witchcraft practices,(many of such not even properly investigated, or at all), and came to demonise the faery-witches as synonymous with the Devil, contrary to God, and evil accordingly. It was, indeed, the established churches that made the equation; fateful for so many poor women who suffered.

'But to assume that a pagan locality is ipso facto a diabolised one is to my mind altogether too naive and conventional a reading of the enigma – even granted that there can be something diabolical about a decaying and overripe paganism.'
(H. E. Massingham, supra:*1932*)

The fire and brimstone, fervour and fear of Victorian times is something we have never gotten over, not least through the malpractices of such as Aleister Crowley ...

**'On a starred night Prince Lucifer uprose.
Tired of his dark dominion swung the fiend
Above the rolling ball in cloud part screened,
Where sinners hugged their spectre of repose ...
He reached a middle height, and at the stars,
Which are the brain of heaven, he looked, and sank.
Around the ancient track marched, rank on rank,
The army of unalterable law.'**
(Lucifer in Starlight: George Meredith; 1883)

The final conclusion is rationalised: witness Witchmarshall Hansen in Appendix C, with the whole phenomenon psychological rather than physical ...

'We must bear in mind that in a society which believes in witchcraft, it works. If you believe in witchcraft and you discover that someone has been melting your wax image over a slow fire or muttering charms over your nail-pairings, the probability is that you will get extremely sick. To be sure, your symptoms will be psychosomatic rather than organic. But the fact that they are obviously not organic will make them only more terrible, since they will seem the result of malefic and demonic power. So it was in seventeenth–century Europe, and so it was in seventeenth–century Massachusetts.'

'They're selling postcards of the hanging'

329

On our own current thinking, a kind of communal mania prevailed, on the footing that there was no developed understanding of the difference between right and wrong; other than by reference to strict religious teaching, which forcefully condemned non-compliance; and the Devil was created as symbolic of the force in opposition to God: yet the treatment of the witches hardly represents the teachings of Jesus Christ; indeed, more devilish than Christian, and simply **EVIL**. A concept for the assessment of guilt in cases of murder (knowing the difference between right and wrong) was not accepted until the 19th century, that is to say 200 years later.

Arguably, something similar prevailed in Nazi Germany.

We cannot pass judgement upon these, nor any other, times, because this is the dirty hole mankind is, and always has been, and forever will be, accustomed to crawl in, witness the sin on the T.V. News (courtesy Anthony Burgess) in the Cauldron ...

'A hungry mob is a (h)angry mob'
(Bob Marley)

The mob is hungry because the crops have failed, and the witches are to blame because they control the weather: see how easily *because* becomes questionable, irrational and hysterical: an awful load of hysteria likely breeds an awful load of contempt for the objectives of it, and a consuming *blood-lust*: making for an awful hateful eyeful ... any crowd can be whipped up this way, if you pull the right lever, and the Jews in the chambers were Adolf Hitler's witches ...

**'Though they murdered six million
In the ovens they fried
The Germans now, too, Have God on their side '**

(Oswald Mosley was pulling a second lever (the other one) on the road we trod to Crickhollow of the Shire, way before where we are now).

*'The mirror's eye smiles back at me

---

*   Maria Iommi, Drain

330

Fed me with your madness
Burnt the cradle to the ground
Created a beast of sadness'

We see a madness through the glass, darkly; and the towering wicker cage of the heathen did, indeed, proceed to create the bestiality of a sadness for so many women falsely condemned of wrong in the witchcraft of the pagan.

In the Cauldron, the Author contemplates the vexed subject of the violent clash of ideologies, forever at variance, between the (nominal) representatives of the Church and those accused of witchcraft through the centuries, in particular the Seventeenth Century. Ironically, (and indeed looking backward ... and forward to the next heading ... in anger) it was compassionate Christian thinking that was absent in the cruellest (to say the very least) dealings with the accused; and religious zeal, masking abuse of power, lust and greed (the accused must be virtually naked for such as the ordeal with pins, and the witchfinders ... Matthew Hopkins in the easterly fenlands being the most notorious ... received substantial payments for success) went right to their brains, loins and on into their wallets.

'You said the brains I had went to my head.'
(Oasis)

We meet Aleister Crowley later, lustfully poetical alongside the Cauldron: motto *Do What Thou Wilt*. This powerful but warped mind went to his head and exploded over the psyche of many. My own personal impression would be (not that it matters one drop of Black Sabbat candlewax) that Crowley was an attention-seeking, self-serving, self-indulgent, money-grabbing villain-pervert who appealed to vulnerable minds with the allure of sex, magic and seeming out of this world experience; all with no foundation, except for histrionics of appeal to those mesmerised by magic tricks; and because you *so* want to know, here is a taster from the John Bull Magazine sketched in *Hutchinson* (below), having to do ...

'... with the violation of a naked woman in front of the 'altar', and her subsequent slaying and 'sacrifice' of a goat, which is made to play a

331

principal part in these disgusting Dionysian rites ... The woman ... who is first given an aphrodisiacal drug, such as hashish ... [which] renders the debauchee 'capable of participating in practices which no normal person could conceive of, much less describe ...''

(Then, again, as I always say down the Pub, **normal** is just a dial on the washing machine).

Nobody in their right mind would succumb: yet many are out of it, stoned; yet we might bear in mind (from the Letters) that Professor J.R.R. Tolkien attended seances, and such as Sir Arthur Conan Doyle experimented with reaching the other side; perhaps darkness for Crowley, yet a search for enlightenment for others; all such being very fashionable during the early part of the Twentieth century.

> ### 'The man standin' next to me,
> ### his head was exploding
> ### Well, I was prayin' the pieces
> ### wouldn't fall on me'

Yet Crowley's dirty tricks are so outerworldly, (the Master melting candlewax of *female* fat only, the only surprise being that you may be surprised, albeit Crowley swung his stinking fiery thurible both ways, so we are told), Crowley, worst luck, calls to mind all such tricksters, their confidence swirling in the evil of duplicity, some named in the Cauldron: as well as, to our communal shame in terms of a blind eye to depravity, the accursed Jimmy Saville.

It also brings to mind the observation of Adolf Hitler, way up the road ahead in Mordor, that it matters not how barmy, bonkers or barbaric is your creed or message, what matters is how loudly and often you shout it out for unceasing impact ... and in the case of Nazi Germany, back it with intolerance and violence as required; Hitler had in mind a mimicry of The Roman Empire, with absolute faith in Caesar; the Kaiser in Germany, revisited in Mordor: even down to imitation of the great demonstrations of Imperial power, in such as the Nuremberg Rallies: ever stranger that the mentality of Two Millennia previous was being revisited.

It is suggested (by the Author) that Crowley researched the mentality and practices, including the Magick … sink your spoon into the Cauldron in Appendix C … of a communality of mind belonging two millennia previous (that of Ancient Egypt, witness focus on the Eye of Horus) and updated its sell-by-date for today's market.

> **'I take possession of man's mind and deed.**
> **I care not what the sects may brawl,**
> **I sit as God holding no form of creed,**
> **But contemplating all.'**
> (The Palace of Art; Tennyson)

Crowley is father in a fakery of Devilry; many contemporaries are in accord: dipping now into the cauldron for *The Beast Demystified* (Roger Hutchinson), and this of Christopher Isherwood unmasking the poison mix …

'The *truly awful thing about Crowley* is that one suspects he didn't *really* believe in anything. Even his wickedness. Perhaps the only thing that wasn't fake was his addiction to heroin and cocaine.'

… and anonymous in the closing paragraph of the Hutchinson book …

'… a poser who had come to believe in his own poses …'

I suppose Crowley may visit in my dreams tonight …

I shall sleep by candle wax …

I have no idea who she is it drips onto…

> **'And the daughters of darkness flame**
> **like Fawkes fires still.'**
> (In The White Giants Thigh; Dylan Thomas)

The foregoing are the Author's inadequate words, and rather than see them perhaps hubbled and bubbled in the Cauldron of Appendix C, we include more now from way back in 1884,

Reprinted *1936*; this leading authority would unequivocally be well known to Professor J.R.R. Tolkien, simply because of the subject-matter ...

'Luther again, and probably everybody else, believed in witchcraft. Hundreds and thousands of poor wretches were burned for the supposed crime of having sold themselves to the powers of evil, and having held communion with evil spirits. And stranger still is it that the number of witches burned was rapidly on the increase. There were more witches burned in the 16th century than any previous one, and more still in the next.

Heresy and witchcraft were looked upon as nearly allied, and probably the zeal against both grew together. Nor was the cruel death allotted to these supposed crimes out of proportion to that of others. Thousands and thousands of people were hung in England for no other crime but that of vagrancy and 'sturdy begging.' The system of criminal law was everywhere brutal.

Soon after the Peasants War, the Prince Bishop of Bamberg published a popular criminal law book for the benefit of his subjects – his poor crushed peasantry among others – in which were inserted wood-cuts of thumb-screws, the rack, the gallows, the stake, pincers for pulling out the tongue, men with their eyes put out or their heads cut off, or mangled on the wheel, or suspended by the arms with weights hung on their feet, and so on; and then, to add the terrors of another world (as if these humanly inflicted tortures were not enough), there was a blasphemous picture representing the day of judgment, ***and the hobgoblins carrying off their victims to hell.*** The Prince Bishop, we may suppose, had learned a lesson from Luther, and produced, as he thought, a good book for the laity, meant, not like Luther's, to dispel men's fears of the Pope, but to frighten his poor subjects into submission to his episcopal and princely authority. This may be taken as an example both of the way in which civil and ecclesiastical power were sometimes blended together, and of the brutality of the times.'
(The Era of the Protestant Revolution; F.Seebohm)

One cannot help notice what a bad press the Faerie Realm gets over the years.

Hunting the Witch

'Not so long and wide the world is,
Not so rude and rough the way is,
That my wrath shall not attain him,
That my vengeance shall not reach him!'
(The Hunting; Song of Hiawatha: Longfellow)

Your author is likewise poser, as inventor and mentor in torture and death; it is unclear whether our victims from Weathertop through to The Ford comprise elves, fairies, druids, pagans or witches, or their hunters and slayers farming tool freaks, hammer or pitchfork geeks, or merely cornflake munchers and crunchers (cereal killers), or Witchfinders, Ringwraiths, Nazgûl, lion-beasts or the Devil incarnate his-self; looking back, we suppose the killer could even be Gollum, a proven murderer once, and very likely again and again in his yearning search for the One Ring. Our imagined histories of foul play are heightened by the presence in the Shire of all so many other hunters on the same search for the witches, in human form, those other evil folk perhaps also seduced by the One Ring; almost definitely, *but we should know more before we end it all.*

It does not matter a newt's testicle (if they have any) which side we, you or they are on, because at one time or another through history, each may have been regarded as wicked and evil; it doesn't matter for a second time because such thoughts of condemnation are those in the communal mind at the relevant point of time in history: minds that can accept setting fire to another human being (such as, say, the minds of the average rabble citizen of the seventeenth century) will not be attuned to the rational, and in any event *belief sustains all*: there is little or no room for objectivity, assuming belief in witchcraft, as Witchmarshall Hansen has observed.

Yet some had rationalised the phenomenon, markedly by the middle of The Great War ...

'TOIL and grow rich,
What's that but to lie
With a foul witch

335

And after, drained dry,
To be brought
To the chamber where
Lies one long sought
With despair.'
(The Witch: W. B. Yeats; 1916)

... and it still and never has mattered because the Devil has been afflicting the people with evil and devil demons of this wicked kind over the centuries since time immemorial ...

'... Great God! I'd rather be
A Pagan suckled in a creed outworn;
So might I, standing on this pleasant lea,
Have glimpses that would make me less forlorn;'
(The World Is Too Much With Us: William
Wordsworth)

... for it is foretold ...

Be sober, be vigilant; because your adversary the devil, as a roaring lion, walketh about, seeking whom he may devour...

(I Peter 5:8)

Gollum (Korova milk bar, on drencrom, sharpened up and ready for a bit of the old ultra-V): ... Forlorn? Forlorn? Why so forlorn? ... we viddys clockwork oranges-ss inner Cauldron, Audiences-ss-ss ... very fruity is-s, ras-ssbry ripples-ss enjoyables-ss cripples-ss is-ss ... plenty whines frommer goblets ... snots-ss an' ruby claretastings-ss-ss, yess, all tolchocks-s luvvly jubblies-ss-ss ...

'... then out comes the red stuff, my brothers,
real beautiful ...'

Binding of the Ring

It is the Author's view that the Severn Bore's impact upon the banks of the Severn itself is the Professor's allusion within the torrents of whitehorse crested waves which engulf the Ringwraiths at the Ford; a cavalry of horsepower bewitched by enchantment from Rivendell ...

> **' And a hundred ranged on the rock**
> **like white sea-birds in a row,**
> **' And a hundred gamboll'd and pranced**
> **on the wrecks in the sand below,**
> **And a hundred splash'd from the ledges,**
> **and bosom'd the burst of the spray, ...'**
> (Voyage of Maeldune; Tennyson)

... Witches within Waves ...

It will be recalled the waves thus save Frodo, carried in the Film by Arwen, before arrival at Rivendell, where he is all but cured of the effects of the stabbing at Weathertop. The Audience may be aware that it is not Arwen who comes to Frodo's rescue at the Ford, but the Elf Gorfindel. Presumably the filmakers wished to introduce Arwen for her future romance with Aragorn. The scene, aided by computer graphics, is one of the most memorable on film.

It is the Author's firm belief that the event of the Professor's description is derived from the effects of the Severn Bore at Upton. For the Author, the allusion is too perfect not to be accurate. We share a lot more of the details of the Severn Bore ahead in Volume II. Yet the primary force must surely be Lord Macauley and Horatius at The Bridge, way back there on the road, granted the Professor's fondness for the classics.

Light Finds the New Places We Tread: Tharbad

> **'Then swift from a bursting sea with bottlecork boats**
> **And out-of-perspective sailors,...**
> **Up through the lubber crust of Wales ...'**
> ('Once Below A Time'; Dylan Thomas)

We have already mentioned the Docklands otherwise known as

Tharbad: Tharbad unlocks the docks cargoing the lubber crust of Wales; whose bottlecork boats burst the seas with hundreds and thousands of tunnelfold tonnages out the *Tir*, the coal crust earth of Wales, merchantmen sailors bringing an entirely outward perspective to the new great wealth of Victorian Britain: to foster and to match England's Glory. Our association was indeed fostered by route of the ancient Doctor Foster rhyme …

… Doctor Foster went to Gloucester, in a shower of rain …

… and the matches of 'England's Glory': whose match factory is an emblem ever here today, one might say still the spill in spirit, afire of old by the Dockyards of Gloucester, rekindled vestament of a proud history.

The Author went to Gloucester, yes, in a shower of rain; and was impressed by the conversion of so many out of work warehouses into bright new retail outlets of all kinds. The Gloucester Quays reminded us of a number of such refurbations; the Docks areas of London for some, Cardiff Bay and Swansea Marina for the pride of Wales, and for our U.S. cousins, Pier 11 at Wall Street of New York City; which we cannot help thinking set the Bar for such innovation: the first among its peers.

> **'Statues made of matchsticks**
> **Crumble into one another**
> **My love laughs, she does not bother**
> **She knows too much to argue or to judge …'**

Gloucester is yet one tough Dockers' community, to be of further mention about Fangorn Forest; yet the Sindarin derivation proved not so tough. The 'Thar' element is perhaps 'y ddaear', pronounced 'ddiar', to rhyme with the mendacious 'liar', minding that the Professor is wont to write 'th'(as in a hard-sounding *mitheithel* for the same-sounding 'dd' of Welsh.

deled dy deyrnas;	Thy Kingdom come
gwneler dy ewyllys,	Thy Will be done
ar y **ddaear** fel yn y nef.	On Earth as it is in Heaven

'Y ddaear' ,with 'Y' simply the definite article 'The', is one of several words of cognate meaning in Welsh for earth, ground land, place or any word implying situation; whilst the 'bad' element means 'boat': thus the hard-prowed and proud boated 'Docklands' of Gloucester. 'Ddaear' to 'Thar' is but baby bath-waterplay in the Professor's wordgames: thus 'Tharbad' is a place for boats.

Gollum (the Misty Mountains and Rivendell in view) (pleading): ... Master, Master ... any more chances precious-ss songs and dances-ss ...?

Voice Off: ... *What about, pray?* ...

Smeagol: ... Boats, Master, boatses ...

Voice Off: ... O Very well ...

(Gollum, nodding, sings): ... the Owls and the Pussycatss went to seas-ss ... in bewtiful pee-green boats-ss-ss... (Whispers): ... ach-ss, hopes-ss they's drownded ... 'We must have it. We wants it, we wants it, we wants It!'

Rambling Man

Having droaned on in so many around and about Bredon Hill (Elmley Castle, Offenham, Wickhamford) we drown in no more herebelow, each such place being equally easy ports of call from Upton under Severn.

And yet we add in here a tale of Romance destined to end happily ever after in Nin-In-Elph ...

> **'A fine romance, with no kisses**
> **A fine romance, my friend this is ...**
> **I've never mussed the crease**
> **In your blue serge pants**
> **I never get the chance**
> **This is a fine romance ...'**

[JRRT] author of Lord of the Rings, married his childhood sweetheart Edith Bratt, who was born in Gloucester and lived in Cheltenham. They didn't have an easy courtship. Both were orphans and found themselves living in the same boarding house in Handsworth, Birmingham when she was 16 and he was 19.

Tolkien was Roman Catholic, Edith wasn't and his guardian, who was a priest, forbade Tolkien from associating with a Protestant...

... To ensure they stayed apart, Edith was banished to Cheltenham where she took up lodgings in Charlton Kings with a retired solicitor and his wife ...

(to be continued at Nin-In-Eilph)

We must recommend 'The Gallant Edith Bratt' by Nancy Bunting of the USA, who knows more about Edit than any other person living. She has even found her first school (Dresden House) in Evesham High Street.

Wandering Star

There are yet further forces at work, exterior to that of the Severn Bore.

As of time of writing in Summer 2010 the breaking wave of news hitting The Swan in Upton is a devastation of itself. Geophysical drill testing by boreholes into the Severn River bank have made the wrong kind of waves. They have undermined (?) the riverbanks to such an extent that the foundations of the Swan are eroded with the result of cracks in the fabric of its structure. The supreme irony is that the drill testing was undertaken in order to establish the strength of the riverbank for installation of a state of the art new flood barrier wall.

The Lord sure works in mysterious ways.

Strike Up The Band

**'Sergeant Pepper's Lonely Hearts Club Band
It's getting very near the end ...'**

RING EII:
Rivendell

'I met a young girl, she gave me a rainbow'

'There comes a murmur from the shore,
And in the close two fair-streams are,
Drawn from the purple hills afar, ...'
(A Garden by the Sea; William Morris)

Through Rivendell we enlist the aid, to rain on our parade ... upwards the high street of Great Malvern ... of poets of whom three (A.E. Houseman, George Bernard Shaw and W.H. Auden) may be considered for their local connection and others (Tennyson, Wordsworth, Shelley, Keats and Coleridge) for their rich romanticism in imagery, and most especially because one assumes these were the classical poets known to Professor Tolkien; indeed, *and recalling the Mantra of Middle-earth,* it sometimes seems to the Author that any number of scenes in The Lord of the Rings have their source in these classic poetical works; the sublime irony, by reason that these poetical works draw almost inevitably upon the mythical imagery of the Roman and Greek poets ...

'Strolling over hills and dales,
Wandering through the land of Wales...'
(Hills and Dales: Shaw)

... there are a few others, amongst them the odd Welsh poet, including (inter haliotosis) the Nogood Boyo; because we wanted to share our adoration: with The Land of Song in sight just over the Shire Ridge. Dylan Thomas is on record for admiration of Auden ... and a postcard picture ever to this day pinned up in the writing shed, Laugharne ... but you wouldn't know it from this ...

'The emotional appeal in Auden wouldn't raise a corresponding emotion in a tick'...

However, Auden will say something on the subject-patter of *Rain* that forecasts the emotion of Mordor more powerfully than any rainbow; likewise, Alun Lewis *patters* with rain, missing from under his umbrella the onomatopoeia of pitter, but that won't matter; except if you fancy yourself a shish kebab …

'Like the touch of rain she was'
(Rain; Edward Thomas)

Aragorn is reunited with Arwen at Rivendell; they are eventually to marry at Minas Tirith: but that is a long way off from Rivendell; some 1000 miles …

'White in the moon the long road lies, The moon stands blank above; White in the moon the long road lies That leads me from my love.'
(Houseman)

We may all remember the luvvy-duvvy film scene with Viggo Mortensen and Liv Tyler … which, personally, I always fast forward over, for me blushing, … and heart bleeding for poor Eowyn unreciprocated in love for Aragorn … but here's one for you old romantics …

'Round full Silvery Moon, Lighting the darkest night. Many a lover did swoon, At such a glorious sight.'
(Shaw)

… or, ignoring lyric restrictions, I must have this …

'Well, it's a marvellous night for a Moondance … … With the stars up above in your eyes … And all the nights ma-a-a-agic seems to whisper and hush And all the soft moonlight seems to shine … in your blush … Can I just have one more Moondance with you, my love, Can I just have one more Moondance with you, my love,

**Can I-I just ha-ave one more Moon – dance
with *you* ...
... My *lo-o-o-ve* ...'**

Gollum (elbows Van the Man, still singing, off stage): ... *My Luv
... My Luv ... My Luv ?* ... No! Our-s It muss be lissnin' to! Ourrs-
ss muss It lissn' to!!It mus-ss be lissnin' to Ourrrs-sss!!! Smeagol
is to do all the songs and dances-ss on this quest, Awffer Mas-sster
... any more chances precious-ss songs and dances-ss so awssums
... in Rivendell, ... Awffer Mas-sster ...? (Whispers)'We must
have it. We wants it, we wants it, we wants It!'

Samwise Gamgee

Rivendell evokes the kernel or core of Middle-earth. Sam says
much later (III, 2640)-

' ... there's something of everything here, the Shire and the Golden
Wood and Gondor and kings' houses and inns and meadows and
mountains all mixed ...'

Yet way before all of the troubles up the road ahead, Samwise is
moved to this; following Gandalf's apparent demise at The Bridge
of Khazad Dum in Moria ...

> **' The finest rockets ever seen:
> they burst in stars of blue and green,
> or after thunder golden showers
> came falling like a rain of flowers.'**

Gollum (elbows Samwise, still in recitation, off stage): ...
Thunders-s? ... Rains-ss?... Mas-sster be doing po'try lyrrix all
inner lightnins-ss-ss next if he gesser chances-ss-ss ...!!!

Smeagol: ... Good Smeagol does all po'try lyrrix on this quest,
Author Master... any more chance fix summore my po'try lyrrix so
lyricals-ss, ... in Rivendell, ...

Gollum: ... Awffer Mas-sster ...? (Whispers) 'We must have it. We wants it, we wants it, we wants It!

> **'The sky is darkening like a stain,**
> **Something is going to fall like rain**
> **And it won't be flowers.'**
> (The Witnesses; Auden)

Three of the most powerful lines in poetry ever. For a personal opinion: inspiration for Sam; and a hard rain's a gonna' fall.

Having about the Trollshaws taken our usual format out of order by re-ordering our 'Light Finds the New Places We Tread' section, we are about to practise the same method; but we think for very good reason: here we cut the light from our association for Rivendell ... the Spa town of Royal Great Malvern ... to a second Spa Town, equally admired in the day for the marvels of its sparkling spring waters; being no distance from Rivendell on the Ring-Maps, nor any distance in mileage on Mother-earth today.

Light Finds the New Places We Tread: Nin-In-Eilph

> **'All visible visibly**
> **Moving things**
> **Spin or swing,**
> **One of the two,**
> **Move, as the limbs**
> **Of a runner do,**
> **To and fro,**
> **Forward and back,**
> **Or, as they swiftly**
> **Carry him**
> **In orbit go ...**
> (The Runner; Auden)

(This poem may focus on human runners;
but if the cap fits: wear it in all colours flying)

Cheltenham is the more sedate and perhaps (but without *any* doubt on the part of the smart young fillies of The Cheltenham Ladies'

345

College) more refined brother or sister to Gloucester (an o so unwanted siblingry, once again without *any* doubt on the part of our charming Ladies); the closest one can call them being in terms of comparative geography; in all other comparative terms the towns are worlds apart.

> '... There were multitudes assembled
> with their tickets at the station
> ... And me eyes began to dazzle
> and they're going to see the races
> ... With me whack fol the dol
> fol the diddlely idle ay ...'
> (The Galway Races; Trad. Ireland)

The Celts and the Fillies: the leetle people with thorough breeds, breeches and tweeds, bound for breezy Cheltenham, whose March Festival springs an invasion of the Irish (horses, trainers, jockeys, shamrock rovers, Guinness gulpers, guzzlers and gangs of roaring no brainers) t' be sure to put your money on. Paddock upon paddock of Paddies, corale and coral, herding and here and hear sing all aloud the Celtic voices: all horses, ... jockeys, shamrock rovers, Guinness gulpers, guzzlers and the finest of trainers.

So many wild rovers, and all very welcome, t' be sure.

One more for the road, and riding, back from the racecourse ...

> 'The time you won your town the race
> We chaired you through the market-place;
> Man and boy stood cheering by,
> And home we brought you shoulder-high.'
> (To An Athlete Dying Young; Houseman)

We shall be acknowledging certain difficulties of etymology; but perceive none of geography: for Cheltenham (as was Gloucester) is in perfect first and second place on the Ring-Maps, at least according to the odds laid by the Author on the Professor's Secret of the Shire.

346

'Far to the west in a haze lay the meres and eyots through which [the Swanfleet] wound its way to the Greyflood: there countless swans housed in a land of reeds.'

(The Return of the King)

'Nin-In-Eilph' is otherwise 'Swanfleet'. We learn that the Swan emblem representing Cheltenham is derived of Royal connection; an acquisition from the designation 'Royal' Cheltenham Spa by Queen Victoria. Such designation confirmed Royal Patronage and was accorded many Spa towns for their distinguished healing waters, including Royal Great Malvern: Rivendell. Of itself the Swan indicates the Royal connection, all Swans being, by history and tradition, in the ownership and protection of the Crown.

Quite apart from a delightful historical account of the connection of the Swan with the River Thames and, indeed, Royalty, Peter Ackroyd provides a further inkling of the 'Swanfleet' derivation …

'The mingling of the tributary and the main river was deemed to be sacred … There is one special god for this purpose. The Celtic god Condatis – who in some late Roman inscriptions associated with Mars, no doubt in his capacity as a healing power – takes his name from the Gallic epithet 'watersmeet'. He is literally the god of the two streams, the *confluens*, and was worshipped as such.'

'Swanfleet' is at the very least evocative of 'watersmeet', noting the ancient usage of 'fleet' as a river or watercourse; and, of course we have appreciated the meeting of the River Churn and the River Chelt, at least so far as concerns Professor Tolkien and the Ring-Maps, by reason of the flow of the Mitheithel, about the foothills of the Trollshaws.

We had yet to decode the 'Nin' or the 'Eilph' of Cheltenham, having no Sindarin/Welsh derivation to offer: with the lame offerance that we must make do with Elf Legolas, arrowing in later. The town is built upon the rivulet of the 'Chelt'; so even without a Sindarin Nin or Eilph, we retain a Celtic ambience.

'The archer with time
as his arrow – has he broken
his strings that the rainbow
is so quiet over our village? ...'
(R.S.Thomas;tbc)

However, we now share what we have heard in our further researches beyond a first silence.

Aelf

'Fays and Fairies haste away!
... Bring the purple lilac here,
Festoons of roses, sweetest flower,
The yellow primrose of the bower,
Blue-ey'd violets wet with dew,
Bring the clustering woodbine too.
... Be the brilliant grotto scene
The palace of the Fairy Queen.'
(Invocation to the Fairies; Felicia Dorothea Hemans)

The Fairy Queen is festooned with the loveliness of flowers; the most memorable on Malvern are in Bluebell Wood: blooming for you now in a field of clouds over Malvern.

The Elf Queen, Lady Galadriel, awaits at Lothlorien up the road ahead.

'The Old English word 'aelf', the linguistic origin of 'elf', has cognate words in Norwegian and Old High German. Because it occurs in such ancient forms of these languages, we know that belief in these beings goes back to very ancient times, when the ancestors of the English, Germans and Norwegians still spoke the same language ... Despite the picture of destructive elves' arrows in the Christian manuscript, they were a positive presence in people's lives ... The elves were often described as beautiful. A considerable compliment for a woman was to compare her appearance with an elf. An Anglo-Saxon poem – found in the same manuscript which contained the epic *Beowulf* – refers to its heroine as 'Judith, wise in thought, a woman as brightly beautiful as an elf ...' The beauty was more than mere physical attractiveness. It was of an iridescent quality – a radiant, pale brightness. This glow is reflected in the Anglo-Saxon word 'aelf', which is cognate with the Latin 'albus', meaning 'white and shining' ... Tolkien revealed in a letter that in *The Lord of the Rings,* his fantasy version of these creatures drew on the elves from the real Middle-earth. His elves, too, shine with goodness ...'

(The Real Middle-earth: Magic and Mystery in the Dark Ages; Brian Bates; 2003)

A Fine Romance

To end the tale of Romance begun at Tharbad ...

> **'A fine romance, with no kisses**
> **A fine romance, my friend this is ...'**

' ... On his 21st birthday and free of his pernickety priest, Tolkien wrote a letter to Edith, declaring his love and asking her to marry him. They arranged to meet and while in Cheltenham, Tolkien stayed at the Moorend Park Hotel, which stood on ground now occupied by the Pinetrees estate, off Moorend Road in Charlton Kings ...'

> **'Things are mending now**
> **I see a rainbow blending now**
> **We'll have a happy ending now**
> **Taking a chance on love ...'**

' ... A weekly newspaper called the Cheltenham Looker-on published a list of visitors to the town. Reproduced here is the entry published on January 11, 1913 ...

'Happily, love conquered all. John and Edith were married for 56 years ...'
(Robin Brooks; Gloucestershire Echo: February 25, 2014)

> '… Let us stand, then, in the interval
> of our wounding, till the silence
> turn golden and love is
> a moment eternally flowing.'
> (Evening; Poems to Elsi: R.S. Thomas)

Rainbows

> 'From rainbow clouds there flow not
> Drops so bright to see
> As from thy presence showers a rain of melody.'
> (To A Skylark; Percy Bysshe Shelley)

Gollum: … Rainbows-ss!? … Rainbows-ss!? … muss mean rain onner forecasts-ss!

Smeagol: … and far beyond rainbows of Rivendells still more rains, My Luv, we wonders, yes we wonders …???

Voice of Genesis 9:12, 15, (HBFV):

> 'I set My rainbow in the cloud, and it shall be the sign of the covenant between Me and the earth … and the waters shall no more become a flood to destroy all flesh.'

Gollum: … The Dead Marshes-ss! O Mercy!! … nuffing but pools-ss in floods of waters-ss and destruction of flesh is-ss there, my precious-ss-ss !!! … (eyes tight-shut, head-shaking grimace): … Is-ss nun Rainbows-ss there, precious … Prufessur's Dead Marshes runs-s wiv rats-ss-ss onnem inner green pools-ss dead faces-ss, Audiences-ss … Is-ss nun Rainbows-ss there, my precious-ss-ss-ss …

> 'The sky is darkening like a stain,
> Something is going to fall like rain
> And it won't be flowers.'

Smeagol: … but there might be signs of pretty colour rainbowses until the leaving of Rivendells, My Luv?

Gollum: ... praps yes-ss, praps no, but only if we'ss all to be *hearing* it so, my precious-ss-ss-ss ... then, yes-ss, indeed, ... is-ss like wot ol' Percy Shelley do say ... '*... thy presence showers a rain of melody ...*' (whispers) ... an' so long as it is ours It is-ss to be hearing ...

'My heart leaps up when I behold
A rainbow in the sky: ...'
(Wordsworth)

The Colour Purple

'... I think it pisses God off
if you walk by the color purple in a field somewhere
and don't notice it ...'

The colour purple is that best befitting the shading of the Malvern Hills which peers from beneath the haze above the mountains ... distant in our current view, yet majestic once we lift those mists ...

'The purple headed mountain,
The river running by,
The sunset and the morning,
That brightens up the sky;
All things bright and beautiful ...'

... this river perhaps the source of the name of the one ('*river running*') running south of Esgaroth in The Hobbit, only Professor J.R.R. Tolkien knows ... we shall indeed be hearing the colour purple plenty more times over the hills, and go on to sing (ever after Aragorn's gift to Arwen and the Professor's song to Edith), yonder rainbows regretful for the rain come but gone ...

Middle-earth

'The rocks are cloven, and through the purple night
I see cars drawn by rainbow-winged steeds
Which trample the dim winds ...

A wild-eyed charioteer urging their flight …'
(Prometheus Unbound; Shelley)

Lo, Shadowfax and Gandalf … here for the Council of Elrond? The Audience might recall that Gandalf acquires Shadowfax in events leading up to The Council: and the cloven rocks and the purple make a flighty path for the charioteer Wizard of Fire.

'Beyond the horizon, behind the sun
At the end of the rainbow life has only begun'

Before we fix the po'try lyrrix of Rivendell, we preview the most shifting experience in the swim of it; the most quickshifting sands for the Author, who went (… with Gollum, as we shall hear …) to the ends of the horizon in tapping the resources of 'The Rhyme of the Ancient Mariner', that legendary poem of the most powerful drama, imagery and mysticism, for aquaduction into the environment of Rivendell, only to discover that we were being deluded by a deluge of dŵr … (circumflex the Welsh rain-water with a roof, ever rattling in from Wales over Offa's Dyke) … by the film-makers; and it is now that we might dehydrate our (s)elves: quick as we were to suggest … 'visualise Rivendell on film', and … rushing down the guttering to drown us all in …

'… water, water, everywhere …'

… we were swimming in the *reel* world, but not in the *real* world; or at least as Professor Tolkien wrote of the surreal world of Middle-earth, there being not the drip, drip, drop of water in the text of The Rings at Rivendell: cast away the watercannon hoses gushing forth on all sides of Rivendell on film; yet perhaps cast one's mind away back to the island of Bushell's Marvells at Neat Enstone, once the target of water shapeshifters: all because here the film-makers have shifted the watershapes of Mother-earth, into Middle-earth, and into the cast of the films.

In *The Fellowship of the Ring, Part I of the Trilogy*, there pour the fabulous streams of water from above, in and about Rivendell, it being perfectly crystal water clear that the researchers of the films have gauged the meter of *Royal Great Malvern*, to pimp the pump and pomp of waters shooting, from every angle, in their towering, showering, power ...

> **'Warming waters washing over me,**
> **It was the time of my baptising.**
> **Things of beauty I did see,**
> **As my spirit was slowly rising.'**
> (Shaw)

Water gushes from every available duct in the film scenery of New Zealand ... so much so, it might be said we are ducked down under ... but, as a matter of deduction, *not at all* in the text of The Rings; yet, yes indeed, *once upon a time, but no longer, in Royal Great Malvern, the Rivendell of Mother-earth.*

> **'I'll walk where my own nature would be leading:**
> **It vexes me to choose another guide:**
> **Where the gray flocks in ferny glens are feeding;**
> **Where the wild wind blows on the mountain side.**
> **What have those lonely mountains worth revealing?'**
> ('Often rebuked ...'; Emily Bronte)

So evocative of our quest in The Hobbit, now pose yourself a question, or, perhaps riddle; consider, also, who there is lurking, lonely, leering all to his-selfs, deep beneath us here ...

> **'It was a den where no insulting light**
> **Could glimmer on their tears; where their own groans**
> **They felt, but heard not, for the solid roar**
> **Of thunderous waterfalls and torrents hoarse,**
> **Pouring a constant bulk, uncertain where.'**
> (Hyperion; John Keats)

Gollum (way, way, way beneath The Misty Mountains): ... We guesses-ss, yes, we knows-ss ... now search for us-s, Audiences-ss, inner darks-ss of recesses-ss wheres we outguesses baggines-ss, you remembers-ss ... ?

Smeagol: … yes, My Luvvs, look into my eyeses … dusn't they hypnotyses …?

'Jeepers, Creepers, Where'd ya get them peepers?'

Gollum: …*fillfy hobbitses-ss* … Ach,-ss! … Yes-ss, my precious-ss, we knows … We guesses, yes,… like allur riggle games wiv bagginses … *an'* wot hobbitses had got in his nas-ssty little pocketses … *an'* wot hobbitses have got round his filffy little neckses-ss … *we hates-ss them forever* …

**'When I consider how my light is spent
Ere half my days in this dark world and wide,…'**
(On His Blindness; Milton)

Smeagol (calming, sad eyes): … and we wants *them* to know, durstn't we, My Luv … Yes, yes indeed, … find them safe paths in the dark for water, yes we will …

Gandalf the Grey in Rivendell: "Well, well, he is gone, 'said Gandalf. 'We may have no time to seek for him again. He must do what he will. But he may play a part yet that neither he nor Saruman have foreseen."

'A skulking gangrel creature with an ill-favoured look'

Gandalf speaks of Gollum at the Council of Elrond in Rivendell, and it is at Rivendell that we first encounter the history of the *creature Gollum*: through Aragorn (whom he had bitten, but who tamed him to crawling, tied on a leash), Gandalf (to whom he told the tale of the One Ring and of his torture in Mordor), and Legolas whom he evaded, escaping capture by the Elves.

Poor, poor … poor Smeagol …

Gollum (sings):

**'Into every life,
a little rain must fall,**

But too much is falling in mine …
(Ella Fitzgerald)

Not to forget the trauma suffered by Gollum, there is, by the end, more to come of what is troubling Gollum on his ventures throughout Middle-earth; and so the creature plays a part in Rivendell not even the Author had foreseen in the script.

Gollum the Great

'We must have it. We wants it, we wants it, we wants It!'

Without foreknowledge of exactly what *It* might be, and beyond the obvious, easy and trite answer that Gollum wants the One Ring, some things are clear: Gollum's ambition covets *greatness* of a kind …

'See my precious: if we has it … praps we grows very strong, stronger than Wraiths. Lord Smeagol? Gollum the Great? *The* Gollum?! Eat fish every day, three times a day, fresh from the sea. Most Precious Gollum! …'

This history of Gollum in the Council at Rivendell being his first real scenario in The Rings, by happy coincidence for the Author it is here at Rivendell of the Quest that Gollum finally begins a search for the Greatness he so secretly craves, interlarkening about, amidst the dark pathways and passages of the Misty Mountains as you will see and hear them, in the search for the waterfalls long since missing from the Rivendell of Mother-earth: for the waters were here, but today they are no more to be seen.

Smeagol (hand to worried forehead): … Author Master flooding us all in waters of Rivendell, My Luv … and them picture peoples been here to see … yes, they sees is-s gone … all waterfallses is lost now …

Gollum: … but still they pitchers-ss waters-s back again … yess, indeed, back again they bring waterfalls-ss in pitchers-sss …

Smeagol(Nodding): … in *pictures*, My Luv …

Gollum: … pitchers-ss is wot the precious says-ss, and pitchers-ss is wot we means-ss …

Smeagol (hand to worried forehead): … so we must find the missing waterfallses ?…

Gollum:(whispers to hisselfs) … Must have it. We wants it, we wants it, we wants It! … yess, yess, nice water, … drink it, drink it, if we can …

Smeagol: … find it, My Luv …

We awaken at Chapter 1 of Book II of the trilogy:

Many Meetings

Frodo wakes up in a bed in the House of Elrond in Rivendell. Gandalf tells Frodo he is just recovering from the wound inflicted at Weathertop.

> **'O plunge your hands in water,**
> **Plunge them in up to the wrist;**
> **Stare, stare in the basin**
> **And wonder what you've missed.'**
> (As I Walked Out One Evening: Auden)

Surprisingly (to the Author), Gandalf says that the Barrow Downs were even more dangerous than Weathertop. Gandalf had been delayed, but does not explain why; the reason is, of course, the trauma of his confrontation with Saruman.

War is to come. The Black Riders are the Ringwraiths, the Nine Servants of the Lord of the Rings; Sauron is such Lord.

They speak of such as Barliman Butterbur; Frodo thought him rather dim, but Gandalf corrects him with the observation that (as they say in Bree) Butterbur can see through a brick wall given time.

Gandalf explains Strider's family history. Aragorn is a King.

Frodo has lost track of time. A splinter of the Morgul blade has been removed.

Gandalf explains that the horses of the Black Riders were real enough and have perished; there are robes too, which were real enough. Otherwise they are spirits.

Gandalf now relates the chase by the Black Riders and the rescue by Gorfindel, who knew of the 'Flood' which was to come. Gandalf comments that the Ringwraiths were carried away by its first assault. This is not the end of the Ringwraiths, but there is nothing to fear for now. Gandalf reveals that it was Elrond that commanded the flooding at the river. Specifically he says that the waves took the form of great white horses with shining white riders, there being great vigour in the waters that flow down from the Misty Mountains. Sam, Merry and Pippin join with Frodo and Gandalf.

Gandalf is keen to point out that the Lord of the Rings is not Frodo, but the master of the Dark Tower of Mordor.

There follows a gathering in the Elven Hall. Elrond and Gorfindel are there, but Frodo sees for the first time a fair, queenly lady who is Arwen, daughter of Elrond. There is also Gloin the Dwarf. Gloin relates that it is not safe between the Misty Mountains and Mirkwood. He lists the names of his band of surviving Dwarves. Three have been lost. He describes Moria with its halls and cavernous streets under the earth, with arches carved like trees.

They enter the 'Hall of Fire'. Bilbo Baggins is there, who explains he has been wandering (very much like the Author) since he left the Shire. He asks Frodo for the Ring, and becomes transfixed and besotted by the sight of the Ring. Frodo sees Aragorn with Arwen, between whom there is clearly a strong bond.

**'Everybody is making love,
or else expecting ra-a-ain ...'**

The Audience will have noticed that the Professor pauses the action of the story at Rivendell. After the 'Many Meetings' those gathered at Rivendell get together for one special Meeting, the Council of Elrond. Rivendell's meetings are something of an interlude between the first and second stages of Frodo's journey.

The Council of Elrond

Naturally there is very little in terms of our investigation of locality, within the primary purpose of the Quest. In any event we summarise the proceedings of the Council for completeness.

Those attending include Elrond, who is as it were chairman of the meeting, together with Gorfindel and others of the Elves. Gandalf accompanies Bilbo, Frodo and Sam, who is not deterred by lack of invitation, the lack of which does preclude Merry and Pippin. Gimli and Gloin represent the Dwarves. Legolas attends on behalf of Thranduil of the Elves. Boromir comes on behalf also of his brother Faramir, heirs to the Kingdom of Gondor.

The Council discusses the prospect of War following the duplicity of Saruman of Isengaard in forming a coalition with the Dark Lord Sauron. His pursuit of the One Ring is fundamental to the discussions. Gollum, who has played little part thus far, is mentioned, with a potholed history of what has happened to him.

The outcome of the deliberations is that Frodo will be the Ring bearer, charged with the responsibility of destroying the Ring in the fires of the Sammath Naur within the realms of Mount Doom.

The Ring goes South in Chapter Three.

The four Hobbits meet Merry and Pippin, envying Sam who had attended the Council. Pippin recommends someone of intelligence to accompany the Ring on its journey, which according to Gandalf, therefore excludes him, Peregrine Took.

They have been two months at the House of Elrond.

Scouts have returned over the High Pass through the Misty Mountains. Elves had passed down the Silverlode into a 'strange country'. The Eagles of the Misty Mountains have profound knowledge and reported many of these things.

We learn that eight out of nine Ringwraiths are 'accounted for'. Elrond regrets that he cannot foresee the future for the association because the future is in Mordor. The association will constitute nine 'Walkers'. Elrond wants Pippin, being the youngest, to stay behind, but Pippin insists upon going as part of the Fellowship.

The sword of Elendil is reforged.

We learn that Bilbo spent his time reading passages from his book, 'which still seemed very incomplete.'

As the Author commented at Bree, the Author so knows that feeling of despair for the magnitude of a task ahead …

'A nice pickle we have landed ourselves in, Mr. Frodo!'

This is Sam's comment at the conclusion of the Council of Elrond and must stand as the greatest understatement in the history of English literature. There is also, of course, Frodo's immortal comment …

'I will take the Ring … though I do not know the way.'

Obvious, trite and facile as may be, yet Frodo is guided by moral compass.

"Ash nazg durbatulûk, ash nazg gimbatul, ash nazg thrakatulûk agh burzum-ishi krimpatul."

Gandalf utters these words of the Dark Speech, (being those of the 3, 7, 9 configuration, and of the One Ring to bind them all) here at Rivendell, provoking a reaction which may only be considered the response of Sauron in wrath and rage …

'The change in the wizard's voice was astounding. Suddenly it became menacing, powerful, harsh as stone. A shadow seemed to pass over the high sun, and the porch for a moment grew dark. All trembled, and the Elves stopped their ears.'

Once before has Frodo entered communication with the other world of Sauron, wearing the Ring at Weathertop, and will do so once more at Amon Hen, yet it seems that Gandalf, a powerful wizard and *Istari*, may do the same. One recalls that Lady Galadriel does likewise, tempted by the One Ring at Lothlorien.

(Mere mortals catch Sauron on skype by Palantir).

'This wheel's on fire, rolling down the road'

On Mount Doom:

'I am naked in the dark, Sam, and there is no veil between me and the wheel of fire.'

The Tolkien Boys (ignoring the derivation in Welsh, for the moment, being far too parochial for a scene written in Rivendell, yet imagined in Mordor) the world over, have puzzled, long and hard, over the following image, in the final reaches of Mount Doom, on the brink of the flaming stretches of the Chambers of Fire …

'Gollum was tearing at his master, trying to get at the chain and the Ring … He fought back with a sudden fury that amazed Sam, and Gollum also … 'Down, down!' he gasped, clutching his hand to his breast, so that beneath the cover of his leather shirt he clasped the Ring…
Then suddenly, … Sam saw these two rivals **with other vision.** *A* **crouching shape,** *scarcely more than the shadow of a living thing, a creature now wholly ruined and defeated, yet filled with hideous lust and rage; and before it stood stern, untouchable now by pity, a* **figure robed in white,** *but at its breast it held a* **wheel of fire. Out of the fire there spoke a commanding voice …**

Then the vision passed and Sam saw Frodo standing, hand on breast ... and Gollum at his feet, resting on his knees with his wide-splayed hands upon the ground.'

Thus, the Wheel of Fire, synonymous with the One Ring, is held at the breast of a figure robed in white ...

... a firelit wheel, perfect for lifting the veil to reveal ... that it is **Gandalf ...** through a throat of thunder wrought under a mounting mountain roar ... tough tongued yet untouched by pity for Gollum, who commands ...

'Begone, and trouble me no more! If you touch me ever again, you shall be cast yourself into the Fire of Doom!'

Thus, in Sam's own vision of the other world, (which he, too, may have entered given the proximity of Sauron), Gandalf impersonates the One Ring (touch **me**) by a voice only the Wizard has the power to personify, that of Sauron, the Dark Lord.

At least, that is the way the Author sees it and tells it.

Yet the Author tells also that the command is accurately prophetic, and immediate, present, premonition, because when Gollum next touches the Ring, a fixture on Frodo's bitten-off finger, the creature **is cast into the Fire of Doom.**

Also it is foreheard here *in Rivendell* ... because, at this stage of the Quest, we have no idea whether we shall ever get to Germany in order to set the scene alight in Mordor.

Frodo's Betrayal of Quest

The following paragraphs, before we pick up on *Premonition* once more, were added as a result of inquiry upon why, in Mount Doom, Professor Tolkien causes Frodo (by voicing a wish to keep the Ring for himself) to somehow betray his Quest, the Fellowship and to turn traitor on its members.

**'I do so dearly believe', he wrote to Edith,
'that no half-heartedness and no worldly fear
must turn us aside from following the light
unflinchingly.'**
(Letter: Biography; Humphrey Carpenter)

It must be stressed that the 'religious' theory outlined here is derived from an understanding of some aspects of Professor J.R.R. Tolkien's staunch Roman Catholicism, the faith readily detectable from the Letters and Biography; indeed the pathways through Continental Europe in Volume III merely serve to accentuate the observation because they take in countless shrines indeed sacred to Roman Catholicism.

Tolkien always strongly held that The Lord of the Rings was not allegorical, particularly in reference to political events of his time such as World War II or the Cold War. At the same time he conceded 'applicability' as being within the 'freedom' of the reader, and indeed many people have been inclined to view the One Ring as a symbol or metaphor.

'There is power, too, of another kind in the Shire.'
(Gandalf, Many Meetings)

The Author's ultimate conclusion is that the One Ring symbolises a perpetual seduction into the evil of original sin, which is bound to fail, given the faith that God's Providence will inevitably overcome all evil: Original Sin means rebellion against the will of God, as it was in the Garden of Eden.

**'Lord of all eagerness, Lord of all faith,...
be there at our homing and give us, we pray,
your love in our hearts, Lord, at the eve of the day.'**

Faith is the key and is the moral of the story in The Lord of the Rings: faith not necessarily in the existence of a god, but in the certainty that good will overcome evil through love. This is the essential doctrine of Christianity: evil being manifested to Roman Catholics in the seven deadly sins.

Gollum: ... inner prufessurs stories-ss we means-ss-ss-ss ... (Aside)... the res-sst is-s up to you, Audiences-ss-ss ...

Smeagol: ... might be right, could be wrong ... come, come, see what Smeagol finds ...

We may be right or wrong, yet we are borne out in the correctness in the direction of our thought process by this, honestly and truly found after the next following paragraphs were laid down, and indicative that the specialist Tolkien Boys may already be aware of what the Author (truly) assumed his own fairly original commentary ...

... in a 1953 letter to Robert Murray, a Jesuit priest:

"The Lord of the Rings' is of course a fundamentally religious and Catholic work; unconsciously so at first, but consciously in the revision. That is why I have not put in, or have cut out practically all references to anything like 'religion,' to cults or practices, in the imaginary world. For the religious element is absorbed into the story and symbolism."

This is, never mind all the places in the Shire that we may find upon our Quest, the most powerful revelation *of all* about the best-read story of the Twentieth Century: one that most readers have no conception of whatsoever; and no more did the Author until the inquiry of these paragraphs provoked that very premise. It also serves us well to remember that this *1953* correspondence *predates* publication of The Lord of the Rings, and was made to garner the reactions of any number of Tolkien intimates *pre*-publication: we have many whose reactions are in the public domain *post*-publication, but none known to the Author who emphasises the *religious* ethic, and where it leaves the professorial dismissal of the concept of *Allegory,* only God knows ... yet I can quite imagine that Professor J.R.R. Tolkien would have absolutely no idea of the mass global popularity his work would achieve; in which event the Professor would presumably be inclined to minimise the publicity for its doctrinal core, avoiding schism in religion.

Since this dawning of awareness, there are indeed any number of web discussions about Catholicism in The Rings out there ...

Smeagol: ... like a dog wivver bone, Author Master is now, My Luvvs, won't leave it alone ...

Gollum: ... curse us-s an' crush us-ss, precious, Ach-ss ... muss' mean more of me an' my nas-ssty nonsenss-ss inner Awffer Mas-ssster Quests-ss ...

Smeagol: ... Dreadful Danger! Dreadful Danger! Smeagol's bones shake to think of it!

Yes, indeed; how true: if only you, the Audience, knew.

The Power of the Ring

'The ambiguous reference to the 'Dark Lord' and the nature of his power adumbrates the ambiguity of Sauron in the story. No-one ever is sure in just what his corruption lies, whether it is the deadly sin of pride, Machiavellian power-perversion, or alliance with death-forces.'
(The Eighth of the Wise and Great)

The One Ring is engine, conduit and symbol of Sauron's subtle, gradual, yet perpetual seduction into evil, held in fear by some men of religion as the evils of the *seven deadly sins* ...

**'... Lead us not into temptation
but deliver us from evil ...'**

... the zenith of that seduction takes place when Frodo falls from Grace by rejecting the destruction of the Ring within Mount Doom, for it is then that Frodo is fallen,(in a biblical sense), in victory by evil over good: at that point Frodo's will is broken, and he does not (at least as a matter of this theoretical) adopt the Ring by free choice: though not broken physically, yet psychologically Frodo is, or would be, lead into the temptation and beyond ...

A number of the Fellowship have already been tempted, for instance, Boromir at Amon Hen ...

All of them, it seemed, had fared alike: each had felt that he was offered a choice between a shadow full of fear that lay ahead, and something that he greatly desired: clear before his mind it lay, and to get it he had only to turn aside from the road and leave the Quest and the war against Sauron to others.

It is significant that Gandalf steadfastly refuses to take physical possession of, or even touch, the Ring, nor will the Lady Galadriel (other than to combat, and to defeat, the seduction ... 'I pass the test' ...), and yet Tom Bombadil might do so, according to Gandalf, with impunity, simply because, as a pure force of nature, Tom is immune to the failings of human beings, and thus to the seduction of evil.

'And there are no truths outside the Gates of Eden'

Original Sin may be defined (there are several nuances) as the rebellion against God's will by consuming the fruit of good *and evil* in the Garden of Eden.

'We have offended against thy holy laws. We have left undone those things which we ought to have done; And we have done those things which we ought not to have done'

Here is perhaps the true significance of the Wheel of Fire; the consequence of the original flaw leading to the fall: we are all, *indeed all*, vulnerable to the human tragedy of the fall from grace with God (whatever be your understanding of what god means, indeed if *god* means anything to you at all) ...

'Unfortunately there is so much original sin in us all that we find evil rather attractive ...'
(Anthony Burgess, cited in Appendix C)

This exceptional insight (introduction, 1982 Edition) into the cruel mind of Alex in 'A Clockwork Orange' (equally exceptional in vision) presupposes that we all have free will to make choices between good and bad. Burgess suggests that we all have that free will. It may be that some of us do not; it may be that we all do in

365

objective terms, but, in subjective terms, there are those who do not know the difference between right and wrong. Indeed some of us do not even know that we don't. Myra Hindley (see Appendix C) recognised that she at least did know the difference, but claimed that Ian Brady did not.

One strand of Roman Catholicism indeed avows that original sin **negates freedom of will,** a comprehension fundamental in this, the Author's theoretical of the power of the One Ring.

This, we believe, is what Professor Tolkien means by the seemingly faithless, and purely selfish, action of Frodo in Mount Doom.

Gollum

'**Father,** *forgive them; for they know not what they do*'

Gollum is so seduced into the sin of selfish greed that he is driven to wickedness in order to achieve it; Gollum is prepared to kill for the Ring, without any first or second thought: it may be that, when so fully consumed into the evil of the One Ring, and with free will gone, Gollum does not know what he is doing, does not know right from wrong, and for, say, legal analysis, is insane.

Sméagol offers a less insane alternative: Sméagol could and would be good, but for the evil temptation into sin radiated by the One Ring through Gollum. In that regard, the creature represents two heads on the couch; splitting personalities in the drama of a schizophrenic trauma; but I wouldn't suppose that even my own shrink understands …

… I need a dump truck, Mama, to unload my head …
Until another shovel-load unveiled a mortal soul soiled in the spoils of evil, yet even so, redeemable …

'For even the very wise cannot see all ends. I have not much hope that Gollum can be cured before he dies, but there is a chance of it. And he is bound up with the fate of the Ring. My heart tells me that he has some part to play yet, for good or ill, before the end; and when that comes, the pity of Bilbo may rule the fate of many – yours not least.'

(Of course Bilbo was the first to spare Gollum in The Hobbit.)

**'If You find it in Your heart, can I be forgiven? …
It gets discouraging at times, but I know I'll make it
By the saving grace that's over me.'**

… because Professor Tolkien sees Gollum as *curable*. That is to say not beyond redemption through turning away from evil, perhaps the sin of Greed in particular: perfectly consistent with the confessional of Roman Catholicism (as the Author understands it) where God recognises human weakness and one may receive forgiveness and be pardoned of sins. The Professor confirms as much in his letter concerning Uruk-hai following hard on our heels below; very much like the chase onwards Amon Hen.

It would go one step further to suggest that Smeagol does indeed represent Gollum on the path towards redemption, … and there is a big temptation in my heart to convert my mind to that school of thought … I do so wonder if it will do me any good …

**'I saw the light I saw the light
No more darkness no more night
Now I'm so happy no sorrow in sight
Praise the Lord I saw the light.'**
(Hank Williams★)

If, consistent with the choice between good and evil which confronts us all, one regards the One Ring as symbol of the seduction into sin, then that symbol is destroyed and thus overcome by the forces for good; for *faith in goodness* overturns evil: thus the consequence of evildoing is *comeuppance, what goes round comes around,* and *just desserts,* which all spring (like a crazed Gollum) to mind …

367

'Your Sins Will Find You Out'

... the irony of the end being that Gollum's greed is the causation of the downfall ... yet an inevitable irony because if Gollum had not been the agency of the destruction of the Ring ... then Frodo's future becomes an unseen, obscene one ...

'... it results in a total deprivation of free will, and without free will, Man is nothing. A body may be enslaved, but that is as nothing if the mind is free. But the deprivation of free will is essentially the death of the soul and the extinguishing of the spirit ...'★★

Imprisonment ... Madness ... Hell ...

We shall be taking you all down there in Volume III; some of it at The Battle of the Somme: because J.R.R. Tolkien was there to witness events; and at this stage (the Author suggests that) the Audience has no idea how closely the Professor documented the scene of that misery.

It is perhaps fundamental to appreciate the purpose, nature and function of the One Ring as Professor Tolkien might have formulated the concept; and so even the erstwhile purest in heart Frodo Baggins succumbs to the temptation of the evil that dwells in the One Ring; given the premise that Frodo no longer enjoys freedom of will at that point.

> **'Well, God is in heaven**
> **And we all want what's his**
> **But power and greed and corruptible seed**
> **Seem to be all that there is'**

If we are right about our perception of the Ring's seductiveness into sin, then (for the Professor, we suggest) evil would be formulated in terms of the *Seven Deadly Sins*, paramount being the *gluttony* of ever-expanding control, abuse and consumption: indeed, Smeagol expresses it so ... for Sauron will *'eat the whole world'* if ever the Ring is repossessed by the Dark Lord ...

*'Tolkien in developing the concept of the Ruling Ring, addressed the issue of why the Dark Lord desired its return, why it was so important, and what was so special about the Ring. It was power and with that power he could see where the other Rings were and be master of their masters. Total domination was the goal. Total, mindless obedience would be the result. A world enslaved would be his kingdom. And ruin, destruction and the putrefaction of all beauteous and living things would be the fate of Middle-earth.'***

Professor Tolkien might readily address the dangers in terms of *excessive consumption,* given an obsession with the degradation of the natural world with which the Professor has become associated: indeed, expressly, given Treebeard, Saruman and his *mind of wheels,* with the 'Scouring of the Shire' chapter a final perception of insult to the landscape.

All in a *world gone wrong,* greedy like Gollum and gluttonous like Sauron …

'The picture of England I had when I arrived as a just and congenial society is as good as ever, but at the same time there's a drift – a tendency to corruption, a vulgarisation through consumerism'
(Tom Stoppard, Telegraph Magazine; February 2017)

Frodo's apparent failure of purpose has been the greatest puzzlement to readers of The Lord of the Rings. Perhaps it is indeed for the reason that, under the power of the One Ring, at its greatest in the near-presence of Sauron, Frodo's free will is wholly eroded by the power of seduction into evil, and into Evil itself; the Original Sin of rebellion against God's protection of goodness: by way of God's *Providence.*

In epigrammatic terms, the One Ring *brings out the worst in us;* yet one must have Faith that *Providence* will intervene.

Good begets Good

'Good begets good; evil begets evil; and even if the good you give is

369

met by evil, you have no choice but to go on giving better than you get. Otherwise … why bother to go on living?'

(Paul Auster)

No doubt that is why we all choose to crawl on in this stinking sewer of our sullen existence, rats in the trap, caged and no way out, each day stained dark with the blemish of some wrongdoing, offence, injustice, battle or war; but, after all this useless self-pity, there is something to cling on to by the skin of a survival instinct in the teeth of a bad storm …

> **'Now at this last we must take a hard road, a road unforeseen. There lies our hope, if hope it be. To walk into peril – to Mordor.'**
> (Elrond at Council)

There is always hope for a mind of free will.

We merely suggest that this analysis represents the function of the Ring contemplated by the Professor: the Author might one day attempt to show that most of the main characters of The Rings are similarly afflicted by the deadly sins … for verily, verily we say unto you … that the primary characters of The Lord of the Rings appear (to the Author) to be the deal for a seven card trick … a deal with magic in it up the road ahead in Volume III … and needless to say Saruman has a hand in it; the white one on the faces of his indomitable Uruk-Hai.

The Professor's Letter number 78-

'Urukhai' is only a figure of speech. There are no genuine Uruks, that is folk made bad by the intention of their maker; and not many so corrupted as to be irredeemable (though I fear it must be admitted that there are human creatures that seem irredeemable short of a special miracle, and that there are probably abnormally many of such creatures in Deutschland and Nippon – but certainly those unhappy countries have no monopoly: I have met them, or thought so, in England's green and pleasant land)…

'Something is happening here, but you don't know what it is, Do you, Mr Jones?'

Mister Jones is of the Manor in George Orwell's 'Animal Farm': he keeps pigs; these ignogrunts are Farve Mitford, with Deluded Diana and Ugly Unity close by in the ranks, both sisters avowed fascists and friends of Herr Hitler: just down Woodentop Lane from the Professor's Oxford, at *Stock*, don't you know ... where any concept of Christianity lay with this mob (collective for *pigs*) is open to question, but one suspects they were paying silver salver lip service; and simply to salve my own conscience (and I have already read hundreds of the Mitford Letters, not wanting any more), there is this ...

We cannot pass judgement upon these, nor any other, times, because this is the dirty hole mankind is, and always has been, and forever will be, accustomed to crawl in, witness the sin on the T.V. News ...

Then again, there is this ...

'I recoil in horror from the foulness of thee
From the squalor and the filth and the misery
How we laugh up here in heaven at the prayers you offer me
That's why I love mankind ...
You really need me ...
That's why I love mankind'
(God's Song; Randy Newman)

More Providence Please

Providence has a second sense, the feeling that one's story in the book of life is, as it were, already written; a sense to which we return in Volume III: epitomised in the words of Gandalf ...

'Do not trouble your hearts overmuch
with thought of the road tonight.
Maybe the paths that you shall each tread
are already laid before your feet,
though you do not see them.'

In the final Wheel of Fire revelation, Gandalf intrudes, to veil and to shield Frodo against the power of Sauron; yet upon Frodo's apparent fall from grace, (but it may not be *voluntary* assuming the question one of free will) it is Gollum who is destroyed along with the One Ring: all because, as we may (if we are very good) discover in Volume II, that *Providence* must by the nature of the dominance of goodness, overcome all patent or latent evil: yet this is where *Faith* comes into it.

It becomes clear that Professor Tolkien intuitively believed in the Providence of God's will: it is the foundation upon which the edifice of The Lord of the Rings is constructed: the sparing of Gollum by Frodo and by Sam are but turns rolling down the road within the wheel of fire. The pity they show are acts of virtue, driven by honorable emotion, and which become duly rewarded in the success of the Quest, albeit by an unforeseen chain of events.

It seems that Professor Tolkien may have believed also in *Providence* in the second sense, tantamount to the inevitability of existence.

'The future belongs to those who believe in the beauty of their dreams'
(Eleanor Roosevelt)

The Alchemist: author Paulo Coelho

The celebrated story carries a similar sensitivity to Providence …

Author's Introduction

… we all need to be aware of our personal calling. What is a personal calling? It is God's blessing, it is the path that God chose for you here on Earth. Whenever we do something that fills us with enthusiasm, we are following our legend …

From the Text …

'In his pursuit of the dream, he was being constantly subjected to tests of his persistence and courage. So he could not be hasty, nor impatient. If he pushed forward impulsively, he would fail to see the signs and omens left by God along his path … God placed them along my path … He had never thought of them in terms of a language used by God to indicate what he should do.'

And, once more, through a glass, darkly …

'The wise men understood that this natural world is only an image and a copy of paradise. The existence of this world is simply a guarantee that there exists a world that is perfect. God created the world so that, through its visible objects, men could understand his spiritual teachings and the marvels of his wisdom.'

Some would argue that all three sensitivities amount to one and the same thing.

The Nobel Voice:

'I think of a hero as someone who understands the degree of responsibility that comes with his freedom.'

We think not only physical freedom, but freedom of will.

Smeagol: … best we summarises to Audiences how we's hypnotyses'd cos of evils eyeses, My Luv …

Gollum: … fink like wot roman caffoliks finks-ss, precious-ss …

Smeagol: … original sins causes aller trubbleses, My Luvvs …

Gollum: … is sevens-ss for them caffoliks folks-ss-ss, Audiences-ss-ss …

Smeagol:… if we chooses bad evilses … one who eats the whole worlds, My Luvvs …

Gollum: … but ignore loving gods-ss like saints-ss etceteras-ss-ss …

373

Smeagol: ... we loses aller nice willpowers freedoms ... wiv horribles, horribles endings, My Luvvs ...

Gollum (warning):... like Master Bagginsess-ss-ss inner Cracks-ss Dooms-ss, an' nas-ssty persons-ss inner Awffer Mas-sster Cauldrons-ss, precious-ss-ss ... an' like poor, poor, miz-zerable me-e-e-e-e, chained inner mizzeries by evil ones-ss-ss is-ss we, precious-ss-ss ...

Smeagol:... is no livin' happilys ever afters if we goes wrong way, Audiences ... no heavens lies that way, My Luvvs ...

Gollum: ... none Prufessur's fairys tales-ss-ss ends happy that way, precious-ss ... be verry's nice lives-ss happilys ever afters-ss-ss, we wishes-ss ... but chained inner mizzeries by evil ones-ss-ss we is-ss, precious-ss ... (thinks about being good) ... whass all that guff about luvving thy neighbour stuff an' nonsenses-ss, precious-ss-ss ...?

(sings):

**'In the human heart an evil spirit can dwell
I am a-tryin' to love my neighbor and do good unto others
But oh, mother, things ain't going well'**

Smeagol: ... but praps we be nice to them all if they be nice to us, My Luv ...?

Gollum: ... yes-s, yes-ss, precious-ss, Hobbit Master is-ss my friend ... even to hobbits-ss, even to the Fat One ... we finks summore about Orcses-ss, verry much dreadul danger we turns-s uvver cheeks-ss on *them* ... isser Providences helps us-ss, Gandalfs-ss Providences helps-ss us all, Audiences-ss ...

Smeagol: ... isser Gandalf Providences, isser Providences we searches for and trusts on, of course we do, ... an' maybe's all sensutivvities the same fings, My Luvvs ...

"What Does Your Heart Tell You?"

The Nobel Voice:

'Destiny is a feeling you have
that you know something about yourself
nobody else does.
The picture you have
in your own mind
of what you're about will come true.'

[... and if it's not looking so good for you, better start searching for the omens of your personal calling and legend, **now** ...]

Gollum: ... a likely fairy storys-ss-ss ... maybe's nifty, maybe's shifty ... maybe's pukker, maybe's clutter ... maybe's true, maybe's false ... only the precious knowss, we sposes-ss-ss ...

Smeagol: ... might be right, could be wrong ... but never forgets it My Luvvs, hobbitses was **meant** to find my Ring ...

Gollum: ... **our** Ring, precious, it is **our** Ring ... they sto-o-o-ole the precious from us-ss-ss ... sto-o-o-ole it, they did ... (screams): ... **sto-o-o-ole** it ...

(Off: Gollum tolchocks some old veck in an alley and viddies him swim in his own blood)

'... then out comes the red stuff, my brothers,
real beautiful ...'*

---

* Hank's eyes were not open that long; he died of the Bottle in 1953, aged 29:

** David Harvey (One Ring To Rule Them All); whose knowledge and understanding of Professor Tolkien's works might have prepared him for Mastermind questions which, in fact, it did, being Champion several times.

Prophecy & Premonition

We are bound to juxtapose yet one further instance of prophecy foretold by Professor Tolkien within the One Ring as wheel of fire. It happens, (just as the interlude involving the Dark Speech) also at Rivendell; and we think, it is often overlooked. The scene with Bilbo transfixed or mesmerised by the presence of the Ring is memorable enough, yet there is this in the text ...

'When he had dressed, Frodo found that while he slept the Ring had been hung about his neck on a new chain, light but strong. Slowly he drew it out. Bilbo put out his hand. But Frodo quickly drew back the Ring. To his distress and amazement he found that he was no longer looking at Bilbo; a shadow seemed to have fallen between them, and through it he found himself eyeing a little wrinkled creature with a hungry face and bony groping hands. He felt a desire to strike him ...'

It seems obvious on re-reading that Frodo is foreseeing an attack by Gollum, perhaps in the Emyn Muil, but more likely, of course, in the approaches of the Chambers of Fire on Mount Doom; where they do, as it were, get into a fighting struggle, as already foretold. We cannot think there is any earlier event, but one might return to haunt us up the road ahead, no doubt blood on the tracks; and having already done several cuts out of It's Alright Ma(I'm only bleedin'), or is it *I'm only dying,* we shall wait and see what the wheel of fire holds in store for the Author...

> **'I must follow in their train**
> **Down the crooked fairy lane**
> **Where the coney-rabbits long ago have gone,**
> **And where silverly they sing**
> **In a moving moonlit ring**
> **All a-twinkle with the jewels they have on ...'**
> (Goblin Feet: J.R.R. Tolkien; tbc)

We sought to begin to explain the theoretical of the Wheel of Fire way back there at The Trollshaws, culminating in the horrors of Weathertop onwards The Ford; and now we consider it complete until we reach Mordor. We omitted the findings of our inquiry for the young ghost of a girl at The Corner Cupboard Inn, just over The Last Bridge which crosses the Mitheithel, with St. Peter's Church a little further on towards Cheltenham. We may just cut the revelation in, retrospectively, before we are finished. Below the site of The Last Bridge, nearby the flow of the Mitheithel, lies the charming glade called Puck Pit Lane, so evocative of Cwm Pwca in Wales, of Midsummer Night's Dream connection,(*pwca* meaning *fairy*, if your memory serves you well), also the fairies dancing by the Fairymaster of our Cauldron in Appendix C, who declared the fairies wore green or brown or red hats or hoods: primarily red, one supposes, with the other colours tending to blend into a leafy background; and assuming, of course, the fairies wish to be seen, if only by other fairies. There were also the fairies dancing in the Welsh legends which have the fairies in military style costume, once again primarily red.

Now we can quite imagine red (our favourite colour) pixie hoods dancing amongst the bracken and reeds down Puck Pit Lane. The Author, returning home, strange to say, from a late evening at The Corner Cupboard, was quite sure he saw one once upon a time, down that Lane, and even once upon a time again, near St. Peter's Church. In our mind, we call her our own little Red Riding Hood; but that of course, is pure Fairy Tale.

Some of the materials intervening here and the final outcome of the Author's efforts are essential to the understanding of our ending; which is an extremely personal one, if I may say so. In order to comprehend, you need better recollection of Gollum's evening on top of St. Peter's Church Roof, in Winchcombe; you may remember Gollum's drunken merrymaking way up there, and no doubt you will recall what Gollum may have seen, and warned the Author about; a search for Little Red Riding Hood, perhaps: which conclusion therefore follows at the end of the Author's final thoughts in this Volume I: indeed, you might call it the last breath he breathes …

That may, or may not, be the final prophesy or premonition of our Quest.

More Water Falling

> '... it is fed and watered
> by God's almighty hand;
> ... the breezes and the sunshine,
> and soft refreshing rain.'
> ('We Plough the Fields and Scatter ...)

Whilst in the vicinity we might review once more the Wilderland of Middle-earth on the Hobbit-Maps; entirely visible from our vantage point up here on the Malvern Hills: the situation of the wilder placed dwellings of Mother-earth: on a high, wild and windy slope of terrain: literally in *The Wilderness*; dew drop in on the dwellings of The Wilderness: just a peek over the Misty Mountains; for, albeit we took the Audience there on our quest in The Hobbit, we shall meet there again in Volume II.

> 'The river of God is full of water: ...
> They shall drop upon the dwellings of the wilderness:
> and the hills shall rejoice on every side.'
> (Psalm 65)

Gollum: ... and so, as we was saying, ... them picture peoples been here to see ... yes, indeed, they sees is-ss gone ... all waterfalls-ss is los-sst now ... so even now the Precious must seek for the missing waterfalls-ss ... and we have searched and searched, of course we have, precious-ss ... we knowss, yess indeed, and we wants It all should knows-ss-ss-ss ...

The search is on with Gollum to find the water, or rather what is left of it to see: just so the Ancient Mariner, fixated by the image of water and the drought of it, with poor Gollum ever craving greatness, albatross around his-ss neck: 143 verses of the Rhyme of the Ancient Mariner to suffer with 'Gollum the Great': all because he wants It so much.

Smeagol: ... far too many for *us*, My Luv ... 143 verses in all ... why din' ol' Coleridge go the whole gross, we wonders, yes, we wonders ... isser funny number, ol' Coleridge musta counted, isser bit likes twenty Rings o' power ...

Gollum: ... we's gonna finish wot ol' Coleridge din' finish, precious-ss ... yess, yess, nice water,... drink it, drink it, if we can find the missing waterfalls-ss-ss ...

The Malvern Hills stretch south west to north east for a substantial length, some 9 miles, fringing the curving and plentiful flowline taken by the River Severn towards its Estuary.

A most significant aspect in terms of association, following the Professor's Secret of the Shire, is that the curve of the Malverns reflects perfectly that of the Misty Mountains of the Ring-Maps in reverse: *if the Map is held to a mirror.*

Sparing our modesty, the Author is seriously thunder and lightning-struck that this (now) obvious correlation appears yet to have occurred to the Tolkien Boys; but when one realises the Secret of the Shire, quite frankly the Professor's code becomes so laughably obvious, one wonders ... but then the Professor was already ahead of us, through the words of Gandalf...

'I have it!' he cried. 'Of course, of course! Absurdly simple, like most riddles when you see the answer ...'

Royal Great Malvern is the town at the heart of the Malvern Hills. It abides in a substantial cleft within the backdrop of the Hills. The Worcester Beacon highpoint, a towering crag, dominates the landscape over 1300 feet directly above the town; and we really do mean 'directly' above: the town is literally gashed out of the foothills of the Malverns.

The incline on its High Street must be 35 Degrees but feels like 45 Degrees upwards. This is unusually strenuous walking for a centre-town street, but most of the superior hill work is tougher. One old yarn in Wales has it that the Valley boys have one leg shorter than the other, from walking the slopes since childhood; if so, our Malvern cousins are gaited in similar fashion.

The town has its own impressive connections with the arts. Sir Edward Elgar of the Enigma Variations (composed here) is immortalised by bronze statue. There is a fountain memorial to him there at the top of the High Street where it reaches a level sufficient to accommodate a transverse connecting road. This road is so much like the alpine road which cuts crossways beneath the hills above, the joinder into which is the only way up or down; and we shall be revisiting the road, for it is the road to the secret of Malvern's missing waters falling.

We cannot resist the remark that the Elgar monument has four hewn segment spikes of solid rock which bear an unusual resemblance to the claw-like projections of the summit of Orthanc, the Tower of Saruman, like a granite banana split into quarters. Such remarkable coincidence; if it happens to be one.

Gollum the Great in Rivendell (Continuing)

Smeagol:… yes, My Luv … the Precious be walking the talk …

Gollum (sly): … *and* talking the walk …

Smeagol: … through the Rhyme of The Ancient Mariner … 'water, water everywhere' … is everywhere … but everywhere …

Gollum (grinning): … yess, my precious-ss … but nowheres on Muvver-erff … 'til I be the Great One who finds … the los-sst … *waterfalls-ss-ss-ss* …

> **'Today it's raining cats and dogs,**
> **Tomorrow it might be raining frogs …**
> **Now this poem is not a weather report,**
> **And if it rains tomorrow, It's not my fault.'**
> (Weather Report; Shaw)

Binding of the Ring

To conjoin the association from the very outset, and quite apart from the many personal associations with Professor Tolkien, Great Malvern is *exactly* where it should be for Rivendell of the Ring-Maps by application of the Secret of the Shire.

'Just like birds of a feather,
a rainbow together we'll find …

A number of events, some personal to Professor Tolkien, and even some personal to this plankton author, came together to promote this association, in the following order:

… We had seen the Professor's own painting of the valleys about Lauterbrunnen in Switzerland, on which Rivendell has traditionally been thought to be based; one captured in the issue of Royal Mail stamps (in 2004), for those into posterity, and more lately philately … to mark 50 years since publication of The Lord of the Rings.

This was much confirmed by the Letters (number 306) of which the following is an extract-

'I am … delighted that you have made the acquaintance of Switzerland, and of the very part that I once knew best and which had the deepest effect on me. The hobbit's (Bilbo's) journey from Rivendell to the other side of the Misty Mountains, including the glissade down the slithering stones into the pine woods, is based on my adventures in 1911 … We went on foot carrying great packs practically all the way from Interlaken, mainly by mountain paths, to Lauterbrunnen and so to Mürren and eventually to the head of the Lauterbrunnenthal in a wilderness of morains.'

Those of the Audience familiar with the Professor's painted image of Rivendell will no doubt be equally familiar with its noted identikit of the Lauterbrunnen in Switzerland, hence the inevitable logic that the image of Rivendell in the Professor's mind is that of Switzerland; but, as we contend, transported geographically to Great Malvern of the Malvern Hills: Rivendell of the Misty Mountains.

The etymology of Rivendell is, of course, split or cleft valley; the Malvern Hills are indeed split by British Camp Pass of Mother-earth, (being the High Pass of Middle-earth) as we became familiar with their topography in Magic Mirror Maps.

Quite late in the day we chanced upon a piece of information which started us off on another piste altogether; some of the street names around the Malvern Hills today bear further Swiss associations: Engadine, Lucerne, Geneva to name but three. We continue to research the connection; yet some local is bound to explain; and if so, perhaps we might hear on the horn(common speech for the telephone); we had thought by Flugelhorn, realized we meant Alpine horn, concluding it doesn't matter which plenties the horn of the streets rolled by the Swiss.

… during the inaugural Broadway Arts Festival of 2010, we learned more of the history of famed American actress Mary Anderson (married name De Navarro)of Broadway who in her (auto) biography apparently knew the Malvern Hills as 'Little Switzerland'. Mary Anderson had a very wide circle of influential friends. Part of the famed American Colony in Broadway which included John Singer Sargent, Frank Millet, Alfred Parsons and Frank Barnard (Dickens's illustrator), she seems to have been at the head of the social whirl, receiving house guests at her Orchard Farm pile such as J.M. Barrie, Sir Arthur Conan Doyle and even, we hear, Victor Hugo. Oscar Wilde was a fan.

Very much the celebrity starlet of stage and Shire of such day: we owe the Broadway Artist Jeremy Houghton for these images of contemporary stars: please do take a look at his own.

… we came upon an extract in Wikipedia which described the walks in the Malverns taken by the Professor in the company of C.S. Lewis. Apparently Professor Tolkien would relive the book as they walked and compared parts of the Malvern Hills to the White Mountains bordering Rohan and Gondor. Please excuse the Author for the suggestion of the Professor's indulgent smile. Assuming our theories have any credence whatsoever, there is no way on (Middle-, or any other) earth that the Malverns might be the Professor's contemplation of the White Mountains.

That is a divergent spread of snowfalling mountain altogether; the White Mountains come to the light in the snows of France and Spain: the Author is ploughing a sledful of tracks now, dogging it onwards to Volume III of our Quest. Those of the Audience not yet mapped onto the White Mountains of Mother-earth are bordering on the realms of fantasy: we look way in the distance, hand shielding eyes, foreseeing genuflexion to the Lordship of those Realms.

Gollum the Great in Rivendell (Continuing)

Smeagol: ... Wot is genuflexion, My Luv ... and wot is that about a Lordship ...?

Gollum: ... On their knees, kneeling they must be, my precious ... we have lead the Audience to the Lords of the Manors of Mother-earth ... Rotherwick in Wychwood, Redesdale of Batsford ... Peers of the Realm ... and we learns of Theoden, a Lordship of the Golden Hall at Edoras, precious ...the Mark of Rohan ... peer of that Realm of Middle-earth, precious ...

Smeagol: ... so they must kneel to the Lordship, in far, far places, My Luv ...? ... The Dark One ... of Mordor ...?

Gollum: ... No, no, my precious; not the evil Lordship ...

Smeagol: ... we must take the Audience to a Lordship, but not of Mordor, My Luv...?

Gollum: ... yeeess-ss, my precious ... kneeling to a Lordship and Peer of the Realm they goes-ss ...yes, yes, through Middle-earth shall we be leading the Audience ...to the Mark of Rohan of which we have spoken ... to Theoden, to the Lordship of that Realm they shall be going ...

Smeagol: ... on their knees to the Lordship ... of Rohan?

Gollum: ... O yess, precious ... yess, yess, indeed, my precious ... ... there to find the *Peer on knees* ... (mischievous): ... no one foresees those pair o' knees in Gladaerial's precious Mirror, does-ss they ... silly hobbitses?

The Arts and Crafts Men and Women of The Malvern Hills

'And on, and on, without a pause,
untired they bounded still
All night from tower to tower they sprang;
they sprang from hill to hill
Till the proud Peak unfurled the flag
o'er Darwin's rocky dales
Till like volcanoes flared to heaven
the stormy hills of Wales,
Till twelve fair counties saw
the blaze on Malvern's lonely height,
Till streamed in crimson on the wind
the Wrekin's crest of light.'
(Lord Macaulay: The Armada)

Lord Macaulay, the Historian and 19th century poet, gives the Malverns a central role in this warning chain of fires in his famous poem 'The Armada'. Reference to Darwin is prescient; so, too, is that to the beacon fires ablaze on 'Malvern's lonely height': Herefordshire Beacon is but a foothold distant.

The fire beacon of reference by Macauley will have warned of the approach of the Spanish Armada in the times of Elizabeth I and Sir Francis Drake of the Sixteenth Century. Looking back in time and place, Queen Elizabeth will have come through Elmley Castle of the Trollshaws on her visit to the area.

'The colors of the rainbow so pretty in the sky
Are also on the faces of people going by ...'

W.H. Auden writes a long poem, The Malverns, about the hills and their views: the text being difficult to unearth, the first time The Malverns have let us down; one for the Rangers: but this is a starter for 9 (miles of the Malvern Hills)...

'And over the Cotswolds now
the thunder mutters ...'

These two lines, important for precision in location on our Quest, are lines following well after the first line: of the rarified air of upper Malvern …

'Here on the cropped grass of the narrow ridge I stand'

… where the next succeeding ten (reduced to five here) lines can only be the landscape viewed from The Misty Mountains: indeed, the Malvern Hills …

'Eastward across the Midland plains …
Westward is Wales …
… Here, which looked north before the Cambrian alignment
Like the cupped hand of the keen excavator
Busy with bones, …'

The let–down may be explained if these lines are what commentators are wont to call 'The Malverns' of Auden: the poem does not carry that official title anywhere we have seen it quoted.

Noting the *cupped hand* of *bones*, the crescent shape of the Malverns, these first two lines are remarkable (for the Tolkien Boys) in their synergy with Professor Tolkien's view from Amon Hen, …

'But eagles golden-feathered, who do tower
Above us in their beauty …'
(Hyperion; John Keats)

… whose outline indeed you might see in the distance with Auden on a good clear day, overhanging the Severn with preying eagles …

Smeagol: … Haresfield Beaconses, My Luvvs …

Moving on from the supposed defeat of Caractacus by the Romans at British Camp (Herefordshire Beacon), here Auden writes of the historical demise of Empire …

**'Altogether elsewhere, vast
Herds of reindeer move across
Miles and miles of golden moss,
Silently and very fast ...'**
(The Fall of Rome; Poem: W.H.Auden)

'Altogether elsewhere' recalls Bilbo within the cave tunnels of Smaug in The Hobbit ... 'altogether alone' ...

Since we are where we are, and Auden's connections are multifaceted, not unlike the Hills, there follow three audiences with Auden:

'Auden was surprised to learn from a third party that Mike de Lisio, his sculptor friend, wrote poetry in his spare time and had had some of his verses published in the New Yorker. 'How nice of him never to have told me,' he said.'

(William Espy, An Almanac of Words at Play, 1975)

Another audience with Auden:

'Auden had total self-confidence, of course. He just thought that he was cleverer than anyone else, but without arrogance, really, just out of his own judgment ... He knew exactly what he was doing, and he was totally indifferent about what anyone said about it. And then being a 'psychoanalyst' helped him a great deal. For instance, when he was so attacked by Randall Jarrell in 1947 or so, he said, 'He must be in love with me; I can't think of any other explanation.' He was genuinely puzzled. He didn't think it was a damaging attack in any way.'
(Stephen Spender in Writers at Work: The Paris Review Interviews, sixth series, 1985)

And the third; Gabriel Carrit was a friend of Auden at Oxford:

'A rather odd aspect of him which I am told he retained in later life was his belief in fate and that he could intervene with the almighty. Once, when we were walking on the downs, he discovered that he has lost three pounds which he had stuffed loose into his trouser pocket. 'Never mind,' he said. 'We will

pick them up on the way back.' Four hours later, in the dusk, as we followed the ridgeway above Letcombe Bassett, we saw three notes fluttering along the grass. He picked them up, put them back loose in the same pocket, and said nothing. On another occasion we were walking along the Roman wall and late at night were reluctantly received at a small inn. When we went to our room, Wystan found under his crumpled pillow a half-full bottle of brandy. He took a drink as if he had just ordered it and passed it on.'
(Gabriel Carritt, 'A Friend of the Family', in Stephen Spender (ed.), W.H. Auden: A Tribute, 1975)

Many games ago, wandering about the Ford (at Upton on Severn), the Author spoke of Football; and now of Sir Edward Elgar to boot. It has emerged that Sir Edward, as we all may know the composer of 'Land of Hope and Glory', composed the first ever Football chant. With many games to go before this season ends, we shall be speaking of the Wolves threatening the association's traverse over the Misty Mountains. It is reported that the Wolves (Wolverhampton Wanderers) were beloved of Sir Edward.

Goal-scoringly orgasmic, Elgar wrote: 'He Banged The Leather For Goal' over a century ago. Banging a leather for goal is surefire ecstasy. Because there is nothing like banging one in (other than really banging one in) we offer this from the Web:

Professor Steven Mithen, author of The Singing Neanderthals: The Origins of Music, Language, Mind and Body, said: 'Football chants are a very sophisticated activity. They come from a point in our evolutionary past before language, when we used music and chanting and dance to bond as social groups.'

We are to hear a lot more chanting from the Celts in Wales. The Author hears the chant: give us the wolverine words of Sir Edward? The second let down, because we have yet to find them. Delivered at a private Charity event, the Author does not believe they are publicly available.

We recall Evelyn Waugh of the Portrait Gallegory: Brideshead is Revisited soon at Madresfield.

And so begins the life of Elizabeth Barrett(Browning)…

'… a few miles from the ancient town of Ledbury, in full view of the beautiful Malvern Hills, Elizabeth Barrett lived from infancy to womanhood. There she wrote verses at the age of eight, and even earlier; at eleven she composed a great epic, called 'The Battle of Marathon,'…'

(Website: 'Female Ancestors')

Yet back with the Mitfords.

In 1833 Miss Mary Russell Mitford, when on a visit to London, became acquainted with Miss Barrett, … In her 'Recollections of a Literary Life,' issued in 1851, she gives a sketch of her young friend, Miss Barrett, as she appeared at the beginning of their acquaintance …

The Malverns let us down for a third time: we have no idea how (if at all) Miss Mary predates the Mitford Girls: one for the Rangers.

We thought to sketch Sir George Bernard Shaw(and his mulberry tree planted personally in Priory Park, Rivendell)and Charles Darwin amongst the literary and other associations of Rivendell; and we do so in the Bureau of Shire-history in Appendix B, in terms of social and scientific history written by these famed men of Great Malvern.

In the backdrop of the Hills, with the ostensible gentility of the surroundings in Victorian times, (yet choking draughts of Victorian manners and mannerisms cloning self-consciously, stiffly and formalistic, classes above all below stairs, following a Queen whose brand of charisma was such as to characterise a generation, and damn its children, and childrens' children, to inhibition), we turn in the Bureau of Shire-history to the appreciation, by George Bernard Shaw, of a musical performance of the day, with refreshingly frank and witty reflections upon polite society.

Victoriana (without the furniture) still stands still if you know the right places to look.

Just as the Author is looking for something of the essence of Charles Darwin, along come Stephen Hawking and our Vicar. The former has been pontificating upon the meaning and existence of God. Our Vicar made it the subject of his Sermon this week in late Summer 2010. The Victorians were in the same debate a Century and a half ago, as our findings of Charles Darwin reveal in the Bureau of Shire History in Appendix B. Charles Darwin often took the cure of the Malvern Waters for illness that befell throughout his life. His beloved daughter died in Malvern, which undermined his faith in a god in favour of scientific origin: as the letter to Asa Gray (1860)) in the Bureau attests.

'They got Charles Darwin trapped out there … … High water everywhere …'

To return to the splendour of the Malvern Hills.

Great Malvern gives the aura of preserved calm gentility where no one offends or wishes to be offended. It retains that polite 'nice to know you' feel of a timewarp of the 1930's or 40's.

'In my own shire, if I was sad, Homely comforters I had: …'

One might slow to nestle a long, long, long time here and the others wouldn't know, even that you were. There is indefinitely something of the Enigma about it. There is the influence of water everywhere about. Its history is one of countless natural springs and fountains, becoming a famous resort for spa waters in Victorian times. Quiet in the mood for water and a drink or two, we wander time in thoughtful search, especially so as to share the pleasure of the capture of rapture in nature …

> **'Whether in the woodland brown
> I heard the beechnut rustle down,
> And saw the purple crocus pale
> Flower about the autumn dale;
> Or littering far the fields of May
> Lady-smocks a-bleaching lay,
> And like a skylit water stood
> The bluebells in the azured wood.'**
> (In My Own Shire … : Houseman)

You already know of Bluebell Wood on the Malvern Hills; and they are indeed up there for you: literally and metaphorically, in the clouds.

Gollum the Great in Rivendell(Continuing)

Gollum (to hisselfs): … we wants it, we wants it, we must have It … now … now … now is the time for my master mariner Coleridge bis-ssness … O yes-ss, on very important bus-ssness the precious is-ss … the Precious knows it … O yes we knows it … O yes, we have 'bin waaaiiting to be telling how Great is the Precious …

Smeagol: … how great is *the Rhyme*, My Luv …

Gollum: … yes-ss, I means Great the pome of Ancient Mariner … yes-ss, yes-ss … yes, preciouss-ss, it is time now we must search for the missing waterfalls …

**'The hills are shadows, and they flow
From form to form, and nothing stands;
They melt like mist, the solid lands,
Like clouds they shape themselves and go.'**
(In Memoriam; Tennyson)

Voice Off: In Biographia Literaria XIV, Samuel Taylor Coleridge writes:

*In this idea originated the plan of the 'Lyrical Ballads'; in which it was agreed, that my endeavours should be directed to persons and characters supernatural, or at least Romantic; yet so as to transfer from our inward nature a human interest and a semblance of truth sufficient to procure for these shadows of imagination that willing **suspension of disbelief** for the moment, which constitutes poetic faith … With this view I wrote …*

Gollum: (in Recitation)

*And every tongue, through utter drought,
Was withered at the root; …
With throats unslaked, with black lips baked,
We could nor laugh nor wail; …*

390

(screams, befuddled, traumatised, crazed like Ancient Mariner)...
where is it? Where is it? They **sto-o-o-le** *it from us ...*

(in Recitation)

> *Water, water, everywhere, . .*
> *Nor any drop to drink ...*

Rain At Last

> **'Over the heather the wet wind blows,...**
> **The rain comes pattering out of the sky,...**
> **The mist creeps over the hard grey stone,...'**
> (Roman Wall Blues; Auden)

Those looking in the Malvern Hills or about Great Malvern for
waterfalls or any fuming falls of white water will be disappointed on
the Mother-earth of today; but one may begin to hear the sound of
water running, perhaps running water ...

> **'By a grove of ash slowly flows a stream,**
> **Following me hauntingly even in dream.**
> **The eddying of water surrounding the stones,**
> **Soothing the aches and pains from out of my bones.**
> **Mine is a wanting for peace, perfect peace,**
> **I find it here in nature's own sweet masterpiece.**
> **The sounds of rippling waters is music to my ears, ...'**
> (Tell Me It's A Dream: Shaw)

... Yet once upon a time there *was* a big waterfall: on that same
crossways alpine-like road of mention, some half mile from the Elgar
monument, lies the Quarry Water Tank. The disused Quarry which
lies high above it was serviced by a genuine waterfall which came
tumbling from the Hills above and was collected in the Tank below ...

> **'All the sad spaces of oblivion,**
> **And every gulf, and every chasm old,**
> **And every height, and every sullen depth,**

Voiceless, or hoarse with loud tormented streams:
And all the everlasting cataracts,
And all the headlong torrents far and near,
Mantled before in darkness and huge shade,
Now saw the light ...
(Hyperion; John Keats)

... The Tank building is quite some edifice, the size of a small house; leach from the collective mind any vision of such as for water in the attic, or tanks for fish ...

'Be it early in the morning or late into the night,
I see the goodness of the earth and it fills me with delight.
A waterfall cascading over the moss piled stones, ...'
(This World: Shaw)

... other than the tanks of the giant Aquaria cast on London's South Bank within the old GLC (Greater London Council) building, big enough for sharks to swim in and the frogmen feeding them; whilst they offer a lot of themselves in work ethic, not literally ...

'Rain cuts the place we tread,
A sparkling fountain for us ...

The substantial building of The Quarry Tank houses little information of its history, excepting a tired photograph of the waterfall at the height of its flow ...

... With no fountain boy but me ...

The building design is something of an Art Deco gem. The modern gates to it, however, resemble the back stage door of a Cairo nightclub ...

... To balance on my palms
The water from a street of clouds.'

Is not The Quarry Tank the watershed of, but also below, a street of clouds on high above?

The following inscription appears on the Clocktower of the Tank:

**YE YOUNG AND AGED POOR PRAY
THAT THE BLESSINGS OF GOD
BE ABUNDANTLY POURED UPON HIM
WHO HAS HERE POURED
ABUNDANT BLESSINGS UPON YOU**

The aura pervading the preservation of the Tank is as of all but forgotten; little prayer, less than abundant pourings, less than abundant blessings: poor Tank, poor ye Young and Aged, poor pun: except the Clocktower poured it down before we have; we prayed 'poor' must have poured forth not consciously, but by consultation with Professor J.R.R. Tolkien, who may well have been pouring past on his way to pouring a Pint at The Unicorn, a favoured Pub in the Rivendell of Great Malvern, (whence, on leaving in the snow in the company of Professor Tolkien, tradition has it C.S. Lewis first contemplated the opening lines of The Chronicles of Narnia), and this on its wall ...

**At this Inn
C.S.LEWIS
1898-1963
scholar and author of
THE NARNIA CHRONICLES
met frequently with literary
and hill-walking friends**

... and I should know, 'cos I have just driven a dozen dells bendered home from the Hic – H-u-u-nicorn – Hic ...

**'I hear leaves drinking rain;
I hear leaves on top
Giving the poor beneath
Drop after drop;
'Tis a sweet noise to hear
These green leaves drinking near.'**
(W.H. Davies)

… or perhaps The Red Lion, crannied into the hillside beneath Worcestershire Beacon (near 1400 feet above), just 50 yards from The Unicorn and, that same(as Elgar)half mile from where we are right now at The Quarry Tank. There was apparently something of a falling out between the two as a result of Lewis's intrusion into the Professor's literary genre …

'I didn't mean to treat you so bad,
You shouldn't take it so personal …'

Smeagol: … We's all gotta say sorry sumtimes, My Luvvs …

'I never meant to cause you any sorrow
I never meant to cause you any pain
I only wanted one time to see you laughing
I only wanted to see you
Laughing in the purple rain …'

'Malverns Stockwatch' Central Hills

Cattle and sheep are on East Pinnacle Hill.

Southern Hills

Sheep are on British Camp, Swinyard Hill and Ragged Stone.

Commons

Sheep and cattle present throughout.

The information in Stockwatch guides people as to where they will find the livestock under the Conservators' grazing schemes. However, the Malvern Hills and Commons are registered Common Land. This means certain local people have legal rights to put livestock onto the land to graze without notice.

Members of the public should therefore be ready to encounter livestock anywhere and at anytime.

Malvern Shepherd

'His clothes, sour with years of sweat
And animal contact, shock the refined,
But affected, sense with their stark naturalness.
Yet this is your prototype, who, season by season
Against siege of rain and the wind's attrition,
Preserves his stock, an impregnable fortress
Not to be stormed, even in death's confusion.
Remember him, then, for he, too, is a winner of wars,
Enduring like a tree under the curious stars.'
(A Peasant; R.S. Thomas)

Smeagol: ... We tells Author Master no Samwises Gamgees in po'try lyrrix ... but there Sam is, My Luvvs ... prototype winner of wars ...

Gollum the Great in Rivendell (Continuing)

'Sweet the rain's new fall,
sunlit from heaven,
Like the first dew fall,
on the first grass ...'

Gollum: (In Recitation):

The silly buckets on the deck,
That had so long remained,
I dreamt that they were filled with dew;
And when I awoke, it rained.

(ecstatic) ... yes, yes, nice water,' ... drink it, drink *more* of it, while we can!

'All day it has rained
... And from the first grey wakening we have found
No refuge from the skirmishing fine rain
... All day the rain has glided, wave and mist and dream,

Drenching the gorse and heather, a gossamer stream
… Pattered against the tent …
… but now it is the rain
Possesses us entirely, the twilight and the rain.'
(All Day It Has Rained; Alun Lewis)

Visualise Rivendell on film. Water gurgles, gushes and geysers from every available mountain source: the Hills are alive with the sound of water. Dunk your doughnut under the furrowed foam falling if you've yet to quaff sufficient …

Gollum: … yes, yes, nice water,' … drink it, drink *more and more* of it, while we can!

'Hence the only prime
And real love-rhyme
That I know by heart,
And that leaves no smart,
Is the purl of a little valley fall
About three spans wide and two spans tall
Over a table of solid rock,
And into a scoop of the self-same block;
The purl of a runlet that never ceases
In stir of kingdoms, in wars, in peaces;
With a hollow boiling voice it speaks
And has spoken since hills were turfless peaks.'
(Under the Waterfall; Thomas Hardy)

The Author tumbled the history of The Quarry Tank and its Clock Tower, to finally unblock our neverdrivellending search for the dribbles of missing waterfallses:

1887 'Great drought' reported with many springs drying up to a trickle from March to November.

1890 Plans to build a new reservoir at British Camp costing £26,000 are adopted at a public meeting. The following year the Malvern Water Act is passed to make way for the reservoir at British Camp.

1895 British Camp Reservoir is opened by the Duchess of Teck, collecting water from many springs.

1900 Above Clock Tower, 'Quarryman's Bridge' is shown in a photo-postcard, but now without the waterfall as this supply has been piped.

1901 Queen Victoria dies.

> **'And the brooks glitter'd on in the light without sound,**
> **and the long waterfall,**
> **Pour'd in a thunderless plunge**
> **to the base of the mountain walls ...'**
> (Voyage Maeldune; Tennyson)

The Poet Laureate is a contemporary of Mirrormere!

Now, at long last, we understand that the waterfall serving The Quarry Tank has been 'piped' for collection in the British Camp Reservoir; of much significance but a few gallons later on in our Quest. The 'photo-postcard' of mention will be *not* the 'tired' one now on display at the Tank. That one shows a healthy waterfall stream to the Quarry. We conclude that the many springs that had flowed down from the Malvern Hills, including the one supplying The Quarry Tank, had been dammed and collected into the single British Camp Reservoir.

> **'For after the rain when with never a stain**
> **The pavilion of Heaven is bare,**
> **And the winds and sunbeams with their convex gleams**
> **Build up the blue dome of air,**
> **I silently laugh at my own cenotaph,**
> **And out of the caverns of rain,**
> **Like a child from the womb, like a ghost from the tomb,**
> **I arise and unbuild it again.'**
> (The Cloud; Percy Bysshe Shelley)

(*Womb* and *Tomb* is, of course, a standard banner for the forces driving the poetry of Dylan Thomas; go straight to the top of Caradhras if you knew it was Shelley: which the Author had not).

Drivell-end

This learning may well may be drivel for the conservators of The Malverns, whose sources of vast knowledge we share in Volume II, (where they enlighten us on many aspects of The Misty Mountains, including, by way of foresight, the High Pass through), but the Author for one has yet to encounter any ready written historical account of the missing waters of Rivendell in such terms, albeit we are sure they exist within the records of the Malvern Hills Conservators in some depth ... yet the linkage between Caradrhas, the most significant peak of The Misty Mountains in The Lord of The Rings, and the Roman armies' capture of British Camp one thousand feet above where we are now, below the ramparts so stoutly defended by the Celtic chieftain Caractacus, will unequivocally not be recorded ... until now ...

> **'Then,'twas before my time, the Roman**
> **At yonder heaving hill would stare:**
> **The blood that warms an English yeoman,**
> **The thoughts that hurt him, they were there.'**
> ('On Wenlock's Edge; Houseman)

So, in the alternative, we have created our own, with the appreciable help of the poets, singers and dancers, ... and ... songwriters ... and ...

Gollum (Resuming Recitation):

> *My lips were wet, my throat was cold,*
> *My garments all were dank;*
> *Sure I had drunken in my dreams,*
> *And still my body drank.*

(gleeful, clapping; half-full water pitcher between knees): ... Ha Haaaaaaaaa! ... there's drinks-s and drinks-ss and drinks-sss of water to come ... mussn't bottle me up no longer ... clever, clever ... clever the Precious one to find the water and for searching, searching and searching again for the missing waterfalls-ss-ss-ss ... (on a ragged rock, dizzyrascal dancing under high falls of water;

joyful, berserk, frenzy): ... yes, yes, nice water,' ... drink it, drink *even more* of it, if we can!

Smeagol: ... dooby doob doob, dooby doob, dooby dooby doob ...

Gollum (sings):

> **'I'm singin' in the rain**
> **Just singin' in the rain**
> **What a glorious feelin'**
> **I'm happy again ...**
> **I'm laughing at clouds,**
> **So dark up above ...**
>
> **Let the stormy clouds chase,**
> **Everyone from the place**
> **Come on with the rain**
> **I've a smile on my face ...**
>
> **I'm**
> **just singin' ... and dancin' ...**
> **... in the raaain ...'**

(calms, comes, closer: further in Recitation)

> *The thick black cloud was cleft, and still*
> *The moon was at its side:*
> *Like waters shot from some high crag,*
> *The lightning fell with never a jag,*
> *A river steep and wide ...*

(tip-toe tip-tap tango dancing through puddles; drowned in lightning): ... there is another way for more water ... O yess, indeed there is ... another way, darker, more difficult to find, more secret ... but we knows-ss it ... Let us-ss show it! ... yess! Yes-ss indeed! We have used eyes and feet and nose to find the way we seeks, yess, yess: we have used eyes, we know that way we seeks ... There is another way. We found it once. Let's go to see if it is still there! Let's go to see if we find more water ... yess, yess indeed ... beneath the trees, besides the Lake … by Caradrhas … Silvertine … and Cloudyhead we goes-ss …

… to the lake of Mirrormere for more water …
(wandering off into distance)

… yess, precious-ss, we goes to find the Mirrormere …

Smeagol: … Caradrhas, Silvertine, and Cloudyhead, besides, My Luv …?

Gollum: (nodding and beckoning) … yes-ss, yes-ss, they mos' certainly is-ss … each of them hills besides-ss …

Rambling Man

… and, as we are about to depart Rivendell, here's one onwards and upwards the challenge of Caradrhas …

> **'Purple haze,**
> **all around,**
> **Don't know if I'm comin'**
> **… up or down …'**

Up … and back down again … Caradrhas, as you may remember: high … high … high … scuseme … while I kiss the sky … and whose skyline we are to visualise in depth from the Citadel of Caradrhas … in Volume II, if by then anyone is interested in such details …

> **'Gettin' light outside, the temperature dropped**
> **… I think the rain has stopped '**

Madresfield

One should not farewell Great Malvern without an appreciation of Madresfield Court, which sits quietly on the road out of Great Malvern on the bottomed out flat side. From the right spot in Madresfield one divines the most clear and perfect image of the outline of the Malvern Hills: stunning in silhouette from green to blue to purple.

One may pay a visit to Madresfield in the Author's words, through the Bureau of Shire-history in Appendix B.

Waugh has gone before, and now for Mulvagh:

The inspiration for Evelyn Waugh's Brideshead Revisited is detailed in a new book showing how closely the author based his fictional characters on a family with whom he spent long periods in the 1930s.

It shows how the character of the flamboyant, teddy bear-owning aristocrat Sebastian Flyte was inspired by an Oxford contemporary with whom Waugh was infatuated and who, like his fictional counterpart, was a tortured alcoholic who died young.

Both 1981's acclaimed television adaptation of the novel, and a Hollywood film due out this year use Castle Howard, the extravagant North Yorkshire country pile, as the setting for Brideshead, the stately home of the Flyte family.

But the real inspiration, according to the work by Jane Mulvagh, was provided by Madresfield, a moated house in the Malvern Hills, in Worcestershire.

For almost 1,000 years, the property has been the home of the Lygons, the family of the Earls Beauchamp. In her history of the building and its owners – Madresfield, The Real Brideshead – Mrs Mulvagh has spoken to the family, including some of those who knew Waugh, studied his letters to them and explored the property.

Sebastian was based on Hugh Lygon, the second son of the seventh Earl of Beauchamp.

Mirroring the relationship with Charles Ryder, the novel's narrator, Waugh, who was from a middle class background, met Lygon while they were both studying at Oxford University, and the friendship catapulted the author into the world of the aristocracy…

Waugh would write Brideshead Revisited almost a decade later, in 1944, looking back, as Charles Ryder does, on his experiences.

(The Telegraph, Julian Copping, 2008, reference Jane Mulvagh, Madresfield: THE REAL BRIDESHEAD: One House, One Family, One Thousand Years)

Fact becomes fiction once more; and the Lygon connection retraces our steps to Broadway and its famed Hotel of the name.

Wandering Star

Malvern Priory is something of a priority on the downward slopes of Great Malvern.

It has a long wall of 13th century tiles, near the Altar.

At the Priory we were so enchanted by a pair of Rivendellesque throne-like chairs, we asked the Verger: where was the rest of the seating for the Council of Elrond?

Not being the Antiques Roadshow, the Verger could not offer a date but he did inform that (as we had already guessed) they bore an Ogee arch finished with a stemmed acorn.

We asked whether copies might be available, possibly at Ikea of Rivendell, but no one would speak of that source. There was ancient talk of fearsome straightlines and minimalism there. The very ikea of the new wave furniture of Ikea and of its ikeaology was altogether so loathsome to us we turned away to thoughts of those older arts and craftsmen.

Speaking as we were of other years, Orlando's Legolas had quite a pair of plastic ones blooming from his elven head.

Better than Spock.

We hear no reference to them in The Rings but then again Elves always have ears pointy; someone must have seen them: the Elves and their Ears.

There were no pointed ears in Rivendell, so far as we could see: even though we looked hard through one of the many arched windows of the Abbey, this one full of fine archery …

Gollum (startled from deep sleep):

'Yeah I looked through a window and
surprised what I saw

A fairy with boots dancin' with a dwarf, …
Yeah, fairies wear boots and you gotta believe me
Yeah I saw it, I saw it, I tell you no lies
Yeah Fairies wear boots and you gotta believe me
I saw it, I saw it with my own two eyes, …'
(Black Sabbath)

Smeagol: … why's the Elf fairy legless wearing bootses, My Luvv, an' dancin' wiv that Gimli dwarfses …

Gollum: … Wellies bootses-ss, precious, … Wellies bootses-ss… is-ss bin raining, my precious … hasen't you bin lis-ssnin'?

Plenty of Arrows about Legolas too; they never ran out, no doubt the Wonder of Woollies of Rivendell, as supplier to the sometime archers amongst the stars. There was one in the Great Malvern of Rivendell: at the bottom of the hill of the High Street. Alas trading now only in spirit.

Things went flat at the bottom, the great hill of Great Malvern expeditioned.

We took pleasure in the breezy contours of the newbuilds at the Morgan motorcar factory parked beneath the Hills. We marvelled at Rivendell being their only garage.

We agreed it would be rather breezy in one of those without a top on, meaning the detachable roof.

We gazed upwards to the blue-red-grey-green-purple silhouette of the 9 miles of Malvern range like a cardboard cut-out against the sky blue sky.

Nine?

We were enchanted and rested there for the spell that girl put on me … Arwen on Aragorn …

Gollum the Great

'We must have it. We wants it, we wants it, we wants It!'

What is *it* … beyond the obvious that Gollum wants the One Ring … ?

'One for the dark Lord on his dark throne …
One Ring to rule them all, one Ring to find them,
One Ring to bring them all
and in the darkness bind them'

The Eighth of the Wise and the Great regards it all of so much uncertainty:

'The ambiguous reference to the 'Dark Lord' and the nature of his power adumbrates the ambiguity of Sauron in the story. No-one ever is sure in just what his corruption lies, whether it is the deadly sin of pride, Machiavellian power-perversion, or alliance with death-forces.'

Gollum is as corrupted by the Ring as is Sauron; so, from the same perspective as the Eighth of the Wise and the Great, we pose the exact same question of *Gollum* on the Quest. Perhaps we should leave it to the greatest and wisest of the Wise and the Great, Professor J.R.R. Tolkien, who regards it thus through Gandalf:

"I have it!' he cried. 'Of course, of course! Absurdly simple, like most riddles when you see the answer.'

So what is 'it' for Gollum on his special quest?

As ambiguous as the Eighth of the Wise and the Great holds it in relation to Sauron, we trust that Gollum 'the Great' has performed often enough for the Audience to guess the answer to our riddle; as absurd and simple as the Professor suggests: for it merely requires a look in the mirror; of itself so reminiscent of the Professor's way of looking at things by the Secret of the Shire.

For Gollum, and for pure contrivance in the course of our Quest …
'it' is all of *you … the members of our Audience* … and the amusement,
attention and attraction we had hoped to sustain through all of
Gollum's po'try lyrrix so lyricals-ss, and songses and dances-ss
so aws-ssums-ss, the continuing recitation of 'The Rhyme of the
Ancient Mariner', the search for the missing waterfalls of Rivendell,
to be continued soon through more great song lyrics: all in a
contrivance of Gollum's craving for Greatness, hopefully to amuse,
even raise a smile, but certainly to lighten the (Author's) burden of
poring over the Professor's scripted pathways to reach Rivendell,
as we pour through Great Malvern onwards the end of our Quest.

'The Eyes are the Windows of the Soul'

Gollum has the ambition to be great, even the greatest of the great; and
so we are about to accommodate that wish by singing three extracts of
lyrics, some of the greatest ever in our opinion … (and it's my book
so a Desert Island Discs senior moment is allowed)… disclosing a
telescope of romantic intellect ever trained on truism … to (more or
less) close the show … but we may just clear my throat with one or
two more songs of the darkness before cutting to our ending …

But to end at the beginning with the Ancient Mariner again and to
begin again at the ending with a Death …

Nightmare Life-in-Death:

> The game is done! I've won! I've won!'
> *Quoth she, and **whistles thrice** …*
> (index finger and thumb cupped
> between broken teeth, whistles …)
> … ***sshhvveeeeett …***

Smeagol to Gollum (sings)…

'How does it feel, ah how does it feel?
To be on your own,
with no direction home

**Like a complete unknown,
like a rolling stone …'**

Smeagol (eyes tight shut in prayer): … ***Forgive me, …***

Gollum: … Shut up … Be quiet … say no more, … and Ach-ss … pray no more …

… sshhvveeeeett …

Smeagol to Gollum (sings) …

**'No, I do not feel that good when I see
the heartbreaks you embrace …
And though I know you're dissatisfied
with your position and your place
Don't you understand, it's not my problem?'**

Smeagol (eyes tight shut in prayer): … ***Forgive me Father, …***

Gollum: … Shaddup! … say no more, … and Ach-ss … pray no more …

… sshhvveeeeett …

Smeagol(thinks; to his-self): … what about a Redemption that is ever there, and which still awaits a creature prepared to think about turning to goodness, to renounce the One Ring and all evil once and for all, and finally to close the window of a tormented soul, one half of the whole damned, devilish, deviant of the Professor's creation …

Smeagol(sings to his-self):

**'Please crawl out your window
Use your arms and legs it won't ruin you
How can you say he will haunt you
You can go back to him any time you want to …'**

Gollum: ... Awffer Mas-sster betrayed us. Wicked. Tricksy, False. We ought to wring his filffy little neck. Kill him! Kill him! Kill him! And then we take the precious ... and we be the Master!

Smeagol: ... But the Author Master, he knows. Eyes always watching ...

Gollum (anger growing): ... Then we stabs them out. Put out *his* eyeses-ss, make not Sméagol to crawl, but *him* to crawl ... wicked, tricksy, false ... filffy Awffer-Mas-sster ... is-ss not right Awffer Mas-ster makes us turn away from the Precious ... O, No! ... is-ss none repentenses-ss-ss for us-ss ... not for us-ss-ss, we's all we's got ...

Smeagol (eyes tight shut in prayer): ... *Forgive me Father, for I ...*

Gollum (growing anger): ... Shurrup the precious says-ss again ... Be quiet ... Ach-ss ... say no more, pray no more ... Shurrup! Shurrup! Shurrup! ... or so help us ... we will ... (whispers) ... *kill* ...

Smeagol (eyes tight shut in prayer): ... *Forgive me Father, for I have* ... Author Master says is to be *no* more questses ... too much temmtayshuns for poor Smeagol there is ... too many temmtayshuns for one who wants to be so good ... fugged about Volume II ... and III, Author Master say ... but there's still enuff time to be good before the end, Author Master promises, and let questses continues ...

Voice Off: ... or no time left at all, as the wheel of fire turns ever onwards and dictates our fate ...

Smeagol (kneels; head bowed): ... *Forgive me Father, for I have sin—* (Trails off, prayer unfinished) ...

Gollum: ... Shurrup, we says-ss, for a verry lars-st time ... we wants it still, wants it, still wants it ... we must have it!!! ... Awffer Mas-sster muss promise ... on the Precious-ss-ss ... we's all we's got, remembers-ss, Awffer Mas-sster ...

Author: … promises, on the precious, to go on with Volume II and III of the Quest, *the same as we ever was* …

Gollum: . . wots that words-s hobbits says-ss to show they means-ss they's promises-ss-ss…?

Author: … Cross My Heart and hope …

Smeagol: … ***Forgive me Father, for I have sinned …***

(In Recitation)

'The selfsame moment I could pray;
And from my neck so free
The Albatross fell off, and sank Like lead into the sea …'

Gollum: … We shall see! O, yes-ss, we shall see !!!

'Lit'l red girlsess, Lit'l red girlsess-ss…
Deadful danger …'

… and keeping a promise we made to the Audience sometime earlier, to share our conclusion of the little girl presence at The Corner Cupboard Inn, very near The Last Bridge, over the river known as Mitheithel in The Lord of the Rings …

'O! the warmth! O! the hum! O! the colours in the dark!
O! the gauzy wings of golden honey-flies!
O! the music of their feet — of their dancing goblin feet!
O! the magic! O! the sorrow when it dies.
(Goblin Feet: J.R.R. Tolkien
(Exeter College) Oxford Poetry (1915))

… albeit added to by our imagination of a little Red Riding Hood fairyscape nearby Puck Pit Lane … here now follow our terminal findings of the visit we made to The Corner Cupboard, strange to tell that same dark night Gollum was up there on the roof of St. Peter's Church, drinking and singing in merriment, and so the Author goes up … in darkness …

... the Author climbed, from the ground floor bar area, many a dark ... ★*flight of stairs, which were spiral, twisting, leading to the floor above ... The Author ran up the stairs after the little girl in red he had glimpsed from afar, who had darted into a room leading off a small landing, and followed her inside and slammed the door. The little girl must be the one Gollum mentioned back at The Corner Cupboard Inn by The Last Bridge; yet this did not seem to be a young girl at all, what with streaks of greyish-green, thin lank hair straggling the outline of the face hidden within the hood which topped her cloak.

The little girl was crouching by the open window, sobbing, crying in an insane cackle ... the way one sometimes weeps with laughter ... into an old piece of rag wool sacking she buried her face in.

'It's all right,' the Author panted, 'it's all right,' and held out his hand, trying to smile.

The little girl struggled to her feet and stood before the Author, the red pixie-hood falling from her head on to the floor. The Author stared at her, incredulity turning to horror, to fear. It was not a little girl Red Riding Hood at all but, when he drew back the red hood, it was *Gollum*, stretching his long neck, and forcing his pale venomous eyes to stare up at him: the creature wasn't sobbing any more, he was grinning like a maniac at the Author, nodding his head up and down ...

'It's either one or the other or neither of two'

Gollum (unlimited, enduring, venom and hatred; screaming, screeching, cackle): ... Nobody likes-ss Awffer Mas-sster! Awffwer Mas-sster hasn't got any friends-ss! Awffwer Mas-sster hasn't got any Audiences-ss! Nobody likes his silly Modus Scribendi! Latin my Loincloff! ... so pons-ssey poetic ... paffetick pretenshussnes-ss ... arty farty, artful fartful, poser, todger, prose-bodger ... We don't like him! We don't want him! We don't need him! We have used eyes and feet and nose to find the way we seeks, yes-s, yes-s: we

---

*   After Don't Look Now; Daphne du Maurier

have used eyes, we know that way we seeks-s … yes-s, we knows-s, like allur riggle games wiv bagginses … an' wot hobbitses had got in his nas-ssty little pocketses … *and* wot hobbitses have got round his filffy little neckses-ss … We wants it! We wants it! We wants it! We must have it …! We's all we's got … We's all we's got, yes-s… Yes-s, we's all we's got … we's got all we needs … for seeking ways-ss by our own selfs-ss-ss, my precious-ss-ss … and we wants it and we must have it!!!

Smeagol: … yes, my Luv, altogether by our own selfs … **the same as we ever was** … altogether alone, together on our ownses!

Gollum: … yes to Mordor on our own quests-s … wiv redemshuns gone all to … Hell, yes-s Hells-ss …

Smeagol: … yes, My Luv, we goes by our own selfses and redemptions gone to Hellses …

Gollum: … They will curse us once more. Murderer they shall call us again. They shall curse us, and drive us away. And we shall weep, Precious, we shall weep to be so alone …

> **'Alone, alone, all, all alone,**
> **Alone on a wide wide sea!**
> **And never a saint took pity on**
> **My soul in agony.'**

Gollum (mutters under breath): … bes-st take no chances-ss-ss, my precious-ss … wiv no more ways-sting times-s kneeling downs-ss, confeshunnals-ss or uvver redemshun nonsensess-ss-ss …

> **'Your bones are weary,**
> **you're about to breathe your last'**

Gollum fumbled in the sleeve of the long red cloak, drawing a knife, and as the creature threw it at the Author with hideous strength, piercing his throat, he stumbled and fell, the sticky mess covering his protecting hands … only to fulfil a recurring premonition …

**'... then out comes the red stuff, my brothers,
*real beautiful ...'***

Gollum was cackling with Smeagol in a dark corner.

**'...it's not dark yet,
but it's getting there ...'**

'Oh God,' the Author thought, 'what a bloody silly way to die ...'

**'*Www ... ooo ... Www ... ooo
Wwwwww ... oooooo
Wwwwwwww ... oooooooo ...*
That long black cloud is a' coming down,
Feel like I'm knocking on Heaven's Door ...'**

Gollum (from dark corner): ... Awffer Mas-sster ...

'The world has gone black before my eyes'

Smeagol (same corner): ... gonner sleep forevvers, My Luvvs ... wot is your wishes Audiences? Is you intrested in more detailses, we wonders, yes, we wonders?

**'But in my spirit will I dwell,
And dream my dream, and hold it true;
For tho' my lips may breathe adieu,
I cannot think the thing farewell.'**
(CXXIII, In Memoriam, Tennyson)

Gollum : ... any chances my po'try lyrrix so lyricals-ss, or my songses and dances-ss so aws-ssums-ss, up the road ahead, Awffer Mas-sster? (sings to Audience):

**'Somewhere over the rainbow, way up high
There's a land that I've heard of, under a Mordor sky
Somewhere over the rainbow,**

411

rats, gorging ghost-eye* cuisine,
Fallen in hell, shell-shock and blood,
Feed red under corpse-light green.'

Scarlet corn poppies (popaver rhoeas) grow naturally in conditions of disturbed earth throughout Western Europe. The destruction brought by the Napoleonic wars of the early 19th Century transformed bare land into fields of blood red poppies, growing around the bodies of the fallen soldiers.

In late 1914, the fields of Northern France and Flanders were once again ripped open as World War One raged through Europe's heart. Once the conflict was over the poppy was one of the only plants to grow on the otherwise barren battlefields.

'The sky is darkening like a stain,
Something is going to fall like rain
And it won't be flowers.'

Coda Volume I

Déjà vu

*... in a cacophony of resurrection in celluloid,
memories young and old are rising from the coffins in the void
beyond the backyard of your cemetery cerebrum,
each dream of coming back characters
one new out the cutting room,
each host of spirits a new one out without repeat,
not coming again to your cinema seat;
no more to video, with most, but by no means all,
forgotten as soon as the lights go up in the hall,
but the odd one out to return, flesh and blood,
sometime later, as you somehow knew it would ...*

'The road that I speak of leads to the Mines of Moria ...
Only Gimli lifted up his head; a smouldering fire was in
his eyes. On all the others a dread fell at the mention of
that name ...'

---

*   Poppy: Llygad Y Bwgan(W): Eye of the Ghost

If there is dread at the mention of the name of Moria, such is as nothing to the tension and consternation, by the Professor's sheer invention, in The Bridge of Khazad-Dum chapter of The Lord of the Rings: particularly so given our attempt to show how the topography of Middle-earth is derived from Mother-earth. A bold statement: the Author doubts whether any reader fully visualises the full drama of the scenery in which the Fellowship first encounters the Goblins and then the Balrog within the chase which starts from **The Twenty-first Hall ... on the Seventh level, that is six above the level of the Gates ... down to** *the First Deep, the level immediately* **below the Gates... and thence** *up a broad stair, along a wide road through the First Hall, and out!* ...

For those who recall Magic Mirror Maps, this conundrum-code is very much like the one that had to be cracked from the text of The Hobbit in order to differentiate the two separate exits from Goblin Town used by Gandalf and the Dwarves, the High Pass, as opposed to Bilbo by the Back Door.

There is nothing that convinces the Author of the integrity of our quests than the clearing up of these questionable areas of logistic ... and that is the case *even if one is confining the quest for meaning to Middle-earth* ... because they may serve to indicate the models of Mother-earth that the Professor was working to, thence the infrastructure of Middle-earth.

'Ghash!'

Perhaps the most ironclad ironical of an ironhelm bursting through any door of perception, the scenery may become explicable upon finding what there is *on Mother-earth*. As the scene stands, one imagines one has wandered into some one off dream, a bad one at that, or some wandered into some one off dream, a bad one at that, or some virtual reality game set with turrets, passages, and walls and halls and steps and depths one really cannot fathom (sic) just yet, or at all. The Author's first reaction to all this new architecture was one of **shock**; waking in a dream, in a daze like Dorothy in Oz: where **am** I? There is a wizard responsible for all of that, too. It seems entirely possible that, in order to reflect Gandalf's own confused

413

state of mind, Professor Tolkien goes about the same business with our own collective consciousness.

The floor plan in the halls of Moria may become a little easier given the virtual tour we have in mind for Volume II of our Quest. The Author was destined to realise that plan *before* this Coda (which would not have been written otherwise) … so deliberately enticing … if indeed the Audience is interested in such details. And it is there we leave you, clinging on the precipice of anticipation, grasping vainly at the stone within a form of Dante's Purgatory …

'Fly, you fools!'

'Come! I will lead you now! … We must obey his last command. Follow me!'

Strike Up The Band (Reprise)

'We're Sergeant Pepper's Lonely Hearts Club Band
We hope you have enjoyed the show …
… You're such a lovely audience
We'd like to take you home with us
We'd love to take you home …
Sergeant Pepper's Lonely Hearts Club Band
We're sorry but it's time to go …'

APPENDIX A

'Annals of the Wise and the Great'

FIRST

'a compelling grandeur of vision, a searing inventiveness and a depth of humanity that give it a rare – and rewarding – greatness.'
(Sunday Times)

'To have created so enthralling an epic-romance, with its own mythology, with such diversity of scene and character, such imaginative invention and description, and such supernatural meaning underlying the wealth of incident, is a most remarkable feat.'
(The Guardian)

'An extraordinary book. It deals with a stupendous theme. It leads us through a succession of strange and astonishing episodes, some of them magnificent, in a region where everything is invented, forest, moor, river, wilderness, town, and the races which inhabit them.'
(The Observer)

SECOND

"Now The Lord of the Rings is certainly not a realistic novel ... It would seem closest to 'myth' except that we generally think of myth as ... what was once either fact, or felt to be fact, or desired to be fact. *But here there is no question of fact at all. It is clearly sheer invention*, and that is the sharp edge of the razor which both friendly and hostile estimators have had to get over. It follows, of course, that to ask the value of invention is to assume a knowledge of, 'reality', and to ask how far, and in what way, and for what reason this invention departs from reality – and whether this invention is justifiable."
(R.J.Reilly, 'Tolkien and the Fairy Story' from Tolkien And The Critics (1968))
(Author's italics)

THIRD

"Many writers of fantasy would have stopped at this point*[the point referred to being 'At the point this History begins ...' being the introductory words of the Prologue]*.But Tolkien has a constitutional aversion to leaving Middle-earth in empty time and place, or perhaps his literary instincts warn him that it needs a local habitation and a name. Consequently he takes the further crucial step of identifying it as our own green and solid earth at some quite remote epoch in the past. He is able to accomplish this most handily in the Prologue and the Appendices ..."
(Author's italics)

"... the hobbits still live in the region they call the Shire, which turns out to be 'the North-West of the Old World, east of the Sea.' This description can only mean north western Europe, however much changed in topography by eons of wind and wave ... the maps of Europe in the Third Age drawn by Tolkien to illustrate his epic show a continent very different from that of today in its coastline, mountains, rivers and other major geographical features. In explanation he points to the forces of erosion, which wear down mountains, and to advances and recessions of the sea that have inundated some lands and uncovered others."
(Paul Kocher: 'Master Of Middle Earth'(1972))

FOURTH

'Aragorn begins 'You are looking now south-west across the north plains of the Riddermark ...Ere long we shall come to the mouth of the Limlight that runs down from Fangorn to join the Great River...

A little before Celeborn had been tracing the course of Anduin 'to the tall island of the Tindrock, that we call 'Tol Brandir', where it falls 'over the cataracts of Rauros, down into the Nindalf, the Wetwang as it is called in your tongue. That is a wide region of sluggish fen ... There the Entwash flows in ... About that stream ,on the side of the Great River, lies Rohan. On the further side are the bleak hills of the Emyn Muil.'
(Tom Shippey, The Road to Middle-Earth (1982))

FIFTH

'In fact, the more I read Tolkien, the more convinced I am that the inside joke (which may of course be quite serious) – is one of his favourite techniques. As in Joyce and Pound, the allusive nature of *The Lord of the Rings* is frequently borne in the linguistic texture of the work, but more like Eliot a vast polycultural background forms the raw material for points of reference. But beyond this we must not push, for unlike Joyce, Pound and Eliot, the allusive nature of Tolkien's work is not designed with the elaborate high seriousness and super-intellectuality of a master puzzle-maker. The *game* of solution is turned by Tolkien to a *play* of nonsolution. Thus, it should be one pursuit of Tolkien critics to pick up the frequent and tantalizing clues for allegory and follow them through to their dead-end.'
(Neil D. Isaacs, Tolkien And The Critics (1968))

SIXTH

'Tolkien's world did not spring full-grown from his head like Minerva, nor did he fully grasp its implications and possibilities immediately on inventing it ...'

'Tolkien had, in other words, hit a dry spell, suffered a momentary imaginative inhibition, chiefly because he was not sure *what ground he stood on* ... he had to shift briefly from map-making to map-reading ... Tolkien had to restudy the realm wherein they lived, the perilous realm of Faerie.'
(Randal Helms: Tolkien's World (1974))

SEVENTH

'To indicate the magnitude of the task Tolkien set himself, let me give a few figures. The area of his world measures some thirteen hundred miles from east(the Gulf of Lune) to west (the Iron Hills) and twelve hundred miles from north(the Bay of Forochel) to south (the mouth of the River Anduin).In our world there is only one species, man, who is capable of speech and has a real history; in Tolkien's there are at least seven ...

The first task of the maker of an imaginary world is the same as that of

Adam in Eden: he has to find names for everyone and everything in it and if, as in Tolkien's world, there is more than one language, he has to invent as many series of names as there are tongues.

In the nominative gift, Tolkien surpasses any writer, living or dead, whom I have ever read; to find the "right" names is hard enough in a comic world; in a serious one success seems almost magical. Moreover, he shows himself capable of inventing not only names, but whole languages which reflect the nature of those who speak them …

An imaginary world must be as real to the senses of the reader as the actual world. For him to find an imaginary journey convincing, he must feel that he is seeing the landscape through which it passes as, given his mode of locomotion and the circumstances of his errand, the fictional traveller himself saw it. Fortunately, Mr. Tolkien's gift for topographical description is equal to his gift for naming and his fertility in inventing incidents …'

(W.H.Auden, 'The Quest Hero', Tolkien And The Critics (1968))

EIGHTH

'Like the riddles of Gandalf, the full meaning of the poem cannot be fathomed unless the listener has special knowledge. Frodo must be told that the ring in his possession was *the* one ring, but only as his quest progresses does he, and the reader, learn of the full extent of the ring's binding force. The poem refers to all the benevolent races with whom the hobbits associate in the Quest – Elves, dwarves, and men. The ambiguous reference to the 'Dark Lord' and the nature of his power adumbrates the ambiguity of Sauron in the story. No-one ever is sure in just what his corruption lies, whether it is the deadly sin of pride, Machiavellian power-perversion, or alliance with death-forces. Significantly, the Ring-poem ends where the Quest ends: "In the Land of Mordor where the Shadows lie." '

(Marion Zimmer Bradley, 'Men, Halflings and Hero Worship', Tolkien And The Critics (1968))

NINTH

'The common reader who is of all the one that matters, finds himself poring over the maps of Mordor, tracing the arrows towards Haradwaith and seeking for the pass over the Misty Mountains through which the Hobbits made it to the Shire. Then the general joy may turn to particular pleasure, for the few aficionados who trace the routes and seek the roots of words. The maps that are appended to The Lord of the Rings were made by hand; the detail is so tiny that a magnifying glass, enlarging the details, fails to give a bird's eye view, and that is what the common reader must obtain if he is to go further than the rivers, roads, fords and forests of Middle-earth. He needs only a general idea of them, and of the tongue and the time that ran in Tolkien's mind when he created them, and should seek for no more.'

(William Ready, Understanding Tolkien (1967))

APPENDIX B

'Bureau of Shire-history'
RING (M:I):HOBBITON

Witham Woods

[In 1943]The last private landowner, Raymond ffennell gave the Woods to the University in memory of his daughter, Hazel, who tragically died at a young age. It was intended from the start that the woods be preserved and used for research and education. ffennell himself had bought the Estate from the seventh Earl of Abingdon whose family had been the principal landowners since the dissolution of Abingdon Abbey between 1538 and 1546. Various charters exist which give clues to the history beyond this date and it seems that the Abbey was granted its land at Wytham by King Eadwig (AD 955-8).

Bushell's Marvells: Neat Enstone

'As we approach Neat Enstone, before crossing the Glyme, we may notice on our left a small rivulet and a pool. There is nothing at all remarkable about them now, and anyone who had never heard of Thomas Bushell would certainly pass them by without notice. Yet here is one of the wonders of Oxfordshire, which every traveller made a point of visiting, and which was long a fashionable resort for all the surrounding gentry.

Thomas Bushell, the contriver of the wonderful Rock of Enstone, entered the household of Francis Bacon early in the reign of James I., and derived from his master a knowledge of what was then called natural philosophy, and a love of mechanical experiments. He devoted a long life to engineering projects for the good of his country – projects which too often landed him in financial difficulties. His principal undertaking was the working of the lead mines in South Wales, which contained a certain proportion of silver mixed with the lead, and were therefore Crown property. Of these he obtained a lease from Charles I., and, when the Civil War broke out, he supplied the king with money coined in a privileged mint of his own establishment. An interesting letter of Charles to Bushell, enumerating his many services, has been preserved. He lived till 1674, and the last project we hear of his being engaged in, is one connected with the lead mines of the Mendips.

About the year 1629 he came to live at Enstone, and one day, when he was cleaning out a spring near his house, he was struck with the idea that here was a capital field for the exercise of his ingenuity. What he accomplished the reader will best understand by a reference to the two fine plates in Plot's Oxfordshire, in which all the details are minutely depicted. In one of them he will behold the trim house built over the rock, "containing one fair room for banqueting, and several other small closets for divers uses, besides room above" : in the other he is taken down into the "grot" beneath the house, and finds himself face to face with the Rock, and all its marvels, which consisted of fountains and spouts of water of various kinds, including certain jets "often used by way of sport to wet the visitants of the grot." This was a kind of practical joke vastly popular in those days, and the chance of repeating it was not to be lost. After the Civil War the Rock and its waterworks, which had suffered from neglect, passed into the possession of the Lees of Ditchley, and Sir Edward Henry Lee, the first Earl of Lichfield, repaired it and added the circular island, which will be seen in the middle of the pool in front of the banqueting house. On this island jets of water are turned on "which water the whole island, and sportively wet any persons within it; which most people striving to avoid get behind the man that turns the cocks, whom he wets with a spout of water that he lets fly over his head, or else, if they endeavour to run out of the island over the bridge, with two other spouts." All these "spouts" are duly represented in the first plate, as well as "the man that turns the cocks," evidently gloating over his unholy devices while a gentleman in full dress, with sword and ruffles, and a walking cane in his hand, is making a dignified retreat across the bridge, pretending to be utterly unconscious of the two jets, one of which strikes him full on "the reins of the back," and the other on his legs.

But the great day in the history of the "Waterworks" was August 23, 1636, when they were honoured by a visit from the King and Queen, and the latter commanded the Rock to be named Henrietta, after her royal self. It appears that Charles had paid Mr. Bushell a surprise visit some time previously, and had been much pleased with his host's ingenious contrivances; but this time their

421

Majesties, who came over from Woodstock, were expected, and an Entertainment had been provided in the orthodox fashion. As the royal party entered the place "there arose a Hermite out of the ground and entertained them with a speech, returning again in the close down to his peaceful urn. Then was the Rock presented in a Song answer'd by an Echo, and after that a Banquet presented also in a Sonnet, within the pillar of the table, with some other songs." These speeches and songs were printed at Oxford by Leonard Lichfield in a small quarto, now very rare.

During the whole of the eighteenth century the waterworks seem to have enjoyed some sort of reputation, and at the beginning of the nineteenth it was still the fashion for strangers who passed through the village to devote a few minutes to their inspection. A tourist of 1806 describes them as "no bad specimen of the taste of the period when jets d'eau were in fashion." In the summer time the leading families of the neighbourhood would assemble there for dancing and social intercourse; the proceedings began about ten o' clock in the morning, and lasted till evening set in; as many as sixteen family coaches-and-four were remembered by an eye-witness to have attended on one of these occasions. At last, about the middle of the century, the banqueting house was pulled down, and the whole of the elaborate structures and devices fell into decay.'
(Highways and Byways in Oxford & the Cotswolds, H.A. Evans, 1927)

'In the Seventeenth century Enstone was famous for its Fantastical Waterworks, a special attraction built by a chap called Bushell, with grottoes, fountains, and nightingales' notes blowing water through underground pipes. It was all so fairy-like that Charles I and Queen Henrietta even visited it, whereupon it became knowed as 'Queen Henrietta's Waterworks'.All this were long before my time. In my young days 'Queen Henrietta's Waterworks' were the privy behind the Harrow Inn. Owen Reagan were the landlord. When a charabang party anchored there on their way to the 1924 Wembley Exhibition a snooty passenger complained about the 'disgusting amenities'.'It were good enough for Queen Henrietta,'Owen says,'it be good enough for thee!"
('Lifting the Latch', Shirley Stewart)

The Marlboroughs

'Charles, 9th Duke of Marlborough (1871–1934) can be credited with saving both the palace and the family. Inheriting the near-bankrupt dukedom in 1892, he was forced to find a quick and drastic solution to the problems. Prevented by the strict social dictates of late 19th-century society from earning money, he was left with one solution; he had to marry money. In November 1896 he coldly and openly without love married the American railroad heiress and renowned beauty Consuelo Vanderbilt.

The marriage was celebrated following lengthy negotiations with her divorced parents: her mother was desperate to see her daughter a Duchess, and the bride's father, William Vanderbilt paid for the privilege. The final price was $2,500,000 (worth about $300m in 2007) in 50,000 shares of the capital stock of the Beech Creek Railway Company with a minimum 4% dividend guaranteed by the New York Central Railroad Company. The couple were given a further annual income each of $100,000 for life. The bride later claimed she had been locked in her room until she agreed to the marriage. The contract was actually signed in the vestry of St. Thomas Episcopal Church, New York immediately after the wedding vows had been made. In the carriage leaving the church, Marlborough told Consuelo he loved another woman, and would never return to America, as he "despised anything that was not British"

Girdley Island
St. Botulph or BOTOLPH.

Abbot, date of birth unknown; died c. 680. St. Botulph, the saint whose name is perpetuated in that of the American city of Boston, Massachusetts, was certainly an historical personage, though the story of his life is very confused and unsatisfactory. What information we possess about him is mainly derived from a short biography by Folcard, monk of St. Bertin and Abbot of Thorney, who wrote in the eleventh century (Hardy, Catalogue of Brit. Hist., I, 373). According to him Botulph was born of noble Saxon parents who were Christians, and was sent with his brother Adulph to the Continent for the purpose of study. Adulph remained aboard, where he is stated to have become Bishop of Utrecht, though his name does not occur in any of the ancient lists. Botulph, returning to England, found favour with a certain Ethelmund, "King of the southern Angles", whose sisters he had known in Germany, and was by him permitted to choose a tract of desolate land upon which to build a monastery. This place, surrounded by water and called Icanhoe (Ox-island), is commonly identified with the town of Boston in Lincolnshire, mainly on account of its name (Boston = Botulph's town). There is, however, something to suggest that the true spot may be the village of Iken in Suffolk which of old was almost encircled by the little river Alde, and in which the church is also dedicated to St. Botulph. In favour of Lincolnshire must be reckoned the fact that St. Botulph was much honoured in the North and in Scotland. Thus his feast was entered in the York calendar but not in that of Sarum. Moreover, even Folcard speaks of the Scots as Botulph's neighbours (vicini). In favour of Suffolk, on the other hand, may be quoted the tradition that St. Botulph, who is also called "bishop", was first buried at Grundisburgh, a village near Woodbridge, and afterwards translated to Bury St. Edmunds. This, however, may be another person, since he is always closely associated with a certain St. Jurmin (Arnold, Memorials of Bury, I, 352). That Botulph really did build a monastery at Icanhoe is attested by an entry in the Anglo-Saxon Chronicle under the year 654: Botulf ongan thoet mynster timbrian oet Yceanho, i.e. Botulph began to build the minster at Icanhoe. That the saint must have lived somewhere in the Eastern counties is proved by the indisputable evidence of the "Historia Abbatum" (Plummer's Bede, I, 389), where we learn that Ceolfrid, Bede's beloved master at Wearmouth, "journied to the East Angles in order that he might see the foundation of Abbot Botulphus, whom fame had proclaimed far and wide to be a man of remarkable life and learning, full of the grace of the Holy Spirit", and the account goes on to say that Ceolfrid "having been abundantly instructed, so far as was possible in a short time, returned home so well equipped that no one could be found more learned than he either in ecclesiastical or monastic traditions". Folcard represents St. Botulph as living and dying at Icanhoe in spite of the molestations of the evil spirits to which he was exposed at his first coming. Later accounts, e.g. the lessons of the Schleswig Breviary, suppose him to have changed his habitation more than once and to have built at one time a monastery upon the bank of the Thames in honour of St. Martin. His relics are said after the incursions of the Danes to have been recovered and divided by St. Aethelwold between Ely, Thorney Abbey, and King Edgar's private chapel. What is more certain is that St. Botulph was honoured by many dedications of churches, over fifty in all, especially in East Anglia and in the North. His name is perpetuated not only by the little town of Boston in Lincolnshire with its American homonym,

but also by Bossal in Yorkshire, Botesdale in Suffolk, Botolph Bridge in Huntingdonshire, and Botolph in Sussex. In England his feast was kept on 17 June, in Scotland on 25 June.
(Catholic Encyclopaedia Online)

Uncle Remus and Uncle Tom's Cabin

Mark Twain read the Uncle Remus stories to his children, who were awed to meet[the author Joel Chandler] Harris himself. In his Autobiography Twain describes him thus:

He was the bashfulest grown person I have ever met. When there were people about he stayed silent, and seemed to suffer until they were gone. But he was lovely, nevertheless; for the sweetness and benignity of the immortal Remus looked out from his eyes, and the graces and sincerities of his character shone in his face.

Uncle Tom's Cabin *was the best-selling novel of the 19th century and the second best-selling book of that century, following the Bible. It is credited with helping fuel the abolitionist cause in the 1850s. In the first year after it was published, 300,000 copies of the book were sold in the United States; one million copies were sold in Great Britain. In 1855, three years after it was published, it was called "the most popular novel of our day." The impact attributed to the book is great, reinforced by a story that when Abraham Lincoln met [the authoress Harriet Beecher]Stowe at the start of the Civil War, Lincoln declared, "So this is the little lady who started this great war." The quote is apocryphal; it did not appear in print until 1896, and it has been argued that "The long-term durability of Lincoln's greeting as an anecdote in literary studies and Stowe scholarship can perhaps be explained in part by the desire among many contemporary intellectuals ... to affirm the role of literature as an agent of social change."*

RING (M:III):the Old Forest

Newell (Newhill) Plain and Fair

The origins of the fair aren't especially ancient, nor were the originators intent on starting the crowded, bawdy spectacle into which it developed. In fact, the three Wesleyian Methodists who were the fathers of the fair wanted to escape from the rowdiness of the Witney Feast, and it began as more of a picnic than a fair. That was in 1796 and the three were Mr Payne of Fawler Mill, Mr Bolton of Finstock and Mr Early of Witney.

John Wesley himself, the founder of Methodism, often preached in the area and said of Finstock in October, 1775:

'I preached at Finstock. How many days should I spend here if I was to do my own will!'

(Historical and Other Notes on Charlbury, Kibble 1927)

The chosen site for these picnics was Newell (Newhill) Plain on the edge of the Cornbury Estate (then known as Blandford Park) near Charlbury. It was held on Wednesday and Thursday in the third week in September, following the St Giles Fair in Oxford and the Witney Feast. It quickly developed a momentum of its own and by 1819 Jackson's Oxford Journal reported:

'The annual Fair of Wychwood Forest was holden on Wednesday last. The unclouded and brilliant and sunny morning attracted a vast concourse of persons.'

(Historical and Other notes on Wychwood Forest and Many of its Border Places, Kibble 1928)

The darker side of the fair

As the fair's reputation grew, the crowds got bigger and it attracted a sizeable lawless element. Villagers from the surrounding area often blamed incomers for any trouble, but because the Forest was extra-parochial, and therefore outside the jurisdication of the parish constables, the fair was known by locals as the place to settle scores, with fights a regular occurrence in the darkening evening light.

The fair was also taking its toll on the Forest. On September 4th 1830, C.R. Henderson, Deputy Ranger of the Forest, placed this notice in Jackson's Oxford Journal:

'Fair to take place on Newhill Plain on Tuesday, not Wednesday. Instruction not to injure growing Timber, Underwood, Mounds or Forest Gates.'

The same edition also contained a notice placed by local Magistrates warning against *'Games of Chance.'*

Clearly the populace didn't heed the Mr Henderson's warning because after the fair he placed this notice:

'in consequence of ... not having attended to the regulations laid down ... not having left the ground at the time appointed, and great damage and

injury having been done to the mounds, gates, roads, underwood and other property within the Forest... such Fair has been the means of bringing the neighbourhood vast numbers of idle and disorderly characters, the Ranger has directed that the Fair ... shall be DISCONTINUED'. Jackson's Oxford Journal, September 25th 1830.

The fair was subsequently banned in 1831, 1832, 1833, 1843 and 1845.

Evidently an entrepreneurial inhabitant of Charlbury wanted to offer the town as replacement home for the fair, because in 1831 a handbill was printed to that effect. It brought a quick response from some of his fellow townsfolk, that such a fair would be

'entirely disapproved (and) discountenanced by many of it's (Charlbury's) inhabitants, as tending to bring a number of idle and disorderly persons into the neighbourhood.'

(Jackson's Oxford Journal, September 10th 1831)

In the years when the fair did go ahead, Newell Plain became a vast pleasure park, with entertainments and refreshments of all kinds. Regular favourites were Wombwell's menagerie of exotic beasts, the Vauxhall Dancing School and freak shows. The Yeomanry Band would march and play and the crowds would be further amused by parades of the local gentry, including the Dukes and Duchess of Marlborough. All in all, it must have been a riot of colour and noise, and welcome escape from the restrictions of everyday life.

The final years

The old fair's demise was at least hastened by two factors. Firstly, in 1853 the Oxford, Worcester and Wolverhampton railway line was opened, with a station at nearby Charlbury. During the line's construction there would have been large numbers of navvies in the neighbourhood, for whom the fair would have been a tempting release from the rigours of the day.

'The sub contractors on the OWW railway in this neighbourhood took a lively interest in suppressing gambling tables two years ago, and should these nuisances make their appearance upon this occasion, their owners may reckon on a ducking in Newhill pond.'

(Jackson's Oxford Journal, September 15th 1852)

Not only did the railway add to the lawlessness, it also allowed more people to get to the fair, and it was during this period that the fair reached the height of its appeal; a popularity that was to be part of its undoing.

The second factor which caused the end of the fair was the Parliamentary

Act of Disafforestation (1853), whereby the 10 sq. miles of Wychwood remaining as Royal Forest was taken out of Forest Law. This resulted in the land on which the fair was held, Newell Plain, being transferred into the ownership of Lord Churchill, ranger and owner of Cornbury. He probably regarded this as an excellent opportunity to rid himself of an event that had become an annual nuisance, especially at a time when much of remaining Forest was being stripped of its trees and converted to farmland.

The last of the old fairs was held in 1856 and whilst it has always been reckoned that the huge crowds it attracted and the consequent lawlessness were the primary reasons for its demise, this may not be so, judging by these reports in Jackson's Oxford Journal of that year.

Cornbury Park Estate

Cornbury Park originated as a hunting lodge in the Royal Forest of Wychwood, erected by Henry I close to his principal lodge at Woodstock (see the Register entry on Blenheim Palace), the Crown keeping large areas of the Forest in hand until the middle of the 17th century. Almost every king and queen up to Charles I visited Cornbury Lodge, and it is connected with many major events of English history. The Rangership was granted to favoured courtiers, tenants including the Harcourts, Beauchamps and Robert Dudley, Earl of Leicester. In 1617 it was granted to Henry Danvers, Earl of Danby, a courtier and founder of Oxford Physic (now Botanic) Garden (see description of this site elsewhere in the Register). Lord Danby died in 1644, having employed the mason Nicholas Stone to build the south wing, as well as the stone gateways at the Physic Garden. **Following the Restoration, the Rangership and the park were given to Edward Hyde, first Earl of Clarendon and Viscount Cornbury. John Evelyn (1620-1705) visited Cornbury in 1664 (the same year that his Sylva or a Discourse of Forest Trees was published) with Hugh May, who had designed the stables and was, in 1666, to build the east, or Clarendon, front. Evelyn advised Clarendon on the planting of the park during his 1664 visit, and possibly again in the 1680s when it was owned by his friend the second Earl, Clarendon's son. In 1689 George London (died 1714) worked on the estate layout with William Talman, although London's exact input is uncertain (Pevsner 1974).** It is possible that Alexander Pope advised at Cornbury in the early 18th century, although there appears to be little surviving evidence for his work (Environmental Design Associates 1994). The estate remained

428

in the Hyde family's ownership until 1751, when it was bought by the third Duke of Marlborough and known as Blandford Park. It was sold by Viscount Churchill in 1896, and bought by Vernon Watney in 1901, remaining in this family until 1966. The House and park remain (1997) in private ownership.

RING (M:IV):THE Three Farthing Stone

Frogmorton

The animal familiar was quite distinct from the familiar in human shape. In England particularly there is abundance of evidence concerning them ...It is worth remark that in other countries the domestic animal familiar is rare ... we find that animals of all kinds were regarded as familiars: dogs, cats, ferrets, weasels ,toads, rats, mice, birds, hedgehogs, hares, even wasps, moths, bees, and flies ... very frequently the witch did actually keep some small animal which she nourished on a diet of milk and bread and her own blood in order that she might divine by its means. The details of this particular method of augury are by no means clear. Probably the witch observed the gait of the animals, its action, the tones of its voice easily interpreted to bear some fanciful meaning, and no doubt a dog, or such a bird as a raven, a daw, could be taught tricks to impress the simplicity of inquirers.

The exceeding importance of blood in life has doubtless been evident to man from the earliest times. Man experienced a feeling of weakness after the loss of blood, therefore blood was strength, life itself ,and throughout the ages blood has been considered to be of the greatest therapeutic, and the profoundest magical, value. The few drops of blood the witch gave her familiar were not only a reward, a renewal of strength, but also they established a closer connection between herself and the dog, cat or bird as the case might be. Blood formed a psychic copula.

(Montague Summers, The History of Witchcraft,(1994))

The Four Shire Stone

'The current stone marker is at the point where four shires used to meet; (there are now three, as the Worcestershire parish of Evenlode boundary was transferred to Gloucestershire in 1931). The monument was probably erected in the late 16th century. It is believed there was a Roman milestone at that point earlier, and at one time individual stones for each county, though this is not well documented. The current stone was described by Samuel Rudder in 1779 as being "A handsome pedestal about 12 feet high with a dial on the top and an inscription to inform travellers that 'This is the Four Shire Stone'"

Speede's map of 1610, Morden's of 1695 and later maps such as Toms of 1741 indicated four stones at the spot, but this is thought to be erroneous, as an earlier tapestry map woven in Barcheston for William Sheldon in the 1580s shows a square with a circle in the centre, labelled 'Fowre Sheer Ston'. The current finial replaced the dial in the late 19th century following vandalism, and the county names added at that time. The stone has been damaged and repaired several times since, and has been protected by iron railings, which can be seen in photographs taken in around 1900 …

'The present stone is built in white oolitic limestone which probably came from quarries near Chipping Campden …the ball at the top is concrete, replaced after the Stone was vandalized some years ago. The names of the four shires of Worcestershire, Gloucestershire, Warwickshire and Oxfordshire are inscribed on the south-west, north-west, north-east and south-east sides respectively. An observant reader immediately notices that Worcestershire seems to be on the wrong side…

Evenlode … became a *detached* part of Worcestershire until it was transferred to Gloucestershire in 1931.

It is now clear why the south-west side of the Four Shire Stone is inscribed 'Worcestershire' – this refers to the *detached* parish of Evenlode … Evenlode was so far from the rest of Worcestershire …'
(Margaret Shepard; Four Shire Memories:Moreton-In-Marsh And District Local History Society,1992).

The Universal Green Man

A Green Man is a sculpture, drawing, or other representation of a face surrounded by or made from leaves. Branches or vines may sprout from the nose, mouth, nostrils or other parts of the face and these shoots may bear flowers or fruit. Commonly used as a decorative architectural ornament, Green Men are frequently found on carvings in churches and other buildings (both secular and ecclesiastical).

The Green Man motif has many variations. Found in many cultures around the world, the Green Man is often related to natural vegetative deities springing up in different cultures throughout the ages. Primarily it is interpreted as a symbol of rebirth, or "renaissance," representing the cycle of growth each spring.

Usually referred to in works on architecture as foliate heads or foliate masks, carvings of the Green Man may take many forms, naturalistic or decorative. The simplest depict a man's face peering out of dense foliage. Some may have leaves for hair, perhaps with a leafy beard. Often leaves or leafy shoots are shown growing from his open mouth and sometimes even from the nose and eyes as well. In the most abstract examples, the carving at first glance appears to be merely stylised foliage, with the facial element only becoming apparent on closer examination. The face is almost always male; green women are rare.

The Green Man, in the form of a foliate mask surrounded by Bacchic figures, appears at the center of the 4th century silver salver in the Mildenhall Treasure, found at a Roman villa site near London.[5]

Superficially the Green Man would appear to be pagan, perhaps a fertility figure or a nature spirit, similar to the woodwose (the wild man of the woods), and yet he frequently appears, carved in wood or stone, in churches, chapels, abbeys and cathedrals, where examples can be found dating from the 11th century through to the 20th century.

In Britain, the image of the Green Man enjoyed a revival in the 19th century, becoming popular with architects during the Gothic revival and the Arts and Crafts era, when it appeared as a decorative motif in and on many buildings, both religious and secular. American architects took up the motif around the same time. The Green Man travelled with the Europeans as they colonized the world. Many variations can be found in Neo-gothic Victorian architecture. He was very popular amongst Australian stonemasons and can be found on many secular and sacred buildings.

Parallels have been drawn between the Green Man and various deities.

Many see him as being connected to the Mesopotamian Tammuz who is thought to symbolize the triumph of Life over Winter and Death,and also [9] Osiris and Odin, as well as later folkloric and literary characters such as the Holly King).

Mythical figures such as Cernunnos, Sylvanus, Derg Corra, Green George, Jack in the green, John Barleycorn, Robin Goodfellow, Puck, and the Green Knight all partake of the Green Man's nature; it has also been suggested that the story of Robin Hood was born of the same mythology. A more modern embodiment is found in Peter Pan, who enters the civilized world from Neverland, clothed in green leaves.

The Green Knight of Sir Gawain and the Green Knight serves as both monster and mentor to Sir Gawain, belonging to a pre-Christian world which seems antagonistic to, but is in the end harmonious with, the Christian one.

In his A Little Book of The Green Man, as well as his website, Mike Harding gives examples of similar figures in Borneo, Nepal, and India: the earliest is a foliate head from an 8th century Jain temple in Rajasthan.[16] He also notes that heads from Lebanon and Iraq can be dated to the 2nd century and that there are early Romanesque foliate heads in 11th century Templar churches in Jerusalem. He tentatively suggests that the symbol may have originated in Asia Minor and been brought to Europe by travelling stonecarvers.*

As early as the 1st Century AD, foliate heads were being treated as ornaments on temple friezes all over the Roman Empire, from Turkey to the Rhine. Similar images also appear in ancient Chinese and Indian cultures. In England, the Green Man appears in the 11th Century – he was rendered by mediaeval masons on many churches and cathedrals. He is the foliate mask made up with the leaves growing from his mouth, around his eyes and from his nose. He embodies the nature spirit, the living pulse of the forest and the Earth as it is felt by mankind. It may be that the Green Man is a pagan reference incorporated into Christian belief.'

RING (M:VI):BREE

Staddle

*The **Battle of Stow-on-the-Wold** took place during the English Civil War. In the Spring of 1646, King Charles I of England was getting ever more desperate* to hold the Royalist cause together whilst waiting for the long promised relief forces from Ireland, Scotland and France. Sir Jacob Astley took command of the Royalist forces in the west and began to gather up the remnants from the handful of Royalist garrisons still left in the west. At this point in the war, Royalist morale was low. However, Astley, a stalwart of the Royalist commanders and an experienced soldier, was able to cobble together a force of 3,000.

Astley was trying to reach Oxford with his force when Parliament got wind of it. What ensued was a period of thrusting and parrying along the river Avon as Astley tried to evade certain defeat. Finally, Astley had no choice, but to stop and fight the harrying Roundhead forces of Colonel Thomas Morgan and Sir William Bretherton. Astley chose a hill to the northwest of Stow-on-the-Wold straddling the present day A424.

The Roundhead forces (the Parliamentarians), who were slightly smaller, lined up to the northwest of Astley's position, also along the current route of the A424. The Roundheads, flush with the confidence of an army on the brink of total victory, charged up the hill at the Royalist positions, near the present day Greenfield Farm. Initially, the Royalists held and even pushed the Parliamentary infantry back. However, the Roundhead cavalry under Brereton rolled up the Royalist cavalry on the right flank. The Royalist cavalry fled the field and the infantry fought a running retreat southeasterly back to Stow Square.

(Wikipedia)

RING (M:VII): WEATHERTOP

The Midgewater Marshes

Ceratopogonidae, or biting midges (including what are called, in the United States and Canada, **punkies**... **no-see-ums**, midgies, and others), are a family of small flies (1–4 mm long).

They are found in almost any aquatic or semiaquatic habitat throughout the world. Females of most species are adapted to suck blood from some kind of host animal.

Larvae are always found in some damp location, such as under bark, in rotten wood, compost, mud, stream margins, tree holes, or water-holding plants.

In humans, their bite can cause intensely itchy, red welts that can persist for more than a week. The discomfort arises from a localized allergic reaction to the proteins in their saliva.

433

The smaller members of the family are tiny enough to pass through the apertures in typical window screens.

The Philleypools

'As for the construction of the aerodrome at such a location, an entry in the Operations Record Book for 21 Operational Training unit(RAF Moreton-in-Marsh)shows that on January 20th,1941,personnel found 'the whole station was a sea of mud, even parts of the roads being knee deep'. Local farmer, Jim Meadows, has said: "I never thought they'd ever put a 'drome on the camp where it is because it was all boggy, especially four acres at the bottom –all under water all the time …

Other local residents have confirmed the existence of a marsh before the building of the aerodrome. Stan Hathaway stated the aerodrome was built on marsh "and a large pool called the philleypool."…

'Beyond … lay the philleypools, and the expanse of marsh mentioned earlier. Fred Thorne recalls that the philleypool consisted of 'seven or eight acres of water and marsh', while other local residents have slightly differing recollections as to what the pool, or pools, looked like. But the fact there was a lot of marsh appears not to be in dispute…

There are no known photographs of the area, and it is fortunate there are people still alive who remember it well enough to give descriptions. In conclusion, it may be considered that Arthur Scarsbrook's poignant words best sum up those recollections:

"Oh, it used to be a lovely place that did … but that's all gone … it is a shame really, but there you are."
(Mark Turner; Four Shire Memories:Moreton-In-Marsh And District Local History Society,1992).

Charles Walton

'When Charles Walton failed to return home by the time darkness fell on 14 February 1945 after a day of hedge-cutting at The Firs farm, Edith called on her neighbour to help her search for her uncle, fearful that he had been taken ill or met with an accident. Alfred Potter, the farmer for whom the old hedger was working on the slopes of Meon Hill, joined in the search. Finding Walton by the light of a torch, pinned to the ground by his pitchfork and his throat slashed in a form of a cross, made grisly reading in the newspapers and the bizarre base for the ensuing lengthy investigations, suspicions, whispers of witchcraft and sacrificial ritual in ancient fertility rites. The famed Fabian of the Yard, a famous inspector, joined forces with the Warwickshire CID and the case took on monumental status. One theory had been that the method of killing was so brutal and ritualistic that it was 'un-English', and every one of the 1,043 prisoners-of-war in the nearby camp at Long Marston was closely interrogated. Of mixed nationality – Italian, German, Ukrainian and Slav – the only prisoner among them found to be a likely suspect was an Italian who had bloodstains on his coat; a laboratory test proved it was rabbit's blood from a crafty bit of poaching for supper. A squad from the Royal Engineers scoured the woods and fields around with metal detectors, searching for clues and the old man's watch that was missing off its chain on his coat; every soul in the villages of Lower and Upper Quinton and Admington was interviewed.

His uncanny affinity with creatures of fur and feather, with an extraordinary ability to commune with and direct them to follow his commands were later considered to be unnatural.'
(Folklore of the Cotswolds, June Lewis-Jones (2003))

'There is evidence to suggest a pre-Christian existence on the hill – an iron-age fort with ditches and ramparts, deposits of gold and pottery dating from the first century BC and ruins of a Roman villa on the northern shoulder. For countless centuries the hill has overlooked the green fields and quiet hamlets of the English countryside.

Long ago, wakes and sabbats were common occurrences on its desolate slops. More recently, a series of macabre events have been reported there – incidents which always remain a mystery.

Winter 1875: At nearby Long Compton the body of an old woman, Ann Turner, was discovered with a pitchfork piercing her throat and pinning her to the ground. Across her face and chest was slashed the sign of the cross. James Heywood, a young farmworker, had long suspected the woman of being a witch.

'It's she who brings the floods and drought,' he once accused. 'Her spells withered the crops in the field. Her curse drove my father to an early grave!'

Often he had protested that the only spilling of her blood would take away the old woman's evil powers. And so when Ann Turner's body was discovered suspicion was aroused and the farmhand was charged with her murder. During his trial at Warwick Assizes, he asked that the victim be weighed against the Holy Bible – a rare custom prevalent in past centuries.

For his crime James Heywood was convicted and sentenced to life imprisonment. But there were many inhabitants of Long Compton and surrounding villages who were never convinced of his guilt. Seventy years were to pass before memories of the incident were awakened.

Autumn 1885: It was dusk when Charles Walton, a fourteen-year-old shepherd boy, was returning home after a day in the hills. The evening was still. Passing through a copse, he heard footsteps rustling among the fallen leaves.

Turning to look over his shoulder, he saw a black dog following him which he later described as a fierce-looking animal with a face resembling that of a bull terrier. It neither growled nor barked, but just stared at him with eyes that smouldered like burning coals.

Each evening as he made his way home the beast followed, sometimes emerging from the trees, at other times trotting behind along the hillside paths. It made no sound and always vanished as mysteriously as it had appeared. When he described how one evening the apparition had transformed into the shape of a woman wearing a black cloak his story was received with chuckles of derision.

Although it was commonly believed that the appearance of a spectral black dog foreshadowed misfortune and bereavement, little was though of the shepherd boy's tales until a day when news was heard of his younger sister's tragic death.

Whether from grief at his loss or fear of the unknown, from that time on the boy spent most of his days alone, suspicious of all strangers. No-one, except perhaps the members of his family, was at ease in his company, for it was believed that the Devil had set his mark on him.

As investigation continued, more sinister motives were uncovered. From past records a comparison was drawn with the murder of an old woman at Long Compton in 1875. Dr. Margaret Murray, the distinguished professor of Egyptology, was consulted. Her research showed that the date of Charles Walton's killing, calculated by the old calendar, coincided with the day when Druids performed rites of human sacrifice to ensure the fertility of their fields. She suggested it was likely a pitchfork had been used to force back the head of the victim so that blood could more easily flow to the soil. There was also an ancient belief that the shedding of a witch's blood exorcised evil spells.

Apart from the company of his niece, Charles Walton had led a solitary life, searching more into the secrets of nature than for the companionship of farmers and shepherds who lived around him. Villagers recalled that he was a vindictive old man, sometimes harnessing toads, yoked with reeds and pieces of ram's horn. These he willed to cross fields, blighting crops and harbouring thistles and briers. They remembered, too, that hidden at the back of his pocket he kept a 'witch's mirror' – a black stone, polished in a mountain stream.

Among the villages in the shadow of Meon Hill, where even today a belief in witchcraft is not dead, the inhabitants have learned to accept that the murder of Charles Walton was either a ritual killing or an act of vengeance.

It was not until the summer of 1960, when outbuildings behind his cottage were demolished, that the old man's pocket watch was discovered. But the sliver of polished stone said to have been concealed in its cavity – his witch's looking glass – the crystal used for weaving spells or seeing into the future was never found.

Was this the talisman for which he was slain? Was the old man's killer some crazed wanton? Or was the motive revenge for an act of witchery? If the true identity of the culprit was known, no-one ever dared tell and the mystery will forever remain unsolved.'
('Fire Burn', Kenneth Radford (1989))

RING (M:VIII) THE LAST BRIDGE

'The Town Hall now houses the Tourist Information Centre and the Folk and Police Museums. It was built in 1853 and extended in 1871. There was a market hall on the ground floor. The stocks have holes for seven limbs – one hole was reportedly for a one-legged rogue who lived in the town.

The George Inn, now the George Mews, was built in the 16th century and used by pilgrims when visiting Winchcombe Abbey. Above the door the initials R.K. can be seen. Richard Kidderminster was Abbot from 1488-1527. Inside the courtyard can be seen the Elizabethan balcony and stone bath used by the pilgrims.

No. 8 Hailes Street is reputed to be built on the site of Winchcombe's Saxon Mint. Mercia, opposite, has an over-hanging first floor and a traditional Cotswold stone roof.

21 and 23 Hailes Street dates from the 16th century. In Victorian times, it was 'The Sudeley Arms'. Many of Winchcombe's old houses are timber framed, but most have been given a stone 'face'.

Tudor House in fact dates from the middle of the 19th century. The wide arched gateway was designed to allow carriages into the courtyard.

The Follies was built in the 17th century, probably as both home and business premises for a wealthy merchant.

No. 52 North Street is a narrow house filling a gap – perhaps the site of an ancient road.

The White Lion is a 17th century gabled building, with stone mullioned windows and an arched stone doorway.

Treacle Mary is named after Mary Yiend, who kept a sweetshop here. She sold cakes, sweets and slabs of cold rice pudding.

There are iron rings in the wall at many points along North Street. They were used for tethering horses during the twice-yearly horse fairs.

The Gate was once a Temperance Hotel. It had a saline well in the courtyard. Horse-drawn coaches set off from here to Cheltenham daily.

From the Library car park can be seen remains of early Winchcombe. Depressions in the fields may mark the site of the Abbey fishponds. Remaining Abbey domestic buildings have been converted to private houses. One report states that the earthen rampart of the Saxon town, along the present Back Lane, had stone revetments and was crowned with a palisade.

Back in the High Street is the sixteenth century Wesley House, where John Wesley is believed to have stayed on Tuesday 16th March 1779.

In Abbey Terrace, several eighteenth and nineteenth century houses are built on older foundations. The road was widened in 1835 by taking in part of the Abbey grounds. Mop fairs, theatrical performances and public meetings used to be held here.

The Dent almshouses were designed by Sir George Gilbert Scott in 1865 for local benefactress Mrs. Emma Dent of Sudeley.

A wall plaque commemorates the 1914-1918 use as a hospital of the 1857 school. The building has also been used as a drill hall, assembly rooms and a working men's club.

Vineyard Street derives its name from the Abbey Vineyard. Its other name, Duck Street, records the ducking stool which was found when the present bridge was constructed.

The Jacobean House was built in 1618 to house the King's School. The master's accommodation was on the first floor, with a seperate entrance at the back. The Chandos Almshouses, to the side of the Jacobean House, were built in 1573 and rebuilt in 1841.

A splendid golden weathercock tops the Parish Church. St. Peter's was built about 1456 in local Cotswold stone, entirely in the perpendicular style. Its many noticeable features include numerous gargoyles; the fierce moustachioed example supposedly represents benefactor Ralph Boteler of Sudeley. A guidebook is available inside the Church.

Three Gables was carefully rebuilt in the Jacobean style for Emma Dent in 1882 by the local stonemason John Oakey.

No. 23 Gloucester Street houses the Winchcombe Railway Museum.

(from the pamphlet Winchcombe Heritage, available locally)

RING(D:I):THE TROLLSHAWS

The Golden Valley

Chalford is a village in the Frome Valley of the Cotswolds in Gloucestershire, England. It is about 8km upstream (4 miles east) of Stroud. It gives its name to Chalford parish, which covers the villages of Chalford, Chalford Hill, France Lynch, Bussage and Brownshill, spread over 2 mi² (5 km²) of the Cotswold countryside. At this point the valley is also called the Golden Valley.

The remains, and known sites, of many barrows indicate that the plateau area of Chalford Hill, France Lynch and Bussage has been an area of continuous settlement for probably at least 4,000 years. Stone Age flints have been found in the area as well as the remains of a Roman Villa. Several of the place names in the area are also Saxon or Danish in origin.

The name Chalford may be derived from Calf (Way) Ford, or possibly from the Saxon cealj or Chalk and the Norman Ford: both possibilities have the same meaning. There were two ancient crossings at Chalford apart from the ford from which the village was named: Stoneford, recorded from the later 12th century, was the crossing-point of a track up Cowcombe hill on the line of the later Cirencester turnpike and by 1413 another track crossed into Minchinhampton by Stephen's bridge at Valley Corner.

Chalford Hill is a recent title for the western end of the hill: Its original name was Chalford Lynch. "Lynch" (lynchet in modern English) means a cultivated terrace following the contours of a hill.

The settling of displaced Flemish Huguenot weavers in the 17th and 18th centuries brought quality silk and woollen cloth manufacturing to the valley. It is thought that they gave their name to the neighbouring village of France Lynch. At this point the Golden Valley is narrow and deep so many weavers' cottages were built clinging to the sides of the hills, giving the village an Alpine air. It is sometimes still referred to as the 'Alpine village'.

As the paths on the hillsides were too narrow for more conventional forms of transport donkeys were used to carry groceries and other goods to houses, this tradition continuing until as recently as the nineteen-fifties. Chalford expanded rapidly with the opening of the Thames and Severn Canal in 1789 and the village became one of the centres for the manufacture of broadcloth. Its wealthy clothiers lived close to their mills and built many fine houses which survive to this day.'

Mary Queen of Scots

Mary, Queen of Scots (8 December 1542 – 8 February 1587), also known as **Mary Stuart** or **Mary I of Scotland**, was queen regnant of Scotland from 14 December 1542 to 24 July 1567 and queen consort of France from 10 July 1559 to 5 December 1560.

Mary was the only surviving legitimate child of King James V of Scotland. She was 6 days old when her father died and she was crowned nine months later. In 1558, she married Francis, dauphin of France. He ascended the French throne as King Francis II in 1559, and Mary became queen consort of France until she was widowed on 5 December 1560. Mary then returned to Scotland, arriving in Leith on 19 August 1561. Four years later, she married her first cousin, Henry Stuart, Lord Darnley. Their union was unhappy and in February 1567, there was a huge explosion at their house, and Darnley was found dead, apparently strangled, in the garden.

She soon married the 4th Earl of Bothwell, who was generally believed to be Darnley's murderer. Following an uprising against the couple, Queen Mary was imprisoned in Loch Leven Castle and forced to abdicate in favour of her one-year-old son, King James VI. After an unsuccessful attempt to regain the throne, Mary fled to England seeking the protection of her first cousin, once removed, Queen Elizabeth I of England. Mary had previously claimed Elizabeth's throne as her own and was considered the legitimate sovereign of England by many English catholics, including participants in the Rising of the North. Perceiving her as a threat, Queen Elizabeth had her arrested. After 19 years in custody in a number of castles and manor houses in England, she was tried and executed for treason.

Bredon Hill

'Bredon Hill – a northern spur of the Cotswolds – has been described as "like a stranded whale," which gives a good idea of its form. It is 980 feet in height, and it stands separate and apart from the adjacent elevations, thus forming a prominent land-mark for many miles in either direction, and interesting as it undoubtedly in that respect, its broad summit is well worth a visit, not only to account of the many and varied views to be obtained there-from, but also in order that an inspection of its antiquarian and historical features may be made…

Near the summit of the hill above Westmancot, stands a curious group of pillar-like rocks called the "King and Queen." They are simply **two** natural rocks which in the course of time have appeared above the surface and evidence of their antiquity is afforded by the fact that they were mentioned as far back as the first Edward's reign, and described as "a great stone hanging under the hill." Until comparatively recent times a Manorial Court was periodically proclaimed at the "King and Queen," and adjourned to the Royal Oak Inn at Bredon, but this practice like many others equally ancient and picturesque has fallen into disuse.

Remembering "that sweet is the lore which nature brings" we cannot abstain from mentioning that it was customary to whitewash their Majesties, that being one of the ceremonies connected with the opening of the Court; also that at one time the practice of passing sickly persons through the narrow passage between the two pillars for the purpose of charming away their aches and pains was observed.'

(Round Bredon Hill, T.H. Packer (1902))

RING (E:I): THE FORD

*'**Upton-upon-Severn** (or Upton-on-Severn) is a small town and civil parish in the Malvern Hills District of Worcestershire, England, on the River Severn. According to the national census 2001 it had a population of 2,859. Located 5 miles (8.0 km) from Malvern, the bridge at Upton is the only one across the river Severn between Worcester and Tewkesbury .*

The present bridge was built in 1940. Upton was founded in 897. Oliver Cromwell's soldiers crossed the Severn here before the Battle of Worcester in the English Civil War. The town has a distinctive tower and copper-clad cupola known locally as the Pepperpot and the only surviving remnant of a former church.'

RING (E:II):RIVENDELL

The Malvern Hills

'At 1100ft the Beacon is another magnificent viewpoint, this time towards the rougher, less inhabited country to the west of the hills. It is also the site of an Iron Age hill fort with some spectacular ramparts and ditches. Comparatively few people venture further south, but this section, through a broken and wooded landscape, makes a pleasant change from the exposed ridge to the north.

The path continues to follow the Shire Ditch★ below Hangman's Hill, passing an outcrop containing the mysteriously-named Clutter's Cave. The obelisk over on the right is in the grounds of Eastnor Castle and commemorates members of the Somers family. Several tracks meet at the point known as Silurian Pass (to mark an underlying bank of younger Silurian stone) and the way lies over or round the modest Swinyard Hill. The dangerous Gullet Quarry lies straight ahead and it is best to skirt it on the right before making for Midsummer Hill (930ft). A track that skirts the hill on the right avoids the climb; otherwise you need to branch east at 150:758387 and pass through the 'north gates' of the Iron Age ramparts. Inside the ramparts there are paths leading to Midsummer Hill or to Hollybush Hill, its neighbour to the east.

In fact the route by way of Hollybush Hill is possibly the more interesting, if longer, because the descent is through the 'south gates' of the fort, which have been extensively excavated, and then through the old Hollybush quarry, a source of valuable roadstone until fairly recently. Either path leads to the hamlet of Hollybush.

Unless it is a point of honour to scale every summit there is little to be gained from climbing Ragged Stone Hill to the south of Hollybush; the recommended route is east along the A438 for 300yd and then into the lane on the right opposite the entrance to the quarry. Keep to the left when the path branches and follow a contour with the hill on the right. The way lies through woodland and emerges at the romantically-named and picturesque hamlet of White-leaved Oak. Chase End Hill, the southernmost summit of the range, lies a short distance away. It is a fairly steep climb to an unfrequented spot, but worth it for the sense of achievement at the end of an exhilarating ten mile walk.

Looking down from the hills at the open countryside stretching across the Severn, it is difficult to believe that the area was once thick forest, part of the 700 acres of woodland that surrounded the Malvern range. From the time of William the Conqueror onwards it was under direct royal jurisdiction with its own officers and laws. When the Earl of Gloucester married the daughter of Edward I, the forest was made over to him and became Malvern Chase. During the next 200 years large areas of the forest were cleared, parts were colonised, and by the time of Charles I a large number of people had claimed squatters' rights. In 1632 the position was regularised by royal decree; the king kept one third and the remainder was made available to the dwellers as 'commoners'.

There is little woodland left now but the area still has the unmistakable air of commonland, with long straight roads linking the hills and the river. Something of the atmosphere of the Chase can be appreciated in the course of a drive from Great Malvern, across the hills and round the southern end to Upton-on-Severn.

*a thirteenth century boundary created by the Earl of Gloucester and the Bishop of Hereford to mark the division between their hunting grounds. Later it was part of the county boundary between Worcestershire and Herefordshire.

(The Visitor's Guide to The Severn and Avon; Lawrence Graner:1986)

Madresfield

Madresfield Court is a large estate surrounded by parkland and gardens, with a wide moat surrounding. Originally Tudor, a manor house grew up around the main hall. Major changes took place in Victorian times, notably in Gothic style, including the Bell Tower added in 1875.

Madresfield has never changed hands for money in its history, but only passed by inheritance. The most famous descendents are the Lygon family and successive Earls Beauchamp lived there until 1979.

The Lygon Arms in Broadway is an obvious connection.

The house is perhaps most notable for its works of the Arts and Crafts movement, by such as William Morris.

The Chapel is a major work carried out in this style. The interior is integrated with various styles along the same theme.

The library contains 8,000 books. The books are for reading, not merely for show, so the official Literature tells us. The books cover interior design, architecture, furniture, craftsmanship as well as agriculture, gardening and flowers. There are also many children's books. C.R Ashbee created the library interior. He later worked from Chipping Campden and quite apart from intricate carvings at Madresfield, is a silversmith of high repute and renown.

The Chapel within is recognised as perhaps the most impressive expression of the Arts and Crafts movement in Britain.

The Long Gallery contains Jacobean and Elizabethan oak furniture in a William Morris setting. The views from here are the best on offer. There stretches an avenue a mile long ending at the Gloucester Gate. It is from here that southwards there is the perfect view of the Malvern Hills.

There is also the Staircase Hall, the Saloon and Drawing Room and also the Dining Room.

Finally, the Gardens were enlarged in 1865 and now cover 69 acres, comprising avenues of Cedar, Oak and Poplar.

Flowers of every variety garland the grounds in the Spring.
(The Author, from literature available from Madresfield Court)

George Bernard Shaw

'*One point I might have put to him, but didn't, is that when you get up a musical entertainment for the exclusive delectation of the nobs, you must either be content with a very scanty audience, in which case the nobs will think this is not good enough to come again, or else pack the room with a contingent of musical deadheads, who are not nobs, nor even respectable philistine snobs, but rank outsiders – though you would be surprised at the costly entertainments, operatic and otherwise, that are [got up] solely for their sake, and that of the jaded pressmen.*

On entering that Bond Street portal which was brought here bodily all the way from Italy, and approaching the stairs which I have so often worn with the wearing feet of an art critic, I found on one side a descending stream of sad and hollow people, and on the other an ascending one, flushed and swollen. By this I perceived that the refreshments were downstairs; and I hurried **up** *with all the convenient speed. Here I found a nob or two, a deadhead or two, and a vast majority of solid snobs. No celebrities, no literary lot, no journalistic lot, no artistic lot, no Bohemian lot, nothing (to speak of) except plain snobbery, more or less choice.*

However, the choicer spirits sat in the front of the room and faithfully listened. The others sat at the back and talked. How they talked! One young lady, who must I should think, be the champion chatterbox of the universe, so outdid with her tongue the most rapid flights of Signor Ducci's fingers that I stole round three times through the east gallery merely to see whether she had stopped from exhaustion: but she was as fresh as an aviary each time. Another lady, who coaches me in the ways of good society, and makes certain pre-arranged warning signals to me when I eat with my knife or help myself to potatoes with my fingers, was very severe with me.

Whenever the subject arose between us, I declared that English society did not care about music – did not know good music from bad. He replied, with great force, that I knew nothing about it; that nobody had ever seen me in really decent society ' that I moved amidst cranks, Bohemians, unbelievers, agitators and – generally speaking – riff-raff of all sorts; and that I was merely theorising emptily about the people whom I called bloated aristocrats.'

Charles Darwin

'With respect to the theological view of the question. This is always painful to me. I am bewildered. I had no intention to write atheistically. But I own that I cannot see as plainly as others do, and as I should wish to do, evidence of design and beneficence on all sides of us. There seems to me too much misery in the world. I cannot persuade myself that a beneficent and omnipotent God would have designedly created the Ichneumonidae with the express intention of their feeding within the living bodies of Caterpillars, or that a cat should play with mice. Not believing this, I see no necessity in the belief that the eye was expressly designed. On the other hand, I cannot anyhow be contented to view this wonderful universe, and especially the nature of man, and to conclude that everything is the result of brute force. I am inclined to look at everything as resulting from designed laws, with the details, whether good or bad, left to the working out of what we may call chance. Not that this notion at all satisfies me. I feel most deeply that the whole subject is too profound for the human intellect. A dog might as well speculate on the mind of Newton. Let each man hope and believe what he can.'

(Letter from Charles Darwin to Asa Gray (22 May 1860))

APPENDIX C

A CAULDRON OF ONE'S OWN

**'Here is wisdom .Let him who has understanding
calculate the number of the beast, for it is the
number of a man: His number is 666.'**
(The Holy Bible, Revelation 13.18)

Many will be familiar with the configuration of the Number.

Perhaps not so many with the source. The Author crystal balls the
prolonged and painful purgatory of this our Cauldron of Appendix
C; so long, involved and complicated, one will probably need to
read it at least three times.

A long stretch: exhaustion for the unfortunate victim under the 'devices'
for the loosening of tongues machined by Sauron in the Tower of
Barad-Dûr; Gollum's tongue: 'Baggins!!!' cries the poor wretch under
the devices; betraying the identity of the keeper of the One Ring.

There are a number of whipping posts still standing in The Shire to
this day: three or so.

Pilloried, racked or hung, even unto the very last long stretch of
the neck by rope: the Witches of England were hung unto their
fatal end, until Dead. We are to learn of the hangman's fate for the
Witches at home; abroad, fire burns out their heart and soul, a hot
trot to the other side. Yet we must not go tearing ourselves apart
between the stretching and the rope; we lighten the burden so far
as we may; we hope to have the Audience screaming its head off by
the end: just so the Witches of England at the end of their tether.

(Bilbo Baggins is, in the words of the Professor, 'stretched' about
leaving The Shire for the last time; perhaps today 'stressed': except
that the Professor's use of language is forever deliberate; we cast
the word into the fires of oblivion, for the metaphor is as butter too
thinly stretched over bread after … toasting …)

Macbeth is the one Shakespeare Play reasonably well known to the Author. Coincidentally, we know that the Professor knew it, but who no doubt would have been familiar with most, if not all of Shakespeare. The Forests and Dunsinane must await another day.

However, we are given to understand he may not have enjoyed reading the works in isolation from performance.

Letter number 76-

'But it emphasised more strongly than anything I have ever seen their folly of reading Shakespeare (and annotating him in the study), except as a concomitant of seeing his plays acted.'

We invoke now Macbeth for its Witches. There is plentiful sorcery to come in the Quest, as of course there is in The Rings; but not the Hobbit, which was written for children, where the supposedly evil Dragon Smaug has the oily unctuous charm of Sheer Khan in The Jungle Book, at least on film ... as Disney has it for the children. Smaug of The Hobbit sounds in the reading, to the Author, much like the sly Tiger in the film of The Book.

Is Smaug smug?

Curiously, the Dragon connotes the evil of the Devil, such connotation also being Biblical-

'Then I saw an angel coming down from heaven ... He laid hold of the dragon, that serpent of old, who is the Devil and Satan, and bound him for a thousand years.'

(Revelation 20:2)

And so Saint George slew ...

Foreshadowing The Hobbit, the Dragons were once Worms. Smaug has a weak spot unprotected by his bejewelled waistcoat; foreshadowing our stripping down the Witchcraft, we are to learn of the fatally weak spot of the Witches: and so; Worm to Dragon to Devil to Witch.

The Nazgûl or Ringwraiths of The Rings, the evil servants of Sauron, are indeed Witches metamorphosised. They represent Sauron, the evil one, in the ultimate form the Devil Satan.

The Dark Lord.

There is of course another contemporary 'Lord' of the same design: William Golding's 'The Lord of the Flies'. Some sources hold Beelzebub the Lord of the Flies, by biblical reference. Suffice for now to say one of the most powerful convocations imaginable of the access to power of the young and the abuse of that power by the young; the evil that unbridled power may unleash in the young, or the old for that matter. Piggy remains forever the victim of the playground bully, on a desert island or in the local schoolyard. One or two with the inclinations of a Roger (corrupted by the authority-power of a Jack) spells trouble for any community.

The Author has been brewing a caustic Cauldron of our own.

We foretell first our peradventure of the 'British Goblins' of Wirt Sikes (1880), by which there we are to be further mesmerised in Wales, when once we get there, in our work on The Hobbit and its Maps; Upon arrival, Wirt Sikes concocts his own special brew of the witches and fairies of Wales.

Our conviction was that it evoked the Witches of Macbeth and their-

'Double, Double Toil and Trouble…' (popularly misquoted 'Hubble, Bubble …')

A bit of this, a bit of that (the 'this' and 'that' being unthinkably and unpalatably unspeakable, other than by the tongue of a Witch of the Sixteenth century) and yet Wirt has been stirring things up for us for over a Century. He heard this tale here in Wales, he was told that one there in Wales: mix them all up together and pass this strange recipe to anyone who might like a taster-

'O well done! I commend your pains;
And every one shall share i' the gains;

And now about the cauldron sing,
Like elves and fairies in a ring
Enchanting all that you put in.'
(Hecate; Macbeth)

We dream a caustic kettle concoction, all mixed-up; warts and all.

The Three Witches are dancing about a Poisoned Chalice –

'Round about the cauldron go;
In the poison'd entrails throw.'

The Audience may taste the same torments, absent the virtue of any coherent, cohesive or conjunctive ingredient in this our Cauldron of Appendix C, that our Cauldron is a mish-mash, hotch-potch or tosspot of pot-luck. We hope to defy such torment; for we have at worst met the pleas of the Witches-

'Say if thoud'st rather hear it from our mouths,
Or from our masters?'

We have already met with our first and most ancient master-general of Witch and Fairy, but Wirt Sikes must await The Hobbit; for he is to convene with us in Wales. We make extensive mention upon the Quest, in relation to The Hobbit most particularly, of the work of the American Wirt Sikes; of 1880. We preview now merely the existence and theme (without detail) of his work, recently republished under the 'British Goblins' title: there are tales aplenty of fairies and, though less so, witches in Wales. Of some interest for our further authorities upon the relation between the lore of the Faerie and the Witch, they are treated by Wirt as part of the same phenomenon. Here endeth for the moment the lessons of Wirt Sikes; never fear, Wirt makes a further apparition in Wales.

Even if one ever thought about it, we doubt the Audience made any connection between the two phenomena. Fairies are a figment of some childlike imagination. Witches represent the cranky comic crone who lives on the corner of the block – weird, but no real harm in the old dame; been a few like her over the years, all faded

451

out since the old days, what with Prozac and all to take away the nasty urges.

Gollum (gloating): We shall see,... O yes, we shall see!

We now encounter two further master-generals of England, the Fairyseeker and the Witchfinder, who, together with the Witchmarshall of the Americas (O! The O so civil charm of our initiation procedure, even unto expatriates into the ranks), he of Salem, one Chadwick Hansen, who are to be the three mouthpieces of our Inquisition.

And so, we invoke Fairyseeker Pennethorne, Witchfinder Olliver and Witchmarshall Hansen to the dark side; we are inducted by each into the Black Arts quite soon.

Now to the brighter side for a split three seconds.

Here's the The Nobel Voice calling now, hopefully to lighten if not altogether cleanse the Spirit:

> **'A telephone was ringing,**
> **It just about blew my mind,**
> **When I picked it up and said 'hello'**
> **This foot came through the line...'**

The Author is in Church and a Mobile (Cell) Phone rings. Ours. Embarrassing for all concerned, especially the Author. The Vicar makes good-natured reference. Service over, the Author tells the Congregation, all agog and eager to cavil: it must have been God;He knew where I'd be; He is paying a call but He chose to come feet first. Some clearly thought the call not from on High; but from the fires flaring far below.

And so to Fairyseeker Pennethorne and Witchfinder Olliver.

Whilst the Author may have thought of the Fairies and the Witches as part of some lost folklore myth, we were never before to hear the very least of the origins of the Fairy Realm ;and never before, to one's growing fascination, to partake of a respectable explanation of what the relationship between the lore of the Fairy and that of the Witch might be; and never before, to one's greater growing fascination, to be initiated into the practices that made the practitioners of Fairy and Witch lore regarded as evil: incarnate.

This was not too dissimilar from the Author's search to better understand the writings of the Professor. What lay behind his thinking in writing The Rings? Just so, how and why on Earth do we recognise the Fairy and Witch phenomena; how do the stories originate and why was there any belief in what most fancy exist only in our imagination and fantasy?

Most reaction, at least to the Fearie Realm (we react perhaps a little less disdainfully to Witches, having a feeling for *some* misery ages ago) is this :all tales of fantasy, made-up for the kids.

How odd that similar, sometimes the same, tales are told all over Mother-earth; there must have been a serial taleteller on the loose. If one really thinks deeply about it, the worldwide phenomenon is shocking. Explanations there are nowhere; even Wirt Sikes who recounts the tales, does not explain the How, Why's and Wherefore's of the Fairy Wings flying circus.

The Author has only so much Cauldron to spare.

The Author did in fact discover these Three, very late in the Quest and we share them however late the hour: not that it matters for the purposes of the Quest, but the Author came upon these authorities in late 2010,when virtually all of the remainder(to some hundreds of pages of typewritten script) was written; and their discovery was as enlightening to us as had been the work and words of Wirt Sikes; such that the three were included belatedly. Wirt awaits in Wales. Wirt is a great act to whom we listen, like and liken to Burl Ives.

About to share them with the Audience, share also the contemplation whether the Professor may have had something of these first two on his mind in his writing of The Rings. An ominous comment, for there was a lot going on in front of the roaring fires of the 1920's in

Oxford. Fairyseeker Pennethorne is indeed to tell all of such goings on.

The Author may be somewhat fanciful at times, nay prone to fantasy, yet we derived massive comfort from this first work which appears to the Author to at last lay some of the ghost of the proposition that Fairies and Witches are 'all make believe', a proposition admittedly more held of the former than the latter. Even if not put to rest forever, at least we have some Inkling. There are sundry place names for webbing derived of their proximity to the Wychwood of Oxfordshire in England; Shipton-under-Wychwood for one. We now spell out our own creation; how appropriate that the source of Fairyseeker Pennethorne should emanate from Oxford-under-Wychwood: our own chosen one.

If any of the Audience is by now lolling, a dumb doll effigied by the potion, we seek further effect upon the Rangers of our Quest; in the oracle that the 'Wychwood' of mention is soon to take the shape of 'the Old Forest' of The Rings; and so we are indeed in the right place for efficacy.

The first work of relevance, reference and now indeed reverance is 'Witchcraft' by Pennethorne Hughes, first written and published in 1952, and recently republished in 2004 as one of the 'History Classics' series of Sutton Publishing.

The Author knows not why, but the 'Pennethorne' of the author's name implied to us a Female. Comforting nevertheless, somehow the Author wished he had a Female authority to underpin (ouch, for we are all over stuck with pins hereafter) a subject which is unequivocally female related. No authority ever mentions a 'Warlock' or, if they do, the Author never found one.

The back cover dispelled our inference, for he is *James* Pennethorne Hughes.

The Author designates Pennethorne Hughes 'Fairyseeker Pennethorne' by way of contrast with the contemporary of his brethren, Charles W. Olliver of the 'Handbook of Magic and Witchcraft', our 'Witchfinder Olliver'; they both sound plausible enough and, in any case, coven or calling, such, according to the Fairyseeker, was the nomenclature initiation rite into the Witches' Sabbat ...

'... there sometimes followed a ceremony of baptism, but this was in all probability a parody of the Christian rite-the mere giving of a name in Satan to counteract the possession of a name in Christ ... [ ]analysed the Christian names of witches and feels that the predominant ones, Joan, Isobel, and so on, are not the most common in general society at the period considered. This implies that witch societies probably avoided normally such very Christian names as Temperance, Faith, or Mary ... '

Joan of Arc('Jeanne D' Arc')burns on in the memory.

The Author came to his senses that 'Witchcraft' was to be a bubble of a pot-boiler, nay ready-made feast provisioned by Fairyseeker Pennethorne for the Cauldron: forthwith upon reading the very first three lines of the tract; the Author open-mouthed, and yet, even so, so – minded –

'This is a serious book, on a serious subject. It was only the original approach which was, perhaps, flippant.'

The Author thought of the Author, but the self-awareness ended abruptly-

'At Oxford University, in 1928, a few of us founded a witch-group. One paper only was read – by a young undergraduate ... who is now a distinguished politician ...'

If such is one's fate, we really must find another group to play in. We mentioned the Professor and his writing of The Rings. One is hardly surprised that the Professor calls up a few spirits of his own given the tender young souls of his teaching community are running around in Covens; covert and unconventional, to say the least: even for Oxford-under-Wychwood.

Apart from a few sporting ones and the oddest drinking ones, the only group the Author was in was the Cub Scouts, so we pathfinder-badger our way on; perhaps to full scouthood; destined to be hoods of green, red or brown according to Fairymaster Pennethorne; Swamps, Robins and Hoodies entering the merriment soon.

Bewitchingly, the Witchfinder's Handbook was likewise written in 1928; this must have been quite a year for the students, certainly those of the darker arts.

We suppose a hunt of its own kind was forming in Germany about this time.

Fairies

And so to the 'Witchcraft' of Fairyseeker Pennethorne Hughes.

We must not be tempted to take out of their unnatural habitat(being a later context, *infra*) the vivid Fairyseeker visions of the peoples thought to originally inhabit the Faerie Realm, for this very first glimpse embodies the whole Realm – behold, the Author becomes so enchanted with the spells cast by Fairyseeker Pennethorne that the words of the Fairyseeker take on a shape of their own, turning into small, dark, bold speech; bold for ones so unbold; it must be we who have emboldened the Little People-

'The palaeolithic peoples of Western Europe were small dark cattlemen, living on the animals which, as has been shown, they were so closely identified in a psychical as well as a physical sense. As the various waves of invaders came, equipped with a higher economic standard and a higher mechanical efficiency and armoury, they retreated into the swamps and the islands, loathing with passion the agriculture, iron and church bells which were their defeat. Some of them intermarried with the invader, particularly when the celts themselves in turn pushed westward by newer Nordic tribes.'

So small yet bold the Audience may need a Ready (Bill's) spyglass to see them.

Herewith the first portion of the notion of the potion; Fairyseeker Pennethorne speaks of an amalgam of races, predating the Celts and the Romans, with certain specifics of characteristic. Again we fast forward in context, for it is as well to know the swamp from which the Fairyseeker emerges in order to understand the progress of the development, both of the subject(ed) peoples and the Fairyseeker's ideas of them-

'The palaeolithic people, dark, shy, small, and swift; probably had the property of moving so quickly to escape detection. '

Overlooking the four-leaf clover of 'probably', what of the 'psychical' aspects of these peoples; certainly differing physically, what were their beliefs, bearing in mind we have yet to fast-forward centuries to any organised 'Religion'-

'The scattered hamlets and villages, most of them self-contained units, miles apart from each other, lay off the ridgeways which the Romans had adapted into military highways, and were surrounded by swamp, forest and devils. It was not surprising that the beliefs they had brought with them when their ancestors first settled there should persist, only superficially affected by the culture of their overlord and the inexplicable doctrines of his religious compatriots...

The palaeolithic peoples of Western Europe were small dark cattlemen ... [SUPRA] ... Some of them intermarried with the invader, particularly when the celts themselves in turn pushed westward by newer Nordic tribes. The original inhabitants of Scandinavia, later known as Dwarves, were, as is pointed out by Sir Walter Scott, who had not even heard of the Diffusionist Theory: "originally the diminutive natives ... who, flying before the conquering weapons of the Asae, sought the most retired regions of the north, and there endeavoured to hide themselves from their eastern invaders. They were a little, diminutive race, but possessed of some skill probably in mining or smelting metals, of which their country abounds. Perhaps also they might, from their acquaintance with the changes of the clouds, or meoteorological phenomena, be judges of weather, and so enjoy another title to supernatural skill. At any rate, it has been plausibly supposed that these poor people, who sought caverns and hiding places ... were in some respects compensated for inferiority in strength and stature by the art and power with which the superstition of the enemy invested them. These oppressed yet dreaded fugitives obtained, naturally enough, the character of the German spirits called Kobold, from which the English goblin and the Scottish bogle, by some inversion and alteration of pronunciation are evidently derived."

Never mind the 'Diffusionist Theory', we have quite enough already, what with Sir Walter and the 'Bogie Man'(to Get You) piping down from Scotland.

Fairyseeker Pennethorne reviews the evidence for the existence of such peoples; which of its nature is open to challenge, even ridicule. The evidence of the swamp is scarce; supposition based on the accounts of others. Until an Archaeologist digs one up (one may have done so: the so called Hobbit Man of Indonesia – but, apart from Peking Man imported soon, zero is to be the current, our Cauldron of Appendix C, presumed state of knowledge of the Author), nobody can or will ever know the truth of the theories synthesised here; we must bear in mind that the theories relate to 'the first two millennia before Christ'(in the words, to come, of the Fairyseeker) being the equivalency in Europe of developments in Egypt (the height of whose Empire was in the course of building at the very start of those two Millennia, two thousand years before Jesus Christ), and whose developments in 'magic' in its widest sense became, as we shall see, for Fairyseeker Pennethorne , the origins of much we might recognise by that terminology.

We barely understand the Pyramids of Egypt; just so how the 'Leetle People' scurrying here and there through the swamp?

The Fairyseeker with a message –

'… it is a truism that the tradition of fairies, whenever it is found, often embalms race-memory of earlier peoples. Even Robert Burton, writing the anatomy of melancholy in 1621, identified fairies and devils, cataloguing "Terrestrial devils, Lares, Genii, Fauns, Satyrs, Wood-nymphs, Foliots, Fairies, Robin Good-fellows, Trulli &c." This identification is almost as well recognised as the freudian revelation that nursery rhymes have only too often a phallic significance.

458

But the very identification of witches and fairies, as being names equally given to the submerged races – more particularly in Europe – is a major theme of Sir Walter Scott's Letters on Demonology and Witchcraft ...

In the popular mind today, fairies are associated chiefly with A Midsummer Night's Dream.

... But fairies were originally far more than this ...

They represented belief in ghosts and nature spirits, and the lesser deities of the Teuton and the Celt. But, more particularly, they were race-memories of the stocks which had inhabited Europe before the coming of the Celts, with their iron-culture, in the first two millennia before Christ ...

... the racial minority lived on, largely with its own customs and beliefs, the magic of the physically defeated but mysterious Little People, became the superstition, and often the justified fear, of the dominant race.'

To enlighten the spirit, we now have the Little People furried, ferried and fairied away into the inaccessible depths of the swamps, forests and glades – shyly but rarely on occasion peeping outwards – we peeking a glimpse of their accustomed, cute yet uncustomised, fairytale fashion–

'Evidence everywhere is insistent on the hoods which the fairies wore. The little green and red hoods of the gnomes are still remembered, which the seven Dwarves share with the witch of charicature, in her high hat with the elf locks peeping from under it. In Germany, the local Hobgoblin was called Hoodekin, or Hutkin, and Robin á Hood may be another manifestation of the devil king of the fairies.'

It being so easy to be poking fun in the direction of that of which there is no evidence, except for folklore ... the unwritten legend passed down orally from one generation to another, say a few thousand years ... and accordingly at theories wholly unproven, that we have poked some on the way over ... to London Town and a folklore of its own ... and beyond *to the other side ...*

... all in a dream, all in a dream, ...

The Road to the Woad

'Que mes cheveux divins n'en donnaient à mon coeur'
'My divine hair gave into my heart'
(La Colere de Samson; Alfred de Vigny)

The Author's heart has ruled our head with this tonsorial pictorial of the smart London 1960's set …

'… high hat with elf locks peeping from under it'

… really is taking hair length a step too far, doing Pudding Lane in the City of London for a basin, or Bread Street for a bun or Billingsgate for a mullet; even a rinse down Gray's Inn Road; and once even a pageboy down Buckingham Palace Road; one had a hairy time when she split down dead ends street with the kinks before Leonard of Mayfair put this frizzy fairy straight, but not so stiff as Leonard is, November 2016: it was he coiff'd the Beatles and the Stones in the first cuts of the 1960's(… the deepest according to some feline called Cat in 1967, a british shorthair in the chair for the lady cutter, since, as the shorthair sings, *she's taken almost all that I've got* …) … and it was there David Bailey did the photographs to make one look like Twiggy: on the way another went for a shag in Soho Street, even a jaunty crop on the bottom end, noticing that each of the haircutting girls were …

'What's it going to be then, eh?'

… dressed in the heighth of fashion too, with purple and green and orange wigs on their gullivers, each one not costing less than three or four weeks of those sharps' wages, I should reckon, and make-up to match (rainbows round the glazzies, that is, and the rot painted very wide). Then they had long black very straight dresses, and on the groody part of them they had little badges of like silver with different malchicks' names on them – Joe and Mike and suchlike. These were supposed to be the names of the different malchicks they'd spatted with before they were fourteen …

One of the girls asked whether any coming for the first time might fancy *a malenky bit of cutter,* right quick and dirty in the back of the shop, on the dressing table if they won't come without looking in a mirror, or even on the ceiling, (the mirror that is, not the cutter, unless she's some kind of gymnast and hanging), and costing only a *malenky bit of cutter;* but the elves declined, all they wanted in 1962 was to read A Clockwork Orange for all the funny words in it.

… Most drew the line with a council house facelift in Croydon like Kate Moss, or a mane down Red Lion Street like Kate Bush in the early days wuthering about her highlights … So, some with twigs in their hair, others with mosses, some more with bushes and others with fishtails or rattails and even one sporting a duck's ass, all were feeling homesick for the swamp and took a quick pixie cut, very short, home to get there …

The Road to the Secret Shire

As much as the Author is intrigued by the motivations of Professor J.R.R. Tolkien in writing The Lord of the Rings, we are equally upon inquiry about our own in furthering the Quest. The motivations are produced from somewhere, and the melting pot of the Cauldron may be the place to view what was melding my mind, on the supposition that the formative years are the ones that represent inspiration. In any event, and for what it may be worth, probably absolutely nothing, as merely a timeline of events which the Audience might find for themselves if they were interested in such details (yet, because many of you never lived these years, one supposes nobody is, that much), here is that timeline, but we would add that the materials within 'The Road to the Toad' section following were equally prevalent in one's mind at the time, and echoing Anthony Burgess …

> *'Unfortunately there is so much original sin*
> *in us all that we find evil rather attractive…'*

If this sounds like an ego-trip, it is not meant to be: merely a trip down memory lane, (down mammary lane in the case of Aleister Crowley's rude bits going down way after the Road to the Toad), a sharing of personal experience, seen and heard, for those interested in such details.

And so quiet, now, please, for we are turning on the Television for a decade of news story, all to the backdrop of the lyrics which capture so evocatively the newsome, sometimes awesome, often unhandsome, picture-world in which it all transpired ... before our very eyes ...

> **'Let's go back to yesterday ...**
> **Turn back the hands of time**
> **Turn back the hands of time**
> **Picture a room with a window**
> **A sofa and some chairs**
> **A television turned on for the night**
> **Watching other people living**
> **Seeing other people play**
> **Having other people's voices fill our minds ...**
> **This is my country, those were my people**
> **Theirs was the world I understand ...**
> **I know 'em like the back of my own hand**
> (My Country: Bad Love; Randy Newman)

1961

> **' ... ask not what your country can do for you,**
> **ask what you can do for your country...'**

1962

The Cuban Missile Crisis has the world on the edge of another World War as the United States and USSR come close to launching nuclear attacks.

1963

> *... Kennedy would remain as the U.S. President*
> *until he was assassinated in November of 1963 ...*

'I have a dream that one day this nation will rise up and live out the true meaning of its creed: 'We hold these truths to be self-evident, that all men are created equal."

1964

'The Times They Are a-Changin''

President Lyndon B. Johnson signs the Civil Rights Act of 1964 into law on July 2nd, 1964. The Civil Rights Act of 1964 made it illegal to discriminate against someone based on their race, religion, sex, national origin, or the colors of their skin.

Nelson Mandela and seven others are sentenced on June 12th to life imprisonment in South Africa.

1965

... the war in Vietnam continues to worsen as whatever the Americans do including major bombing of North Vietnam they continue to lose more men, at the same time the Anti-War movement grows and on November 13th 35,000 march on Washington as a protest against the war.

'Like a Rolling Stone' ... is considered one of the most influential compositions in postwar popular music. Rolling Stone magazine listed the song at number one in their '500 Greatest Songs of All Time' list.

'After writing that I wasn't interested in writing a novel, or a play. I just had too much, I want to write songs.'

'Like a Rolling Stone' being about Edie Sedgwick within Andy Warhol's circle, as something that Dylan saw from the outside, not being personally involved with either of them, but as something he saw and was scared by and saw disaster looming and wrote a song as a warning, and it was compelling ...

1966

'Some people are on the pitch, they think it's all over ... [BANG] .. it IS now ...

1967

Sgt. Pepper's Lonely Hearts Club Band is ... released on 1 June 1967 ...

In 'The Times' prominent critic Kenneth Tynan described Sgt. Pepper as 'a decisive moment in the history of Western civilisation'. Others … were similarly expansive in their praise … 'listening to the Sgt. Pepper album one thinks not simply of the history of popular music but the history of this century.'

1968

Civil Rights leader Martin Luther King Jr. is assassinated in April by James Earl Ray.

Richard Nixon wins the United States presidential election.

The first manned Apollo mission, Apollo 7, is launched by NASA.

1969

'giant leap for mankind'

Neil Armstrong and Buzz Aldrin become the first men to arrive on the Moon during NASA's Apollo 11 mission.

The Woodstock music festival takes place in New York …

> *'We are stardust*
> *We are golden*
> *And we've got to get ourselves*
> *Back to the garden'*

Much of the following *diabolique* had been, and still was, (… except for the Victorian bloodcurdling, and the filth of Reg Christie in the previous decade …), disgorging itself from our history during the very same timeline …

The Road to the Toad

> **'In the human heart an evil spirit can dwell …'**

**(Voices over Victorian London:
gibbering, jarring psychobabble)
' ... Im gonna wring your neck ...
You're going down the road, baby,
and you can't come back'**

... fancy a drink on the way ... where's the shampoo, or, lowering the tone above the screaming from under the pavement, my favourite, Bloody Mary? ... at the end of the day we get quaffed, maybe half-cut, in Prince Henry's Room within the Prince's Arms down Fleet Street, with St. Dunstan's Church next door; you know it, right next Sweeney Todd's barbering shop by The Strand; you may even like a pie with your gargle, and as you gaily splash your tonsils, the Demon Barber has a mind to slash them wide open downstairs, revolving chair downwards the cellar where Margery Lovett gives you blood to drink ... your own ... before farewell forever in a ...

Bye Bye London Pie

And with a bland and courtly air the bishop smiled as he ascended the steps of St Dunstan's church.

'That's all very well, but what a terrible stink there is here!'

'Is this horrid charnel-house sort of smell always here?'

And so it was, for it seemed to come up through all the crevices of the flooring of the church with a power and perseverance that was positively dreadful.

'Isn't it dreadful? – did you ever before know the smell in St Dunstan's so bad before?' ...

'You are getting dissatisfied, and therefore it becomes necessary to explain to you your real position, which is simply this: you are a prisoner, and were such from the first moment that you set foot where you now are; and you will find that, unless you are resolved upon sacrificing your life, your best plan will be to quietly give in to the circumstances in which you find yourself placed. Without

465

going into any argument or details upon the subject, it is sufficient to inform you that so long as you continue to make the pies, you will be safe; but if you refuse, then the first time you are caught sleeping your throat will be cut.'

Bang! went the little square orifice at the top of the door, and the voice was heard no more. The jeering mockery of those tones, however, still lingered upon the ear of the unhappy prisoner, and he clasped his head in his hands with a fearful impression upon his brain that he surely must be going mad …

In the space of about a quarter of a minute, there came from the next room a sound like the rapid drawing of a heavy bolt, and then in an instant the shaving-chair disappeared beneath the floor; and the circumstances by which Sweeney Todd's customers disappeared was evident.

There was a piece of the flooring turning upon a centre, and the weight of the chair when a bolt was withdrawn, by means of a simple leverage from the inner room, weighed down upon one end of the top, which, by a little apparatus, was to swing completely round, there being another chair on the under surface, which thus became the upper, exactly resembling the one in which the unhappy customer was supposed to be 'polished off'.

Hence was it that in one moment, as if by magic, Sweeney Todd's visitors disappeared, and there was the empty chair. No doubt, he trusted to a fall of about twenty feet below, on to a stone floor, to be the death of them, or, at all events, to stun them until he could go down to finish the murder, and – to cut them up for Mrs Lovett's pies!

'Secure him well, my men,' said the magistrate, and don't let him lay violent hands upon himself. Ah! Miss Oakley, you are in time. This man is a murderer. I found out all the secret about the chair last night, after twelve, by exploring the vaults under the old church. Thank God, …'

(extract Text, London Penny Dreadful, 1846/7; 'The String of Pearls': Sweeney Todd, Demon Barber of Fleet Street)

The Ripper

Jack is in the pub, 'The Ten Bells', less than a mile from here …

On the wall opposite the bar is a giant sign listing the victims of Jack the Ripper. Although it is generally accepted by most ripperologists that Jack the Ripper murdered only 5 victims, the large sign shows six, with Martha Tabram being named first. This was based on the theory that the murders were based on black magic. Five mutilated victims were needed for the black magic theory to work. Elizabeth Stride was not mutilated. Her throat was cut. The theorist therefore, had to go back in time to find another victim that was mutilated in order for the theory to work. Since Martha Tabram (aka Turner) was stabbed 39 times, he counted this murder as a mutilation. Thus Martha Tabram now becomes the first victim on the giant Jack the Ripper board at the Ten Bells.

Black Magic Rituals

(Ivor Edwards, 2002)
'And the wind cries, Mary … '
(1967)

On the finding of the mutilated body of Mary Kelly, the rent collector, Mr. Bowyer, rushed to get his boss, Mr. McCarthy, who stated …

'The sight we saw I cannot drive away from my mind. It looked more like the work of a devil than of a man. I had heard a great deal about the Whitechapel murders, but I declare to God I had never expected to see such a sight as this. The whole scene is more than I can describe. I hope I may never see such a sight as this again.'

(She had been gutted, dissected and partly skinned. This victim had had her heart removed and stolen.)

The Black Magic theories are reviewed on the web, and the notorious wizard Aleister Crowley conspires in the theoretical, as he is on our quest here, later, raving and revelling with the beasts; bowing to the Devil. Incidentally, there he is in 1967, second left back row, Sergeant Pepper cover: both Dylans in attendance …

'We hope you will enjoy the horrorshow …'

'the conviction of Timothy Evans

467

is now recognised to have been
one of the most notorious,
if not the most notorious, miscarriages of justice.'

I'm in Notting Hill in west London with a 76-year-old man who doesn't want to be named. He moved into his house after the area was rebuilt in 1978, and seems to regret it. 'I think the place is cursed,' he says. 'I've had bad luck since I've been here. I've been here 40 years. My health's gone. Everything's gone.'

If you're superstitious, you could say he has a good reason to be concerned, for he lives just beside where 10 Rillington Place used to be, and where John Reginald Christie used to live. You may have heard his name already: Christie killed at least eight women – including his own wife – over a 10-year period during the 1940s and 1950s.

It is now widely accepted that he was completely depraved – a necrophile posing as a backstreet abortionist who preyed on vulnerable women. He would invite his victims back to his flat and trick them into inhaling cooking gas. Once this knocked them out he would then rape their unconscious bodies, before strangling them to death. This was the case for Beryl Evans, who reportedly came to him as she had become pregnant again and couldn't afford to have another child.

Until his arrest in 1953, Christie stored all of his victims' bodies on his property. Some he buried in his garden, while others he stashed beneath his floorboard, or hid away in a secret alcove in his kitchen.

… focus on two of Christie's victims: Beryl Evans and her one-year-old daughter Geraldine. The mother and her child moved into the top floor flat of 10 Rillington Place in 1948. Christie killed them both a year later, then framed her husband Timothy Evans, a 24-year-old lorry driver from Wales. Evans – who had an IQ of 70 and seems to have been forced into giving a false confession – was charged and executed for the murder of his daughter in 1950.

It took another three years until Christie was brought to justice, although by then he had already killed three more women. When it became clear Evans had not killed his wife and child, his case was key in turning the tide against capital punishment, which was abolished in 1965.

In 1946 [Christie] was digging in his garden when he unearthed a femur … You'd think Christie would have panicked upon seeing the thigh bone – the largest in the human body, with an average length of almost half a metre.

But instead of hiding it away, he was completely nonchalant, and used it to prop up a rickety trellis on the right-hand side of his garden. He left it there for the next seven years ...

A Clockwork Orange (1962)

'You naughty old veck, you,' I said, and then we began to filly about with him. Pete held his rookers and Georgie sort of hooked his rot wide open for him and Dim yanked out his false zoobies, upper and lower. He threw these down on the pavement and then I treated them to the old boot-crush, though they were hard bastards like, being made of some new horrorshow plastic stuff. The old veck began to make sort of chumbling shooms – 'wuf waf wof' – so Georgie let go of holding his goobers apart and just let him have one in the toothless rot with his ringy fist, and that made the old veck start moaning a lot then, then out comes the blood, my brothers, real beautiful. So all we did then was to pull his outer platties off, stripping him down to his vest and long underpants (very starry; Dim smecked his head off near), and then Pete kicks him lovely in his pot, and we let him go. He went sort of staggering off, it not having been too hard of a tolchock really, going 'Oh oh oh', not knowing where or what was what really, and we had a snigger at him and then riffled through his pockets, Dim dancing round with his crappy umbrella meanwhile, but there wasn't much in them. There were a few starry letters, some of them dating right back to 1960 with 'My dearest dearest' in them and all that chepooka, and a keyring and a starry leaky pen. Old Dim gave up his umbrella dance and of course had to start reading one of the letters out loud, like to show the empty street he could read. 'My darling one,' he recited, in this very high type goloss, 'I shall be thinking of you while you are away and hope you will remember to wrap up warm when you go out at night.' Then he let out a very shoomny smeck – 'Ho ho ho' – pretending to start wiping his yahma with it. 'All right,' I said. 'Let it go, O my brothers.' In the trousers of this starry veck there was only a malenky bit of cutter (money, that is) –

'Hindley wakes and says:
Hindley wakes, Hindley wakes, Hindley wakes, and says:
'Oh, whatever he has done, I have done ...'
(The Smiths)

At first glance it's the very picture of suburban normality.
But the blonde woman leaning casually in her doorway is Moors murderer Myra Hindley.

The smartly dressed man at her side is her vile partner in crime Ian Brady.

And when this cosy snap was taken, at least one helpless child had already been tortured and killed in the house of horror behind them …

Taken in 1965, the black and white photograph shows Brady, then 27, and Hindley, then 23, with her younger sister Maureen outside 16 Wardle Brook Avenue, a two-bedroom council house in Hyde, near Manchester.

A year earlier 10-year-old Lesley Ann Downey was strangled at the house where Hindley lived with her grandmother.

But before they killed her the twisted pair taped themselves abusing and torturing the terrified little girl as she pleaded pitifully for her mum.

The sickening 16-minute recording was later played at the trial of the murderers.

Just a few months after this picture was taken, Edward Evans, 17, was also killed in the house when Brady hit him 14 times with a hatchet before strangling him.

It is believed Hindley's brother-in-law David Smith took the photograph of his wife Maureen and the sick couple.

David, who died in 2012, witnessed the murder of Edward and phoned the police the following morning, finally bringing the killings to an end.

Unlike Brady and Hindley's other victims, Edward's body was not buried on the Moors. Police found his corpse wrapped in plastic in a spare room at Wardle Brook Avenue when they turned up that day.

**'I had covered lots of big trials
involving all sorts of killers
but I had never seen grown men cry before
as they did listening to Lesley.'**

(1966)

'You're not laughing now, are ya?'

… 'cos your larffing gear's all over the bleedin' floor …

Ronald Kray shoots George Cornell in the head; The Blind Beggar: London March, 1966, less than a mile away from The Ten Bells …

'The sun ain't gonna shine anymore'

… the Walker Brothers song plays over and over and over again on the jukebox jammed by a stray bullet …

'Now is the time for Helter Skelter.' (1969)

August 9: After midnight, acting on Manson's instruction, three Family members including Tex Watson murder Sharon Tate and four other persons on the premises of 10050 Cielo Drive. Susan Atkins, one of the killers, writes 'Pig' on the house's front door, in Sharon Tate's blood. When the killers and a fourth Family member, who accompanied them, return to Spahn Ranch, Watson assures Manson it was Helter Skelter.

August 10: After midnight, three Family members acting on Manson's instruction murder Leno and Rosemary La Bianca at their Los Feliz home, next door to a house at which Manson and Family members had attended a party the previous year. Using La Bianca blood, one of the killers writes 'Rise' and 'Death to Pigs' on the living room walls. She writes 'Healter [*sic*] Skelter' on the refrigerator.

'He's as queer as a clockwork orange,' meant he was queer to the limit of queerness.'

'… by definition, a human being is endowed with free will. He can use this to choose between good and evil. If he can only perform good or only perform evil, then he is a clockwork orange-meaning that he has the appearance of an organism lovely with colour and juice but is in fact only a clockwork toy to be wound up by God or the Devil or (since this is increasingly replacing both) the Almighty State. *It is as inhuman to be totally good as it is to be totally evil. The important thing is moral choice. Evil has to exist along with good, in order that moral choice may operate.* Life is sustained by the grinding opposition of moral entities. *This is what the television news is about.* Unfortunately there is so much original sin in us all that we find evil rather attractive. To devastate is easier and more spectacular than to create …'

(Anthony Burgess; 1986)

The Professor's Letter number 78-

"Urukhai' is only a figure of speech. There are no genuine Uruks, that is folk made bad by the intention of their maker; and not many so corrupted as to be irredeemable …'

Many believe that, for some, one's choice is captive: that free will degrades itself despicably, in shackles set by the Beast in the desert of the second coming …

> **'Things fall apart; the centre cannot hold;**
> **Mere anarchy is loosed upon the world,**
> **The blood-dimmed tide is loosed, and everywhere**
> **The ceremony of innocence is drowned;**
> **The best lack all conviction, while the worst**
> **Are full of passionate intensity.'**
> (The Second Coming; W.B.Yeats, supra)

'Be sober, be vigilant; because your adversary the devil, as a roaring lion, walketh about, seeking whom he may devour…'

(I Peter 5:8)

For those interested in such details, the Author recalls reading many of the main authorities in these regards, by way of follow up to the news breaking, and only upon writing up the foregoing, did we realise that, in fact, we had; they are …

Sweeney Todd: that same Penny Dreadful;

Jack the Ripper: many, but with Stephen Knight's 'The Final Solution' the most challenging;

Christie: 'Ten Rillington Place': Ludovic Kennedy;

A Clockwork Orange: Book and Film;

Moors Murderers: 'Beyond Belief': Emlyn Williams;

The Krays: The Profession of Violence; John Pearson;

Manson Murders: Helter Skelter; Vincent Bugliosi and Curt Gentry.

'And there are no truths outside the Gates of Eden'

To this day, I do not know the answer to the simple question, Why? … but might Anthony Burgess know something I don't? All that talk of Original Sin … I have no idea what Original Sin is, after all, do I, Coven Master …?

> *'Oh had our simple Eve*
> *Seen through the make-believe!*
> *Had she but known the*
> *Pretender he was!*
> *Out of the boughs he came,*
> *Whispering still her name,*
> *Tumbling in twenty rings*
> *Into the grass …*
> *Picture the lewd delight*
> *Under the hill to-night –*
> *'Eva!' the toast goes round,*
> *'Eva!' again.*
> (Eve; Ralph Hodgson)

… noticing there are *Twenty* rings…

All the Fun of the Hair

We tease with the (French) hairstuff only as we all do when the Faerie Realm imagines itself into our 'psychical'; for the Professor, and to fairy-boot the Author, if not the Audience, the topic is enchanted of its nature. We have a little fun with Fairyseeker Pennethorne's history; and yet we take it seriously: it might just be a respectable explanation.

And so with all Fairy Stories, like Children, we inquire open-mouthed – What Happened Next? Did It All End Happily Ever After?

We fear not: for any number of the progeny of the Fairy Little People were burned as Witches.

Of itself a cruel portend of the Biblical reference –

'And the ten horns that you saw on the beast, these will hate the harlot, make her desolate and naked, eat her flesh and burn her with fire.'

(Revelation 17:16)

Before we Burn, Baby, Burn we must recount the tale of the next Millennium and a Half or so, from the time of Christ to perhaps the Sixteenth or Seventeenth Century; after all, Children, what is a 100 years between us and the Fairies and Witches, if Rip Van Winkle slept through a dream of 100 years; we may dream our own dreams: and the Fairies are growing, up, and into Witches ,and so is their manner of speech: ***growing in status*** –

'As the Middle Ages proceeded, travel of every sort increased. Norman adaptability helped to spread and organise society, and the church itself, in spite of every sort of difficulty and individual incompetence, secured the adherence, and often the passionate adherence, of all classes. Without it there was only extermination – physical if heresy was openly avowed, spiritual and eternal if cherished secretly. Throughout the period, and even, perhaps, down into the seventeenth century, there were other groups of villages. These, not usually on the main trade routes, uncritically accepted both religions as occasion dictated, and beliefs had been recognised as surviving paganism. From the eighteenth century onwards, the remaining traces, disguised as custom and folk-lore, were to be tolerated as amiable antiquarianism. But, for some four centuries, the organised asceticism of Christianity suppressed with blood and fire the scattered, degenerate, but still persistent organisation of the cults, and successfully purged their challenge as a rival faith.

This Old Religion – of the Horned god and the emotional reunion with nature through the dance and the practice of long established taboos – was not, of course, pure.

The adherent of the mediaeval cults, in their degenerate thirteenth-century form, would have been even more inarticulate and ill-informed in his beliefs – a jumble of phallic-Druidism, the dregs of Mediterranean ritual, this does not invalidate the fact that the beliefs

474

did exist, and the extraordinary feature is how far the evidence of trials, even as late as the seventeenth century, shows this.

The practitioners of the cult were originally merely the people of those racial fringes of Europe which still represented palaeolithic culture. The worshippers were known variously as witches or fairies ...

Witches, then, were early known as fairies, and until the later middle ages represented the remaining pockets of pre-Nordic peoples which Christendom still contained in its valleys, behind its swamps, or living in the lonely islands which Rome had never reached and where the converts of Rome, except as colonial exploiters or consciously adventurous missionaries, had barely penetrated. These people still retained the old customs, totems, and festivals which belonged to the pre-agricultural peoples, and something of the palaeolithic fertility system – the other-consciousness, and the power to manipulate it, which material advance had made increasingly rare and increasingly mysterious to peoples in a later stage of development. To Christian priests, bred in a tradition of pietistic asceticism, it was all both incomprehensible and disgusting ...

It certainly appears that the suppressed peoples kept some of their beliefs and their organisation into the seventeenth century, and that the king and queen, though perhaps ordinary enough to the uninitiate, were revered and obeyed by those who belonged to the cult, much as are the king and queen of the gipsies today. '

Just as one will never, ever slip one by the tired yet alert child, Fairytale or otherwise; nor even slip a word or paragraph by even the slip of a slumbering girl or boy, on the edge or threshold and very nearly there in Dreamland; of which you, Parent, Ma or Pa, will certainly know this truth: the easy Fairyseeker slippage from 'Fairy' to 'Witch' slips by in the slipstream of dream. It may never come true (or have been the truth, yet we all suspect it so), so why spoil the dream of the dreamer; believe the make-believe: that it might just have been so, all over Mother-earth; and the pan-european element is recognisable:

> 'We have strayed, we've lost the trail.
> What can we do, when a devil
> Drives us, whirls us round the vale? ...
> Swaying, flittering and swirling
> Like the leaves in autumn days...

What a crowd! Where are they carried?
What's the plaintive song I hear?
Is a goblin being buried,
Or a sorceress married there?'
(The Devils; Pushkin 1830)

Notice that goblins, sorcerers and Devils are all mixed together in the Russian pot; bearing in mind this is in translation, one supposes there are word equivalents for all of the spirits.

'... Witches, then, were early known as fairies...'

The Author loves this Fairytale of Fairyseeker Pennethorne; especially the bit about the little dark hoodie people scurrying about; we had never had it read to us before nor any story like it; it is our favourite …

… after The Hobbit and The Lord of The Rings.

Peking Man

Whysoever might the Author now ferry us away with the fairies, and to China?

Given the Author is to refer to China for the purposes of 'Pangu', the Chinese 'Green Man', in our musings of Tom Bombadil; alongside our discovery of the Hobbit Man in our Revelations, we found much of great interest in the work of Harry L.Shapiro: Peking Man (1974).

The early 1970's has proven a most fertile breeding ground for the Quest; so many of our resources are of the time.

Likewise, so many researches are sourced in the later 1920's; for example the Fairyseeker and the Witchfinder; our subjects of China were buried until that era,to be dug up there and then: fragments of Prehistoric man and woman known to the author of 'Peking Man' as just exactly that.

We have so little room left in the Cauldron, even for the Little People, that we must not regress or digress to or transgress upon the history of the Peking Man; and we do not now mean Pre 1928,but Post. Some interloper went off and half-inched (pinched) the 1928 finds of bones; unforgiveable with the Peking Man having so few to spare; inches that is. Never found since. Ossorific espionage, but not grand scale, Peking Man being of far lesser.

No doubting there will be countless other sources, the Author has no knowledge of Archaeology. This becomes self-evident, big-time this time, when we Regain the Precious, on account of our falling out with certain of the Archetypes over the science of the Precious – also over them and down their private dark holes. That fight must await our future history of The Battle of the Two Armies: a miniaturised Battle of the Five Armies of The Hobbit; yet we found the following series of statements stimulating(as much as labouring with one's Tripod) for three factors; first ,they are three, second they appear eminently reasonable for the average Archetype, whose tendency is to self-preservation, and third they are ,for an Archetype(with the exception of Sir Mortimer Wheeler with whose style, notably at The Mines of Moria, we are quite taken)written in a minimalistically readable style:

' … the stature of the males was estimated to have been 5 feet 1[and a half]inches, and of the female 4 feet 8 [and a half] inches… By our standards, then, the Peking men and women were distinctly short –at the very lowest margin of present day variation …'

'There has been, in other words, a steady progressive increase from the earliest accepted hominids – … – to recent man, with Peking man standing about halfway between these two extremes…'

'Among the primates, the order to which man and the closely related hominids belong, the progressive enlargement of body size in the course of evolution crops up repeatedly … the first primates back in the Paleoscene, some 60-odd million years ago, were only about the size of a small mouse …'

We knew not what to make of the statement that the first Primates were the size of mice; but we were terrorised by the nightmare of a mouse-size, rat-like, little-people Audience gnawing us to the bone, with the prescience of Winston's Room 101,which is, by the way, a portend of Volume III of the Quest, yet a long way away. There we deal with the vagaries of mind that so beset us all: more Horror.

Back to the future: Room 101 awaits in Volume III.

Yet one must readily acknowledge, another measure of stature for the theory of the Little People sought by Fairyseeker Pennythorne.

With forever a keen ear to the ground,the The Nobel Voice will have been the first to dream of the little people; and perhaps of the fate we are to explore for ourselves: the surefire death of the Fairies and Witches-

> 'King Kong little elves and the rooftops they dance
> Valentino-type tangoes while the heroes clean hands
> Shut the eyes of the Dead,
> not to embarrass anyone … '

Witches

We seek now the contribution of the Witchfinder, Charles W. Olliver.

We forever wondered what name his middle 'W' initial stands for, seeking for it like the Fairies of the swamp, without success. We hunted through the Handbook for it, to no joy; concluding that it must be so obvious that it need not be spelled out.

We were doubly spooked by the double 'ell of the surname.

We strove for the significance of 'Handbook' – casting aside with an Abracadabra the David Copperfield or David Blane (back home in England, just like that Tommy Cooper or the mercurial Derren Brown)hand-book of how to do magic tricks – conjuring that the depths of knowledge, intelligence and resourcing of the Witchfinder are as devastating as the very thickest smoke and deceptive mirrors; leaving one breathless, gobsmacked and dumbstruck; the mathematical explanations are of themselves, pure 'Magic'.

Perhaps the reason for 'Handbook' might be that the book is so handy; so handy we toss it in the Cauldron, just as the Witches of the Heath, yet wrecking the hand down –

'Here I have a pilot's thumb,
Wrack'd as homeward he did come.'

– and the Witches go digital –

'Finger of birth-strangled babe
Ditch-delivered by a drab ...'

Doubtless the Weird Sisters foresaw the 'Tyger, Tyger' of William Blake, burning bright centuries later; having the guts to throw them in, and rhyming for Cauldron to boot ...

'Scale of dragon, tooth of wolf ...
Make the gruel thick and slab:
Add thereto a tiger's chaudron,
For the ingredients of our cauldron.'

... or, if not the whole bootful; toe and leg –

'Eye of newt, and toe of frog,
Wool of bat, and tongue of dog,
Adder's fork, and blind-worm's sting,
Lizard's leg, and howlet's wing,
For a charm of powerful trouble,
Like a hell-broth boil and bubble.'
(Third Witch, Macbeth of Shakespeare; Act IV, Scene I)

The Author knows only one (self-acknowledged, definitively not 'confessed') Witch, of the White(better or good) variety and next time we broomstick by one another, the Author shall inquire of the perceived standing of Witchfinder Olliver in the stakes of the witchfire gatherings: crass confetti, of the cognoscenti, or all the rage conflagranti –

Ember, smouldering, smoking, aflame, burning bright or raging truth?

Six burning questions; firing up the Author with Olliver's own brand of Witchfinder fireworks.

The Witches bestow an effect upon our speech of greater materiality,density and intensity than the Fairies, portending curling, as in smoke, black phantoms of letters; and so Witchfinder Olliver is at last upon the record –

'At some period the theory or secret of life, which is to be found universally in all religions and physical systems as a symbol or condensed expression of the three [and four] fold mystery, makes its appearance, and this essentially simple creed may be taken as the origin and foundation of all symbols and initiatic rites. Briefly stated, it consists of the conception of the unity of Spirit, the existence of which presupposes the necessary existence of matter or duality, which in turn entails the existence of a bond or relation between the two, thus forming a Trinity.'

Hence the Holy Trinity of God the Father, God the Son and The Holy Ghost are the blessed Trinity of Christianity, symbolised by the Cross: as to which the Author aptly here acknowledges his first baptism in the principle that the intersection of the two limbs of the cross equates to the relation between the two limbs; and thus the third element of the triad.

The disclosure has supervening import for the significance of the Swashtika of Nazi Germany, whose origin is also the simple cross; more of this at some stage, no doubt the latter part of the Quest in Volume III.

This explanation becomes relevant for that in turn of Devil worship, whose symbolism involves the inverted or upside down Triangle, representative of itself of the Trinity; notably when superimposed upon the original, to form the pentagram.

Suffice to say that the threefold symbolism is quite enough for now ;the fourfold of the Witchfinder taking us into mathematics higher than the Author's for present purposes; but we shall perhaps arrive at that magic number 4 some time hence.

Seeking for the moment the duality of a second inquisition, we shone the fairylights back on Fairyseeker Pennethorne, who also takes the birth of Witchcraft back to the very origin of religious thought-

'Witchcraft is the degeneration of one of the earliest stages of religious belief and practice. In its history it has added parodies of the various later religions which have challenged it, and which, after generations of struggle, have usually swamped it. The story of the witch cult is only comprehensible against the background of religious development as a whole.'

We crow with a wicked black beak that Fairyseeker Pennethorne is forever seeking in the swamp.

The Nobel Voice's Motorpsycho Nitemare:…

**'… without freedom of speech,
I might be in the swamp…'**

'… religious systems were built up from a fundamental subjective Trinitarian creed for which a more objective form was later substituted, Phallic worship in its broadest sense … The original creed is a complimentary duality, the other a duality of opposition …

The new dual system originated in the conception of opposition, the opposition of a principle of good to a principle of evil, of a dark god to a god of light, and, although it occurred in ,or spread to, every religious system, it is comparatively recent [dating to the Manichean sect of the early Third Century A.D.]…

… it will be shown that the Sabbats were corruptions of religious rituals by sects who were slowly reverting to the original Phallic worship, and who, through analogy with sorcerers and witches amalgamated with these for the joint purpose of sexual excess and crime…'

Ably assisted by Fairymaster Pennethorne in the Inquisition –

'Witchcraft, almost everywhere, had two main derivatives to which its other formative influences became attached-the fertility cults persisting from the indigenous inhabitants of any area, and the later

481

'magical' practices derived through direct or distorting channels from the centralising Egyptian source ...

Witchcraft, as it emerges into European history and literature, represents the old palaeolithic fertility cult, plus the magical idea, plus various parodies of contemporary religions.'

The numbers (which are everything to Witchfinder Olliver: summarise his theory of the Kabbala: quite simply beyond this Author) become complicated. The original concept (of regeneration) was two becoming Three, but the complimentary pairing becomes a force of opposition in good versus evil (Godevil): and in addition to which (not conceptually, but as the constituent elements)we have three elements of the emerging Witchcraft: the phallic fertility cult, the magic and the corruption of standard religious practice.

This latter three has no significance as a trio, except that it helped the Author to remember their sum; three again; and that both authorities, Fairyseeker and Witchfinder, concur broadly threefold indications of the features of the development of Witchcraft.

In the result a cacophony of Cult (Phallic), Conjurors(Magic) and Corruption(Ritual).

If the Audience misses the Witchfinder's indication of 'Magic', his reference to 'sorcerers' is such; the Handbook indicating in a Chapter of its own the illicit trickery of the Sorcerer; Witchfinder Olliver devotes an entire Chapter to the White and Black Magic of Sorcery.

We hear a further ribald, rude, racy crescendo: what of the 'sexual excess': what of the goings on there?

Strictly Come Dancing for the Witches' Sabbat; we neither take your partner, do the dance; nor ogle the caresses, dresses or excesses. Those of the Audience wishing to peep for more may join The Witches' Sabbat amongst The Black Paintings of Goya; albeit wanting sexual excess. Others will favour Luis Falero's Witch of 1880.Those cruising for one Helluva sexy Witch will admire The

Magic Circle of John William Waterhouse,(1886); the Author's personal favourite. In case we forget the Sexy Witch website from which we spirited Falero's: we are bound to return, in Wales, to the remarkable similarity between the Witches' hat envisioned in the images of that site ,well known to us all (every Witch – except those of Goya, Falero and Waterhouse – wears one)and that of traditional costume for the women of Wales, whose black bonnet is disported every Saint's Day (March 1st,of Saint David)by the women and young girls of Wales to this day and ever in the future: we leave the mix bubbling under for now, trusting Wirt Sikes to have an answer: what, pray, is that hat and cat all about, Wirt?

The Author knew the Goya and the Waterhouse (not the Falero) before the site visit: the broomstick has since taken on a whole new position in the Author's imagination; with thoughts of sweeping your chimney.

If you can't stand the heat of Falero's Hell's Kitchen, get out and don't stir the Cauldron.

Whew!

'The Wickedest Man in the World'

And so we summon one who ought to know: the role of Aleister Crowley in modern day 'witchcraft practice' is legend of itself, called in his time 'the wickedest man ... '; and, indeed, you may find him in the clouds for yourselves: we invoke the Wizard for his poetry of their kind in 'The Wizard Way'; and here is summary ...

'He had learnt the elvish sign;
Given the Token of the Nine:
Once to rave, and once to revel,
Once to bow before the devil,
Once to swing the thurible,
Once to kiss the goat of hell,
Once to dance the aspen spring,
Once to croak, and once to sing,
Once to oil the savoury thighs

**Of the witch with sea-green eyes
With the unguents magical.'**

Three sections seem to reveal the same threefold tenets of Black Magic witchcraft:

Phallic Cult and Pact in lines 4 and 9 to 11: possibly, lines 1 and 2, with the Author going through Hell in the Shire searching for *the elvish sign* and *the Token of the Nine;* **Magic and Sorcery** in lines 7 and 8, the Aspen long held to have magic powers, and hear the ensemble croak like a frog; **Desecration by Perversity** in lines 3, 5 and 6, the worshipful party being orgiastic, with the thurible (swung incense burner) in use in obscene context, with a kiss for the abomination, where one might kiss holy artefacts.

Despite an earlier smirk, elves and witchcraft are indeed spoken in the same context. Crowley will have ogled so much and so many with such orgiastic, grandstanding high, hard and handsome cock-tail, we shall stare all agog in grim voyeurism; and many a maidenhead and false godhead slapped and slabbed out: each vexed headed section of the next three carries lines from within the poem, evidential of practice … Crowley ought to know, he was there agogling, such that his poetic input precedes the formal comments of the Witchfinder and the Fairyseeker …

Cult and Pact

> 'Give thy body to the beasts!
> Give thy spirit to the priests! …
> Seal my speech with ecstasy,
> *★Till a babe is born of me*
> That is silent more than I;
> For its inarticulate cry
> Hushes as its mouth is pressed
> To the pearl, her honey breast;
> While its breath divinely ripples
> The rose-petals of her nipples,
> And the jetted milk he laps

From the soft delicious paps, …'

Lactation in bizarre context.

Witchfinder Olliver knows something of the *Phallic Cult-*

'… the Phallic cult, from being primarily the symbol of an abstract doctrine, became not merely the deification of the generative function in man, but a widespread and universal Nature worship, the cult of fecundation, a natural religion deprived of its primitive demonology.'

The Author might have indulged **'widespread'** but resisted the temptation for the time being.

Ably assisted by Fairymaster Pennethorne in the knowledge –

'For a period in world history, phallic religions, with fertility rites led by the magicians … dominate the early religious exercises of mankind. The woman's position remains all-important, both as the repository of tradition, the guardian of the home round the fire, and the symbol in herself of sexual fecundity.'

The Author might have indulged **'The woman's position remains all-important'** but resisted the temptation for the time being.

Magic and Sorcery

> 'Oh the honey and the gall
> Of that black *enchanter's* lips
> As he croons to the eclipse …
> Mixed with fat of many a maid
> Slain by the *inchauntments* cold
> Of the witches wild and old.'

Witchfinder Olliver knows something of the *Magic* –

---

*　　*Enchantment* is the magical pathway …

485

'Sorcery and Black Magic can be traced to the fear and superstition of the Middle Ages and darker civilisations when all things were endowed with demons and spirits, and hence, anyone having even a slight knowledge of any form of science such as Physics, Chemistry or Medicine would be naturally regarded with awe, and as one commanding spirits. That in order to do this he must have signed a pact with the evil one, king of the spirits of darkness, was a foregone conclusion.'

Ably assisted by Fairyseeker Pennethorne in the knowledge –

'The darker and more sophisticated activities of the adepts – thaunaturgic and goetic magic – were the pursuits of the intellectual. Rites of criminal curiosity, rationalised perversion, mathematical magic, the evocation of evil spirits, talismans, and aspects of astrology, derived from the Egyptian mysteries, the Kabbalah, Pythagoras, and the aristocratic stream of diabolism ... Against the witch, or those mistaken as witches, the accusations were mainly of natural magic, venefic magic, spell-casting, fire or storm raising, lycanthropy and the keeping of familiars ... '

For those not aware of thaunaturgic, goetic, and venefic Magic, neither is the Author, one for you would-be Witches with a dictionary. Lycanthropy means adoption of animal form; like Dracula and the Bat, werewolves or, indeed, Beorn in The Hobbit. *Familiars* are considered at Frogmorton; Graymalkin' is the one in Macbeth, a grey cat: or (when we're hosting one of our more formal Phallic Cult gatherings with all the trimmings, and Crowley head lubes boy), a greasy pussy, lapping up the baby milk left over from the (divine) ripples of her nipples, if indeed she's pumped up for it tonight, just in time to catch the Wizard's magic show, with star guest Paul Daniels who has come from afar for this; to include nothing of 'rationalised perversion', whatever that may entail, but hold tight ... someone is ringing the back door down in the swamp so deep, saying they are all well into it, the practice is perfectly acceptable, and that is what all the boys go in for ...

Desecration by Corruption of Ritual

'He had crucified a toad
In the basilisk abode,
Muttering the Runes *averse*[*]
Mad with many a mocking curse ...
Smote the blasting hazel rod
On the scarlet lips of God;
Trampled Cross and rosy core; ...'

Witchfinder Olliver knows something of the *corruption of ritual*:-

'The principle which forms the very essence of the Devil, the idea of opposition, also underlies the whole ritual of Black Magic and Black Masses. Such ideas as repeating prayers backwards, reversing the cross, consecrating obscene or filthy objects are typical of this sense of opposition or desecration ... the key word to the whole of the practices of Black Magic is desecration ... '

Ably assisted by Fairyseeker Pennethorne in the knowledge –

'It is now time to discuss the pact with the Devil, and the witch mark ... there was a direct vow to the Devil himself, in the person of the local master of the coven ... or a symbolic burning of the theological boats, as when a person 'useth the Words or Signs which Sorcerers use, knowing them to be such'. In other words, there was formal entry into the coven, or there was personal desertion of Christianity and adoption of magic ritual ... First, the new witch denied the Christian faith and baptism ... insulting the Virgin Mary (known as the Anomalous Woman), spitting on the Cross, and so on. This was followed by vows to the adopted god, the Devil ... the witch received a mark from the Devil.'

Personification of the Devil must take a strong will, or no free will at all; there being plenty of substances available for that end, if you're not warped enough in the first place.

**'If you're going to do something, do it well.
And leave something witchy.'**

---

[*]   backwards

487

(Charles Manson)

Desecration is, without reference to OED, the contrary and reverse of 'sacer' the Latin for 'sacred' 'holy' 'devotional', thus to desanctify, render unholy or negate devotion.

Now, to the reason for the Author's interest in the details of Witchcraft: simply that our Inquisition reveals far more than we ever thought, or thought to know, of the Craft of the Witch: this is a subject with its own tortuous history, and with its own historians, researchers and scribes: what it is **not** is some Disney-esque, green-faced drag-queen out of The Wizard of Oz; hundreds of thousands of **women** were persecuted as Witches, tortured and died. Often in the fire. One may have imagined the occasional firework; wrong: Witchcraft was everywhere: fearful and feared of the fearsome witchfinders; fatal for the deemed, unredeemed and doomed participators.

The truth is the complete contrary and reverse of the rather kindly, wildly cranky, berserkly demented, crone image stuffed down our throats.

The Professor, of course, knew all of this.

Witchfinder Olliver screams of it for us all-

'All over Europe witch-finders and the like arose in countless numbers. Their favourite method consisted in sticking long pins into the victims' bodies, and should a spot be discovered that was not sensitive to pain they were found guilty and burnt; in either case they were tortured and executed.'

Ably assisted by Fairymaster Pennethorne, now screaming the same scream-

'... This Mark which the Devil made upon the witch was regarded ... as final and irrefutable evidence of guilt ... when a mark had been discovered and had been pricked without bleeding or appearing to cause pain ... conviction followed more or less automatically ...'

But still Why the Witch-hunt?

Fairyseeker Pennethorne tells all; bluntly enough –

'For the Faithful, it was an Age of Faith and, as such, all-embracing. Criticism was madness and witches were lynched with the terrified cruelty with which animals will dispatch one of their own kind which suffers from a deformity. It Totality admits toleration, its case is lost. There was a concept of Universality: of unity and authority and law.'

Witchfinder Olliver decries all, no prisoners taken; leaving no stones for turning, nor any bones about, in the silencing of the Crones-

'It must be remembered that the Church, and the Church alone, was responsible for the creation of the Devil-Myth, no trace of this existing in the earlier forms of demonology ...

The concrete idea of a Devil or evil god did not arise all at once, and only gradually took shape ...

... other partial myths such as Beelzebub, Python, Asmodeus, Belial, Lucifer and Shatan all embodying some sort of belief in an evil force or forces ... give us about the third century B.C. a more or less mythical, indefinite entity of evil inimical to man. During His life, Christ, finding some rudimentary idea of a Devil or evil influence amongst the Jews, makes use of it as a symbol to illustrate His teachings ... The third century brings us to Manicheism ...

... The Devil is first defined at the Council of Toledo in 447, and the Council of Constantinople in 547 bestows upon him the gift of immortality. The monster is born ... the Christian religion has become a creed of terror, while other religions the world over are suffering from the same influence, but to a lesser extent ...

... The Devil and Hell, curiously enough, were not developed simultaneously, nor did they arise from the same origins. Whereas the Devil was born from the duality of opposition, Hell was derived from the idea of reincarnation, from the houses of pain, or lives of suffering which became the portion of the wicked after death. Hell was conceived as the counterpart of Heaven, so the Devil, become naturally king in Hell, a god opposed to a god, Christianity unconsciously fell into the Manichean error.'

(As the theory of two eternal principles, good and evil is predominant in this fusion of ideas and gives color to the whole, Manicaeism is classified as a form of religious Dualism: the belief in two supreme opposed powers or gods, or sets of divine or demonic beings, that caused the world to exist.)

The Author knows not the truth of the inquisition of Witchfinder Olliver.

Let the Audience be the Judge.

The New World

'Let me have my own way;
Let others promulge the laws—
I will make no account of the laws;
Let others praise eminent men and hold up peace—
I hold up agitation and conflict;
I praise no eminent man—
*I rebuke to his face the one
that was thought most worthy.'*
(Me and Mine; Walt Whitman: Author's Italics)

And yet there is to be one last Rattle at the Death; for we have not inquisition'd, known and told quite all. To that end we must invoke the aid of our Pilgrim Fathers. What of the goings-on elsewhere in the World, notably the New World of the founding fathers of America?

We shall be returning to Salem later in the hour of this our Cauldron of Appendix C; but for this brief moment we partake of the inquisition, knowledge and the retelling of the Witchmarshall(*ever*, for the second time, a clever calling into the Craft) Chadwick Hansen in 'Witchcraft at Salem'(Century Hutchinson 1970)and we do so for clarity of record: leaving the subjectivity of the events of Salem for that later hour.

---

*   chaos; conflict; desecration …

'Witchcraft at Salem' has a following of its own –

'An instructive and intelligent study of the trials, perhaps the best that has ever been written' (Sunday Telegraph).

(Ah-ha! The Sabbath!)

Witchmarshall Hansen now records a burning truth-

'Witches were burned on the Continent and in Scotland, where witchcraft was a heresy, but hanged in England and in New England, where it was a felony. Burning seems not to have been motivated by the wish to inflict a particularly painful death; Scottish witches, for instance, were first garrotted by the executioner, who then proceeded to burn the corpse and scatter its ashes. Most probably burning was an attempt to prevent the resurrection of the body.'

'While Europe hanged and burned literally thousands …'; even so, …

'The full horror of that warfare will never be known in all of its details. Even the statistics of convicted witches who were executed vary from one authority to another. But it is clear that the battle reached its height during the first half of the seventeenth century, when, for example, approximately nine hundred witches were burned in the single city of Bamberg, and approximately five thousand in the single province of Alsace.'

We truly do put an end to the Witch-hunt – Hellhag, Hellhole, and Hellfire, at last in Europe, for we must yet hear the fullness of account of Salem through Witchmarshall Hansen, – with the following, which is the frontispiece to a work subtitled 'Tales of Witchery'. We scream the scream of screams in a haunting, harrowing, hideous, lament of cruelty-

'For all those who died – stripped naked, shaved, shorn.
For all those who screamed in vain to the Great Goddess, only to have their tongues ripped out by the root.
For those who were pricked, racked, broken on the wheel for the sins of their inquisitors.

For all those whose beauty stirred their torturers to fury; and for those whose ugliness did the same.
For all those who were neither ugly nor beautiful, but only women who would not submit.
For all those quick fingers, broken in the vice.
For all those soft arms, pulled from their sockets.
For all those budding breasts, ripped with hot pincers.
For all those midwives, killed merely for the sin of delivering man into an imperfect world.
For all those witch women, my sisters who breathed freer as the flames took them knowing as they shed their female bodies, the seared flesh falling like fruit in the flames, that death alone would cleanse them of the sin for which they died – the sin of being born a woman who is more than the sum of her parts.'

Anon, 16th Century
(Published in E. Jong, Witches, New York, 1981)
(From 'Fire Burn': Kenneth Radford (1989))

The Author had invoked 'Amen', so be it, for the Future; but let it lie there; in the Past, where it belongs.

The Three Witches cry from the Heath-

**'When shall we three meet again,
In thunder, lightning or in rain?'**
(Act I, Scene I, Macbeth of Shakespeare)

Wirt Sikes haunts The Withered Heath of The Hobbit; we have already said so three times.

Which the Three to meet? The Fairyseeker and Witchfinder are already in place; we seek addition to the want of order; from disorder to order such that we may be three by our end: we evoke Three! Three! Three! …

Voice Off (of New England): *Put us out of our misery and go get the Witchmarshall, will ya'?*

... And so to Salem ...

And so the Witchmarshall is third to throw his lot in the Cauldron. Finally to our Triumvirate at last! Three Cheers for the Witchmarshall, convened so craftily into the Cauldron, this third and last time.

We have no case study as yet in this our Cauldron of Appendix C, other than passing reference to Joan of Arc. And so the souls of the Witches of Salem must indeed be purged along our miserable, wicked and tortured way. Perhaps the most notorious locality of Witchcraft of history; Salem: the frontispiece of 'Witchcraft at Salem'(Chadwick Hansen, 1970)announces the perplexed, vexed and hexed subject-matter, but denounces failure to do justice to the incumbents –

'For most people in this country the Salem witches are simply the subject matter of Arthur Miller's play The Crucible – standing for all victims of bigotry and persecution. But were all the witches innocent of the charges levelled against them?'

We are obliged first to set the scene as succinctly as we may.

'Early in the year 1692 several girls of Salem Village (now Danvers), Massachusetts, began to sicken and display alarming symptoms. The most disturbing and most frequent of these symptoms were convulsive fits: fits so grotesque and so violent that eyewitnesses agreed the girls could not possibly be acting.'

Reverends Lawson and Hale respectively-

'Their motions in their fits are preternatural, both as to manner, which is so strange as a well person could not screw their body into; and as to the violence also it is preternatural, being much beyond the ordinary force of the same person when they are in their right mind'
'Their arms, necks, and backs were turned this way and that way, and returned back again, so as it was impossible for them to do of themselves, and beyond the power of any epileptic fits, or natural

493

disease to effect.'

The Witchmarshall tells of a dialogue between John Hathorne, ostensibly impartial investigator but more 'prosecuting attorney than a magistrate' as the Witchmarshall recounts, and two of the accused: Sarah Good and Sarah Osburn.

Of these two, some specifics selected by the Author, not of the Courtroom dialogue, but of the commentary of the Witchmarshall, there being many others and more-

Sarah Good –

'… [a] precedent was set at this examination when Hathorne asked the children to look at Sarah Good and say whether she was the one who afflicted them. They accused her to her face,' upon which they were all dreadfully tortured and tormented for a short space of time. When they recovered from their fits they charged her with causing them, saying that her *specter* [Author's Italics] had come and tormented them …'

This was spectral evidence, that is, evidence concerning a specter or apparition of the accused, rather than her bodily person. It was eventually to become the central legal issue of the trials …'

Sarah Osburn –

' … was the first at Salem to assert the principle that the Devil can impersonate an innocent person.'

The Author offers precis of the Witchmarshall's account of experimentation with 'fortunetelling' by two other children, not identified definitively('probably' Elizabeth Parris and Abigail Williams), notably with the egg and glass –

' … the white of an egg poured into a glass being substituted for the fortuneteller's crystal ball.'

Spooked?

'Paddock calls'
(Second Witch, Macbeth of Shakespeare, Act I, Scene I)

The Witchmarshall resumes; as 'Tituba' calls:

' ... But the major event of that first day of March was the examination of Tituba.'

' ... [the children Parris and Williams] were assisted in their occult experiments by Tituba, a slave woman ... brought to New England from Barbados ... a Carib Indian(*not* a Negro)... [who]may well have been involved from the beginning. Certainly she would often have been charged with the care of the [two]children ... '

Interrogated thus-

''Did you ever see the Devil?'

''The Devil' said Tituba, 'came to me and bid me serve him.''

'She went on ... to provide a detailed confession of witchcraft, the first of approximately fifty that were made during the Salem trials ... At the end of Tituba's first examination the children were in fits ... Tituba said she saw the shape of Sarah Good tormenting them, and the girls confirmed it ... The most likely conclusion is that her confession was the product both of experience with the occult and of hysterical hallucinations as vivid and as terrifying as those of the afflicted girls.'

No doubt we have enough subjectivity for now; the Author has indeed, for his Heart is beating, racing and pounding as a man possessed.

And so to the apparent objectivity of the conclusions of Witchmarshall Hansen; these are to be judged by the Audience for itself, the Author knowing as much or little as the Audience. They are broadly and in summary the following: this is the summary of the Author: the Author feared to toss the sketch of a thumbnail

495

in the Cauldron: these *three* should not be disintegrated, all being integral to the integrity of the work of the Witchmarshall-

One

'We must bear in mind that in a society which believes in witchcraft, it works. If you believe in witchcraft and you discover that someone has been melting your wax image over a slow fire or muttering charms over your nail-pairings, the probability is that you will get extremely sick. To be sure, your symptoms will be psychosomatic rather than organic. But the fact that they are obviously not organic will make them only more terrible, since they will seem the result of malefic and demonic power. So it was in seventeenth–century Europe, and so it was in seventeenth –century Massachusetts.'

Two

'The primary causes should now be clear. There was an outbreak of epidemic hysteria in Salem Village which originated in experiments with the occult. And the hysterical hallucinations of the afflicted persons were confirmed by some concrete evidence of actual witchcraft and by many confessions, the majority of them also hysterical.'

Three

The third tissue is of itself deep-seated enough for it serves to form a triumph of opinion with those previous of this our Cauldron of Appendix C, those of Fairyseeker Pennethorne and Witchfinder Olliver; the Audience will have heard an incantation of this nature before:

'Witchcraft is not easy to define, because it is not, like the major formal religions, a coherent body of belief. But in Western civilisation since prehistoric times there has been a loosely grouped body of magical lore-charms, spells and so forth-having to do primarily with fertility and infertility, … Such lore has obvious, if tenuous, connections with pre-Christian fertility worship, whose tutelary deity was a fertility god.'

Cult; Conjurors; Corruption?

We awaited the third element of Witchcraft ascribed by the Fairyseeker and the Witchfinder; we have the Phallic culture and the Magic charms and spells; what of the corruption of accepted Religious ritual? Where is the blasphemous Desecration?

Lo and Behold, Witchmarshall Hansen gives us his Threesome of Corruption, within a *'Black'* Magic-

'But the degree of peril was relative, and proportionate to the degree of witchcraft which, like murder, comes in three degrees.

The first is the practice of white magic …

The second degree of witchcraft is black magic …

The third degree is pact, where the witch … actually believes she has made a contract to serve [the Devil].'

> **'Thrice to thine, and thrice to mine,**
> **And thrice again, to make up nine.**
> **Peace! The charm's wound up.'**
> (All *Three* Witches in Macbeth of Shakespeare, Act
> IV, Scene 1).

And so: we have Three authorities of some substance upon the essential elements of Witchcraft, which are Three; of which the third is made up of Three degrees.

Uncanny; but not so troubling as this: we are to remember that the broad findings of the Salem Witch Trials were mixed; many hanged, many escaped death by confession:

Sarah Good told Rev. Nicholas Noyes:

> *'I am no more a witch than you are a wizard,*
> *and if you take away my life*
> *God will give you blood to drink.'*

Twenty-five years later, as Noyes lay dying of a haemorrhage, apparently caused by a burst blood vessel in his head, he reportedly choked on his own blood…
… which no doubt proves she was hanged with some justification.

The Coven Closeth

Fair is foul and foul is fair, have we not hovered long through the fog and filthy air? Toiling over the Cauldron at least Nine times; troubling over the Cauldron at least Six months; and all the while our Cauldron hubbled, bubbled and boiled to the cackling, raucous, chorus of all Three Witches.

So, at last, Peace; and the Charm's wound up!

'Hecate' of Macbeth is yet waiting in the wings and the darkness. The Queen of Witches speaks last of all; except for the Lord. O My God: **Sauron**?

Voice Off: *Don't forget to say your Prayers.*

The final words of the Inquisition of our Cauldron of Appendix C shall be the final Plea of the Lord.

Our Cauldron was cast not only because the Author wished to share the Why? Why? Why? of the Witch-hunt, but because of the influence of the Realm of Fairy and of the evil craft of the Witches in The Rings.

We must never forget that the dark identity of the Lord of the Ringwraiths or Nazgûl is the Witch-King of Angmar; nor the Witchlike manifestation afforded the King upon Weathertop in the Film version; nor at the Battle of Pellenor Fields fronting Minas Tirith, where the Witch-King may not be slain by Man; but bewitchingly only by Woman.

The thought occurs that Eowyn may evidence Professor Tolkien's revenge for all such injustice; a challenge for Volume III?

The Author adopts a magic spell in the words of Witchfinder Olliver, thus-

'The belief in another world, in ghosts and haunting, in some secret and awful power wielded for good and evil by Magicians and Sorcerers has always appealed to human nature and is one of the most persistent heirlooms of the past, traceable to the fearsome creeds and corrupted demonologies of the origin of religions.'

'Writers at all times have found a rich mine to exploit, and an endless source of inspiration in the lore and legends of the past, and more particularly in the mysterious beliefs and strange events connected with what is commonly known as Magic and Witchcraft.'

'I Confess' screams the Author …

Not yet Hellbent, bound or fired, the Author soldiers onward in Christianity through Chronicles, Epistles and our ultimate Exodus with the final plea of our Lord.

Chronicles

Gandalf: 'I alone of you have ever been in the dungeons of the Dark Lord… those who pass the gates of Barad-dûr do not return…'

The Audience is bound to remain captive in our dungeon of the mind: in the depths of the Threefold towers constructed by the Dark Lord; and so, we foresee in that mind's eye, the third number is to waste the mind of the Audience, for as long as one cares to imagine; for we are all by now psychoanalysed psychosomatic: the psychology of Three; from which, we fear, there is no escape.

And so to the Chronicles of the The Nobel Voice, in the context of a newly envisioned pattern in his art of music:

'You're always at some unexploited fix point. It's not a heavy theorised thing, it's geometrical. I'm not that good at math but I do know that the universe is formed with mathematical principles whether I understand them or not, and I was going to let that guide me ...'

' ... I'm not a numerologist, I don't know why the number 3 is more metaphysically powerful than the number two, but it is ...'

As if the contribution of the The Nobel Voice were not enough to convince the doubters amongst us, we have it as such from our own Wizard, from notes in the midst of development of The Rings-

'Tolkien had made a note at the end of the three chapters that he had already written:'[Frodo] is going to do something about the Necromancer who is planning an attack on the Shire. They have to find Gollum, and find where he got the ring, for 3 are wanted.' ('J.R.R. Tolkien A Biography' by Humphrey Carpenter).

Three Chapters in, the Professor calls for three into the dialogue.

Epistles

Gandalf, already one left with Barliman Butterbur for reading at Bree, sends a letter Farewelling us now, clearly bearing the following Post-Mark and -Code ...

Mark

The Devil's own:

'and that no one may buy or sell except one who has the mark or the number of the beast, or the number of his name ... '

Farewell all Humanity.

Code:

We now comprehend a little better the symbolism of odd numbers: 3, 6 and 9.

It is, of course, mere numerical chance that Hobbits transcend rites of passage at 33. Professor Tolkien tells us as much-

' ... Frodo was still in his *tweens*, as the hobbits called the irresponsible twenties between childhood and coming of age at thirty-three ... Twelve more years passed ... Frodo was going to be *thirty-three,* an important number: the date of his 'coming of age'.

It may be numerical chance that Peter denies Jesus Christ thrice; and that the Resurrection is on the third day.

It may be further numerical chance that (some say) He is crucified at age 33.

Postscript:

We post the script that, the Professor having commenced writing of The Rings around and about 1936, that careful observer of all developing theory will not have failed to observe-

(I)

The Professor already fully expert upon the Faerie Realm (on record for the well documented Lectures),a developing theorisation of the Witchcraft; such that perhaps, and only that, the novel theorisation may have been of pervasive influence; the Fairyseeker and the Witchfinder being vintage 1928;

(II)

Peking Man, of discovery in 1928, is the greatest advance in Archaeological knowledge of its time; the Little People: away in China; The Hobbit, written in 1937, has ten years to grow to fruition.

We were seeking in the swamp, Fairyseeker in mind, for a third script to post, but just so the Little People, this one had all but escaped us: the area of Oxford-Under-Wychwood (a cauldron of our own creation), that of the Old Forest in The Rings, is steeped in the lore of the Witchcraft; and what is more, writers contemporary with the Professor sensed, felt and wrote of it. Most peculiarly of their senses and feelings about and in the Wychwood. We revisit the 'Wold Without End' of H.J.Massingham *(1932)* in RING M:III. There 'Massers' writes in the most serious terms of the lugubrious aura hanging over the Wychwood area, so much so a spiritual phenomenon. Even so Massers clearly enjoyed a cackle:

Wold Without End … Amen.

It is beyond belief that the Professor would not have known of this work, much celebrated in its day.

Exodus

Once more we turn matters backwards, to reverse, regressing to where it all started, the Second Book of the Bible retrospects our introduction to Macbeth, to our initiation into the Craft of the Witches, and thence our departure for new pastures.

And so; truly very near our departure, with the bard upon Avon and the song of the Witch Queen that Witches *were* like Fairies; elves too. For our recipe is foretold; long centuries, ago; and Will ought to know; for they were everywhere about then, in place and time –

> 'O well done! I commend your pains;
> And every one shall share i' the gains;
> And now about the cauldron sing,
> Like elves and fairies in a ring
> Enchanting all that you put in.'
> (Hecate, Macbeth (ibid))

We had made the promise, now fulfilled, of the final Plea of our Lord-

'Get Thee Behind Me Satan'

The tosspot of our cauldron within this Appendix C, relates how Druids (priests derived of the once upon a time Faerie Realm, and we are not going there beyond what's already input the Cauldron) were Pagan, worshipping the earth as mother and all nature, the sun, the moon, the stars, the weather and especially trees, accordingly; yet human sacrifice, by fire or otherwise, was accepted in order to adore the worshipful earth; for some, there were also the other indicia of the witchcraft wicked; which is not necessarily so; there exists witchcraft of the purest intention, purpose and result: indeed, the Author has good friends who teach it. The established Church sought to centralise worship and avowed the 'wickedness' of any number of the witchcraft practices,(many of which were not even properly investigated), and came to demonise the faery-witches as synonymous with the Devil, contrary to God, and evil accordingly.

'With an host of furious fancies
Whereof I am commander,
With a burning spear and a horse of air,
To the wilderness I wander.
By a knight of ghosts and shadows,
I summoned am to a tourney
Ten leagues beyond the wide world's end
Methinks it is no journey.'
(Loving Old Tom/Tom O' Bedlam; Anon.)
(... Altogether Now ...)

'... Onward Christian Soldiers ...'

'... Fight the Good Fight with all Thy Might ...'

'Mine eyes have seen the glory of the coming of the Lord
He is trampling out the vintage
where the grapes of wrath are stored,

He has loosed the fateful lightning
of His terrible swift sword
His truth is marching on
Glory! Glory! Hallelujah!
Glory! Glory! Hallelujah!
Glory! Glory! Hallelujah!
His truth is marching on.'

Lo and behold,…
… witness Frodo loosen Sting's swift lightning …
O Christ!

O Dark Lord!
(January 2017)

Dylann Roof, who shot dead nine black churchgoers who had invited him in to worship with them, has been sentenced to death in South Carolina.

Roof, who defended himself in the sentencing, never explained his actions to jurors, saying only that 'anyone who hates anything in their mind has a good reason for it'.

In his FBI confession, he said that he hoped the massacre would bring back segregation or start a race war.

'Be sober, be vigilant; because your adversary the devil, as a roaring lion, walketh about, seeking whom he may devour…'

(I Peter 5:8)

'But this is terrible!' … 'Far worse than the worst that I imagined from your hints and warnings… What am I to do? For now I am really afraid. 'I am sorry,' … 'But *I am frightened* …'

There are many Biblical references on our Quest: the Author wishes not to be judged devout or otherwise, and prefers (if you don't mind) not to be judged at all until the time and place are right, and Thy Kingdom come, yet offers such references merely for their aptitude in the illustration of some fundamental truths; rather like Frodo who was *meant* to find the Ring, Providence dictates … a Volume II?

APPENDIX D

DOOR THROUGH THE PORTRAIT GALLEGORY

Portrait Gallegory

The sheer volume (sic) of the Quest dictates that a few words of introduction at the Crossroads give rise to some truncated words of entry into the Portrait Gallegory in this Appendix D. The doors may be thrown fully open, of necessity within the Shire, but on our return from Mordor, close to the Scouring of the Shire materials up the road ahead. That is appropriate enough, because the materials of Fascism are indeed those on canvas within the gallery: many of the literati, glitterati and other scatty members of the dignitary classes are there; from Edward and Mrs. Simpson down to Oswald Mosley: and we may go even lower with such as Unity Mitford, who probably couldn't help her sense for indignity, being brazenly bonkers.

> 'The boy I love is up in the gallery,
> The boy I love is looking now at me,
> There he is, can't you see, waving his handkerchief,
> As merry as a robin that sings on a tree.'

The Professor's Letter number 78-

'Urukhai' is only a figure of speech. There are no genuine Uruks, that is folk made bad by the intention of their maker; and not many so corrupted as to be irredeemable (though I fear it must be admitted that there are human creatures that seem irredeemable short of a special miracle, and that there are probably abnormally many of such creatures in Deutschland and Nippon – but certainly those unhappy countries have no monopoly: I have met them, or thought so, in England's green and pleasant land)...

Professor J.R.R. Tolkien was slap, bang, wallop ... what a picture ... in the midst of the fuss, not only in the timing ... the Professor commences to writing The Rings in 1936 ... but in the geography; for besides our cauldron of Witchcraft about Oxford of the 1920's, the blood of all banks(Coutts to the CO-Op)is boiling beastly within the shadow of the Dreamlike Spires; the full-up roaring for greater fulfilment; the empty whimpering, come the General Strike of 1926, for a little more.

The Mitford Letters evoke most succinctly(in the 'Preview' of our Portrait Gallegory) the environment of what all the fuss was about then, and … we merely suggest, Old Bean, Wooster to Jeeves, by surname only one's manservant … thus the Professor's covertly; and now the Author's with the benefit of hindsight.

The Preview sets the wider scene very nicely, but in terms of our own view, limited of necessity, we might also join with the sentiment expressed in the following of the Editor's Note-

'Letters make a fragmentary biography at best and I have not attempted to present a comprehensive picture of the Mitfords' lives'; those seeking a more complete account can turn to the plentiful books by and about the family. In order to weave a coherent narrative out of the vast archive and link the six voices, I have focused my choice of letters on the relationship between the sisters. I have also selected striking, interesting or entertaining passages, as well as those that are particularly relevant to the story of their lives … '

But we are not to join in that sentiment entirely, for those wishing to do so must surely study the Mitford Letters with the attention they deserve, nor do we claim to link the six voices with coherence; but more or less (but fleetingly) most incoherently only those of three, being, the most 'striking, interesting or entertaining passages' of particular relevance to the story of the lives of Nancy, Diana and Unity: which in our perception are those which most readily portray the vagaries of these times and lives; and, specifically where, in our view, they impact the writing of The Rings, *however obliquely*.

Ever the egalitarian, we shall no doubt let each of the other sisters have a bash; recalling that Diana and Unity alone could be said to favour the use of the truncheon,(even if, in their defiant defence, wielded by another), no doubt to the Anthem:

'Deutschland, Deutschland, Rubber Alles ...'

It must go without saying that, whatever the Author's recommendation of the 'Mitford Letters' is worth; we do. If Harry Potter approves, then who are we to argue:

'The story of the extraordinary Mitford sisters has never been told as well as they tell it themselves'
(J.K. Rowling)

'The world is becoming like a lunatic asylum run by lunatics'
(David Lloyd George in 1933)

APPENDIX E

THE SHIRE MAP ENIGMA

Solving the Enigma of the Shire Map

Barliman Butterbur to Frodo following his antics in the Prancing Pony at Bree:

*'But if you're going to do any more tumbling, or conjuring, or whatever it was, you'd best warn folk beforehand – and warn **me**...'*

The Author now forewarns **us all** of a deal of whatever it is, which we may indeed liken to the magic of conjuring as opposed to conjecturing, that we are going to do with the Shire Map.

We are further reminded of the primary requirement of the Quest: the requisite patience, which may lead to the hidden strength of Barliman Butterbur-

'... he can see though a brick wall in time(as they say in Bree).'

We exhort the members of our Audience thus:

'Here is the patience of the saints;
here are those who keep the commandments of God
and the faith of Jesus.'
(Revelation 14.12)

We shall all need to call upon the virtue to the degree of blind faith in order to share the theories of our solving the enigma of the Shire Map: even unto the final Peace; we may get there in the final end, with much patience required in the meantime.

And that patience will hold the Audience in good stead, because there are so many new difficulties discovered at time of writing (February 2017) that the Author has made the easy decision to withhold the details of the Shire Map Enigma for a possible Volume II; should anyone still be interested in such details; merely to add that the text of the Enigma already runs to some 40 pages of A4 text.

Gollum: … Gerron wivvit, Awffer Mas-sster …

Smeagol: … yes, indeed, My Luv, make haste! Time is short … (grinning) … a bit like wot hobbitses is like! …

Gollum: … we knows-ss, yess, we knows-ss where Green Hill Country is-ss, precious-ss …

Smeagol: … and we wants *them* to know, durstn't we, My Luv … Yes, yes indeed, … find them safe paths in the dark for green countries, yes we will … and here we throws downs elf jewelses for Rangers, My Luvvs …

'assuming the area of the Greens commences with Bletchley at some [25] miles to the east of Oxford on Mother-earth, finding in turn Pin Green some [25]miles to the east of Bletchley, and, through Bishop's Stortford at some[15]miles further away to the east, finding next Braintree at the furthest extremity [15] more miles on, then there is a total distance of some 55 miles from Bletchley to Braintree;'

Voice Off; Professor J.R.R. Tolkien, reads from The Two Towers …

'And so Gollum found them hours later, when he returned, crawling and creeping down the path out of the gloom ahead …'

APPENDIX F

Fanfare of the Tolling of The Rings

**'You say you want a revolution
Well, you know
We all want to change the world
You say you'll change the constitution
Well, you know
We all want to change your head
You tell me it's the institution
Well, you know
You'd better free your mind instead …'**

The Audience is requested kindly to be a patient (like Alex, the Main Feature Coming Soon) whilst the Author unburdens himself and revisits a youth. This should not last very long: neither did that; we must all know that feeling of regret.

Cringes if this fun burns rather like 'The Sun' and it's favourite, the Pun.

Here It Comes, anyway.

For those not old enough to have been around at the time to which we regress, but also and perhaps principally for those who are, let us try to hear the first we were told of The Rings. One supposes one could not write this if not there to listen, even if little was heard by some.

Jagger was there but cannot remember. He is on record for the amnaesia: dunno about Keef.

So goes the cliche:'if you can remember it clearly, you clearly weren't there'.

Like many others it is tolled, too far away: clapped and out of it.

Tolling reverberated the chimes of freedom; and so the Rings told for a whole generation of youth.

We remember School Bells.

We were in middle school (say 13 or 14 years of age) and we heard tell of The Rings, and so, like so many others, we tuned in.

Lennon eggman'd us on …

'Man, you should have seen them kicking Edgar Allen Poe'…

… (the reality of which is a real kick in the head) …

Jagger kicked Brian Jones off in a white smock-dress and a Poem by Shelley; even so we pay a visit near Rivendell.

The times they were a changin', all about us, and a day in the life was flowers, peace, love, high life, magic and… wizards .

There were baubles, bangles, beads, Biba and Bus Stop:

'Please take my umbrella…'

Holly'd out ,N joined CSY for the Four Way Street.

There were Carnaby Street, Kaftans, Afghans and Kinks, Warholed up for 15 minutes:

'Everyone's in ShowBiz, Everyone's a Star … It doesn't matter who you are…' (Ray Davies, Kinks).

There was Donovan getting on Dylan's finale of a nerve:

'I looked in the closet; *Donovan* was there…' (Royal Albert Hall, 1966. 'Don't Look Back') – Pennebaker's microcosm of our hero at 25: cool, cutting and a bit of a beast; the apology to the Sheffield student was, looking back, cool, Bobby, cool.

There were grass, weed and speed.

There was Lucy in the Sky.

The psychedelic eclectic electric- or air-guitared a voodoo chil', and adoorned the piano, breaking on through to the other side.

We went to electric ladyland: the album *cover* urged us ahead.

Timetabled to read Shakespeare, we much preferred The Rings.

Undercover we covertly read 007, because of the rude bits.

Hormones were not a new band but raged away, anyway: before we read what they were, or knew we had them.

Hail Mary and the quantum of the pelmet skirt.

The Author was cool Fourteen in 1968.

Dylan nailed her: I Want You.

He sings of his chambermaid at the Queen of Spades.

She *knows* he is not afraid to *look at* her.

She *knows* where he'd like to be but it doesn't *matter*.

'I want you, I want you. Honey I want you, sooo bad.'

We were to cool down.

The later sedated invitation reads 'Lay Lady Lay'.

Across his big brass bed.

'She got pictures on the wall,
They make me look up,
From her big brass bed…'

We are all so spaced out; Man, like these paragraphs.

Catch Woodstock or Frodo's pilgrim progress through Fangorn.

Some of us resembled Treebeard.

Woods and Woodstock: 1968, the Summer of Love.

Dylan chose the Isle of Wight; so the organisers fairied to his back-garden: Yasgur's Farm. Here Came The Sun very early. This haven of talent had so much; he offered us the Sun and everything but: stonehenge brilliant, son, the first performance at Woodstock: the riches of the, now Grey, Havens.

This was 1968, the year Bill Ready rode a wave into town.

Don't Look Back In Anger: we do look back; trumpetting Burton's Osborne-spawn of Angry Young Man. There was Burton and then there was Taylor: the Taylor-Burtons: perhaps the first British celebrity couple; and, hey Man, have they a lot to answer for.

The Rings was an integral part of the burgeoning youth culture, then; and then on. The Rings was coooool (so *many* Rings): Floyd, pink on the dark side; The Boss Born, to Run; Amis, Money and London Fields; Jammed, Strangled and Clashed ;a full circle of the Ring to Oasis: Don't Look Back In Anger.

'Where were you when we were getting high?'

Cool Kurt smells like teen spirit; so cool it kills.

All straight-outa-the-fridge-cool.

Nouvelle Vague after vague: The Rings was the vogue way back when.

The crest of a New Wave, pounding the shore for each generation.

This froth of trippery, frippery and flippancy waves by not to diffuse, deride or delude the deluge flooding the heavenly young in the mid-1960's, and beyond; but for celebration of its depths.

One great rocking and rolling cool tidal wave of music and words.

The cool blind optimism of youth is eternal, recognised by Wordsworth centuries before:

> 'Bliss was it in that dawn to be alive,
> But to be young was very heaven!
> (Wordsworth)

It gets dark, even in Heaven.

Manson rode a mansion all the way down on a crazed and twisted helter skelter.

There was Napalm and Vietnam.

This Is The End.

Back to the top.

The Quest does many lines of songwriting material of – or of just beyond – the era of the tolling of The Rings.One (our Cauldron of Appendix C) is darkly biblical and so has bedevilled us forever.

The songs were included out of deference of the Author to, and to the words of, those songwriters who in the estimation of the Author (the Audience may or may not agree, but at least might show interest in such details) were and are skilled in the art of descriptive writing to music; who craft the meaning of the words they sing; and who are part of the Author's subconscious.

We borrow the lyrics of these throughout the Quest: or had done; until we went classical (in poetry) instead.

We have designated Bob Dylan as The Nobel Voice of the opera of our generation; having borrowed the 'Voice' idea from the other Dylan; Thomas: Under Milk Wood .We borrow our apt name for Thomas also from the Milk Wood: he is forever our 'the Nogood Boyo'.

We have played with several Voices Off; but so did Shakespeare.

Many will simply not be interested.

We speak along the Quest of the lack of interest, yet intrigue and irritation we suffer when Tom Bombadil appears on the scene in The Rings; and offer generally the frank admission that we more or less skip the Professor's Songs and Verses, whether or not Tom is involved; making a further parallel for justification of our musical interludes: the Professor included Songs and Verses, and so do we: the Author is prone to ignore the Songs and Verses, as, so too, is our Audience free to ignore our musical and other offerings.

The popular music of generations has changed the World: it has transcended barriers: geographical, historical and above all emotional: who in this modern World does not know of The Beatles and of the genius that was John Lennon?

'The way things are going, they're gonna crucify me...'

Executed in any event, Chapman is carrying a copy of 'Catcher in the Rye' when he shoots Lennon. We catch a little more later. We have been to Strawberry Fields, and imagined.

The difference between these writers and the commercialised, commercial song is that you won't catch it first time, second time or however many times. You pick up more each play. Number one's and number two's are flushed down the toilet of the Dime Store of the USA or the Charity Shop of the UK. We have all seen them in the Stores and the Shops. Stuck in the middle of the shelf, without you. Destined for Landfill. The more intelligent writers form part of one's own collection, like favourite and memorable Books and Films .One does not discard these, like waste or trash: one savours them, like old friends and fond memories. One shares them.

The young guns may have no idea what we are talking about.

But they do; we do look back once more. Horrendously conceited and disdainful, one interviewer questions the The Nobel Voice ('Don't Look Back') whether his songs and lyrics are so complicated, complex or difficult ('whatever'), his young audience might simply not *understand* them; implying of course that *one does*. Polite but sacrificial reply-

'The kids get it ... the kids get it OK ... Next question ...'

The Nobel Voice's torture and sacrifice of the more pompous interviewers is delicious if one enjoys that kind of cruel spectacle.

Of his sources-

'It's all been done before, Man, it's all been written in a Book.'

He didn't say which book.

We do so get off track.

O well, whatever, Nevermind.

The Nogood Boyo had written his best by the age of Eighteen.

One wonders what Shakespeare was doing at such age.

If we look back to the anger of the young man overmuch, come up to date with the death of J.D. Salinger in the year of our writing, 2010. Salinger writes the classic epitome of the genre: Catcher in the Rye: all, we repeat, all, teenagers might (we must not say 'must') read it for the evocation of disaffected youth.

Better still, maybe their parents might, but we must not say that either.

Wikipedia has a searing account of the history of the Novel, including the 'challenges' to it; which was a concept unfamiliar to the Author until he hit Wikipedia. Read that account and you will surely be bound to read the Novel.

The Novel is awesome reading and amounts to the converse of our ecstasy of youth. Every positive has a negative. Every youth has a struggle going on, and, O boy, or girl, does it show in Holden Caulfield, with the 'blinding sight' of the Nogood Boyo. It has not least the accolade that it entirely represents youth-culture language of the day-

'... propaganda, all is phoney ...' (The Nobel Voice)

Much of the world of his existence is, for Holden, 'phoney'.

It also shows that, generation to generation, some things never change. Salinger writes Catcher in the Rye in 1951.

Yet it shows, in turn, the reverse.

Everything *has* changed: one cannot imagine anyone challenging 'Catcher in the Rye' today.

We read him on a Monday and our heart stood still; somebody told us that his name was Bill; Ready, that is.

This look back to 1968 dadooronronned the roar of phoney applause for the work of William Ready (Understanding Tolkien) –

'... personal, original, creative, brilliant, captivating ... a model of excellence ... '

This is entirely true of Catcher in the Rye.

THIS IS YOUR BOOK!

Puuurlease read it, My Luvvs; for you will see yourself through a glass, darkly.

A belated Revelation of the Revolution; it was the last thing conceived here .We had been tolling the birth of The Rings amidst and amongst all the psychadelia –

'Lend me your ears while I call you a fool.
You were kissed by a Witch one night in the wood,
And later insisted your feelings were true,
The Witch's promise is coming,

Believing he listened while laughing you flew…'

'I dreamed I saw the knights in armour coming,
Saying something about a Queen,
There were Peasants singing, and Drummers drumming,
and the Archer split the tree…'

'We are Stardust,we are Golden,
And we got to get ourselves back to the Garden…'

What of the Witch-King of Angmar for kiss of Death atop Weathertop?

What of Legolas for Archer?

What of the Phial of Galadriel for Stardust and Lothlorien, the Golden Garden?

Applicability and Application, Application, Application …

The Author shot into reverse with this revelation. We remain in reverse throughout the Quest. We venture that The Rings did not toll for the Woodstock Generation already assembled ,but seeded, conceived, flowered and powered its birth:get back to Nature and Love. Whence sprang the spirit of a worldwide youth revolution of culture? Lothlorien? The Rings? The Professor?

Much, much later in the Quest we venture into the realm of Archaeology, whose representatives there speak (somewhat critically) of the interweaving of romantic history, such as that of The Rings, into the popular 'Rock' mode of the day, and intrusively into the hallowed realm of their turf; our prescription, to be observed there in Volume II(where we lose and regain the Precious),is a dose of the proverbials.

This is exactly how the Author remembers the period; and, nostalgist we may be, but the Author feels sure that The Lord of the Rings was at the very heart of the burgeoning of this popular and worldwide youth culture.

We have this from 1968, referencing the work of William Ready-

'The enormous popularity of J.R.R. Tolkien's books-particularly The Lord of the Rings-has created one of the largest " in " circles ever built up around one man's work;at the same time, the critics are in violent disagreement over their value and even their meaning. In the face of this confusion, many non-Tolkien-readers are baffled by buttons that read 'Frodo Lives' and by the special language and subtleties that are understood by those who have immersed themselves in the world of the Hobbits.'
(Back Cover, William Ready's 'Understanding Tolkien').

Peace and Love didn't last.

The Rings has and will.

Why has the World Gone Wrong?

'We Won't Get Fooled Again'.

Yet we have: we have taken another turn; the youth culture has in parts turned rather, well, 'nasty': we don't have to tell the Audience.

Take a look on the Web.

Perhaps we should all be getting back to where we belong.

Ultimately every negative will have a positive:

'Now there's so many sinking, we gotta keep thinkin'
We can make it through these waves...
Acid, booze and ass, needles, guns and grass,
Lots o' laughs, lots o' laughs ...'

It is only a matter of time before the wheel turns on itself.

Heed the warning of the The Nobel Voice in the meantime-

'This wheel's on fire,
Rolling Down the Road
Please notify your next of Kin-
This wheel shall explode…'

Some believed the World would end in 2012; apparently Biblical, or an interpretation thereof: better get on with this; and Volumes II and III.

So too, '1984' was a year feared for Apocalypse Now.

Eric Blair for one.

Our ending, almost final, finale:

'And in the end,
The love you take
Is equal to the love
You make …'

With Her Majesty to end our Road to the Abbey (and Priory of Rivendell), with the most understandable of demurrals:

'Her Majesty's a pretty nice girl …
I wanna tell her that I love her a lot
But I gotta get a bellyful of wine …'

For those interested in such details, the 'book' of mention by The Nobel Voice will be The Holy Bible.

Professor Tolkien knew it, The Nobel Voice too, and they have had the milk of human kindness to share it with us.

This is The End.

These are the words of The Author.

This is the 'End of Ends'.

Those are the words of The Professor.